DESIGN WITHOUT BOUNDARIES

DESIGN WITHOUT BOUNDARIES

VISUAL
COMMUNICATION
IN TRANSITION

RICK POYNOR

BOOTH-CLIBBORN EDITIONS, LONDON

First published in 1998
by Booth-Clibborn Editions
12 Percy Street
London W1P 9FB
info@internos.co.uk
www.booth-clibborn-editions.co.uk

A CIP catalogue record for
this book is available from
the British Library

ISBN 1-86154-006-X

Cover and book design
by Stephen Coates
Design assistance
by Jason Beard
Additional photography
by Anthony Oliver

Printed and bound
in Hong Kong

For Jane and Rachel

CONTENTS

INTRODUCTION

"Art = Design = Art . . .? The boundaries are not so
clear now. I would like to make them much less clear."
Gaetano Pesce, 1988

This book collects articles on visual communication written over the last ten years.
For those in design, it has been a period of head-spinning change and this, more than
anything, seems the best reason for taking the unusual step (unusual within design)
of assembling a collection such as this. Books of new design work, full of seductive
imagery, appear by the week. Books of writing on the subject have never been in great
supply and remain a rarity. For students within the field of communication design,
there is an unmet need for even basic analysis, in book form, of recent developments.
Libraries are often patchy in their subscriptions to the professional magazines and
journals that carry such material, and back issues can be hard to locate, particularly
those published abroad. The lack of introductory critical surveys makes it even harder
for students and practitioners in neighbouring disciplines such as art, film-making,
journalism and the media to find their bearings in this fast-moving field.

The received wisdom among design insiders is that new design "languages" are
changing the semantics of visual communication. Yet if this is really the case and
the work discussed in *Design Without Boundaries* does portend new forms of mediation
and new kinds of media literacy, then outside the professional design magazines
a phenomenon of the utmost significance is going largely unnoticed, or being touched
on in only the most superficial terms. What is this new work? How does it differ from
established forms of communication design? What do its makers think they are up
to and say the work is about? What *is* the work about, since this is by no means
necessarily the same thing?

Much talked about in academic circles in the last few years, the criticism of graphic
communication is still at an early stage. Looked at internationally, its development is
far from uniform, nor does it necessarily correspond with areas of high activity in
design. In Britain, where I write, the last ten years have seen an upsurge of creative
energy that has commanded worldwide admiration, but this has not been matched by
a comparable level of critical ambition or sophistication in the trade publications that
showcase this work. There have been few calls from practitioners for the development
of a graphic design criticism. Professional organisations show no awareness of history or
theory and express no discernible interest in the development of critical thinking. With
no visual education, some of those writing about graphic design lack even basic skills of
looking. Individual designers are fêted, but it is rare for bodies of work to be examined
critically, let alone for individual pieces of design to receive the degree of analytical
attention routinely given to art, photography or film in their specialist presses and in
the media at large. Publishing aside, one sign of a healthy design criticism would be
writers of identifiable and differing critical positions engaged in purposeful public

debate with their subjects and with each other. In Britain, this has yet to happen.

In the US, the process of developing such a criticism is further advanced. The crucial difference, compared to the British situation, is one of self-consciousness. The most interesting American writers on graphic communication are prepared to talk critically about their procedures as critics and to theorise the process of writing itself. The recent emergence of distinct and sometimes antagonistic critical positions suggests that American writing on graphic communication has reached critical adolescence if not full maturity. Such openness – the making explicit of the assumptions, preoccupations and positions that underlie the writing – is a vital first step before a mature critical discourse can occur. My own response, as a writer and editor, to the different speeds at which design writing is moving on either side of the Atlantic has been to discover ways of addressing both audiences. As an editor, I tried to forge links, through the pages of *Eye*, with American subject matter, themes and critical writing. As a writer, my understanding of recent developments in British and European graphic communication is informed, at least in part, by insights and perspectives gleaned from a close examination, over the last decade, of the American scene. Many of the pieces gathered here, including some of the most critical, were commissioned by American publications or deal with American subjects.

These articles were not written with a view to eventual publication as a collection, but they were written in conscious pursuit of particular themes. I started out, in the mid-1980s, as a writer with the broadest interest in design and the visual arts, and for three years worked full-time on the staff of *Blueprint*. As a magazine of both architecture and design, *Blueprint* was committed, under editor Deyan Sudjic, to the belief that there were obvious continuities and overlaps between design's component disciplines and that a reader interested in one area would be just as concerned to know what was happening over the wall. As deputy editor, I was free to pursue my own preoccupations wherever they led me. A journalist has a wonderful *carte blanche* to knock on doors. I could write about all forms of design – graphic, industrial and interior – as well as architecture and art. The dedication, knowingness and verve of the magazine's writers provided the most demanding of models. *Blueprint*'s laser-sharp sense of the mood and needs of its historical moment, the "design decade", was unequalled in British design publishing.

I studied art history before turning to design and I was predisposed from the beginning towards the idea that there need be no rigid categorical distinction between "design" and "art". It wasn't necessary to know anything about the theoretical justifications for this way of working (which, in the case of graphics, were at that stage taking shape in the US) to feel that the new design and communication hybrids of the 1980s made an, admittedly complex, kind of sense. One reason I began to pay closer attention to graphic design in 1976–84 was the era-defining album covers and style magazines of the post-punk period; and this trajectory of growing interest was exactly matched, I found, by many of the designers I went on to interview. The first industrial designer I was sent to profile, in September 1986, showed me a collection of deconstructed, see-through bag radios of liberating audacity and great conceptual brilliance. The sense of aesthetic discovery and intellectual delight I felt examining them is one of the motors for the writing in this book. To underline *Design Without Boundaries'* cross-disciplinary message and its origins in the broadest conception of design, I include my second interview with the designer of the visionary radios, Daniel Weil, plus a few similar pieces, in the final "Crossovers" section.

If *Blueprint* had a weakness in its early years, it lay in its desultory treatment of graphic design. There seemed to be no reason, apart from lack of enthusiasm for the task, why graphic communication could not be covered by the magazine with the same vigorous inquiry. I began to concentrate on writing about graphics and in the context of a publication as committed to the progressive as *Blueprint* it was natural to seek out equivalent forms of graphic experimentation. The conviction that there was a great deal more to say about the subject than could be encompassed in a generalist publication led to the publisher's agreement, in 1990, to launch *Eye*, where some of these pieces first appeared. In the 1990s, as new technology continued its inexorable meltdown of professional practices and standards, while architecture went into recession, there was a real sense that the focus of critical debate had changed. The most timely, memorable and exploratory writing was coming out of the once marginalised field of graphic design. Compared to a building, or even a sofa, a sliver of paper is never going to look very impressive or important. Seen as a single node of meaning in a vast network of graphic signification that interpenetrates every corner of our lives, shaping contemporary reality, it takes on much greater weight. Today, it is writing about furniture and industrial design that seems most in need of an injection of new critical energy.

In the late 1990s, the proposition that art and design may be moving closer together – that design in some of its forms may be taking on some of the characteristics of art (while art becomes increasingly absorbed by design processes and media themes) – is close to becoming a commonplace. While some designers and design commentators belatedly trumpet the cause of intuition, subjectivity and unresolved meaning, others are questioning whether design's personality cult and introspective tendencies threaten to obscure or disrupt the collaborative qualities and problem-solving function that are special to design as a discipline. The problematic nature of the client relationship, for artistically minded designers, is one of the themes running through this book.

Design Without Boundaries seeks to show that the project of developing a more "artistic" graphic design is in any case a collaborative one; it involves the work of many hands over many years. The book's title is a salute to an earlier volume, *Art Without Boundaries* by Gerald Woods, Philip Thompson and John Williams, published in 1972, an alphabetical survey of painting, sculpture, photography, design and film-making which explores the steady erosion of traditional boundaries between disciplines in the post-war period and argues that conventional classifications have become irrelevant. Although its focus is the 1990s, *Design Without Boundaries* includes discussion of work from the 1960s, 1970s and 1980s because a familiarity with earlier developments is essential to any understanding of the condition, concerns and potential of visual communication today. Ideas of personal authorship within a commercial medium and greater collaborative involvement in the process of message-making that are now taken for granted in graphic design, were, in Britain, first proposed and applied twenty or more years ago by illustrators at the Royal College of Art. These radical image-makers looked to art and film for inspiration and were themselves encouraged by the broader interpretation of visual communication and opening up of cultural possibilities recorded in a book such as *Art Without Boundaries*. There is an alternative lineage that stretches from Stewart Mackinnon at *Oz* and *Nova*, to Russell Mills's art/music crossovers, to Neville Brody's innovations of the 1980s, to Dirk van Dooren at Tomato. In the 1990s, experimental graphic design has pushed illustration aside. Any attempt to plot and explain design's development will need to re-examine these links.

Design Without Boundaries has been edited in a way that I hope will shed light on these themes. Most of the pieces – reviews, profiles, essays and interviews – are reprinted as first published. In a few articles, small deletions and adjustments have been made to avoid repetition or to make better sense of their position in this collection. A handful of minor cuts made by the commissioning publications for reasons of length have been restored. Some titles have been changed or added; these pieces are marked at the end with an asterisk. The essay on Russell Mills was originally written for an exhibition I curated at the School of Visual Arts in New York. Only some of it was used then and it is printed here in full for the first time. It would betray the tone of these pieces to introduce footnotes after the event, but for anyone who wishes to pursue any of my sources I have tried, as fully as memory and my filing system allow, to provide references keyed to page numbers in the bibliography. I hope the issues explored in these pieces keep them reasonably current (or retrospectively illuminating) even where their subjects have moved on, but a few "where are they nows?" may be useful:

Hard Werken amalgamated with the Dutch packaging specialists Ten Cate Bergmans in 1994 and changed their name to Inízio. Gerard Hadders and Rick Vermeulen are now pursuing solo careers.

Doublespace never did relaunch *Fetish*. David Sterling left the team in 1994 to set up World Studio and launched *World Studio Sphere* magazine. Jane Kosstrin continues at Doublespace.

Peter Saville left Pentagram, London in 1992; Daniel Weil joined as partner.

Sean Perkins quit Cartlidge Levene, later followed by Simon Browning. They joined forces in 1995 as the London-based design studio North.

Richard Saul Wurman sold Access Press to HarperCollins Publishers in 1991.

In early summer 1997, Jeffery Keedy was still working towards the launch of his Cipher typefoundry.

It remains only to thank the people who made this book possible. My greatest debt is owed to Deyan Sudjic for giving me the freedom to write and providing, through his example as writer and editor, the best kind of inspiration. I owe him a double debt, since, as a director of Wordsearch, *Blueprint*'s publisher, he, together with Peter Murray, underwrote the hugely risky and ambitious launch of *Eye*. At *I.D.*, one of the world's finest design magazines, Chee Pearlman has been a consistent source of encouragement in recent years. Her high editorial standards and thoughtful feedback invariably pay off. Steven Heller, editor of the *AIGA Journal of Graphic Design*, and Matthew Slotover, co-editor of *Frieze*, have given me regular venues in which to stretch out as a reviewer. I should also like to thank Nick Tite (*RA*), Renny Ramakers (*Industrieel ontwerpen*), Nick Barley and Rowan Moore (*Blueprint*), Rowan Crowley (*Eye*), Gert Dumbar, Dan Fern, April Greiman, and Deborah Orr (*Guardian*). Thanks, too, to Jackie Monnier and to all the designers and artists who gave permission to show their work in the book; detailed credits are included in the picture captions. Finally, a tip of the hat to my publisher, Edward Booth-Clibborn, to Vicky Hayward, Diana Allan, Martin Barr, Robert Timms and Jason Beard, and to my two regular collaborators at *Blueprint* and *Eye*, Vicky Wilson, who copy-edited many of these pieces, and Stephen Coates, who likewise designed them and has now reformatted them with an exemplary sense of style.

Rick Poynor, London, July 1997

1. REDEFINITIONS

Select Your Network. Poster.
Designer: P. Scott Makela.
Self-published, Cranbrook
Academy of Art, USA, 1990

DESIGN WITHOUT BOUNDARIES

I am looking at a poster designed by a student at the Cranbrook Academy of Art in 1990 and, quite frankly, I don't know what to make of it. It's more or less square, divided into nine unequal units, or maybe it is eight. It's called *Select Your Network* and those words are printed one by one across three disparate images. At the top, the words "Invention Intuition Ideology" run together in a rectangular panel that crosses a furrowed brow, a closed eye and a wide-open mouth. At the bottom, it reads "Medium of Distribution". There is a fire in a tub, a distorted running foot and train tracks stretching to the horizon.

I said I didn't know what to make of the poster and probably that sounded like a criticism. Often it can be, but not in this case. Here, the uncertainty is the key to the poster's mystery; it is what keeps you looking at it long after an image that yields its meaning immediately has ceased to be of interest. Formal restraint and clarity also play a crucial role. They give the poster the appearance of purpose and authority. Except at the bottom, the "layering" is basic, conceptual rather than actual, the density more a matter of association than visual effect. The meaning, however, moves in and out of focus across the image. The conjunction of "invention" and brow, or "network" and telegraph, is obvious, but "medium" and flaming tub? And how do the component ideas relate to the whole? Are the visual and verbal linkages merely intuitive and "poetic", with no precise intended meaning, or are they supposed to combine to frame some larger statement or argument?

One thing is certain: the poster does not solve a communication problem so much as present the viewer with a communication problem to solve. So is it really graphic design? The question will seem pointless to some and pressing to others, and this divide is itself revealing of the deep divisions among graphic designers – between older and younger, professional mainstream and fringe – as to what graphic design is, or should be. "[A] graphic designer is one who creates ideas that are expressed in words and/or pictures, and generally solves problems of visual communication," writes Paul Rand in *A Designer's Art*. But if we decide, according to the second half of this still widely held definition, that a project like *Select Your Network* is not graphic design, even though it was created by a professional graphic designer (P. Scott Makela) in the course of his design studies, then what is it? The usual dismissive answer is that it is art. But passing the buck in this way does not solve the categorical problem, since the art world does not in any institutional or critical sense recognise such work as art and is probably not even aware of its existence in the first place. Why should it be? It doesn't display it, or write about it, or sell it.

I am particularly interested in work that emerges from the nexus of art and design because this is where we see the clearest signs of how exploratory graphics will develop. For better or worse, ideas tested out under laboratory conditions, in design schools or in personal projects, often find their way into the mainstream. I am less concerned here, though, with mainstream take-up (which often just means watering down or, at worst, thoughtless plunder) than with the possibilities opened up by the purer forms of visual research.

There have been signs for several years that the relationship between art and design is going through a major period of transition. Historically, of course, graphic design has closely shadowed developments in the fine arts, borrowing from Cubism, Futurism, Dada, Constructivism, Surrealism and so on. The Bauhaus offered designers a paradigm of the way in which fine and applied art might be integrated. Mid-century Americans like Lester Beall and European émigrés like Will Burtin brought a similar synthesising consciousness to their work. "The great cultures of the past had neither the concept of 'art for art's sake' nor 'art for use's sake,'" wrote Alvin Lustig, predicting an imminent fusion of the two functions.

It didn't happen. In the post-war period, with the growing professionalisation of both art and design, the divergence began. Graphic designers did still sometimes look to art for ideas and inspiration (and vice versa) but the dominant rhetoric, embodied above all in the Swiss Style, proposed a new objectivity in communication design and an end, in Josef Müller-Brockmann's words, to the "old free subjective manner of representation". Such totalising dreams were, as we know, shattered by the arrival of postmodernism and the Weingart-propelled New Wave. Subjectivity was back with a vengeance and openly declared as an end in itself. For April Greiman the priorities were all but reversed: "Design must seduce, shape, and perhaps more importantly, evoke emotional response."

Select Your Network is an heir to this subjective tradition. Its brutal conjunctions do more than evoke an emotional response, they demand one. But where the formal innovations of the New Wave were to a large degree internal and derived from design itself – a disruptive response to the mechanism of the grid – Makela's reference points for his black-and-white digitally mixed construction stretch from 1920s photomontage to the 1980s media art of Barbara Kruger.

One could perhaps see this as a retrograde step. Why should graphic design decide once again to follow in art's wake? The answer seems to lie in the way art itself has changed and the new possibilities this opens up for designers. The 1980s saw a convergence of technology, subject matter and techniques of representation. Artists' continuing preoccupation with media – photography, film, video, television, advertising and print – has a self-evident appeal for media-obsessed designers. The British designer Peter Saville, now based in Los Angeles, has been one of the most deft and persistent appropriationists – a word he uses himself – with references in his designs to Futurism, Surrealism, Conceptual Art and gallery advertising. In a sleeve for the English rock band New Order's single "Regret", Saville reclaims for print the style of Marlboro Man advertising imagery first appropriated by artist Richard Prince, giving us, in effect, a simulation of a photograph of a photograph of something that was not "real" in the first place. Saville completes the circle of repetitions and underscores a note of plangency by using a movie-style title piece emblazoned across the two cigarette-smoking cowboys, reminding us of the celluloid origins of such mythic imagery.

The most successful examples of such borrowings don't merely quote or rehash the source, they add something new in the process. Saville clearly hopes the viewer will "get" the reference (though it isn't essential for the record-buyer to enjoy the design) but in other cases the art influence is so completely assimilated by the designer as to be apparent in only the most general sense. This is the case with "New York City", a three-page self-promotional by the London-based team Cartlidge Levene. "We wanted to promote ourselves in ways that weren't so obvious," says designer Sean Perkins of this "alternative advertising". The designers began with the plan to document a weekend trip to New York, but rejected most of the photographs taken as too "descriptive". The use of blocks of flat colour and extreme fragmentation – details of the Brooklyn Bridge are unidentifiable, recognisable landmarks are eliminated – were suggested by the conceptual photoworks of Dutch artist Oscar van Alphen. But the formality and precision of the composition is entirely their own. Although they were their own clients, Perkins insists that they "are not trying to be artists". The firm treated the advertisement, one of a series, as a form of research and development. These strategies were later applied, though admittedly in less concentrated form, to commercial projects.

Any definition of what differentiates art from design returns sooner or later to the controlling presence of the client. It is the client, after all, who sets the brief and picks up the tab. This distinction between "free" art and constrained design is a professional reflex so deeply ingrained that designers continue to hold to it in even the most unrestricted of circumstances. "Design is always something given from the outside," says Edward Fella, though it would be hard to imagine less constrained design work than his promotional flyers for the Detroit Focus Gallery.

The Dutch design duo Mevis & van Deursen have also benefited from their associations with the art world. For a poster/flyer to advertise Gerald van der Kaap's "Total Hoverty" exhibition, held in Tokyo in 1992, the artist presented them with a pile of pictures and text to use entirely as they liked. "By choosing us he knows what to expect," says designer Armand Mevis. "But the work is still not our own. For me it can never be art because we are telling a story for someone else." The poster is nonetheless an enigmatic amalgam of photographs, optical patterns, alienating jargon-bites and ambivalent slogans such as "Our method is techno. Our aim is total hoverty." Once again the design, like the mysterious "hoverty" neologism in the title, is open-ended; it asks viewers to make of it what they will.

In the face of work like this, the question "art or design?" seems increasingly beside the point. Here, artist and designers collaborated on largely equal terms in a shared artistic venture. What does it matter, finally, who set the project in motion? If the category no longer fits the activity with sufficient accuracy, and the activity shows every sign of being here to stay, perhaps it is time we enlarged the category or replaced it with something more flexible. This is certainly not a new argument, but given the level of resistance from the professions and institutions with a vested interest in maintaining the status quo, it still needs making.

Seen in broader terms, the work of P. Scott Makela, Mevis & van Deursen and other designers of similar outlook is a good deal less problematic. It is neither design nor art as traditionally defined, though it has qualities in common with both. It permits an unusual degree of self-expression, but it does acknowledge constraints. It may address a "problem", but it is absolved from the need to find a solution in the closed, objective, rational sense that still informs so much rhetoric about graphic design. The reduction of the debate to a generational clash between superficial "style" and supposedly laudable "idea" has been misleading because it never seems to acknowledge that the solution to a communication problem might – as in some of the examples here – be a mood, emotion, or atmosphere.

For those designers who see themselves as more than simply "visual communicators", who are determined to push for the same degree of self-expressive freedom, and perhaps the concomitant status, enjoyed by artists, the openings are few; the perils of self-indulgence, one might add, are great. Few are given the licence to please themselves that Venice Biennale contributor Oliviero Toscani brings to international advertising at Benetton ("I've got the walls of the world"); that Vaughan Oliver can take for granted as cover artist-in-residence at 4AD Records in London; or that Rick Valicenti (motto: "art with function") has won from Gilbert Paper; a recent promotion, "Give & Take", advises the reader: "Warning: This Collection of Words and Images May be Seen as Art."

Given the lack of outlets, Valicenti, for one, believes in creating his own venues. In the July/August 1992 issue of *I.D.* he bought a double-page ad in which he declared "Fuck Apathy ... Demand the President act as if aidshouldie ... If money talks why won't it listen." As art it was a touch unsophisticated – the very speediness of Valicenti's style can look glib – but as a gesture it made you wonder what would happen if more designers began as a matter of course (or even once in a while) to exploit the communication channels at their disposal. Why, for instance, has graphic design failed to produce a genre equivalent to the artist's book? As art and graphic design continue to converge (with design, which perhaps has less to lose, making most of the running) this may yet happen. Valicenti talks of starting the design version of a record label, offering other designers the chance to release their own printed projects. However we decide to categorise such exploratory ventures, self-initiated or otherwise, their restorative effect on the culture and practice of visual communications can only be beneficial.

I.D., November 1993

PERFECTION OF AN EMPTY PAGE

The Japanese poster tradition has given us some of the most beautiful and, to western eyes, baffling images in all of graphic design. You can never escape the suspicion that however deeply the posters might move you and their technical excellence impress, you are almost certainly missing the point. It is not just a question of failing to understand the language – for the more fanciful and poetic copylines, not even a translation would help. To make these images even half as resonant and meaningful to us as they are to a Japanese audience, a much deeper level of cultural translation is required.

This is the daunting task that *Kirei – Posters from Japan* sets itself and which it only partly achieves. The book is based on the collection of posters in the Museum für Gestaltung, Zurich and feels like a catalogue, but essays by Catherine Bürer, Josef Müller-Brockmann and Japanese poster designer Koichi Sato offer valuable insights. Large-format pages enact the posters' drive for lightness and transparency by surrounding them with white space.

The essayists range widely but come back to one point on which they all agree. While there is no one style of Japanese poster, but rather a multiplicity of personal approaches, the single characteristic that most distinguishes them is a reduction of elements until only the essential remains. *Kirei*, the almost untranslatable Japanese adjective that gives the book its title, can mean "beautiful", "simple", "fair", "pure", "plain" or "clean". To make something *kirei* is not to prettify it with pointless decoration, but to purify it of all superfluous matter. "The perfect embodiment of *kirei*," writes Sato, "is logically a blank sheet of paper. Whiteness is colour without impurity and the plane is necessarily simpler than the cube."

And yet, as Müller-Brockmann points out, in Buddhist philosophy these blank spaces are not considered empty, or of lesser importance. The void in these posters is simultaneously both foreground and background. It is not "a mere lack of presence, but rather a sign of seeing beyond things, a site of inner reflection, meditation and utmost quiet". Its meaning is spiritual and religious.

Even if we are unwilling to follow the Japanese into the thorny garden of Zen metaphysics, these posters still have much to teach us in the West. Their radical difference from the norms of our own graphic design is a timely reminder of the contingency that underpins our definitions of the discipline. These are cultural conventions, no more, and there is nothing inevitable, or permanent, or universal about them. When culture changes, as it must, there is no reason why design should not change along with it. Try stopping it.

Apply Bob Gill's famous definition of a successful graphic idea, however, and many of these posters would not qualify as good design. If you described the content of one

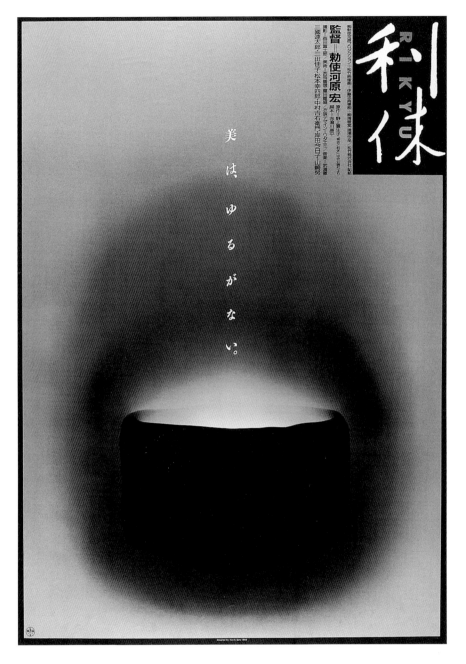

Rikyu. Film poster. Koichi Sato.
Japan, 1988. Collection
Museum für Gestaltung,
Zurich, Switzerland

of Koichi Sato's over the phone – "a box with light flooding out of it" – the person on the other end would have no trouble drawing their own version. They would not have captured Sato's "idea", though, because this lies in the precise way in which the image is realised: the idea is a complex function of the designer's sensibility, style, understanding of his own culture and technique. Unless the receiver's qualities happened to match Sato's, they would not be able to reproduce the effect.

If this collection has a failing, it is the familiar graphic design book ploy of over-generalisation. It would be hard to imagine a guide to Japanese film or literature that omitted to substantiate its arguments by citing a single film or book, but that, in effect, is what we have here. Bürer notes how artistic individuality makes it difficult to speak of the Japanese poster as if it were a definable entity, then proceeds to do just that.

Many of the posters consequently refuse to fit the patterns the writers have established. "In Japan photographs of identifiable subject matter are relatively rare," writes Müller-Brockmann, a surprising assertion when many of these examples are unambiguously photographic. It is hard to detect much "immanence" or sense of "ethereal floating" in routine, albeit superbly photographed images of a bare-chested girl on a beach, a bottle of fizzy drink seen against the sky, or an immaculately coiffured model nibbling fish from the bone (copyline: "Crunch, Crunch, What a Delicious Noise"). Bürer's "inner tremor" and "moment of poetic repose" seem a touch elevated as descriptions of the sort of response images like this are meant to evoke. To western eyes they look as vacuous as many of our own ads.

A closer examination of individual cases sometimes reveals the same chasm within a designer's body of work. Makoto Saito's Parco department store poster of 1981, showing a young woman and boyfriend, is standard fare – literal-minded and unpromising. By the mid-1980s, he is slicing the photographic figure into discontinuous fragments and building cool surrealist montages from bodies, heads and limbs. More recent examples are intricate and painterly: a fashion poster has the selectively applied colour and abstracted details of a Richard Hamilton Pop Art screenprint. What are the personal and external factors that propel such developments?

Nothing about Saito's typography or image for this poster suggests that it comes from Japan, and many of his colleagues have also set their eyes on the West. Shigeo Fukuda's familiar puns, echoes and inversions have as much in common with Sato's mysterious intuitions as a stand up comic's punchline has with a haiku. There is a questioning of local traditions and even a disregard for them in some of these posters that the book's slender, concluding section on the "Occident" has barely even begun to address.

Eye, no. 13 vol. 4, 1994

TRUST THE EXPERTS

It says something about the sometimes arbitrary and certainly incomplete nature of graphic design and typography publishing that Jan Tschichold's "epoch-making" text, originally published in Berlin in 1928, has had to wait 67 years for its first publication in English.

Tschichold himself asked Ruari McLean to undertake the translation of *Die neue Typographie* in 1967 (the same year that McLean's 1947 translation of Tschichold's *Typographische Gestaltung* was finally published as *Asymmetric Typography*). Tschichold had many years earlier rejected the new typography's Germanic "will-to-order" and criticised his own youthful alliance to it, and his intention was to publish an amended edition of his first book deleting material he no longer considered to be relevant as well as revising the typography. No publisher could be found, however, and McLean placed his translation in the St Bride Printing Library, London.

McLean's new translation of *The New Typography* treats the book as a historical document and returns to the original text, though it includes two specimen pages showing Tschichold's proposed revisions as well as translations of his self-criticisms. Where in 1928 he had scoffed at "a fear of pure appearance", in the 1960s he no longer believed it was so simple: "The desire for ornament is elemental and not childish-naïve."

Reading the book today it will be impossible for many designers not to share some of Tschichold's impatience with the unwavering convictions of his younger self. While *The New Typography* does, as McLean suggests, embody some "fundamental tenets" of continuing validity, only the most doctrinaire of latter-day modernists could possibly embrace it as the "Handbook for Modern Designers" that its subtitle announces. The practical advice contained in its second half on the design of letterheads, postcards, advertisements and so on has, for the most part, long since been superseded.

Tschichold wrote at a time when the mass-produced wonders evoked in his opening pages in an unpunctuated rush – "Car Aeroplane Telephone Wireless Factory Neon-advertising New York!" – seemed to herald a radically new world free of all tradition. The hero of this new age of electro-mechanisation was the engineer and standardisation was his aim. Human expression would be stripped down to its purest, most exact and truthful forms. In pursuit of the collective good the designer would dissolve selflessly into his own work. "Just as every human being is part of the greater whole, and is conscious of his connection with it, so his work should also be an expression of this general feeling of wholeness," writes Tschichold.

He constantly harps on this theme. The fault of the early advertising artists was the way they made their own "handwriting" so central to their work. Photography's advantage over drawing is its freedom from the "overwhelming" personality of the artist. The efficient forms needed to express the modern world could "never be found in the work of a single personality and its 'private' language".

Tschichold's insistence on the need for objectivity became one of the cornerstones of modernist graphic design. The typographic demands that follow from this precept are so familiar they need little restatement here: asymmetrical composition employed as a "principle of freedom"; sanserif type because it is in "spiritual accordance" with the times; the use of type and photography in a unified image (typophoto); orthographic reform – the removal of capital letters is desirable, Tschichold suggests, but not essential. Less familiar, perhaps, will be the book's arguments for the standardisation of paper sizes, a section which Tschichold planned to drop from the proposed 1960s edition of the book.

How will this important document be received in the 1990s? In his excellent introduction, Robin Kinross briefly describes some of Tschichold's own objections to the New Typography in his 1950s exchanges with the Swiss typographers. Kinross concludes by noting, with careful understatement, that the "context of the present edition . . . is different from any that its author knew". That's one way of putting it. One could also say (to use a Kinross-ism) that in the prevailing winds of postmodernism many of the tenets that *The New Typography* holds most sacred have been turned on their head.

The individualistic expression that Tschichold and his colleagues rejected is almost an orthodoxy among younger designers now, and this is a conviction as consistent with wider social and cultural patterns as Tschichold's beliefs were with those of his own society and time. Where Tschichold argued that the enormous mass of printed matter meant that speed of reading was essential and form should be clarified to match, many now counter that the huge mass of competing messages requires completely new strategies to capture fickle attention and slow down the jaded reader. (It's ironic that *The New Typography*'s careful rendering into a close approximation of the original design – a pale, loosely spaced sanserif across a wide measure – should make it such a tiring and slow book to read.) Meanwhile, even the rubric "New Typography" has been co-opted. To many younger designers, it will suggest work not from the 1920s but the 1990s.

There is an even more fundamental sense, though, in which the context has changed. *The New Typography* is semiotically innocent. There are no intimations in this ringing manifesto nor, perhaps, could there be – that the developments that form its background are anything other than benign and progressive. Advertising's content is taken for granted. Design's role is to serve it with "impersonal creativity". Tschichold's only stated concern is for the quality of the text, but this is little more than another call for technical proficiency. The writing of ads, he instructs, "should always be entrusted to the expert". It is precisely this unproblematic presentation of the relationship of the designer to his or her material that the more thoughtful postmodern graphic design now questions. *The New Typography* is a lucid, logical, impassioned and challenging text, but within the circumstances of its own time, not ours.

AIGA Journal of Graphic Design, vol. 14 no. 1, 1996*

REREADING RAND

Whether Paul Rand anticipated it or not, the essay with which he concludes *Design, Form and Chaos* has come to occupy a central position in the argument about recent developments in graphic design. The essay was first published as a lead story in the *AIGA Journal of Graphic Design*, then picked up by the British magazine *Design Review*. As a "trailer" for the book itself, it inevitably suggested – as did the book's title – that Rand's attack on contemporary design would form a major theme. As it turned out, the essay, "From Cassandre to Chaos", carries the burden of his case. By using it to close the book, Rand has endowed it with the qualities of warning and lament.

Paul Rand has become an emblematic figure, polarising designers and critics for or against. So I should make it clear right away that I side with neither the out-and-out formalists, like Rand himself, nor with those who put their social and political agendas above everything else. As a writer interested in the development of graphic design criticism, I would like to see a judicious mixture of the two approaches. While I have no particular axe to grind when it comes to Paul Rand and find much of his output superb, I am intrigued by any point of view that discovers so little to admire or respect in contemporary work. However, when I came to take a closer look at what Rand says in "From Cassandre to Chaos", I realised, once the initial sense that "the oracle has spoken" had passed, that I simply was not convinced. Even on his own terms, he fails to make the case.

The nub of Rand's complaint comes in his second paragraph, where he lists the signs of graphic chaos and confusion that cause him such regret: "squiggles, pixels, doodles . . . turquoise, peach, pea green, and lavender . . . corny wood-cuts on moody browns and russets . . . indecipherable, zany typography." It's a long list that manages to seem all-encompassing, while saying nothing remotely specific: not a single designer is named and no examples are shown or discussed. Memphis is mentioned, but Memphis was primarily about furniture and objects; it won't do as a stand-in for graphic design. We can make guesses at the guilty parties (Michael Bierut, writing in *Eye*, suggests, respectively, April Greiman, the Michaels, Joe Duffy/Charles Anderson, and Rick Valicenti), but the fact that we are obliged to fill in the blanks for ourselves highlights the problem with Rand's truculent yet overpolite critical approach. Without a proper sense of context and a great deal more supporting detail and analysis of individual cases, it is impossible to judge the truth of his position. Are all these stylistic attributes invariably bad, wherever or however they are used? So at first it seems. When Rand concedes that "some of these ideas and images may be useful from time to time", he begins to unpick his own argument. So there is, after all, good work. Would he want the validity of his own methods judged on the basis of pale copies by third-rate imitators?

In his opening statement Rand appears to be muddling many different kinds of design into a single catch-all category. By the following page, this compound has been further reduced to "graffiti-like design", a style that has "a certain affinity", he tells us, with Dada. This assessment too seems curiously wide of the mark. Which contemporary designers, apart from those connected with punk, a movement now fifteen or more years old, have explicitly linked themselves to Dada? Rand doesn't say. But the invocation of historical Dada provides a touchstone that allows him, once again, to find contemporary designers wanting. It is easy to say now that Dada was "serious, witty and always interesting"; this was hardly the consensus in bourgeois drawing rooms in 1917 and it might suggest that a degree of caution is advisable when speculating on who will or will not be "remembered in fifty years". Meanwhile, the univocal "'new' style" on which Rand insists is in fact a multiplicity of styles (as his original list has established), many of them contradictory and each with its own aims and audience. If there is a link between, say, April Greiman and Joe Duffy, it certainly cannot be made at the level of style.

By the third text page of his essay, Rand's blinkered tour of contemporary practice is more or less complete. Having erected the flimsiest of paper targets, he now proceeds to blast it apart with some of the heaviest cultural guns he can find: John Dewey, Jacques Barzun, A. N. Whitehead. To give just one of several instances, Rand doesn't cite any actual examples of "extravagantly obscure, modish, opaque verbal shenanigans" and impenetrability in graphic design. He brings on Roger Kimball, writing in *Tenured Radicals*, to assure us they exist (Kimball was in any case talking about architecture, not graphics). If Rand's swipe at "the obsession with theory" is aimed at Cranbrook or CalArts – yet again we can only guess – then intellectual honesty demands that he should say so and offer some representative examples we can assess for ourselves. This evasion of the specific is typical of the way that his argument unfolds. He quotes at length from authorities who support his position, while neglecting to cite a single statement of intention or explanation by those he opposes. Instead he relies on generalities and impressions. This denies the neutral reader a proper point of entry into the debate and makes it impossible for the sceptic to respond to his criticisms with any precision, let alone mount a detailed defence.

I am less concerned with the remainder of his essay. It contains quite a bit with which I would ordinarily be inclined to agree – about the lessons of history, the exigencies of form, and the confusion of aesthetics with sociology – if Rand's method had not left me suspicious. Rereading "From Cassandre to Chaos", I felt, as I had done originally, that it ran out of steam half-way – that Rand did not quite have the stomach, when it came down to it, for the stinging critique that he seemingly set out to mount. He is a generous and erudite guide to the past, willing to turn over a whole paragraph to a roll-call of those he admires, but when it comes to present developments, in this essay he comes across as being completely out of touch.

AIGA Journal of Graphic Design, vol. 11 no. 3, 1993

BUILDING BRIDGES BETWEEN THEORY AND PRACTICE

For a non-American looking across at America, the future – our future – ceases to be a matter of wholly untestable speculation. At least one possible version of it is already happening in the US. This is as true of graphic design as it is of diet crazes, plastic surgery and television. To anyone who keeps a weather eye on the climate changes of international graphics, the American scene is fascinating because the issues that will shape the future course of the discipline become apparent earlier and they are thrown into higher relief. The American graphic design community is exceptional for its edgy mixture of self-confidence and doubt and its up-front willingness at conferences, in competitions and in the pages of the professional magazines, to keep asking itself what exactly it should become. In the 1990s, this introspection shows signs of maturing into a practice founded in critical reflection.

The generational rift runs deeper than might at first have been supposed and there is no going back. The younger radicals still talk as though they were beleaguered, marginalised and misunderstood – and for a long time they were. But while the fundamental changes that are occurring may not yet be fully reflected in mainstream practice, where the power, money and professional kudos are concentrated (and may, in fact, be antithetical to it), when it comes to the argument itself, the passion, tenacity and intellectual conviction of the new guard is winning the day, even if the curmudgeons of modernism have yet to wake fully up to it. The new guard's victory finds symbolic expression, at an institutional level, in the recent redesign by Lisa Naftolin of the *AIGA Journal of Graphic Design.* Even as Rudy VanderLans was excoriating the old design as "amateurish, tasteless and bland", the journal was outfitting itself in funkily serious, unmistakably 1990s garb.

In the 1990s, once radical and transgressive digital styles have burst their subcultural boundaries (design school, music scene, art gallery catalogue) and infiltrated the mainstream, and while the stylistic details will evolve and change and double back on themselves, the rule-breaking pluralism is here to stay. For me, chairing the American Center for Design's "100 Show" this summer, one of the most unexpected and telling entries was *Say* magazine, designed by Johnson & Wolverton of Portland, Oregon, for Amnesty International. Here was the fractured idiom of West Coast youth culture magazines like *Ray Gun, Blur* and *Plazm* applied with undeniable power, though debatable taste, to the hugely sensitive issue of human-rights abuses. If this seems unremarkable, no more than you might expect these days – and if it does, that is exactly my point – it may be worth mentioning that Britain's equivalent newsletter is a piece of sober, conventional, up-and-down desktop publishing.

Most promising for the development of American graphics in the coming years is

Design as

Ellen Lupton and J. Abbott Miller

research

David Peschel was strolling through Child World in Seekonk, Massachusetts with a friend one day. There he happened upon four Harlequin Romance jigsaw puzzles, which he bought, took home, and began to put together.
As he lost himself in their tales of erotic love and exotic travel, he realized that the puzzles were linked to each other by more than just their illustrative style of candied romance: the pieces of the four puzzles are identical. The puzzles are printed with different pictures, but are cut with the same die. Peschel expressed his discovery by shifting an inside section from one puzzle to the outside section of another. This minimal gesture engages the play of sameness and difference which runs across the series of puzzles. With this gesture, the literary and illustrative "language" of the pictures is both torn apart and sewn together by an industrial process.

The cross is a reference to the gothic tradition of romance novels as well as a prototypical modernist device, a two-dimensional diagram of the picture plane which cuts through and splices together scenes of hot love and deep space.

7

The 100 Show: The Sixteenth Annual of the American Center for Design. Opening spread of an essay. Designer: Ellen Lupton, Design Writing Research. American Center for Design, USA, 1994

the gradual emergence of a new spirit of critical inquiry and reflection. The critical discussion fostered in the pages of *I.D.*, *Print*, the *AIGA Journal of Graphic Design* and *Emigre*, the "100 Show" book and at Steven Heller's "Modernism and Eclecticism" symposium is helping to create a profession with a more sophisticated sense of its history, its practice and the function of its products in society. It is perhaps a sign that real progress is being made that such strong dissatisfaction is now being voiced about the nature and aims of this criticism: is there enough of it, who is it for and what is it about? Andrew Blauvelt, currently setting up a graduate programme at North Carolina State University, argues that journalistic criticism's main shortcoming is that it fails to make its assumptions explicit. Blauvelt believes we need a more rigorous form of criticism, closer in its methods to the literary kind, in which critical positions are clearly stated and defended. Such a criticism would build a "bridge between theory and practice". Its goal, he told *Emigre* recently, would be to function as a form of research and development – "to drive the profession".

   To some degree, perhaps in a less systematic way than Blauvelt envisages, this is already happening. Some of the most challenging new design is being forged at the controversial interface of theory and practice, education and the profession. Designer–educators such as Katherine McCoy (Cranbrook), Jeffery Keedy and Lorraine Wild (CalArts) and Michael Rock (Yale) combine design work, teaching and critical writing. The future of Cranbrook's design department may be uncertain with the departure of the long-resident McCoys, but it has created a legacy of critically minded graduates – including Keedy, Wild and Blauvelt – now in positions of influence. The critical fusion of media and methods is nicely summarised in the name of the New York studio founded in the 1980s by Ellen Lupton and J. Abbott Miller: Design Writing Research. Design fuels reflection and the process of research and reflection, in turn, feeds back into design. As a result of this process, "critical positions" evolve.

Designers who wonder what any of this has to do with the daily realities of commercial practice may doubt that there is much to be gained. In American graphic design, as elsewhere, there is a manifest tension between the pragmatics of the studio and the academy's more speculative flights. There is a real danger, if the critical process takes a wrong turn and becomes too inward-looking and insistent on its own theoretical agenda, that it will be rejected by the wider design community as the narrow concern of a minority of design school-based initiates, a useful source of provocative new styles, but nothing more. Such a development at this crucial moment would rob the profession of one of the most obvious and valuable benefits of the new criticism – its critical insight and judgement.

What American graphic design needs now more than ever is to establish new grounds for making assessments of effectiveness and value. With the old consensus of what constitutes "good" graphic design in tatters and professional standards in free-fall, the problem of quality has become one of the central dilemmas faced by designers. Is there such a thing as good graphic design any more? And how do we decide what it is?

Few graphic designers, despite the mood of uncertainty, will answer "no" to the first question. Anyone struggling to keep up with the pace of change can see that the need for evaluative criteria has not only not gone away, it has become more acute. It is a matter, as much as anything, of professional definition. If all graphic design is equally good, and one response to a brief has no more to recommend it than any other, then graphic designers can make no claim to provide anything other than a technical service. While this may be the implicit promise of a "democratising" technology and the breaching of craft's closed circle, no self-respecting designer with several years of hard-won education (or self-education) and many years of experience believes it is that simple. Learning how to use a page layout program does not in itself make you an editorial designer. Design for multimedia's coursing stream of words, sounds and images requires great sensitivity and skill. As a matter of urgency, designers need to convince clients with computers loaded to the gunnels with cheap fonts that they have special talents to offer.

Developing new evaluative criteria is another matter. American graphic design is fragmenting. As it moves toward the millennium, the new pluralism is a necessary response to a multicultural society which, if the profession is to remain relevant, it must more fully reflect. "We need more graphic design particular to the tribes," says Lorraine Wild, "not less." Or to put it another way: design that talks to diverse groups in specially made visual languages each group will understand. A handful of well-worn professional yardsticks with claims to universalism, evolved in simpler times, will be of no help in judging the effectiveness of such work. Instead, a new set of critical yardsticks is needed for the new diversity of applications – many of them still emerging from new media with, as yet, no established conventions. It will be a slow process of trial and error that will mean abandoning our comfortable preconceptions ("this typeface is ugly") and responding to the particularities of context ("does it communicate here?"). And if, as observers and critics, we fail to understand the context, because it falls outside our experience or sphere of expertise, we will have to leave it to those who do understand it. The accepted standards of one sphere will not necessarily apply in another.

But talk of tribes raises a larger dilemma and it is here, perhaps, that graphic design's thorniest problem lies. For, despite regular handwringing and a torrent of platitudes, the "tribes" themselves are still hardly represented at all at the heart of the successful design community. This is as true of the group now assuming the mantle of influence and leadership as it was of their predecessors. The new leaders are in the main white, middle-class alumni of a small group of highly visible, vigorously self-promoting graduate schools. They are diverse, but nowhere near as diverse as American society. Only the increasing proportion of women in their ranks suggests anything is really changing as the baton is passed, and some would dispute even this. Nevertheless, the profession's "underground matriarchy" of women designers (to use Ellen Lupton and Laurie Haycock Makela's phrase) has been in recent years, and remains, the source of many of the most original and constructive ideas.

Now, to build on this progress, the profession must reconcile demands which, though not ultimately incompatible, can often find themselves at odds with each other. It needs to be more inclusive, more genuinely multicultural, while at the same time maintaining the highest educational, conceptual and technical standards. It will be a difficult task, but the best hopes for achieving this necessary evolution lie in the spirit of critical reflection, energy and vision that are transforming the theory and practice of graphic design in the 1990s.

I.D., November 1994

CRITICAL HISTORIES

Graphic design history has become one of the unexpected flashpoints of design debate in the 1990s. Three volumes of *Visible Language* – the quarterly journal concerned, somewhat inelegantly, "with all that is involved with being literate" – combine to make the most concerted and detailed statement of the principles, problems and *bêtes noires* of the new graphic design history published to date. Their almost simultaneous arrival, like buses in a convoy, suggests that this is a subject of rapidly growing interest.

Written by academics for an audience of colleagues, *New Perspectives: Critical Histories of Graphic Design* will feature on the reading lists of few practising designers. But these three issues, stimulating and irksome in roughly equal measure, are worth searching out. Their subject, directly or indirectly, is practice itself, not just in a historical sense, but as it is presently configured. "Graphic design history," notes guest editor Andrew Blauvelt, himself a designer and teacher of future professionals, "has been constructed in service to the legitimisation of professional practice."

Blauvelt has emerged in the last year or so, primarily in the pages of *Emigre*, as a combative critic of the earlier generation of graphic design writers and historians. His complaint, developed at length here, is that the "allergic reaction to theory" seen in the work of these writers shows us that a state of affairs we regard as "natural", the only way things could be, is in reality a self-serving construct that operates to exclude anything that challenges it. It is time, he argues, that graphic design history caught up with the menu of methodologies – revisionist Marxist, feminist, structuralist, post-structuralist and deconstructionist – that has been applied to other subjects in the humanities and social sciences since the 1960s.

The fourteen papers, by designers, art and design theorists, and historians, are divided thematically by volume into "Critiques", "Practices", and "Interpretations". For me, "Critiques" was much the most rewarding. Most histories blur graphic design into a generalised narrative of "visual communication". Victor Margolin argues persuasively here for a tighter definition. With similar rigour, Gérard Mermoz retraces the steps of Edward Gottshall in *Typographic Communications Today* and Philip Meggs in *A History of Graphic Design* to show how their accounts of Futurist typography overlook its coherent critique of typographic orthodoxy and, consequently, its contemporary relevance. To write typographic histories in the 1990s, Mermoz insists, the historian must draw on linguistics, semiotics, literary theory, art history, bibliography and philosophy.

Mermoz concludes by regretting the oversimplifications encouraged by the unilinear format of the academic paper. An alternative hypertext history writing, he suggests, could help to develop "multilinear accounts of typographic pluralism". Steve Baker, in his paper "A poetics of Graphic Design?" takes this rejection of "Pevsnerian" linearity a step further by proposing a form of history writing that would reflect the nature of its subject matter by bringing "the visual and the verbal into a closer relation". Teetering on the brink of absurdity, Baker borrows heavily from the French feminist theorists Luce Irigaray and Hélène Cixous to conjecture a graphic design history that would be "thick and treacly", opaque to itself, as historically self-conscious as other, less naïve forms of history writing, and propelled by the "unfamiliarity and outlandishness" of its ideas.

Intriguing as such an unbuttoned scholarship sounds, Baker's paper contains no clues to how such an approach might be applied to the objects, processes, people or contexts of graphic design history. As the three volumes unfold, their ostensible subject keeps slipping from view. In "Practices", Marilyn Crafton Smith attempts to move beyond graphic design's over-reliance on formalist principles and show how cultural studies might reveal the medium as a "dynamic component of a larger discursive field where meanings are negotiated through cultural forms". But while she is aware of the dangers inherent in cultural studies' "decentring" of the text, and wants to recuperate form rather than relinquish it altogether, her brief examples of possible research to show how audiences produce meaning from graphic design are disappointingly thin: "For example, we could ask how audiences traverse museum displays – (are they connoisseurs or are they there to pick up a date?)." Even if such a question really were worth asking in the present, Smith offers no discussion of how historians might go about asking it of the past.

Given the scale of the revisionist task Blauvelt and his team have set themselves, it is perhaps inevitable that two of the three volumes should be devoted to clearing the site and laying new theoretical foundations. With the third volume, "Interpretations", it is reasonable to expect a better idea of the building itself. Of the four papers, however, only one, Susan Sellers's examination of "*Harper's Bazaar, Funny Face* and the Construction of the Modernist Woman," ventures very far back into graphic design history, though it could equally well be placed in a film journal. Jack Williamson's essay on "hidden narratives" has bafflingly little to say about graphic design, while Frances Butler's study, "New Demotic Typography", and Teal Triggs's paper on British fanzines are as much about the present as the past. The latter's newness as critical history lies more in its recovery of the fanzine from the margins and its repositioning within the context of graphic design discourse than in its intrinsic content.

While there are many insights to be gleaned from these "interpretations", none of them lives up to the radical promise of Blauvelt's programme as editor, or the more imaginative theoretical speculations of the other two volumes. Speaking as a reader, what I particularly like about Steve Baker's paper is its emphasis on history writing as writing. Some of the more turgid contributors to *Visible Language* should perhaps take note. It is also disconcerting to find quite so many spelling mistakes (accomodate, insistance) and typos (distiction, heterosixist) in a learned journal. But I don't want to carp. These volumes are a considerable achievement and, with some tidying up and additional editing, they deserve collection as a book. As for the new graphic design history: there is much work still to be done.

AIGA Journal of Graphic Design, vol. 13 no. 1, 1995*

WHO ARE YOU CALLING STYLISH?

Poor old style has had a bumpy ride since the 1980s. It used to cruise along so confidently, with the top down, its shades on, and the radio turned up high. These days it is a sneer word, the ultimate put-down in the graphic design lexicon. Even designers who made their names as stylists are at pains to put as much distance as they can between themselves and the hated word.

Style did not leave town, of course. It just stopped talking about itself all the time. As Bruce Mau proved at Zone Books, even those hard-nosed radical academics who are always sounding off about pernicious social ills such as, well, style like their textbooks clad in impeccable wraps. And here, in the shape of *The Edge of the Millennium* essay collection and media philosophy guide *Imagologies*, are two more state-of-the-art examples with cool-to-the-fingertips, matt-laminated covers, those nifty flaps that make a paperback feel valuable and important, and titles floating across mysterious backgrounds that suggest something huge, imprecise, and uncertain – history in ferment, ideas in transition, a culture in flux.

In its art historical sense – exemplified, for instance, by Steven Heller and Seymour Chwast's 1988 book *Graphic Style* – style is a useful tool for description and classification. As a synonym for commercial styling, it has been debased into a much too convenient shorthand for everything that is empty, superficial, misguided, or socially irresponsible about contemporary design. "If there weren't so much style," write Karrie Jacobs and Tibor Kalman in "The End", an essay in *The Edge of the Millennium*, "maybe there would be more time for content." Their "modest proposal" for the new millennium: "Why don't we get rid of graphic [and just about every other form of] design?"

Now, I can live without Black & Decker's One-at-a-Time™ coffee filter dispenser – "emblematic" for Jacobs and Kalman "of everything that is wrong with society in general and the profession of design in particular" – but I do think their simple opposition of style and content, and the implication that you have to prefer one or the other, is just plain wrong. Yet it is an opposition you hear all the time from designers and it has become a sign of high seriousness to make a stand for content over style.

Is it really this straightforward, though, in design or any other cultural form? Let's apply the style/content distinction to Jacobs and Kalman's essay. The fact is, you cannot separate them. Jacobs has the most recognisable style of any American design journalist, and through her collaborations with Kalman this has become his voice, too. Jacobs has plenty of "content" and she has a distinctive point of view. For the reader who has never met her, this viewpoint is embedded in her style, her tone. Style here is not just an optional extra, something to brush on for effect – it is the medium of the writer's meaning and sensibility.

Jacobs's style gives the essay authority. The short paragraphs, the punchy, telegraphic rhythms say let's not waste words, let's tell it like it is. At the same time these devices are acutely self-conscious. This writing wants to set itself apart, it wants to be noticed. Nothing else in the book looks or reads remotely like it. The style hooks you, reels you in, and keeps you reading.

This seems perfectly reasonable to me. The competition for attention is fierce. It is odd, though, that Jacobs, Kalman, and so many other design moralists don't see that in the visual world, too, style (the look of the thing) is just as much a medium of content (what the thing says) as it is in writing or speech. The implication, always, is that visual style is trivial, untrustworthy, and beneath the consideration of the serious-minded because it is partly to do with visual seduction and pleasure. Visual styling can, of course, be excessive, just as prose can be purple – that doesn't make every attempt at it invalid. "The concern is style, not content," complain Jacobs and Kalman. But why should it just be content? Why not both?

If there is something rather reassuring about Jacobs and Kalman's old-fashioned moralism, Mark C. Taylor and Esa Saarinen's *Imagologies* offers no such certainties. Taylor, an American, and Saarinen, a Finn, are philosophers of some notoriety and their book will be interesting to designers partly for what it says, but also for how it says it. Structurally, this is the most unusual text book since Avital Ronell's *The Telephone Book* appeared in 1989.

Taylor and Saarinen have no problems with appearances. As self-styled "imagologists", they actively embrace them. "Ours is an age of images and simulacra," they write. "Philosophy must be ready to operate within the realm of images because that is where the 'real' is taking form. Since market forces produce images, philosophy must join the struggle of creating images by marketing its products through mass media . . ." The media philosopher abandons the rational, systematic, uncommercial, hopelessly hidebound academy to become a kind of star turn, a televisual embodiment of his own groovy propositions, and indeed this is what Saarinen has done. He is forever popping up on Finnish TV to talk about . . . whatever you want him to talk about, including his wife and twins.

Negotiating *Imagologies'* flow of fragmentary texts is surprisingly easy. On that level it works. Passages are rarely longer than a page. Some are two-line theory-bites. But whatever you think about the oddball arguments, there is something deeply unsatisfactory about this book. It might have had the elegant subversion of Richard Eckersley's design for *The Telephone Book*, or the cool intelligence Lorraine Wild brings to *The Edge of the Millennium*. Instead, it is a gridless jumble of ill-matched type styles and type sizes, horribly expanded display faces, and clumsily applied graphic effects. These hipster proselytes of the image stumbled at the first hurdle and fluffed the first task of effective visual rhetoric. The styling of their book is a mess.

AIGA Journal of Graphic Design, vol. 12 no. 2, 1994*

CULT OF THE UGLY REVISITED

In May 1993, *Eye* published an essay entitled "Cult of the ugly" by the American writer
Steven Heller, a prolific and well-respected contributor to *Eye* and many other graphic
design publications. Heller's purposefully controversial polemic provoked a remarkable
response over the ensuing months, particularly in the US – its principal focus – where it
cut deep into a very raw nerve. It is unusual for a single article to make such a sustained
impact within the sometimes hard to perturb field of graphic design and for this reason
it seems worthwhile to trace the way in which the debate has developed, to draw
together some of the main strands, and to see what they have to tell us.

It is clearly not possible here, or necessary, to summarise all of Heller's essay.
Contrasting "ugly design" with the classical qualities of balance and harmony, he defines
it as "the layering of unharmonious graphic forms in a way that results in confusing
messages". He criticises *Output*, a student project produced at the Cranbrook Academy
of Art ("the word experiment has come to justify a multitude of sins") and a design
conference brochure by the Chicago designer Carlos Segura ("a catalogue of disharmony
in the service of contemporaneity"). Edward Fella's work is rejected as a model for
commercial practice – a "dead end" – and design schools are accused of pushing their
experiments out into the world, where they will be reduced by thoughtless imitators
into style without substance, furthering the cause of ambiguity and ugliness.

The reaction to this polemic was immediate and came inititally from some of the
people involved. *Output* was robustly defended as the educators closed ranks. *Eye*
received long letters from Katherine McCoy of Cranbrook, from Joani Spadaro, who
initiated the *Output* series at Herron School of Art, and from Teal Triggs, whose
Ravensbourne students were later contributors to the project. All three have returned
to the subject elsewhere, in *Design Statements*, the *AIGA Journal of Graphic Design*
and *Emigre*.

Emigre itself had been criticised in passing by Heller – "a blip . . . in the continuum
of design" – and it is strongly identified with several of the designers taken to task.
In spring 1994, *Emigre* devoted half an issue, ironically titled "Fallout" (no. 30), to a
response. Editor Rudy VanderLans at first planned to publish an essay, but ended up
running a series of interviews by Los Angeles art director Michael Dooley (who has
written sympathetically about *Emigre* in *Print* magazine) with Heller, Fella, Jeffery
Keedy and David Shields, one of the Cranbrook students responsible for *Output*.

This was perhaps a pity. An essay would have allowed a tighter focus on the issues at
stake and would have amounted to a much clearer statement of Dooley's (and *Emigre*'s?)
position. As it is, the interviews ramble. Some excellent questions and revealing replies
get lost among the digressions and chat. Both Fella and Shields come across as slightly

bemused by Heller's attack rather than troubled by it or eager to mount a counter-offensive, so why give them so much space? Only a few of the points made by Heller are dealt with directly in the questions they are asked. Shields makes fewer claims for *Output* than Spadaro and Triggs and one is left thinking that too much attention is being given to one of the weaker contributions to the continuing project. This suspicion receives unexpected confirmation in the next *Emigre*, when another of the Cranbrook *Output* designers, Brian Smith, now a teacher himself, writes to say it is a "(non) issue" and he didn't like the project anyway.

Keedy is more combative and states the heart of the case against Heller's "ugly" thesis: "You can no longer make these quick and easy calls. Simple ideas of good and bad, ugly and beautiful, are just not useful." He also makes the American geographical politics at work in this argument explicit – something that it is easy for the non-American reader untroubled by such local considerations to miss. But if New York-based Heller is guilty, as Keedy claims, of a bias against "anything past the Hudson", it is hard to avoid the suspicion from the tenor of these comments that the bias also operates in reverse.

Emigre's use of the interview format has some significant effects. By asking the writer to account for what he wrote rather than simply analysing it on its own terms, then perhaps rejecting it, it switches attention from the original arguments – whatever their strengths of shortcomings – to the critic's personality and motivations for writing. Sure enough, in the next issue of *Emigre* (no. 31, "Raising Voices"), the letters received by the magazine focus, sometimes abusively, on Heller and his responses in the interview. Meanwhile, an essay by Andrew Blauvelt, titled "The Cult(ivation) of Discrimination: The Taste-making Politics of Steven Heller", sets out to address and seemingly condemn Heller's entire practice as a critic of contemporary graphics, with "Cult of the ugly" seen as the "*summation*" (Blauvelt's emphasis) of his thinking. For Blauvelt, "the real debate is not simply about ugliness, 'theory' or Cranbrook but about the role that education plays, or fails to play, in the practice of graphic design." Like the other prominent voices in the debate, Blauvelt writes from the standpoint of teacher.

The forcefulness and articulacy of the educational defence is only to be expected, and many of the points strike home. But this should not blind us to the fact that this commentary is also highly selective. Heller's central example of what he sees as dubious mainstream practice is Carlos Segura's "Creative Vision" conference booklet. This is as important to his argument as *Output* – the inclusion of three illustrations underscores this – and possibly more so, since it moves the discussion away from the Cranbrook–*Emigre* axis. Heller attempts to show how signature styles that may be perfectly valid as "personal research" or "personal art" within a design school will be taken up and "misused" in the marketplace.

This is problematic. Is Heller really saying that talented people should not experiment in case less talented people copy them? It is an idea which Keedy, among others, rejects: "[Heller] doesn't want a bunch of people imitating them with 'style without substance' because that will 'diminish all design.' That way of thinking about the evolution of style in culture – as a controlled linear progression of mostly 'great white men' is too simplistic." But Keedy's analysis stops short with this somewhat misleading assertion (Heller at no point mentions race or gender). Keedy could have developed this idea with reference to the Segura project, but he does not mention it. Nor, despite its obvious centrality to Heller's essay and argument, does Dooley ask any questions about it in any of his four *Emigre* interviews. If *Emigre*'s aim was to give those criticised by Heller the

Experience the exhilaration of 20/20 creative vision IN CHICAGO. Plan now to attend the one conference that focuses on both the business and creative aspects of design. Focus on your success in graphic design at the 1993 HOW Design Conference April 25th thru 28th at the Westin Hotel in Chicago. Choose from an eclectic collection of enlightening and inspiring sessions for improving your business skills and stimulating your creativity: How to run a design studio, Inside MTV networks, The nuts and bolts of self promotion success, New dimensions in computer design, Designing on a tight budget, Pricing your work, Type design, Interactive and 3D design, Stress management, Innovative business deals, Secrets of Pentagram's success, and more. Plus special sessions covering new dimensions in computer design sponsored by The International Design By Electronics Association (IDEA).

You'll meet and share ideas with designers from around the globe. And you'll return to work inspired by the knowledge and wisdom of these world-class speakers: Marshall Arisman ○ Primo Angeli ○ Michael Bierut ○ Joe Duffy Patrick Fiorentino ○ Louis Fishauf ○ Joel Fuller ○ Mike Hicks ○ Alexander Isley ○ John Jensen ○ Judy Kirpich ○ Nancy Kullis ○ Leslie Leventman Lori Siebert ○ Bruce Turkel ○ Rick Valicenti ○ John Waters ○ and more.

creative

visiON The 1993 How Design Conference on Business and The Creative Process.

April 25th thru 28th, 1993. The Westin Hotel, **Chicago**, Illinois.

Creative Vision: The 1993 How Design Conference on Business and The Creative Process. Designers: Segura Inc. USA, 1993

right of reply, then it would have been more revealing to interview Segura rather than both Keedy and Fella, who represent broadly similar points of view and have talked to the magazine before.

What are we to make of this exclusion? It would be going too far to conclude that the various debaters agree point for point with Heller in his assessment of Segura's piece. But clearly none of the respondents to *Eye* or *Emigre* cared enough for it, or about it, to mount even a passing defence (this was left to Carlos Segura himself in a letter to *Eye*). For Heller's critics, it just wasn't part of the argument. Instead, they concentrated – with relentless particularity in the case of *Output* – on areas where they felt themselves to be under attack.

The implication of Segura's exclusion is that even within the ostensibly open and non-judgmental field of experimental design a value system obtains. "Simple ideas of good and bad, ugly and beautiful" may be dismissed as inadequate, but some alternative, unstated yardstick is clearly being used by the experimentalists to distinguish between cases and to decide who, for instance, is worthy of inclusion in *Emigre* and who isn't, which work merits a defence and which doesn't. But what exactly is it? The language is no clearer on the experimentalists' side than they claim it is on Heller's. "Good solid work is always good solid work," Fella tells Dooley before, only moments later, seeming to contradict himself: "I don't like to use terms like 'good,' 'bad,' 'beautiful,' 'ugly,' because they continually take on different meanings." Few people would seriously argue with the last point; the briefest visit to a museum confirms it. The unaddressed question is how, when the culture changes, as it is so clearly doing now, we decide what the "good solid work" is? The new conventions which are emerging within education and the profession do not in themselves constitute a set of critical standards, however much some of Heller's critics would like to think they do.

Heller himself seems to acknowledge this problem. "It is possible," he writes, "that the most convention-busting graphics design . . . could become the foundation for new standards based on contemporary sensibilities." But it is a weakness of his essay that he does not pursue this, leaving readers with the inaccurate impression that he rejects *all* theory-driven experimental design. In their acute defensiveness, Heller's critics also miss the chance to develop this line of thought. It serves no one except the mediocre, confused and intellectually dishonest to pretend that much of the new typography and graphic design is not intensely problematic, challenging us to begin a complex and sometimes painful process of re-evaluation as we rethink, revise and perhaps abandon our existing models of what graphic design should be, and also, when necessary, our failed experiments. Yet only one of the letters or contributions published by *Eye* or *Emigre* was prepared to concede in plain language so much as a hint of difficulty. "There are many good reasons to make a message offensive (visually or otherwise)," writes Gunnar Swanson in *Emigre*. "But a considerable amount of graphic design seems to say 'fuck you' without really meaning it. Is this merely faddishness, a desperate desire to 'stay on the edge', or some sort of visual Tourette's Syndrome . . . Form makes a claim and designers are responsible for the claims their work makes."

Implicit in Swanson's remarks is a larger issue, also touched on by Heller. What are the cultural catalysts for the current wave of "ugly" design and what is its meaning? Heller expresses doubt that the "current social and cultural condition" requires such "critical ugliness". And he is not alone among critics of recent work in suggesting that radical form without radical content is little more than a "stylish conceit". Robin Kinross, writing on postmodernism in *Modern Typography*, argues that, "Forms that once carried a charge of social criticism become domesticated in the comfortable circumstances of western design culture." Measured by these demanding standards, plenty of contemporary experimentation looks frivolous. But it is too sweeping and strangely blinkered to imply that while Dada was a perfectly legitimate and necessary response to the First World War, there is *nothing* about our present cultural condition that justifies anything other than orderly, harmonious work. Moreover, Heller's insistence on the marketplace as the ultimate arbiter is at odds with his own politics and would effectively foreclose the possibility that radical form might still be put to radical uses beyond, in spite of, and sometimes within, the compromised arena of the marketplace.

Gunnar Swanson is right: form makes a claim. "Ugly" work can be authentic. "Beautiful" work can lie. And the opposite is also the case. Now that the shouting has died down, the real critical task – and nobody said it would be easy – is to decide which is which.

Eye, no. 15 vol. 4, 1994*

2. INTERNATIONAL GRAPHIC DESIGN

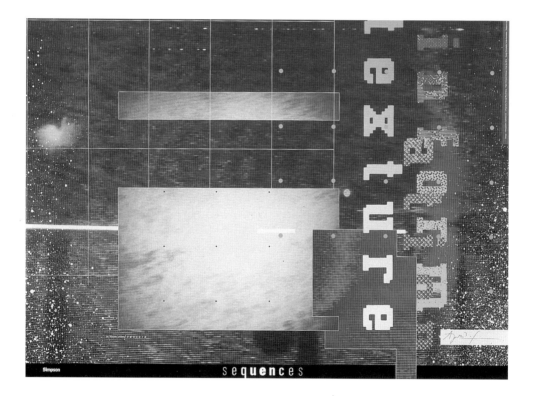

Information/Texture.
Promotional poster. Designer:
April Greiman. Simpson
Paper Company, USA, 1985

DRIFT AND FLOAT
APRIL GREIMAN

American graphic design has come so far in the last few years that it is hard to recapture what it was about April Greiman's work that made it so startling to viewers in the late 1970s. The devices she made her signature – the complex pictorial spaces, mysterious details, and dense layering of elements – have been seen so often in other people's work that very little of their shock value remains. By comparison with the typographic experiments of a more recent generation of designers, Greiman's early, post-Basel innovations look modest, while her emphasis on feeling, emotion and exploring her own "personal agenda" has evolved among those who followed her into an extreme subjectivity of content and form. The technology she was one of the first graphic designers to endorse and explore – the Apple Macintosh – is everywhere now. Today, Greiman is one of the profession's most celebrated figures and even the elder statesmen who once viewed her work with bafflement have come round to her cause.

Yet none of this should obscure the exceptional feat of imagination and synthesis which Greiman's career represents. The body of work she has created in the last fifteen years remains one of the most sustained and intelligent investigations of the nebulous zone where art, design and technology come together. Greiman, we can now see, was a harbinger and the problems she highlighted in her early design work are, if anything, all the more pressing today. How much "noise" or redundancy will a graphic message stand? Should it be as simple as possible, or as layered and exciting as the contemporary culture it reflects? Must it be purified of the designer's personality, or can the preoccupations of that personality be allowed to permeate and colour its content? If they can, where does graphic design stop and art begin? And what will be the graphic designer's role in the coming age of digital multimedia, when as yet static graphics perform in time as well as space?

Greiman graduated in graphic design from Kansas City Art Institute in 1970 during the heyday of corporate modernism. Inspired by three teachers of Swiss graphics at the school, she enrolled at the Kunstgewerbeschule in Basel, studying for six months with Armin Hofmann and New Wave typographer Wolfgang Weingart. Greiman plays down the influence of Swiss typography on her work, citing a more generalised lesson in elegance and refinement. But the sense of "structural integrity" she absorbed during this brief period is fundamental because, as she notes, "you can't have chaos without order [and] I think I've pushed everything else as far into chaos as I can." Typography provides the anchor against which the more freeform elements in her designs are allowed to play and pull. After Switzerland, she taught at Philadelphia College of Art, then freelanced in New York. In 1976, seduced by the light, colour, desert and ocean on a trip to California, she moved to Los Angeles.

With great rapidity Greiman established herself as a leader of the emerging New Wave. She found clients in the high-tech industries and the city's entertainment sector and devised fashionable identities for clothing stores and restaurants. Working with photographer Jayme Odgers, she made intricate, texture-loaded collages from cut-outs, colour Xeroxes, Japanese papers, airbrushing, and paint splatters. These multi-layered constructions were then photographed as a single composite image. A 1978 poster/mailer for the California Institute of the Arts confronts the viewer with a widescreen shot of a zero-gravity interior in which scale is surreally distorted – a pencil bulks as large as a dancer – and people, objects and typography drift and scatter through space. A cover for *Wet* magazine from 1979 fuses angular sheets of gradated colour dots and ornamental texture with a leaf, a fish, a cloud, a Japanese mask and the face of singer Ricky Nelson to achieve an image both casual and hieratically ordered – a homage to popular culture with a mystical edge.

Greiman's term for such designs is "hybrid imagery". This encapsulates both the collaging process which is the basis of all her work and the fusion of related technologies (photography, Xerox, video, or Macintosh) to make a single design. Greiman's approach is essentially additive. She doesn't refine and simplify her message until she reaches some unambiguous essence. Instead, she layers together a set of possibilities or options, then leaves the viewer to sort them out. "Am I making a more meaningful message by reducing and simplifying it," she asks, "or am I making a more meaningful message by throwing it all in?"

It is an increasingly familiar argument: design is overloaded and chaotic because the media landscape is overloaded and chaotic; why should the designer presume to decide what it is important to show, or not to show? "Designers of my age are making images of our own culture," says Greiman. "Ultimately the viewer would sift [the design] rather than me."

Perhaps her boldest essay in this regard is the special issue of *Design Quarterly* magazine (no. 133) she designed in 1986, a six foot-long double-sided poster which comes folded up in a paper wallet. The imagery inside, forming a sort of cosmological self-portrait, includes a timeline beginning with the birth of the solar system, a dinosaur, a disembodied brain, an astronaut, and a digitised image of a life-sized naked Greiman and her "spiritual double". On the cover Greiman asks the question "Does it make sense?" and answers with a quotation from Wittgenstein – "If you give it a sense, it makes sense" – that drives the ball firmly back into the viewer's court.

In practice, of course, a design can never be quite as open-ended and egalitarian as Greiman's invitation suggests. The designer is still the agent who shapes the image, even if she decides to include ten or a hundred components rather than one, and this act of selection already begins to narrow the range of possible readings. But maybe "readings" is not quite the word, since it suggests that designs like the *Wet* cover, *Design Quarterly* or Greiman's many other digital projects might, given sufficient insight, be reducible to particular rational "meanings". This is not, I think, their primary purpose, and it has never been Greiman's central concern, as many of her other statements confirm. It is noticeable how in discussions of her work, both in interviews and writing, Greiman usually prefers to concentrate on the technical means by which a design was achieved; she is unusually meticulous, in fact, in her documentation of these processes (the *Design Quarterly* poster, for instance, has extensive production notes). Intentionally or not, the effect is to deflect discussion from the question of content.

Greiman's designs, to borrow Susan Sontag's phrase, are against interpretation. "Interpretation," writes Sontag, "is the revenge of the intellect upon the world. To interpret is to impoverish, to deplete the world – in order to set up a shadow world of meanings." For Greiman, intuition comes first: meaning is more a matter of unconscious recognition than rational explanation. As she told an interviewer in 1982, her New Wave designs "have very much to do with the water and the mystery and the excitement and the irrational and the unexplained". She believes in the existence of universal shapes which have a collective significance and finds guidance in Carl Jung's *Man and his Symbols*. Colour, representing different kinds of energy, is another important source of symbolism. Like the painter De Chirico, she believes every object has two aspects – the visible, everyday aspect and the metaphysical aspect seen only in the moments of clairvoyance. Many of her designs are charged with this almost clairvoyant (one might equally say hallucinatory) glow.

Texture is also a crucial source of feeling. Discussing her early explorations of video at CalArts, Greiman notes how "parts of the images looked like a weaving or blanket. It was very relaxing for me. So I decided to incorporate these textures into what I was doing. I felt they evoked an emotional response. And that became a very important challenge for my design: to communicate about emotion." A stunning mid-period example of this approach is the *Information/Texture* poster she designed in 1985 for the Simpson Paper Company. Pulsing with energy like a distant galaxy seen through a telescope, the poster is a metaphorical star map pieced together from sections of open grid, rough-hewn computer-generated letterforms, and irregular slabs of video texture blown up to different sizes.

Information/Texture is a spectacular demonstration of Greiman's claim that form itself is the content of her work. Typography aside, it consists of only geometry, texture and colour yet it contrives to be infinitely suggestive. Form does not follow from content, Greiman argues, it *in*forms it. "Form is so plastic in [the digital] environment that it helps you discover your idea as you seek to realise it – to be more daring or more insightful with your idea than you had thought." The liquid imagery Greiman uses to describe this process of discovery-by-technology using video, Macintosh and Quantel Paintbox recalls her early description of the formal qualities of New Wave work: "the thing that I think is most interesting about technology is not having a result in mind; to suspend making judgements about things; to use it as a watery, intuitive, playful form of primary consciousness . . . To drift and float is the profound aspect of the dialogue between you and that tool."

Like many artists before her, Greiman welcomes the operations of chance. The designer's inexperience with new software and the bugs and imperfections of the technology allow accidents to happen which suggest unanticipated directions for the design. The lack of any established tradition or aesthetic restrictions for this kind of work makes the design process an exhilarating journey into unknown territory. And yet, despite her position in the vanguard of technological design, Greiman is not some unquestioning adherent of the digital box. She regards the computer as "just another pencil" and it is the ordinary pencil, she observed as recently as 1991, which she continues to favour. The starting points for many of her designs are pencil sketches which her assistants scan directly into the computer.

Greiman's impact on American graphic design has been considerable; the very "Americanness" of her design, its luxuriance, sun-drenched Californian colour and futurist conviction, means that her influence is perhaps less evident outside the country. She stands at the beginning of the postmodern period which has seen controversial and far-reaching changes in the way contemporary designers think about and practise their discipline. With Greiman, American graphics began to repair its broken relationship with art. Her legacy can be seen in the work issuing from CalArts, where she was director of the visual communications programme from 1982–84, and in the experimental graphics produced by students and graduates of the Cranbrook Academy of Art. If Greiman's work has sometimes been dismissed, discounted or just misunderstood, it is more a measure of its originality and piercing X-ray eye on the times than of its failure as "design". Greiman may not "solve" graphic design "problems" in the limited textbook sense of these terms, but for the adventurous clients who seek her out, her uncompromisingly personal vision is right for the job.

As a banner to rally under, the phrase "hybrid imagery" is well chosen. Greiman's 1990 book-cum-manifesto looks back over her career, but it also points forwards to the future. With the new digital platforms, media with once separate production and delivery technologies – text, image, sound, music, video, animation – are compressed into a single powerful tool. At this relatively early stage in the process it is hard to imagine quite what the new moving digital graphics will be like – graphics will, after all, be only one component in the multimedia mix – but Greiman's hybridising approach to the static graphic image provides one of the best models we have of the conceptual tools that the next wave of digital communicators will need. As graphic design completes the leap from paper to screen, Greiman's own future somewhere in this continuing process of exploration seems assured.

From: *April Greiman: it's not what you think it is,* 1994

LAYERS OF MEANING
KATHERINE McCOY

What attracted you to design?

I wanted to be an architect, but this was the early 1960s and the male high-school counsellor said, "Oh, you wouldn't like architecture, it has too much math. You should be an interior decorator." Industrial design was the university course that covered interior design. When I got in I discovered this whole discussion of problem-solving. For the first project we had to do 50 thumbnail sketches before we could go any further – 50 alternative concepts! – and I thought, "This is the way I want to approach my life. This is the way I think about life." It was so natural after trying other directions and thinking I was an artist, and the high school teacher trying to turn me into a painter.

How did you make the move from industrial design to graphic design?

I'm really grateful that I have a foundation in industrial design because graphic design still isn't taught with much conceptual methodology other than the "Aha!" method of intuition: have your brainstorm, get the idea and then turn it into form. Industrial design has so much more method to it. I discovered typography in the course of industrial design. I took one graphic design course at university, but it was a really weak programme: ten weeks of Chancery Italic calligraphy. It didn't seem to make a lot of sense, but I began to develop a love of typeforms.

I graduated with an industrial design portfolio that included some interiors and graphic design. My first job was with Unimark International, which was fortunate because it was interdisciplinary and that is what I wanted. The bulk of our work was corporate identity and I learned graphic design from several graphic designers at Unimark. It wasn't the ideal training because there was no formal structure, but it was very valuable because the designers were so good. I found I had a natural affinity for the logic of grids. Unimark was dedicated to what they called European design. Basically, they were bringing Swiss graphic design to the US, based on rationality and systems, objectivity, clarity, all those things inherited from the Bauhaus. It felt right with my earlier attraction to problem-solving. It was the way I wanted to see the world.

You became co-chair at Cranbrook with Mike McCoy after just five years of this. Did you have an early ambition to teach?

No, I never wanted to teach. The subject came up every once in a while – Mike would bring it up – and I was sure I didn't want to do it. The position at Cranbrook really just fell into our laps. It was something you could never have thought out, or planned for. On the other hand, when I look back on it, both Mike and I began having students in the studios where we were each working. Working for Chrysler Corporation after Unimark, I had a friend who would keep bringing his design work over to me, and I'd keep slapping his hand: "No! You used too many point sizes here, you violated the

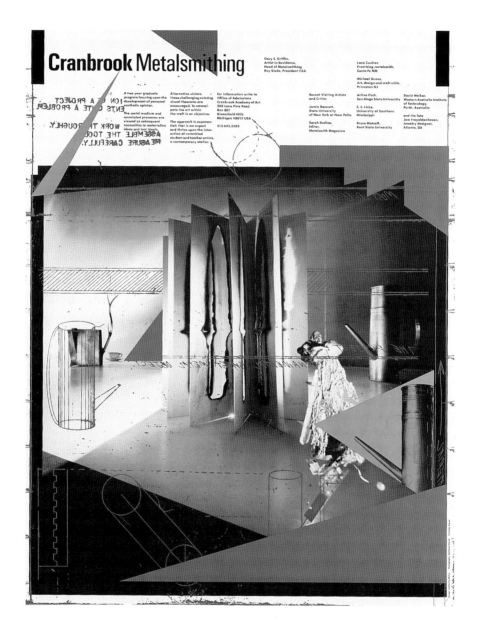

Cranbrook Metalsmithing

Gary S. Griffin,
Artist in Residence,
Head of Metalsmithing
Roy Slade, President CAA

A two year graduate
program focusing upon the
development of personal
aesthetic opinion.

The metal medium and
associated processes are
viewed as subsequent
necessities to materialize
ideas and test ideals.

Alternative visions,
those challenging existing
visual theorems are
encouraged. To emancipate the art within
the craft is an objective.

The approach is exponential; that is we expect
and thrive upon the interaction of committed
student and teacher artists,
a contemporary atelier.

For information write to
Office of Admissions
Cranbrook Academy of Art
500 Lone Pine Road
Box 801
Bloomfield Hills
Michigan 48013 USA

313.645.3303

Lana Coulter,
Practicing metalsmith,
Santa Fe NM

Michael Dunas,
Art, design and craft critic,
Princeton NJ

Recent Visiting Artists
and Critics

Jamie Bennett,
State University
of New York at New Paltz

Sarah Bodine,
Editor,
Metalsmith Magazine

Arline Fisch,
San Diego State University

C. E. Licka,
University of Southern
Mississippi

Bruce Metcalf,
Kent State University

David Walker,
Western Australia Institute
of Technology,
Perth, Australia

and the late
Jan Freydaahoven,
Jewelry designer,
Atlanta, GA

Cranbrook Metalsmithing.
Promotional poster. Designer:
Katherine McCoy. Cranbrook
Academy of Art, USA, 1986

grid there!" It was relatively easy to teach graphic design because there were these nice
rules. So it was fairly natural to start teaching and I do find I always have an urge to
teach. Even with ice-skating, which is an enthusiasm of mine, I find myself teaching
people who just know a little less than me.

What kept you at Cranbrook for such a long time – 24 years?

That's a long time, for sure, but at this point I could never see myself not teaching,
because you learn so much. I'm totally convinced that the teacher learns the most!
So that's my motivation for teaching – it is almost self-interest. It is so stimulating, it
challenges you to grow. Why stay at Cranbrook for so long? Because it is such a flexible
situation. At Cranbrook a department chair is everything from teacher to janitor to
alumni relations director. There is no one to argue with about philosophical direction.
If you want change, you can change. The only real requirement from the administration
is that you attract good students and produce strong graduates who find their way in the
profession. So we have turned a lot of corners over the years. We kept getting interested
in new things and the programme kept growing. It wasn't just from changes that we
made, but also from new directions initiated by the students. They kept evolving and
becoming interested in new things, so it was constantly changing.

Why are you leaving now, given that it turned out so well?

The cost of all that teaching freedom at Cranbrook is that it is a very intense, demanding
situation for nine and a half months of the year. I have experienced whatever revelations
come from being in charge, being responsible for a whole programme. In that sense
there is nothing left to prove to myself. I would now like to teach in a place where
someone will just hand me some terrific students, and drop into a stimulating
programme, while being more free to do other things. I would like to write more
and have more time for personal work at our "electronic cottage" in Colorado. We are
planning to teach at Chicago's Institute of Design at Illinois Institute of Technology
for one semester a year. This could be seen as a change of environment for us, since
many have characterised Cranbrook as the art of design and ID as the science of design.
But the commonality we see is the cultural function of design – the cultural human
factors of objects and communications.

**What sort of students has Cranbrook attracted over the years, and what are they looking for when
they come to you?**

One of the first things we felt we needed to do when we began teaching at Cranbrook
was to define what we had to offer and, in a sense, define our market to attract the kind
of students we wanted. I really enjoy working with mature students in their mid-20s
and early 30s – we have also had some very mature students! – with some professional
experience. A strong undergraduate foundation in design is good but, on the other hand,
some of our most interesting students come from very different backgrounds and found
their way into design informally, on the job, and are now looking for a more structured
experience to focus their design work.

   We insist that students be absolutely motivated and dedicated to their work, with
a lot of initiative. The most important thing is not to know, but to know how to know.
We also get very polished professionals who feel as if they have reached a plateau in
their work. They have learnt a role and they are practising it, but they want to look
inside as well as outside to find a personal voice and vision.

**In the 1980s theoretical ideas assumed considerable importance at the Academy. How did that
come about?**

We always encourage students to read. It is an unstructured programme so we have never had courses with official reading lists. Instead, because of the personal nature of each student's programme, they independently construct their own focus. We have an ongoing department bibliography, and it has been a long-term project of mine to expand it and keep it as current as possible. It all comes back to my early interest in problem-solving. Part of the students' goal for the two years is to develop their own conceptual strategies as designers. We encourage them to capitalise on their strengths, to become aware of their natural abilities, but also to incorporate external methods for conceptualising. We are continually looking for additional theories. Semiotics was always something we discussed – not as a major focus, as at Rhode Island School of Design – but trying to make sure the students understood the fundamentals and its potential as a design tool. Also, in the 1970s we brought the structured planning processes developed at Illinois Institute of Technology into the design department.

The department is fortunate to have a really good fine art photography programme next door to us in the same building, where they are also very interested in visual theory. Fine art photography was the first field to apply post-structuralism to visual media, such as the idea that you can read a photograph and decode it. I think a lot of these ideas have been communicated informally by talk between room-mates, in studio romances and hanging around each other's studios.

In the mid to late 1970s there was a move away from minimalism, but it was mainly a formal investigation influenced by people like Weingart and April Greiman. It was not so much a questioning of the conceptual foundations of modernism as a questioning of its formal expression. By the early 1980s that seemed to be pretty thoroughly explored. Every new group asks itself: "What's the contribution we're going to make?" There were a couple of itchy years when students were searching for new approaches and finding little things here or there that didn't quite come to fruition. But the next direction really began to emerge with the class Jeffery Keedy was in, around 1984 – a group of avid theory hunters! That class and several in succession, including the class Edward Fella was in, very aggressively searched out and explored post-structuralist theories and philosophy. For a while it seemed like the theory-of-the-week club – structuralism, post-structuralism, deconstruction, phenomenology, critical theory, reception theory, hermeneutics, lettrism, Venturi vernacularism, postmodern art theory – but gradually the ideas were sifted through, assimilated, and the most applicable began to emerge.

I have been told that you resisted some of those ideas at first.

Yes, and I still do! Isn't that appropriate? Because post-structuralism is all about resistance. The excitement of discovery leads to great enthusiasm and the nature of a lot of these post-structuralist writers is to question all the fundamental values of culture. Frankly, I wasn't ready to remake my value system completely and I do think that there have been a couple of useful contributions among all those dead white men. I wasn't sure how all of this was going to fit, plus I was searching for the forms it would take. There is a recent quote of Jeff Keedy's where he says that I kept asking, "But what does it look like? What does this mean in terms of design? How do you make it work as a design tool?"

One of your graduates, Andrew Blauvelt, made a comment recently in *Emigre*, which I would like to hear your views on. He talked about graphic design as symptom and cure. "We had the cure in modernism. In the other camp, graphic design as symptom, we have Cranbrook." Do you agree with this analysis?

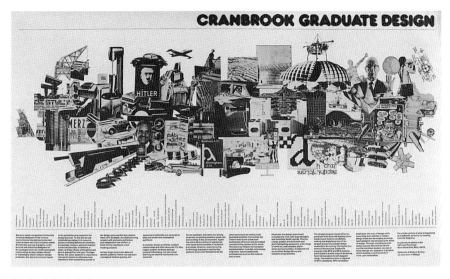

Cranbrook Graduate Design.
Promotional poster. Designer:
Katherine McCoy. Cranbrook
Academy of Art, USA, 1971

It does seem that graphic design should reflect its cultural milieu if it is honest to its time and its audiences. Designers are responsible for a significant part of our society's cultural production, so I think we have a responsibility to produce culturally current work. If a designer takes a nihilistic view of the cacophony of modern life, then I suppose confused complexity would be an honest expression, although that certainly is not my view.

One thing I would like to point out is that a lot of work coming out of Cranbrook is not formally complex. If you look at the *New Discourse* book some of the work has only three elements to it. That is not, to me, formally complex design. Most people think of Cranbrook as only doing layered work, but a lot of this goes back to the pre-poststructuralist period – the "high formalism" – although certainly Allen Hori's work, for instance, continues to be very complex and layered. But the complexity I'm interested in is complexity of meaning. I'm not so much interested in the layers of form as the layers of meaning. The first reading is the ostensible first layer of objective meaning. But what is the second? The third? If you were to live with a poster in your dining room for the next three months, what would you continue to find as you spent more time with it? I think this approach fits modern society because the contemporary world is subtle and complex. Simple black and white dualisms no longer work. Graphic design that tries to make things simple is not doing anybody any real benefit. Society needs to understand how to deal with the subtlety, complexity and contradiction in contemporary life. I also think it is possible and necessary to have both complexity and intelligibility in graphic design.

To say "This is the primary information layer, but there are other layers too" is to create a meaningful hierarchy and imply a degree of resolution. There is a fundamental difference, though, between what you're saying and the student who says: "The world is confusing and impossible to make sense of and I'm going to reflect this confusion in my work."

I do believe that the rationalism and objectivity of the modernist tradition have an important place in the design process. The informational content of a message must be ordered into comprehensible hierarchies, typically the first layer of reading. I teach a method of message analysis in our first graphic sequence project and it is always there in my own work. I think a lot of people assume that because a piece is formally complex, the information will be difficult to penetrate. But if you look closely at a lot of the more pragmatic student printed work, I think you will find that the first layer of content is quite direct and well ordered.

On the other hand, sometimes students assume that there is meaning inherent in complexity itself – if it is obscure, it must be profound. I have a big problem with that.
What is your concern about the "deconstructionist" label that Cranbrook and other recent work have attracted?
Deconstruction is a term originally used by only a few French theorists. When you add that "ist" to it, then it is reduced to a faddish term. "Deconstructionist" now seems to mean forms deconstructed or taken apart, disassemblage. One of the regrettable things about the term is that people who haven't read about it very deeply conclude that it is just about form and, more than that, that it is about the disassembling of visual language. That is part of the process, but I am interested in the idea of deconstructing the relationship of written and visual language to understand the dynamics and intentions in communication. Analysis is breaking down existing things to understand what is happening. The second half of it is: what do you learn from that? How can you build from there, as a proactive, synthetic strategy? Student experiments search for signposts in their conceptual processes to create new methods of communication. I am interested in discovering new options for our audiences such as the idea of encouraging the participation of the audience, opening up meaning so that they can be involved in the construction of meaning and make individual interpretations. This is one strategy for turning the analytical process into a synthetic process.
Is it possible to produce a genuinely probing contemporary graphic design without addressing theory in some way?
Yes and no. Even the most intuitive designers are influenced by the thinking of their professional milieu. These theories become absorbed by the mainstream so quickly that all these ideas are potential resources. I think of design as a pluralistic activity. Having started out with the big ideology of high modernism, and seeing the limitations of one theory for all messages and audiences, I am now interested in the more modest idea of looking for pragmatic tools so that each designer can develop an effective personal process. Every designer is an individual. The idea of a designer swallowing any one method whole and then becoming that is not right or honest. We each should try to find our own best method of working, a synthesis of many different methods combined with our native talents and inclinations.

A lot of people feel that there is a certain pretension in theory and I probably felt that too, early on. There is an idea that the people involved in theory are poseurs and are trying to make graphic design more than it really is. None of us really understands what theory is very well. It would be useful for us to look at other fields to see the role theory plays in assembling a body of knowledge, structuring it, and guiding professional practice. Another thing one hears frequently when explaining a little theory to a group of designers is, "Well, I knew that anyway." In a way that is exactly right. That is the whole point of theory – theory explains phenomena and dynamics that exist out there. You might have known instinctively that a piece of graphic design is successful, but

theory helps to explain why it is successful – or unsuccessful – and hopefully the
theory can also translate into some sort of a guiding strategy as well.

**Do you see much evidence that more theoretical approaches to design are being applied intelligently
within the American mainstream?**

Some theoretical strategies are finding their way into professional work. Maybe the
most prevalent is the opening up of meaning through multivalent shifting symbols
and language – constructive ambiguity – for more active audience interpretation.
I am thinking of the Time Warner annual reports and the Burton snowboard graphics
in entertainment and youth-oriented markets. Of course, there is always the issue of
appropriateness; opening up meaning and multiple interpretations might not be
appropriate for certain types of communication problems – a stop sign, for instance!
An earlier example would be Venturi's ideas about the encoded power of commercial
vernacular styles. We see postmodern eclecticism all over, but much of that
demonstrates the downside of the dissemination of theoretical ideas. So often only
the visual look of the theory gets appropriated and not the underlying ideas.

What are your personal criteria for evaluating the quality of a design?

That is a really crucial point. That is half the challenge for each student who comes to
our programme – to develop a personal set of standards for judging design. Actually, that
is one of the things I felt most uncomfortable about with the first use of deconstructive
theory: the rejection of dominant paradigms. Does that mean that everything is OK?
That there are no valid standards? I have come to think that a different view of standards
is needed, something each designer needs to define for themselves. Every graphic work
has relative degrees of success and failure; each designer must define their own value
system and therefore their own criteria for evaluating relative success and failure.

**The logic of that might be that everyone arrives at such a radically different value system that
there could be no conversation. Can any form of consensus be reached?**

Certainly that is the crucial question for a contemporary multicultural democratic
society. As much as I believe in pluralism, I am also convinced of the necessity for
consensus. In design, it is possible to have a conversation because we really aren't all
that different; we share a common history and communicate intensely. Occasionally
you will find a piece of graphic design that is so clearly successful that everybody can
agree on its quality, regardless of their biases.

How would you characterise that quality?

Resonance, an instinctive recognition and response from a viewer/reader. The resonance
I am thinking of is resonance within our audience. I think it has to do with some sort
of interaction with individual experiences and value systems. Of course, that is more
and more difficult to do in these days of highly segmented multicultural audiences.

**Graphic design is in a time of real transition. How are things going to change for graphic designers
in the next few years?**

I think the process of professionalisation is continuing. Some basic theories and
methodologies are being codified, offering alternatives to the intuitive "Aha!" method.
The educational level of our schools is improving. Many graduates are coming out
of graphic design programmes with something closer to a true education these days.
On the other hand, the refusal to consider accreditation and educational standards is
a big threat in the US. Every other design field has these, but not graphic design. I hope
that will change as the older generation, which feels it would stifle creativity, moves out
of the picture. Another problem is that graphic design is a cash-cow for universities.

There are great numbers of students interested in graphic design now, and market forces are hurting educational quality. There are over 1,000 schools in the US, maybe 2,000, that say they teach graphic design. Of all these, there are maybe 30 good schools.

There has been an immense growth and improvement in professionalism in the last fifteen years. Professional practice as we know it will continue to improve conceptually to the point where design is seen as a strategic process in business and society, operating on a higher level in the business hierarchy. On the other hand, there is a media revolution and an aggressive new area is developing: dynamic multimedia, design digitally produced and digitally delivered as well. It is more than a subset of graphic design, because it involves time, motion and interactivity.

Is the average graphic designer necessarily the right person to do that kind of work?

They might not be, at least for the moment, since multimedia is so new and no one is an expert. But the tools we have now are not sufficient to really understand non-linear interactivity. We need to know so much more about cognitive psychology, about orientation and navigation, as well as our other visual communication tools. I would like to think that a new field might come out of these two areas. It will still be about visual communications, but it will be a much greater intellectual and conceptual challenge than graphic design has been up to now. Multimedia is not just another subset in the school programme, like editorial design, typeface design and so on. It is much more demanding technically and will probably require a masters degree.

What are your goals post-Cranbrook?

I would like to draw on our ongoing experiments in form and strategy to develop some modest theoretical structures specifically for visual communications, which can then be taught. I want to do more graphic design work too, and write and/or design books. I have some other informal interests that will not replace design, but are important to me to develop further: figure-skating, ceramics and the history of the American West. Figure-skating and ceramics both have a lot to do with design. With ceramics, there is a physicality and immediate response from the clay as it takes form. Its instant gratification is a wonderful counterpoint to design's abstractions and planning.

Figure-skating makes a really interesting analogy to issues of form and style. In figure-skating there are a set number of moves, like in ballet. Ballet is all constructed, a system, and there is some of that in figure-skating. Then there is the physics of it. The better form you have the more power you have and the less effort you must expend. You maximise your input as you refine your form. In graphic design, the Bauhaus taught us to distrust form and style as superficial. But taken on a deeper level, might it not be possible that, just as in athletics, the more form and style are developed and refined, the more communicative power is possible?

Eye, no. 16 vol. 4, 1995*

THE GOOD, THE BAD AND THE GOOFY
HARD WERKEN

The clash between Wim Crouwel and Jan van Toorn has entered the folklore of Dutch design. At a public debate in November 1972, the ideological opponents squared up to the nature of graphic communication. Crouwel, austere principal of Total Design, put the case for functionalism and an analytical, systems-building method. Van Toorn, a radical freelance and now, like Crouwel, an elder statesman of Dutch design, rejected what he saw as lifeless standardisation in favour of the personal and subjective. For all their antipathy, both in their way were modernists, heirs to the typophotographic legacy of Zwart, Schuitema and Kiljan. Many of their listeners, versed in the same tradition, fell into one camp or the other.

Not everyone, however, was convinced. "I was still a student," recalls Gerard Hadders. "I looked at the work they were doing and I said, 'Fuck them! I'd rather look at a copy of Italian *Vogue*.'" Hadders and his partners in Hard Werken have been looking for inspiration where a Dutch designer might least expect to find it ever since. Quite deliberately they have broken every rule in the handbook. Scattershot layouts, jarring mismatches of type, shrieking colours and a veneer of industrial grime seem calculated to assault the sensibilities of more delicate colleagues. Hard Werken's critics, and even some of their friends, accuse them of "decadence". One writer on a Dutch newspaper loathed their work so much he demanded Hadders be slung into jail for his offences against good taste – with an extra year inside for his by British standards wholly conventional cover for *The Name of the Rose*.

Even now, almost a decade after Hard Werken was formed, the impression persists that they are a bunch of freebooting anarchists, wilfully courting obscurity and ugliness. *The Graphic Design Source Book*, published in 1987, quotes them as saying: "Everything is done for no reason at all." Maybe they did once say something to this effect (it's hard to tell, the *Source Book* doesn't give a source). They certainly deny it now, declaring the opposite to be the case. Everything is done for a reason and the reason could not be more ordinary: Hard Werken simply want to communicate the client's message. If they use brutal, confrontational imagery for an exhibition poster, it will be because the artist's work is brutal and confrontational, not because they set out to shock. Next to Gert Dumbar's more anarchistic provocations, Hard Werken come across as the epitome of responsible professionalism.

What continues to set them apart from the two main streams of Dutch graphic design is the variety of means they are prepared to use. For an outsider accustomed to the anything-goes eclecticism and intellectual sterility of British graphics, one of the pleasures of Dutch graphic design is its rigour and consistency, the sense that each new piece of "information" is being filtered through a highly developed (and necessarily

Hard Werken. Cover of
issue 10. Designer: Gerard
Hadders, Hard Werken.
The Netherlands, 1982

Perfo2 including the
Symphonie Perfomantique.
Album cover. Designer:
Tom van den Haspel, Hard
Werken. Lantaren Venster,
The Netherlands, 1984

reductive) language of typography and form. Dutch graphic design is instantly identifiable and this structural and stylistic coherence extends to the work of its individual practitioners. For Hard Werken, though, the very consistency of national and individual style militates against the uniqueness of a particular message; the culture of design is bigger than the thing it describes and content loses out to form. "We don't talk about style," they say. "We talk about method."

The group began life as a magazine of the same name, formed with the backing of Rotterdam's authorities in 1978 to show that cultural life didn't stop at the city limits of Amsterdam. In 1980, several of its editor–designers decided to band together as Hard Werken Association to undertake other design projects outside the magazine (which continued for ten issues until 1982). Today five of the original group remain: Willem Kars, Rick Vermeulen, Tom van den Haspel, Gerard Hadders and Henk Elenga, who runs Hard Werken LA Desk, their Los Angeles office.

Hard Werken's Rotterdam studio is tucked away in the light industrial landscape that marks the beginning of the city's sprawling dockland and even the taxi drivers find it hard to locate. Ecologically-sound bicycles are parked in the hall, the stairs are decorated by Hard Werken's early posters and the landing outside their office is dominated by theatrical furniture by Tom van den Haspel. Inside, there is no obvious reception and the atmosphere, with rock music playing, is informal rather than businesslike.

Kars, Vermeulen and Hadders are much the same. Their conversational style, like the group name, is jokey, irreverent and ironic. "Goofy" is a favourite word; "this is an example of our non-grid layout capacity" a typical observation. Hadders, burly and outspoken, does most of the talking, but the attitudes he expresses are shared. "You must have irony to be able to operate well in the design business. A lot of people take themselves much too seriously – moneywise, but also in the content of their work. You can be very serious about your stuff, but that has to do with your intentions, your method. No single piece of print is sacred, because it's the output of the moment."

Hard Werken's not inconsiderable output is currently running, they estimate, at about 500 items a year. In the past most of their clients have come from the cultural domain: art galleries, museums, publishing houses, film festivals, universities, the ministry of culture, architects and furniture companies. Their aim now is to pursue corporate identity work, to build up the interior design side of the company and to "expand to a European scale" (they have a staff of fifteen) without sacrificing their identity. They have very little choice. Most of the founders are 40 or so, and they can't play at being *enfants terribles* for ever. Nor is the cultural arena alone sufficiently large to support all the Dutch design groups vying for its services. Even more worrying, from their point of view, are the advances being made in the Netherlands by commercially aggressive British companies like Fitch & Co, David Davies Associates and Wolff Olins.

Preferring not to see themselves as a "Dutch" design group, Hard Werken show every sign of being prepared to compete on the same terms. They feel much closer to the "emotional" use of letterforms found in British graphics than they do to Dutch austerity. "Typographically speaking we go back to William Morris. Stanley Morison is too modern for us," says Hadders. "Gutenberg is too modern for us!" adds Kars. Wolff Olins, rather than any of their Dutch colleagues, is the design group they most often invoke (and occasionally visit). They joke about what would happen if they were bought by the company or, even more wishfully, if they were to buy out Olins. They are mastering marketing-speak.

The priority now is to learn how to approach, convince and satisfy a new kind of client. "Recently I had a meeting with Wim Beeren, director of the Stedelijk Museum," says a slightly bruised Hadders. "He's said to be a difficult man to handle, but I can deal with him very well. We got along and I can work for him. A day later I was confronted with the PR person of a medium-sized manufacturing company. I couldn't handle this person at all."

Hard Werken grew out of a "graphic workshop" with its own printing press and a first-hand understanding of technical processes remains the cornerstone of their work. They learned the rules before they presumed to break them. Few Dutch graphic designers, they say, pay sufficient attention to the technical developments that can determine design; of the previous generation, only Anthon Beeke, formerly of Total Design, has in their view fully embraced the opportunities afforded by offset litho printing. While some Dutch designers with international reputations still think in terms of letterpress or rubbing down Letraset, Hard Werken claim to astound penny-pinching colleagues by their willingness to pay advertising rates for the best quality photosetting. They have forged strong links with the Macintosh pioneers at *Emigre* magazine in California.

It's this knowledge of what can be done and urge to experiment that seems to drive many of their more controversial efforts. In recent years some of their most interesting work has been for the publisher, Bert Bakker. In Britain and the US, the gold-foil blocking of towering book titles has long been a commonplace of potboiler publishing. Not so in the Netherlands, where Hard Werken's decision to apply it to a title of more literary outlook, *The Name of the Rose*, contributed to a rumpus only relieved by the book's commercial success. "They say it changed the face of Dutch publishing," notes Hadders wryly. "But it wasn't on purpose, I can tell you that. Right now we are in the middle of a foil-stamping war."

This was one of Hard Werken's more "classical" covers. Others, such as a volume of short stories whose title translates as "A Butcher's Son With Glasses On", are, well, goofier. Here, right-handed Hadders used his left hand to scrawl the title, author's name and a pair of spectacles, which he then superimposed on a boyhood photograph of the writer. It's an engaging, oddly beatnik image. The typographer–critic who had called for his incarceration was once again outraged. Not that Hadders or the rest of the team are losing any sleep over it. "If someone can't understand that a cover like this is made in relation to the contents of the book," Hadders says simply, "they must either be stupid or blind."

Blueprint, July/August 1989

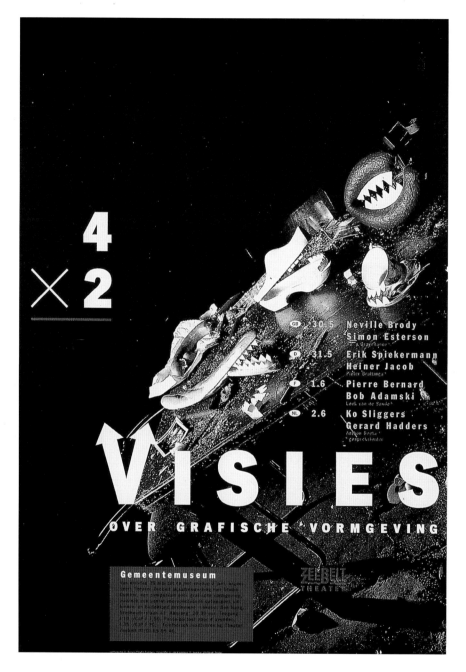

*Visies over Grafische
Vormgeving*. Poster for a
series of design debates.
Designer: Gert Dumbar.
Typographer: Robert Nakata,
Studio Dumbar. Photographer:
Lex van Pieterson. Zeebelt
Theatre, The Netherlands, 1989

FUNCTION AND PLEASURE
STUDIO DUMBAR

Almost two decades after it was founded Studio Dumbar occupies a highly unusual position in contemporary design. While Gert Dumbar's graphic laboratory is still a watchword for uncompromising experimentation of a kind that seems, from outside the country at least, to embody a freedom that is essentially Dutch, it is at the same time a responsible organisation entrusted with serious business projects by clients at the highest level. Experimentalists are often taken to task for producing work that is commercially unviable and therefore of supposedly limited relevance. Equally at home working for an avant-garde theatre group or the Dutch police force, Studio Dumbar has shown time and again that it is possible to extend the graphic conventions of the corporate mainstream. Any account of design innovation in the 1980s would put the studio at the forefront, yet it would not be out of place in a group that included such commercial heavyweights as Wolff Olins, Chermayeff & Geismar, and Pentagram.

Studio Dumbar has always attracted controversy. "Frivolous", "decorative" and "visual entertainment" are some of the milder criticisms thrown at it over the years. Its output has been less tolerantly blasted as "random", "gratuitous" and "irresponsible". To promise function and not deliver it, a critic declared of one project, is to descend into "graphical decadence". Dumbar himself has often seemed to delight in these spluttering expressions of aesthetic and moral outrage. Either deliberately, or because he genuinely cannot help himself, he has supplied his detractors with plenty of ammunition. "People ask, 'What is this for?'" he once said. "But there is no logic to what we do: it is an emotional thing." In the same interview, he followed this startling admission with a claim that makes no sense other than as a deliberate provocation of anyone stuffy enough to take him at his word. "I would love," he said, "to present a timetable which is completely unreadable."

For Dumbar, the emotional, expressive content of a piece of work is of central importance. "Think with your heart" he told his students during his brief professorship at the Royal College of Art in London in the mid-1980s. The deliberate "nonsense" he likes to inject into the studio's work is there to spice things up because without it projects would be duller, less engaging, less human and more ordinary. Dumbar makes no bones about "stealing" ideas from the launchpad of fine art, but he is ambiguous as to whether he thinks what the studio creates is art: "If people wish to call it art, then that is their choice and not ours." His fear of restriction and conformity, of finding himself trapped within an inflexible bureaucratic system, extends to the day-to-day organisation of the studio, which allows individual designers an exceptional degree of autonomy in dealing with the studio's clients. Dumbar himself has been famously outspoken on what he calls the "curious and contradictory" relationship between designers and clients. "To get around the client and his marketing experts," he has written, "you sometimes have to resort to subterfuge, even guerrilla tactics." Clients in a meeting with Dumbar are likely to find themselves on their knees on the floor studying drawings and plans alongside the designers. Once everyone is in it together it is harder to say no.

Yet it is immediately clear, on looking through the studio's output, that Dumbar's teasing public utterances have given a somewhat one-sided picture of his actual concerns. On paper, Studio Dumbar's work is determined not so much by a wilful rejection of reason as by a series of elemental tensions present to some degree (with inevitable variations, depending on the project) in almost everything they do: order and anarchy, function and pleasure, restraint and emotion, decorum and humour, observance and innovation, reason and the irrational. One of the studio's most expressive metaphors for this tension of opposites is seen in a series of posters for the Zeebelt Theatre in which an area of floor is covered by smashed eggs and tomatoes carefully separated from each other into two groups in a way that would never have occurred if they had been randomly thrown or dropped. The visual contradiction, true to the contradictions of everyday life, is suggestive and engaging in a way that design that is either faultlessly logical or entirely abandoned can never be.

Studio Dumbar is a collective endeavour in which to date some 50 designers from all over the world have taken part, yet its formal development, under Gert Dumbar's direction, displays a remarkable degree of coherence. Elements of the studio's mature style are present in embryonic form in its earliest work. A party invitation of 1980 makes use of arbitrary props, such as a snaking electrical cord, which would rapidly bloom (or degenerate) over the next few years into intricately entropic, staged photography tableaux cobbled together by Dumbar and Lex van Pieterson – a collaboration which dates back to the late 1960s. The typography is equally prophetic. With its exaggerated letter- and number-spacing, use of irregular boxes and dotted rules, and dynamic contrasts of size and weight, it anticipates the PTT identity of nearly a decade later.

It was the two annuals designed for *European Illustration*, though, which helped to introduce Studio Dumbar's irreverent humour to a wider international audience. The 82/83 annual's cover by Ko Sliggers, a key figure in the early years of the studio, is a spoof map of trends in illustration which reveals, among other phenomena, a dense area of pen and ink drawing in Macedonia and an outbreak of mixed media along the coast of France. Inside, the publisher's logo is randomly scattered across the pages along with mysteriously repeated details – a cloud, a bar stool, a lightbulb – from some of the illustrations. The following year's annual is altogether harder-edged. The jury portraits are constructed as puppets and, violating the rectangular norm, photographs are twisted into brutal shapes. Staged photographs resembling cities of rubbish are additionally layered and masked by tracing paper cut by Michel de Boer to create jagged windows. In both books, however, the text and caption treatments are a calm and unexceptionable modernist sanserif of uniform size in one of two weights. It is as though the books contain two unreconciled systems, the typographic and the imagistic, respectively embodying communicative order and emotional chaos. The image is treated aggressively as a territory for disruption, but at this early stage such incursions do not extend to the type.

In the *European Illustration* annuals type and image are held apart, but in the Rijksmuseum signing project of the same period these tensions achieve a satisfying degree of resolution. Functionalist pictograms representing lifts, telephone, information, cloakroom, the exit, and so on are superimposed on details from paintings in the museum's collection. The lift, for instance, reduced as graphic information to paired arrows for up and down, is simultaneously expressed as an ascending angel. The typography of more elaborate directional signs unfolds against a visible grid consisting of broken and dotted rules, arrows, mathematical signs, symbols and names of people, painters and paintings in the collection. The grid is not made to account for itself; it just is. Its purpose, in Dumbar's words, is "pure fun", but there is more to it than this. What makes the project so remarkable is the way that its components cohere to make both graphic and cultural sense. Beyond its primary function as a means of making the museum legible while expressing its identity, the signing conveys a strong sense of continuity between the historical achievements of Dutch painting and the visual landscape of the present. It offers a suggestively compressed history lesson, while acting as a declaration of faith on the part of the museum in the continuation of the visual tradition.

In the course of the 1980s, the studio demonstrated time and again that it was possible for a progressive, even wayward, visual spirit to coexist with the most ordinary functional and commercial needs. Dumbar first designed the Spoorboekje, the Dutch railway timetables, in the early 1970s, with his team at Tel Design. At the functional level, in the composition of their pages, these books achieve what he calls "stylistic durability"; in other words they are made to last. By the mid-1980s, the studio was illustrating the covers with mysterious, irregularly-cut photographic details of speeding trains – in one clouds are clipped into the approximate shape of a crown – linked as if to suggest diagrammatic meaning by curved and straight rules. This love of the irregular almost for its own sake culminated in the well-known poster series for Artifort in which the distinctive lines and shapes of the Quadrio sofa, Series 1200/1300 chair and other pieces became generators for virtuoso feats of die-cutting.

An equally free graphic language was applied to the corporate identity projects of the period. Michel de Boer's identity manual for the Dutch automobile organistion, the ANWB, treats the logo based on a 65 degree grid as the starting point for a complex geometry of thick and thin rules cut by a single yellow curve that turns out, on closer inspection, to link the copyright symbol and date. The inside is anything but arid. Rectilinear page structures are breached by type elements and soft edges. Illustrations by the New York-based artist Andrzej Dudzinski establish a playful tone. A sun rises progressively into the "sky" of the page, at one point appearing on a graph. Towards the end of the book, night begins to fall, the pages darken and the sun is replaced by the moon. Other motifs and shapes appear at random. "It's full of those things which have to do with the joy of life," notes Dumbar.

While Studio Dumbar has a strong presence within the Netherlands' corporate and institutional landscape, it has also shown a high degree of commitment to the performing arts. It is here, in projects for the Holland Festival and Zeebelt Theatre (co-founded by Gert Dumbar), that the studio's method has been at its most experimental and extreme. The exceptional flexibility of the Holland Festival logo, designed in three versions by Edward McDonald, can be seen in the "Uit de Muziek Sovjetunie" poster of 1989, which achieves a perfect marriage between staged photography and the dominant typographic layer. The model's hand becomes a fulcrum, resting against a tilted list of musicians, while the festival logo overlaps and fuses with the title, its usual terminating dot replaced by a reprise of the Holland "H" set in a circle poised at her fingertips.

Antichambre. Theatre poster.
Designer: Albert Leeflang,
Studio Dumbar. Photographer:
Lex van Pieterson. Het
Nationale Toneel, The
Netherlands, 1995

De Dood en de Duivel. Theatre
poster. Designer: Bob van Dijk,
Studio Dumbar. Photographer:
Lex van Pieterson. Het
Nationale Toneel, The
Netherlands, 1994

Where Studio Dumbar's corporate typography usually follows the conventions and practice of continental modernism, in the cultural projects type plays a much more assertive role. For reasons of economy as well as consistent identity, the studio has often used a two-stage process for promotional posters, in which a standard litho-printed image of a staged photograph (created by Dumbar and Lex van Pieterson) is screen-printed in a single colour with different typographic information for each new event or performance. The Zeebelt backgrounds, for instance, were used for a year or even longer. Over time, this has the effect of switching attention from the image – which, however wild, becomes predictable and familiar with repetition – to the typography's role as protagonist. In an inversion of their usual relationship, the photograph takes on the role of the "grid" while the type becomes the illustration allowed to play freely across this stable base. In one Holland Festival series based on a classical face garlanded with surrealist musical instruments, purple boxes of type zig-zag across the base image in a way that serves largely to cancel it out.

Typographic experimentation became progressively more marked in the second half of the 1980s. At Katherine McCoy's invitation, Dumbar lectured at the Cranbrook Academy of Art in 1985 and since then there has been a regular procession of pilgrims from Michigan to The Hague, chief among them Robert Nakata, who stayed on to become an important member of the studio. While Dumbar has never shared the theoretical preoccupations of McCoy and her students – "For the Dutch," Jan Jancourt, the first Cranbrook intern, said later, "form is enough" – their reciprocal influence had a significant impact on the studio's work, above all in the treatment of type.

In the Zeebelt posters, the lack of a client in the ordinary sense meant the designers and interns could experiment with impunity. In some cases, the over-printing of type and areas of flat colour all but obliterates the image below. The distinction seen in the *European Illustration* annuals between type as sacrosanct provider of information and image as theatre of chaos finally collapses. Nothing is safe. In the Oktober at Zeebelt poster, designed in 1993, two equally disordered systems – typographic and photographic – jostle for precedence as the event information meanders its way across broken crockery strewn on the floor. Allen Hori's posters for "Contemporary Improvised Music" and the "Laboratory of Plastic Sound", staged by Ooyevaer Desk at the Zeebelt Theatre in 1990, are at first sight dauntingly intricate structures which attempt to give largely typographic expression to the complexities of the new music and experimental films they advertise. Recent posters for Het Nationale Toneel (The National Theatre) are fewer in their elements and simpler in construction, but show a similar reliance on typography for narrative effect. The staged photography tableaux made notorious by the studio are abandoned. In their place, the theatre's clear perspex logo takes on the role of typographic "actor", casting long theatrical shadows and duetting in different ways, from poster to poster, with the play's title.

The experimental urge behind such projects found its most remarkable public expression in early 1989 in the studio's house style for the newly privatised postal and telecommunications company, the PTT. Based on the colours, Univers type and squares of the existing identity, its starting point was a "deconstruction sketch" by studio member Ton van Bragt which showed the geometrical extrapolations that would be possible using its grid. The aim, Dumbar observed with his usual disregard for corporate received wisdom, was "totally anti-clarity because clarity can be very boring". With the new house style, "clarity" of company image would come from its radical difference from competitors in the marketplace. The "dogmatic forms" of the basic identity – red for Post, green for Telecom, blue for other divisions – would be undogmatically reinterpreted by Studio Dumbar, as well as other design groups, like a piece of music improvised around a familiar theme. In the more advanced abstractions, from canteen crockery to wall-sized murals, the PTT's identity is playfully expressed through wordless geometry and colours alone.

Dumbar has written candidly about the sleights of hand involved in winning approval for the house style's wilder offshoots from the board of the PTT. At the same time, the identity has been criticised in the Netherlands by those who see such exercises as little more than empty decoration, as a colourful but ultimately frivolous way of diverting attention while a once great public institution re-groups in the cause of global competition. Yet it is hard, as a visitor to the Netherlands, observing the identity's impact in the streets, on phone booths, on the sides of passing vans and trains, not to view it in a positive light. If a country's post and telecommunications services are among the most public, visible and used of its resources, then the PTT's implementation of such an identity projects a powerful commitment to the potential of contemporary design. Maybe you have to inhabit a culture weighed down by nostalgia for the past and shot through with ambivalence for the present to appreciate fully how unusual this is. The identity's presence as an ordinary part of life, encountered wherever you turn, contributes to a culture of possibility in which other kinds of freedom and experimentation can also flourish.

The PTT house style, like the Rijksmuseum signing, the Zeebelt theatre posters, and many other projects from this most unpredictable of studios, reasserts and extends a visual tradition intrinsic to the Netherlands' sense of its own identity. For anyone who believes, as Dumbar himself does, that plastic expression through design is a fundamental and "life-enhancing" part of contemporary culture, there is no higher achievement than this.

From: *Behind the Seen: Studio Dumbar,* 1996

CORPORATE RAIDERS
UNA

To the outsider it sometimes seems as though Dutch designers are blessed with an unlimited supply of clients, denied to everybody else, who simply never say no. Ideas that a British consultancy would not dare to propose to a company chairman, for fear of looking like a pack of anarchists and being shown the door, routinely find their way into the pages of brochures and annual reports. How else could Gert Dumbar have got away with the whimsical drawings of sunsets he sprinkled through a corporate identity manual, or the entirely irrelevant cactus it pleased him to put on the cover of a brochure about computers? It can't only have been the personal magnetism of the man. Surely such notable indulgences have something to do with the enlightenment, sympathy and visual literacy of the client?

Well no, not according to Hans Bockting, Will de l'Ecluse and Henk Hoebé of the Amsterdam design group, Una. They insist that Dutch clients are no more certain about what they want, or need, than any other nation's clients. A designer waiting for a corporate client to exhibit signs of deep yearning for wild experimentation will wait forever. No bank is ever going to ask for an annual report illustrated with images of Saint Sebastian pierced by arrows, piles of sand, and a couple of lobsters. Nor is an office-equipment and paper supplier likely to arrive, without a good deal of prompting, at the decision to interleave pages of year-end figures with a pictorial essay on the history of communication, from hieroglyphics to the neon sign.

In both cases Una's strategy was the same. Bockting has worked with the bank, F. van Lanschot, for almost a decade; de l'Ecluse has put in five years with the paper supplier, VRG. They started by producing designs that conformed more or less to company expectations. As trust developed, so did the opportunities to experiment and Una were quick to grab them. It's as simple as that, they say. But how many ordinary business readers understand these arcane collages and random cut-ups? "We know that most people are not really interested," admits Bockting. "But that shouldn't keep you from doing it." Surely they would not say as much to the client? "Yes, of course we would, because if you present an annual report like this, people recognise the quality. If they buy a pair of shoes, they don't know anything about the quality of the leather, but they know where to go. It's the same thing."

Una's collective personality embodies the same contradictory sense of time-biding restraint and seize-the-moment conviction. Dutch graphic design is in many ways a hermetic world – intense, inward-looking and, on an international level at least, not especially competitive. "We can do whatever we like here, so why worry?", as Bockting puts it. Una seem torn between waiting modestly for the world to acknowledge their worth and an awareness that PR is there for the taking. Since they formed two years ago they have twice entered the international section of D&AD, and they are one of two design groups to show a portrait of themselves in the book of projects published by the Dutch graphic design organisation, bNO.

Una work in a light industrial building on Mauritskade, to the east of Amsterdam. The first thing a visitor sees on entering their vast, double-height studio is a long central display, almost a conveyor belt, of completed work. Una's library, an expensive resource maintained with evident care, occupies a curved bay at one end. It's an immediate signal of the bookishness that Bockting in particular projects. A broad face, elliptical glasses and silvery hair give the designer the look of a benign antiquarian. Bockting makes no secret of preferring art, literature and music to his chosen form of expression. Writing, he says, matters more than design.

If Bockting is a reflective designer, more concerned, at least in the early stages of a project, with library research and the development of a conceptual framework, then de l'Ecluse is more impulsive and intuitive, organising his designs according to visual effect rather than meaning. In conversation, too, Bockting holds back, while de l'Ecluse plunges in. They previously worked together as partners in Concepts, also in Amsterdam, and a number of their clients (such as F. van Lanschot and VRG) date back to those days. Hoebé is the quiet man of the group. With experience at Total Design, Studio Dumbar and Anthon Beeke and Associates, he must have one of the best-rounded CVs in Dutch graphic design. He now specialises in exhibition work for The Hague's Mauritshuis and other museums.

Una's designs, along with those of Jan van Toorn and Gert Dumbar, belong to what Dutch critics like to term the "post-functionalist" school. In functionalist typography, as practised by Wim Crouwel in the 1960s, "transparency" is achieved when all redundancy is eliminated (superfluous rules, duplicated emphasis, unnecessary changes of typeface and type weight) and nothing on the page comes between the reader and the clear articulation of the text. Although Bockting and de l'Ecluse concur that text is for reading, their designs incorporate many expressive elements with no purpose other than to attract attention – no small consideration in the age of electronic media. A favourite device, seen in the programme they designed for the Design 87 conference, is the use of the page grid as an exposed ornamental framework for the type. At times,

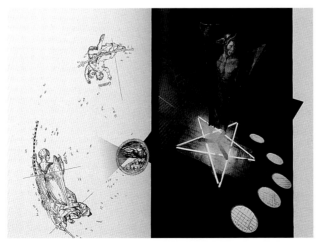

Jaarverslag 1988. Spread from an annual report. Designer: Hans Bockting, Una. Photographer: Lex van Pieterson. F. van Lanschot Bankiers, The Netherlands, 1988

as in some of the promotional work for VRG, this background noise rises to the level of distracting clamour. But the main text is usually handled with respect and care, though they are guilty of the occasional solecism such as letter-spaced Baskerville (anathematised by one unforgiving Dutch critic as a "modish blunder"). In any event, it is impossible to imagine Una chipping blocks of type into the mannerist contortions deployed in the practice brochure that Total Design, Crouwel's former consultancy, published last year.

The group's more outrageous effects are reserved for their image-making; any company submitting to the full Una treatment has to hold its breath and hope. Una's brand of last-minute *mise-en-page* means that roughs are never an option. What the more compliant client gets instead is a description of the proposed approach, emphasising the content rather than the look. When this is agreed, one representative spread from, say, an annual report will be photographed, designed and proofed. Assuming this receives a nod of approval, if not full comprehension, Una will go ahead with the other images. The next thing the client sees is the colour proofs.

There is plenty of time in this nerve-racking process for the checking of text and figures. The images, however, are only finalised at the drawing board. British and American art directors minimise risk and all too frequently block invention by commissioning illustrations in predictable styles to fill pre-defined slots in the design. Una, like other Dutch designers, prefer to improvise their own. One set of images by de l'Ecluse for a VRG annual report was created by cutting tedious supplied transparencies of forklifts, containers and planes into irregular shards, which were then layered and scanned by the printer.

Others are the result of close collaboration between Una and "staged" photography specialists such as Lex van Pieterson, well known for his work with Studio Dumbar. The designers decamp to the photographer's studio in The Hague and work side by side to conceive and construct three-dimensional tableaux that are rarely less than bizarre. Bockting's 1989 annual report for F. van Lanschot, for instance, illustrating the numbers four, six, seven and nine (he had tackled one, two, three, five and eight the previous year), featured, among other sideshow attractions, a naked couple – Mars and Venus, an art historical note explains – heaps of Bacchanalian grapes and a squadron of airborne cherubim.

Confronted by such abandoned images in so conventional a setting, it's clear that the designer is pleasing himself. Bockting owns up to this readily enough – "I'm always trying to see how far I can go" – but maintains that the method intrigues its intended audience and therefore works. It is doubtful that Dutch financial journalists understood all of the imagery, but they still singled out the "enthusiasm" of the reports and the company for comment. "To me," says Bockting, "that's proof that the energy you put into it is not lost." No corporate client is going to volunteer to be a graphic designer's guinea pig, argues Bockting, but when conditions of trust exist and the marketing people are held at bay, the most outwardly conservative clients can be much more open to the excitement of unusual ideas and approaches than is generally taken for granted.

Blueprint, July 1990

*Modern Times Again: Gaetano
Pesce.* Folding exhibition
catalogue. Designers:
Doublespace. Steelcase Design
Partnership, USA, 1988

EMOTION PICTURES
DOUBLESPACE

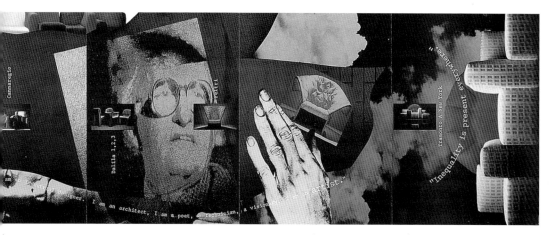

When graphic designers Jane Kosstrin and David Sterling arrived in New York in the late 1970s the art world was buzzing. New rock groups were forming almost by the day and the video, performance art and new music scenes were in ferment. Kosstrin and Sterling's chosen profession, however, was largely untouched by the euphoria of non-stop downtown experimentation. New York graphic design of the post-punk period was corporate, inflexible and, to their minds, stultifyingly dull.

Kosstrin and Sterling's response was to start their own magazine. *Fetish* was to provide them with a purpose-built vehicle for graphic exploration, but what to put in it? "We realised that the thing we spent a lot of time thinking and reading about was stuff – as in clothes and cars and pictures and movies, everything from man-made culture." Launched in 1979, *Fetish* styled itself a "magazine of the material world", ran stories on pachinko parlours, synthetics, love hotels and Barbie dolls, and rapidly achieved a visual and editorial impact that it would take Britain's emerging style magazines two or three years to attain. If the magazine is now a largely forgotten blip in American publishing history, a great idea that peaked too soon, it's because the money ran out after three issues.

It was during this early frenetic phase that Kosstrin and Sterling arrived at their enigmatic name, Doublespace. "All this new music was happening," remembers Sterling, "and we were going from club to club at night and coming into work next morning after three hours sleep exhausted and hungover. One Saturday we were working on the magazine, as we did every weekend, and we were all sitting and staring into space and somebody said 'Oh, I'm so spaced out'. Then someone else, no one quite remembers

Rei Momo. CD insert booklet cover for David Byrne. Designers: Doublespace and David Byrne. Sire Records, USA, 1989

who, said 'I'm double-spaced'. We liked it because it had the connotation of typography."

Nearly ten years on, Doublespace are on the verge of carrying out an often made promise and launching *Fetish* again. "It's got a bit more funky and a little less cerebral," says Sterling. "It's the exact same idea but expanded a bit, really looking at the opposites of culture: treasure and trash." If they do finally relaunch, it will be from a position of much greater authority and far wider acceptance than before. For much of the 1980s Doublespace continued to operate as the uncompromising outsiders of New York graphics. Lately, though, they have moved closer to the commercial mainstream. They still work for prestigious clients such as the Brooklyn Academy of Music, the Museum of the Moving Image and the Bard College of Liberal Arts and Sciences and their approach remains grounded in the collage principles they learned at Cranbrook Academy of Art from the avant-garde masters of the 1920s. But these days they are surprised but apparently happy to find themselves producing press kits for Bill Cosby and the movie *Superboy.*

Partly because of the rate at which they are now compelled to work, the designs have evolved. Early pieces were complex assemblages of type and found imagery in which figures in motion and faces in stress deliver an electrifying emotional charge, while colour was less significant. A poster for the choreographer Pina Bausch in 1984, for instance, uses an austere constructivist palette of red, white and black with most of the drama concentrated in the composition. Now more of a pop sensibility is finding its way into their work. Doublespace's designs for David Byrne's Latin dance album, *Rei Momo,* see a lurch into shrieking Fauvist colours, with yellow polka dots (it took fifteen tries, they say, to get the right shade) on a blood-red heart. The collage is confined to just two layers: Byrne's face peering through the circular apertures and the heart itself, a wax anatomical model suggested by the musician. Again the effect is forcefully emotional, comparable, suggests Sterling, to the disquieting impact of an African mask.

Byrne, it seems, was an exacting collaborator, arriving at the Doublespace offices loaded with favourite images by Francis Picabia and Tadanori Yokoo. Yet far from being bothered by his prescriptions on point sizes and colours, Doublespace appear to have welcomed them as unusually informed. Byrne studied at the Rhode Island School of Design, after all. Then again, for Kosstrin and Sterling, collage is a principle of interaction whose imperatives must be observed in the studio as well as on the picture plane. "There's a lot of interchange," says Kosstrin. "It's never 'this is mine and that's yours'. We like to get a lot of input. The banging together of two heads creates a product that's greater than the two of us could make singly."

Nor is the process as strictly intellectual as it sometimes appears. Doublespace might admire the technical facility of fellow Cranbrook graduate Nancy Skolos, but they feel little regard for work that appears to issue exclusively from the head. For Doublespace, expression and emotion come first; graphic design should be more of an organic, intuitive art than the analytical science it pretended to be in the 1970s. It's a debatable distinction, but a brochure-cum-poster for a recent exhibition of work by Gaetano Pesce in New York shows their method as its most convincing. Kosstrin and Sterling's turbulent, multi-levelled compositions aren't so much a neutral presentation of the Italian expressionist's ideas and objects as a highly sympathetic representation of the ideas in action.

"Most designers in New York, if you told them to promote Gaetano Pesce, would have done a nice little brochure with big photographs of Gaetano's work on each page and pretty little type around it," says Kosstrin. "That is something we would never consider. When we met Gaetano it was like finding a brother. Here was this wonderful man who is delving into architecture and furniture design and doing paintings. He didn't want any boundaries, he didn't care what you called him, he was just doing his art. What mattered was the passion with which he did it. Passion is really important to us. With so many designers, my sense of them is that, as David would say, they are the janitors of society, custodians. They go round and clean things up and organise them so that even if you want to react to them you can't."

Blueprint, February 1990*

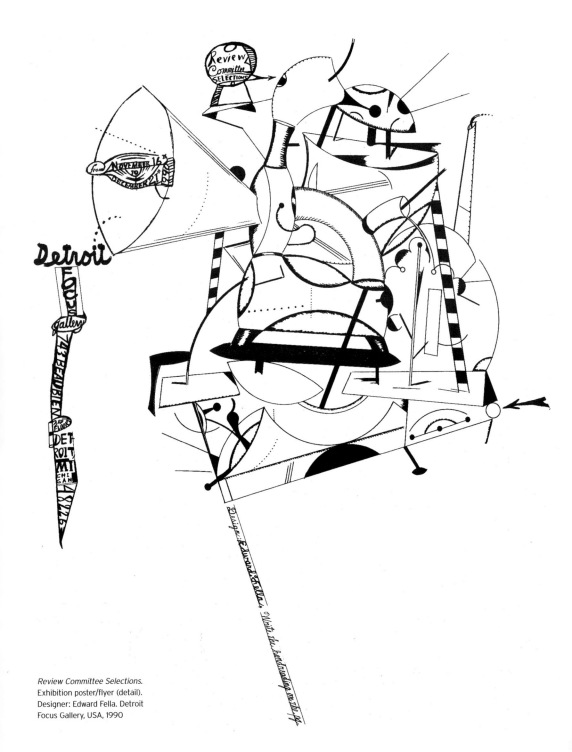

Review Committee Selections.
Exhibition poster/flyer (detail).
Designer: Edward Fella. Detroit
Focus Gallery, USA, 1990

OUT THERE
EDWARD FELLA

The difficulty in placing the work of Edward Fella is that his activity lies outside the established discourses of visual culture. It is not art – not as most galleries, critics or art magazines would construe the term – and it is not graphic design as the profession would generally define it. From the outside it might seem to be design. It is ostensibly commercial, though the rewards are small or even non-existent; it is created for a client; it has a "function", which is promotional; it uses standard reprographic techniques; it is printed in multiple copies with no redeemable value, and it usually arrives in the mail. But to graphic designers, on all the most crucial counts it fails. With only occasional exceptions it has nothing to do with the subjects it advertises and concedes nothing to the demands or wishes of the client beyond the basic need to be announced. It solves no problems. It is completely unprofessional in appearance and riddled with graphic design solecisms and errors. It looks bungled, amateurish, incompetent, ugly. It inhabits a self-contained world of its own.

Fella, it quickly becomes apparent, is an expert at the inept. Letters are scrawled, scribbled, stencilled, typeset in different weights and styles then jumbled, or handwritten in a laborious antiquated script anchored to guide-lines that look like they have been cut from a schoolchild's exercise book. Pictograms, samples of clip art (the commercial illustrator's stand-by), wayward clusters of curves, solids and rules, and drawings with the irrational precision and purposeless conviction of ink-blotter doodles are scattered, apparently at random and for no obvious reason, across the page. Fella's word-pictures are never so extreme or chaotic as to render the words themselves unreadable. A degree of connective logic is always preserved. But the designer's false starts, wrong turnings, interruptions and digressions repeatedly confront us with the process and effort of reading, and the way in which typography, layout and incidental detail can be used to construct meaning, colour the message, or sometimes deny it.

The fact that Fella's clients are artists and that his subject matter is art only complicates the issue. Fella takes the artist's vision and, without compunction, apology or the artist's permission, replaces it with his own. Often he has not even seen the work he is presenting. He lives in California, where he teaches in the graphic design faculty at CalArts, and his clients are based in Detroit. In his commissions for the publicly-funded Detroit Focus Gallery, from 1987 to 1990, Fella was given *carte blanche* by the director, Geri Baskin, to use the gallery's posters, flyers and catalogues as a starting point for his own investigations. Implicit in Baskin's invitation, and Fella's response, is a claim that the designer has a right to the same freedom, autonomy and status within his own sphere that the artist enjoys in his. The Detroit artists' reactions to this proposition were not surprisingly mixed. Some were supportive, especially once the series was established and Fella's subversive intentions had become clear. Others took exception to the idea that their art should be treated as little more than fodder for the designer's personal experiments.

Fella's challenge might have less pertinence, though it would be no less intriguing, were he working alone; he is, in fact, a leading figure in a group of American graphic designers who in the last decade have attempted – with some controversy – to apply the tenets of French critical theory and deconstruction to their craft. The movement is centred on Cranbrook Academy of Art, Michigan and the more significant work of the academy's tutors, students and graduates was collected in the book *Cranbrook Design: The New Discourse* (1990). Fella himself belatedly became a masters student at Cranbrook in the mid-1980s, at the age of 48, though his influence at the academy goes back to the previous decade when he gave lectures showing his private experimental work. For 30 years he worked as a commercial artist, knocking out decorative illustrations to order, often in a parody Art Deco style. "I was like those people that Robert Venturi wrote about," he told *Emigre* magazine. "The guys that made the signs in Las Vegas." Fella's interest in folk art and the vernacular was far from naïve, however, and he read voraciously in literature and art. He absorbed structuralism, semiotics, Nabokov and Barthes. He was fascinated by issues of meaning, interpretation, double-coding and self-reflexivity. While waiting between commercial assignments he would create books of collages, using photostats of found imagery and type, a habit he maintains with great energy to this day.

In his work for the Detroit Focus Gallery and for his other Detroit art scene clients, Fella was finally able to mesh these interests – high culture and low vernacular, autonomous art and applied design – without compromise or constraint. The series came to an end with the appointment of a new gallery director, but the wonder is that he should have got away with it for so long. Most design for Anglo-American artists and art institutions habitually adopts a subordinate role. In the words of the American designer and critic Lorraine Wild, it is one of art's "invisible support systems". Its aim is transparency. We are not supposed to notice it because we have far more important things to look at: the art. The formula is rarely broken: titles, text type and captions in discreet sizes (serif or sanserif, it doesn't matter) and fields of white space surround images with the visual equivalent of a reverential hush. In other contexts graphic design articulates, comments on, and sometimes even shouts down its subject. Occasionally, in more image-conscious art catalogues, a certain fashionable inflection is allowed. But the principal measure of success in design for art's sake is its restraint, its dignity, its obeisance, its absence. Art undertakes a dialogue with the world and the critic pursues a dialogue with art, while design, the medium through which this interaction takes place on the page, is given the role of mute and witless observer. Art's grand purpose is to pose searching questions about social relations, political power structures, the hierarchy of values: design, like a good servant, must meekly tow the line.

Fella describes the contrived ineptitude and vernacular energy with which he assaults these conventions and counters graphic design's slickness and perfection as a kind of "anti-mastery". "I hate fine anythings," he says. His two-sided posters, which double as flyers, are cheaply printed on low quality paper in a single colour. We are accustomed to expect a degree of basic quality and seamlessness in printed communications, especially from art galleries, and the absence of these reassuring signifiers in Fella's work is genuinely perturbing, particularly to other graphic designers. However much designers might talk about finding the most appropriate visual solution, as though their ideas were boundless and literally any outcome were possible, most are inhibited by their knowledge of the discipline's history and rules, by contemporary trends, by habit, and by their own innate, or learned, good taste. The more accomplished a designer is in these narrow, professionally defined terms, the harder it is to break with convention in the use of typefaces, letter-spacing, line-spacing and layout.

Yet this, somehow, is what Fella's anti-mastery has achieved. By drawing on what he understands as an artist, he has produced "designs" that fly in the face of everything he knows as a designer to be correct. Nothing is sacrosanct, everything is open to re-evaluation, no area of the sheet or page is off limits. Fella's scatter-grams of tumbling type and delinquent letterforms make one realise quite how circumscribed our conception of "appropriate" design has become. His fluid distortions force the tired and predictable typographic palette into dramatic new relationships; rejecting utterly the modernist conception of type as a neutral message-bearer, they are continual reminders of the expressive possibilities of the word as image and of the word-image itself as a carrier of meaning.

So where, to restate our original dilemma, does Fella fit in? Although his work has received some attention in the last year and a half (two magazine features, inclusion in

Of Light/Primitive Processes.
Exhibition poster/flyer.
Designer: Edward Fella. Detroit
Focus Gallery, USA, 1989

two anthologies) it is not widely known. The Detroit art scene is obviously parochial compared to those of Los Angeles or New York. The professional design magazines, particularly in Britain, offer designers the chance of instant publication – today's annual report is tomorrow's news – but Fella has luckily eluded such trivialising coverage. Unnoticed, except by a small circle of interested colleagues and his own students, he has taken his own time to develop a highly idiosyncratic body of work loaded with implications for the dialogue between art and design, if only it were more widely seen or discussed.

But this blurring of categories is precisely the reason for the critical silence that has greeted Fella's experiments, and Cranbrook projects in general. Depressingly few magazines address the complete spectrum of visual culture. Critics in the design camp, if they comment at all, say that the work is "design about design", that it is visually and conceptually too complicated, that it is preoccupied with style, that it is too personal, that it is meaningless, that it is art – that it is anything but design. Critics on the art side, unaccustomed to paying much attention to design, or seeing it as a fertile source of cultural ideas, say nothing at all. Neither side has yet developed, or shown much inclination to develop, an adequate critical framework for assessing the hybrid media and new cultural forms which are beginning to emerge at their interface, and which will be further driven by the use of computers like the Macintosh. (Fella's work has until now been created by hand, but its elastic freedoms are a virtual manifesto for the manipulative possibilities of the new digital tools.)

We could, of course, go on saying that anything which falls outside the established boundaries and self-perpetuating discourses of art and graphic design is "failed art", because it is tainted by commerce and the client relationship, or "failed design", because it is tainted by supposed pretensions to art. Or we could say: yes, this art-about-design or design-about-art really is something new and specific to our times, an extension of what we know, a different kind of communication – what is its potential, how can we develop it, and how and where might it be applied?

Frieze, June/July/August 1992

REMOVE SPECIFICS AND CONVERT TO AMBIGUITIES
JEFFERY KEEDY

Jeffery Keedy may be the first graphic designer to try to transform himself into a brand name. In the cantankerous guise of "Mr Keedy", as he has signed himself on and off since the mid-1980s, the Los Angeles-based California Institute of the Arts instructor has earned a reputation as a pugnacious, entertaining and rarely less than controversial observer of the contemporary graphic design scene. Lately, Keedy has begun to travel outside the US, with thoughtful appearances at the *Fuse* conferences in London and Berlin. In Europe, though, he is still probably best known for his *Fuse* magazine typeface LushUS – "more is not a bore" – and for Keedy Sans, an increasingly popular postmodern chameleon that basks with equal assurance on the cover of a book about underground film or emblazoned across a billboard for Colgate toothpaste.

Mr Keedy is an educator with attitude, a critic of waspish insight, and an apologist for the uncertainties of postmodernism who publicly chastises the faint-hearted with unflagging conviction and zeal. Where most in his tenured position would proceed with some caution, Keedy has chosen time after time to "stick my neck out", naming names, telling it like he sees it, and enraging the opposition. "This was the most immature and ridiculous article I have read by someone professing to be an academic," was one reader's response to a Keedy diatribe in *Emigre* on the subject of "Zombie Modernism". But while his bullishness has, Keedy admits, entailed some personal costs, ultimately it seems to have worked both for him and for CalArts. The graphic design programme he developed with Lorraine Wild and Edward Fella and directed from 1991 to 1995 is widely perceived as one of the most progressive and conceptually challenging in the US and for the students Keedy's high profile helps to attract, he is a demanding and inspirational figure.

"My interest has been for designers to become authors," says Keedy. And in essays such as "I like the vernacular . . . NOT!" and the public lectures which he insists on scripting as a mark of respect for the audience he has practised what he preaches. Anyone who has been on the receiving end of a Mr Keedy broadside quickly senses that he relishes the debates and clashes of opinion to an unusual degree. "I enjoy them a lot because that's where you really learn," he agrees. "You start to put your money where your mouth is. You really put to the test what you are thinking. The reward is intellectual exercise, helping you think and figure things out."

As a designer, though, Keedy, now 38, has a much less definite air. There is a disjointed character to his output that is probably to be expected in someone whose primary commitment is teaching. More surprising, perhaps, in a designer of declared authorial intention is that his work, though intellectually coherent, shows no unifying stylistic themes; unlike a Brody, Valicenti or Fella, you would not recognise a Keedy at a glance. It may be that he is a late developer, with his most significant design work still to come.

Since 1989 he has been working towards the launch of his own type design company, Cipher, and he hopes finally to achieve this in April 1996. "In the print world, in a lot of what I've done I have a bit more interest in the ideas and I knock things out," he explains. "But with a typeface, once it's out there it's literally out there forever and I'm interested in showing that quality is part of the new work."

To understand the passion that informs Keedy's position you have to go back to his time as an undergraduate, studying graphic design and photography at Western Michigan University. After the energy and invention of the 1960s, the following decade had witnessed "The Triumph of the Corporate Style" – as a *Print* magazine cover story dubbed it in 1980. Seventies design was highly professional, but slick, formulaic and empty. "It was the tail end of modernism, when it was at its very worst," remembers Keedy. "There was nothing left at that point." The only interesting work was coming from New Wavers such as April Greiman and Dan Friedman, whose innovations were vigorously opposed by the modernists.

Advised by a New York head-hunter that he would never find a job with his New Wave portfolio, Keedy nevertheless landed a position in 1981 designing advertising and promotions at CBS television in Boston. The following year he moved to Honolulu, where he designed corporate signing, logos and symbols for Clarence Lee Design and Associates. Keedy was rapidly coming to the conclusion that his future lay not in practice but in teaching. "I knew that something was wrong and I had a gut feeling that there was more to design than that – that it was more interesting somehow and more important."

In 1983 he started an MFA at Cranbrook Academy of Art, where he began for the first time to read theorists such as J. Christopher Jones, but above all Roland Barthes. "He brought low cultural critique into the self-referential high practice of literary criticism," notes Keedy. "The reason I was particularly interested in Barthes – more than the other post-structuralists and deconstructionists – was because he was engaged in a pop culture critique, a critique of his own discipline, literature, and because he was a 'formalist'."

How Keedy's emerging conception of design as cultural practice rather than problem-solving tool might be translated into practice itself was at this stage unclear. Confronted by course director Katherine McCoy's inevitable question "What does it look like?" he could only answer that these ideas were intended to generate a new kind of thought process; there was no one-to-one correlation with visual form. Some of the eventual consequences of this theoretical reading (fragmentation, layering, degenerative imagery, anti-mastery) are already apparent in a poster Keedy designed for Cranbrook's fibre studies programme, which caused some consternation in the design department. Dozens of tiny student sketchbook drawings and notations are distributed across the surface in a graphically even weave to form a metaphor of creative process which has none of the clear, hierarchical organisation usually expected of a poster. It is a design that makes considerably more sense now, in the light of what followed, than it could have made at the time.

After Cranbrook, Keedy moved to Los Angeles, encouraged by the offer of a part-time teaching job at CalArts. He had never been to the city before and it seemed to offer unlimited possibilities. In the late 1980s he worked for cultural institutions such as the Museum of Contemporary Art and the San Francisco Artspace and for two years designed a series of calendars for Los Angeles Contemporary Exhibitions

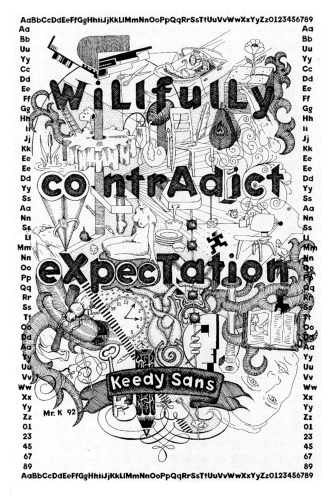

Willfully Contradict Expectation. Full-page advertisement for the typeface Keedy Sans. Designer/artist: Jeffery Keedy. Emigre Graphics, USA, 1992

(LACE) in which he introduced early versions of his own typefaces. Drawing on chaos theory – fashionable at the time – they represent his most extreme explorations of the "anti-aesthetic".

Keedy's growing reputation for working with experimental artists culminated in the *Helter Skelter: L.A. Art in the 1990s* catalogue (1992), where he was an "equal partner" with curator Paul Schimmel and editor Catherine Gudis. His first intervention was to challenge conventional catalogue structure and emphasise the book's status as an anthology of art and creative writing by replacing the contents page with a seven-page contributors section that mixed artists, writers and essayists together. Keedy proposed augmenting the art's alarming mood of impending social breakdown and urban apocalypse by using the Macintosh to cut into the text columns with smooth "razor" slashes and irregular tears.

"When the editor first saw them she was dumbfounded," he recalls. "She thought it was a computer error. When she realised it was intentional she was mortified." In the end Keedy was allowed just a handful of the less destructive incisions in the book's introductory texts, though the effect – in the setting – was startling enough.

"It looks tame by today's standards," he concedes. "But not in the context of 'serious' art catalogues."

Once again, Keedy used two of his own typefaces. Hard Times, representing the writers, had previously featured in the Californian art magazine *Shift* and in the 91/93 CalArts catalogue; Skelter, representing the artists and critics – an "angst-ridden retro-fit" – was designed specially for the book. They combine most powerfully in the titlepiece, where "Skelter" is fractured across three lines. (Both typefaces were later licensed to Condé Nast's *Details* magazine.)

Keedy's method as a type designer, he told his Berlin *Fuse* audience, is to have two or three contradictory ideas operating in each typeface because the resulting complexity and ambiguity give the typographer a greater potential range of expression. "In Hard Times," he explained, "the old jagged irregularity [of Times Roman] is juxtaposed with the new smooth ovals and the sloping 'e'-bar, oblique serifs, opened counters and other details." Skelter's large x-height, on the other hand, gives it a "cartoony and cute aspect" that can be either cheerful or sinister depending on how it is used.

The current vogue for Keedy Sans, released by Emigre Fonts in 1991, suggests that popular taste is now catching up with his double-codings. At first, Keedy recalls, the face just looked "illegible and weird" (it was also, perhaps, slightly too strongly identified with *Emigre* itself). "Most typefaces are logically systematic," he says. "If you see a few letters you can pretty much guess what the rest of the font will look like. I wanted a typeface that would wilfully contradict those expectations. It was a typically postmodern strategy for a work to call attention to the flaws and artifice of its own construction." Four years on, the face's open-endedness can signify the technological avant-garde in the pages of the *Cyborg Handbook*, or mass-audience popular culture, announcing the evening's attractions on London Weekend Television. Where it functions less successfully – see, for instance, its use across Elvis's face for a B&W loudspeakers ad in *Arena* – is as a middlebrow signifier of "contemporary style".

But to use Keedy Sans in this way is to miss the point. Keedy intends the Cipher typefaces – Hard Times, Hard Line, Skelter, Jot, Manu Sans and others in preparation – to act as catalysts for a new kind of design. Planning, increasingly, to be his own client, he sees his role as a typeface publisher as that of both author-by-proxy and "enabler". "We're at a critical point with the millennium where no one seems to know what to do," he explains. "In the postmodern sense everything is now possible. There's the new technology and there's a lot of confusion and directionlessness. What I want to do with Cipher is to make a pretty specific statement and to provide a set of directions. I like to see the typefaces as a set of opportunities – new tools that have inherent within them a set of ideas and options that people can act on."

While Keedy has shown an exceptional commitment to new work and new ideas in graphic design, the larger purpose of his critique is less certain than his plain-speaking might lead one to expect. Despite his repeated plea for a cultural criticism of design's role in production and consumption that would (presumably) link what designers do and how they think about their practice to its consequences in the world, his own published commentary is on the whole centred self-referentially on design as a goal in itself. "It has never been my ambition to 'change the world' with design," Keedy wrote in a "Designer's Statement" in 1995. "Even the modest and vague ambition 'to make the world a better place' is too naïve, and difficult to qualify or quantify. My only hope is that my design be a rumination of life in all of its complexity and contradictions, and that it exists in the world with vitality."

Pressed to explain this *laissez-faire* credo, Keedy seems to backtrack slightly. He says that design as a total practice is "affirmative" and that by making things work better and look more aesthetically pleasing, "it can't help but make the world a better place". At the same time, he points out, there is nothing inherently liberal about graphic design: it can be used to affirm any kind of agenda, even the most dangerous. It seems reasonable at this point to ask Keedy about his own politics, especially since he claims in "Zombie Modernism" to detect a similarity of rhetoric between supposedly modernist design critics and figures of the American far right such as Newt Gingrich and radio commentator Rush Limbaugh. The implication of this strange equation is that aesthetic radicals such as Keedy must necessarily adhere to a liberal agenda.

But Keedy, usually so loquacious, declines to answer. "I don't know if that's interesting for graphic designers, or if that's an important part of it. Probably not. In fact, that's the problem I had with 'Zombie Modernism'. The minute I barely mentioned politics, everyone focuses on that and it goes way off in left-field. Who cares what my political views are? I don't think I'm politically that savvy. I do think I am savvy about design, so people should care about my views on that." Fair enough. Except that if, as Keedy once suggested to me, deconstruction's lesson is that those who are engaged in cultural production and criticism are also engaged in the "politics of power" – manifested in form and style – then it is not at all clear how one could engage meaningfully in such a criticism without being willing to make one's political assumptions explicit.

What it is easy to miss about Keedy is the degree to which the public postmodernist nurtures what he himself calls "traditional values" at heart. One of his complaints about modernism is precisely that it sought to put an end to tradition. Keedy wants Cipher to show that the new design is just as committed to the idea of quality as the old. Asked to define what this quality is and how we will recognise it, he gives the oldest answer in the book. "Your experience tells you. If you've seen 10,000 typefaces and studied typography for several years, that will help you decide. The only thing you have to go on in that respect is experience. You can't have an overriding theoretical idea. Maybe you could use that at some point, but you can't rely on it."

Keedy likes to think of Cipher as an operation on the lines of the traditional American "mom-and-pop shop". It will be a garage-sized company, with an international dimension, much of its distribution, at least in the US, being accomplished through the Internet. Keedy identifies with the American type design lineage of Goudy, Dwiggins and Cooper and, like his literate forebears, he will continue to publish as well as design. "My writing is on a very specific trajectory," he reveals, explaining that little by little the essays are building into a book. And the next contentious instalment? "I may even talk about the problems of postmodernism," says Mr Keedy with more than a hint of irony.

Eye, no. 20 vol. 5, 1996

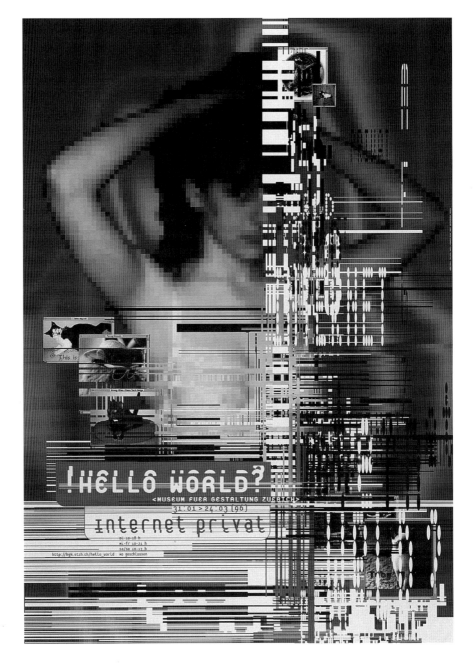

!Hello World? Internet Privat.
Exhibition poster. Designer:
Cornel Windlin. Museum für
Gestaltung, Zurich,
Switzerland, 1996

THIS SIGNIFIER IS LOADED
CORNEL WINDLIN

Signifiers don't come much more heavily loaded than Cornel Windlin's posters for the Rote Fabrik, a performance space located a couple of kilometres south of Zurich's city centre. Windlin's first communiqué, based on a firing-range target, rounded up concert-goers with a pistol-brandishing silhouette. If this suggested the arrival of a designer who, conceptually at least, should be regarded as armed and dangerous, it paled beside a later creation, in which Zurich's good townsfolk were treated to a scarily alluring Uzi, presented without apology against a brilliant yellow background.

It is easy to see how such hair-raising visual tactics might have come as a jolt to the peace-loving collective that operates the lakeside centre, set up fifteen years ago to mollify Zurich's young people in the wake of city riots. Windlin is sure the Uzi poster lost him the job (though enquiries suggest this was not the case). But the willingness – or need – to believe the worst says something in itself. Client relationships are distinctly uneasy for Windlin. "It's always a problem," he says, "If I'm lucky I can get away with things – if it's a good client. If it's a bad one, then I'm the one who's going to walk away with the money, but I've lost the fight somehow. I don't seem to fit in. I don't seem to find people who are willing to do what I want to do." When he won a prestigious Swiss prize for the applied arts in 1995, he illustrated his citation with a prostitute card that read "I'm young, naughty and need to be punished."

Looking at the range, consistency and power of Windlin's work since he returned to Zurich in early 1993 confirms the impression of a designer for whom dissatisfaction may just be a natural state. It is hard to imagine many London-based venues or arts organisations sanctioning the sustained vernacular experiments conducted in his 33 concert posters for the Rote Fabrik (Red Factory), or allowing anything as graphically adventurous and resolutely unpopulist as his exhibition posters for the city's Museum für Gestaltung. Yet Windlin worries. He worries that Zurich might be too small, too parochial, too cosy and that the Rote Fabrik series, meant for a particular audience, might not work out of context, or seem very interesting. But most of all he worries about what to do next: "What is there to say?" he asks. "What do *you* have to say? And *how* do you do it?"

Now 32, Windlin belongs – like British colleagues such as David Crow and Ian Swift – to a mid-1980s generation attracted into the profession by the pop-culture triumvirate of Neville Brody, Peter Saville and Malcolm Garrett. "I was very interested in music," he says. "I still am. And a lot of graphic design that was new and fresh was associated with music. It came on record sleeves and it came primarily from England." An unsatisfactory interlude in a Zurich advertising agency as designer and copywriter, as part of his studies at the Schule für Gestaltung in Lucerne, confirmed his aptitude for language, while

convincing him that he wasn't the agency type. In the summer of 1987, he completed
a second placement assisting Brody in his Tottenham Court Road studio and returned
in late 1988 to take up a full-time position at Brody's new east London base.

Windlin gained invaluable experience helping Brody on projects for Nike, Swatch,
London's Photographer's Gallery, and the Haus der Kulturen der Welt, a cultural
institute in Berlin. But everything inevitably left the studio with the design star's
value-conferring signature on it and Windlin faced the usual assistant's problem of
establishing himself as a designer in his own right. After taking the decision to leave
the studio in 1990, he put in the best part of a year as assistant designer at *The Face* – the
magazine was going through a period of awkward transition – then became a freelance.
"I did get work immediately," he remembers, "but it was a very difficult time."

Up to this point it would be fair to say that Windlin was a designer of promise
who had never quite found the setting to give of his best. When he decided to return
to Zurich, it was for personal reasons rather than a strong desire to go back. Three and
a half years on, securely established in studio space at the offices of *Parkett*, the Swiss
art magazine, he seems thoroughly disenchanted with the city. Yet within Zurich's
bourgeois precincts – "It's like being in a model town," he complains – he has found
the freedom to create a body of work that has rapidly marked him out as one of the
most thoughtful and original young graphic designers working in Europe in the 1990s.

One of Windlin's first initiatives was to start his own dance music club, Reefer
Madness, with a couple of friends. In the membership cards and flyers he designed
for the club's monthly gatherings he began to play referential games with everyday
graphic language – crude street flyers, the Rolex crown, a well-known brand of Swiss
cigarettes – and this approach became the mainstay of the posters that Reefer Madness
co-founder Bernd Blankenberg began to commission a year later, as concert organiser
for the Rote Fabrik.

Windlin's problem with each of the Rote Fabrik posters was to find a way of
announcing four or five concerts by musicians playing wildly different styles.
Sometimes the choice of visual theme relates directly to one or more of the artists – as
with the April 1994 firing-range target. "Violence and guns are very present in hip-hop
lyrics and the whole culture of hip-hop," explains Windlin, whose use of gay icon Rock
Hudson on another poster was a similarly pointed allusion to hip-hop's homophobia.
More often, though, there is no direct link between the chosen imagery and musicians.

Windlin's response to an open brief has been to create what is, in effect, a library
of vernacular references. The posters, usually printed in runs of 2,000, take their graphic
form from hazard-warning labels, newspaper lonely hearts ads, holiday postcards,
Hollywood star portraits, doctrinaire Swiss modernism, and the "big idea" – though
there is a larger sense in which the series as a whole might be considered as an
example of a conceptual graphics that relies for its effect on the regular audience's
awareness of the unfolding image-play. Contemporary styles are similarly appropriated,
with several posters based on expressionistic type manipulation, whether by the
Macintosh or by hand.

Appropriation, in the postmodern sense, seems the best word for what Windlin has
done. His purpose isn't parody – there is no intensification or distortion for satirical
effect – and his method is too forensic in its analysis of the precise nuances of the
original to be dismissed as pastiche. The Rote Fabrik series is quite different, for instance,
from US designer Charles Anderson's construction of an idealised "bonehead"

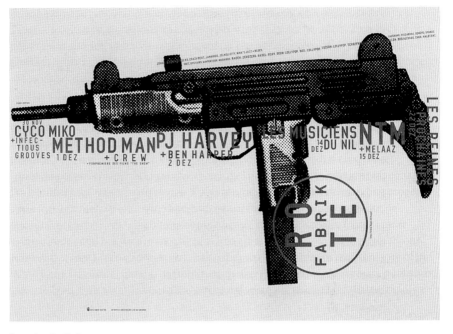

Concert poster. Designer:
Cornel Windlin. Rote Fabrik,
Zurich, Switzerland, 1995

Americana out of the mid-century commercial vernacular. On the other hand, as with
Anderson, the sources have been unmistakably tweaked in the process of acquisition.
Windlin's "Designers Republic" is more accomplished than its inspiration (a Joey
Beltram CD) and easily the equal of more elaborate DR pieces.

On one level, these posters could be considered as finger exercises, with Windlin
emerging as a craftsman of unusually versatile technique. He himself compares the
series to a student project: "There were a lot of things I wanted to do, that I had to get
out of my system. It's also about excitement for myself." Invocations of postmodernism
succeed only in reducing him to silence. "If I think about postmodern architecture,
for instance, it just makes me cringe, it makes me want to say I haven't got anything to
do with that. It certainly goes beyond simple plays of style, appropriations." He is not
particularly concerned, though, by whether the viewer succeeds in penetrating the
referential image-play or not. For Windlin, the stylistic sleights of hand seem, more
than anything, to be ways of avoiding what he regards as the "trap" of personal style.

His undogmatic talent for discovering appropriate form is seen to more directed effect
in projects for Zurich's design museum. In a poster for the exhibition "!Hello World?
Internet Privat" – about digital communication with strangers – a bra-clad girl displayed
in her boyfriend's homepage becomes a poignant and at the same time ambiguous icon
for the public disclosure of private self-image. The girl's pixelised body is overlaid by
sampled images of cats (one squashed by a car) and dense fields of electronic interference
which intensify the sense of voycuristic compulsion. Another Museum für Gestaltung
poster for the exhibition "Zeitreise" (Journey through time) finds an almost mystical
metaphor for dreams of escaping time using technology in the chance encounter of
a bicycle wheel and a jet of water from a drinking fountain as it overshoots the basin.

Windlin speaks warmly of the museum's director, Martin Heller. "He's a client who's not against you – which is very often the situation. He understands and he's on your side but he also has his own agenda, so it's a really interesting collaboration." Heller for his part regards Windlin as a conceptualist of unusual ability.

Windlin's relationships with commercial clients have been less happy. A retail identity for a new youth department at the Globus department store on Zurich's well-heeled Bahnhofstrasse was cancelled the day before its official opening when the shop started to have belated misgivings (in a city notorious for its drug problem) about Windlin's modest proposal for the name: Overdose. In London, a billboard concept for Foster's Ice Beer, aimed at 18–24-year-olds, began as a typographically brutal restatement of the advertiser's brief – "Approachable – irreverent – dangerous – great taste – Ours! (Humour, 'Go for it')" – and was watered down into harmlessness.

Perhaps the most surprising aspect of these outcomes is that Windlin himself seems quite so surprised by them. For a designer with such a strong drive to express his own criticisms of the communication processes he is commissioned to serve, these might seem to be highly unpromising choices of client. "What I do find a problem, more and more," agrees Windlin, "is that all the time I'm solving other people's problems and arranging someone else's work. That's not terribly exciting for me and I'm not very good at it."

The Swiss typographer Hans-Rudolf Lutz, his former teacher and continuing mentor, advises Windlin to follow his own example and go into teaching, using the hours that remain to work on his own projects. This would offer a time-honoured solution to his need for conditions in which self-authorship might flourish, but Windlin prefers to test his mettle in the marketplace and resists such an arrangement as too big a compromise. At the same time, he pinpoints a dilemma facing any would-be experimentalist dependent on the whims of commerce. "In graphic design, if you are trying to push the boundaries, it seems you end up being a laboratory rat for new aesthetic forms. And as soon as they're seen as probably successful in the marketplace, people can adapt them and do it themselves." What Windlin needs now is to find or create a position where he can run his own lab.

Eye, no. 22 vol. 6, 1996

3. BRITISH GRAPHIC DESIGN

AFTER THE GOLDRUSH

Nineteen-ninety was not a happy year for the huge consultancies that dominated British design in the 1980s. Business empires which had once been the toast of City analysts and bankers proved to have been built on the most unstable foundations. Few large design groups remained untouched by the darkening economic climate as Britain moved inexorably into recession, clients cut commissioning budgets, and share prices tumbled. The worst hit companies broke up in spectacular crashes that only a few years ago would have seemed impossible.

None was more spectacular – or more representative – than that of the Michael Peters Group, one of Britain's best regarded consultancies. On 23 August, Peters's design empire was put in the hands of the receivers, City accountants Arthur Andersen & Co. The company's shares, which had peaked in 1985 at 278p, were suspended at 5p. There had been speculation for months about the future of the group as it laid off staff and struggled with debts estimated at up to £5 million. In 1988, in an ambitious bid to break into the American market, Peters had bought the New York retail consultancy Hambrecht Terrell for £5.7 million. The terminal illness of the company's founder and the sudden loss of its main department store client was a blow Peters's ailing business could not sustain. After an eleventh-hour rescue bid by the marketing group Brunning fell through, it remained only for the receivers to break up the Michael Peters Group and sell what they could.

The downfall of one of British design's favourite sons left the profession in shock. The remarkable growth of the British design business in the 1980s had been sustained by a seemingly unlimited supply of clients and a belief that anything was possible. To organisations like the Michael Peters Group, the prospects for expansion seemed virtually limitless. When the decade began Peters employed just twenty staff; at the height of his success he had an international workforce of more than 700. In 1983, he was one of the first to float his company on the London Stock Exchange, and it began to seem as though the soft industry of design would at last achieve credibility in the eyes of the money men. In the course of the decade many others were to follow Peters into the City. In Prime Minister Thatcher's Britain, designers took on the trappings, preoccupations and priorities of the business world as never before. If the archetypal British designer of the 1960s and 1970s had been a Bohemian, slightly marginal figure, in the 1980s he wore a suit, drove a Porsche and was as comfortable in the boardroom as hc was at the drawing board. The British advertising business had undergone similar changes in the 1950s and 1960s, and it was advertising – a flamboyant profession with outspoken stars, a self-congratulatory weekly newpaper, and a high public profile – that provided the most obvious model of what the design industry might become.

What designers didn't perhaps foresee, as they made their pacts with the City, is how a stock market listing could so quickly turn into a treadmill. Shareholders are never content to see their investment ticking over: they demand constant growth, and the only way such growth can be sustained is through diversification, takeover and merger. Whatever the core of their business – graphics, product design, interiors, or a combination – consultancies bent on expansion are almost invariably drawn into related services, such as management consultancy, market research, public relations and recruitment. In the large, impersonal, unfocused, accountant-led organisations that result, the spirit and purpose that originally animated a company can all too easily go missing.

In a recent interview, Steve Smith of Addison gave *Design* magazine a telling picture of the Byzantine business manoeuvres into which his publicly-listed company was drawn. "We did mergers with a new company emerging [from] the two companies merging, we did a contested takeover bid of a company, we bought lots of private companies, we demerged a company, we did just about everything, culminating in [a] management buyout." Older, wiser and once again the owner of his own company, Smith now says that he should never have gone public.

Michael Peters is equally emphatic about the pitfalls of a public quotation. "We have seen the waste and misunderstanding which arises from misinformed investor pressure, and the incalculable long-term damage caused by the headlong pursuit of the quick buck," he said in a speech shortly before his company crashed. Later he told *Direction* magazine: "Every day you get letters from shareholders saying, 'Tell me about x, y and z', 'Why isn't the share price higher?' You're not your own master. You're very much at the behest and the request of shareholders and the City." This bitter lesson is being learned by a community that still prides itself on belonging to the design capital of the world. Almost as salutary as Michael Peters is the example of Fitch RS (formerly Fitch & Company). Founder Rodney Fitch has seen his once buoyant share price sink from 330p on 23 January 1988 to just 33p on 24 January 1991. In the course of 1990, the company shed more than 100 staff, many of them from the architecture and retail divisions worst hit by the downturn in client spending.

Confronted by signs that the design bonanza is over, not everyone is sympathetic. To some critical observers inside the industry, many of the bigger practices were little more than factories churning out mediocre projects for the sake of their annual turnover. "The Fitches of this world didn't grow on consultancy, but on rows and rows of drawing boards. It's mass production," Klaus Schmidt of Henrion Ludlow & Schmidt told *Design*. Such designers argue that the logistical need for vast consultancies has been much exaggerated and that clients are too easily impressed by size, when, in fact, it has always been possible for relatively small, dedicated design teams to produce work of the highest quality. Neville Brody has been consistently outspoken on this point. "Huge overheads and onerous commitments to shareholders and the City means no creative risktaking," he wrote in an editorial for *Eye*. "The important ideas during the next decade will come from small design groups or individuals; the more human scale of these outfits will allow for a more humanistic attitude to design." David Pocknell, president of the Chartered Society of Designers, spoke for many when he concluded: "The City and design do not seem to mix."

But Michael Peters, despite his recent experiences, is adamant that this is not necessarily the case. "I would refute completely that creativity and the City don't mix.

I don't see that one has got anything to do with the other." Like many designers, he has been obliged by circumstances to reassess his priorities. The core of Peters's old business – devoted to packaging, brand development and corporate identity – was bought by Craton Lodge & Knight, owned by Hillsdown Investment Trust, which is owned, in turn, by Hillsdown Holdings. This time round, however, Peters has taken care to insulate himself from personal contacts with bankers and the City: his partners take care of that for him. As chairman of Michael Peters Ltd he employs just 80 people. These days, he claims, the main thing he has to worry about is which typeface he should use, not whether he will be able to pay back the banks.

Time will tell whether Peters's early optimism is well founded. But it is certainly the case that his new company, by concentrating on what it does best, is following the pattern of the British design groups which most smoothly negotiated the financial rapids of the 1980s. Consultancies such as Minale Tattersfield (established in 1964) and Pentagram (established in 1972) held back from the City jamboree. The Pentagram partners insisted, in a way that seemed positively old-fashioned at the time, that creative freedom would continue to be their main priority. "What turns people on here," says founding partner Alan Fletcher, "is being proud of the job, not how much money they earned for it. I can't see a suit coming in from the City and saying, 'Look, you can't do this. You've got to do that.' They'd throw him out of the window."

In the mid to late 1980s British designers began, increasingly, to look abroad for new business. Flushed with success at the ease with which they had transformed the high streets of Britain, the retail consultancies, in particular, began to dream of delivering the gospel to Europe and the world. Now, in a much starker economic climate, the super-consultancies are planning their global strategies with a new sense of urgency – the shrinking market for their services at home leaves them little alternative. Rightly or wrongly, they believe that if they are to have any hope of winning and holding the accounts of multinational corporations, then they must be able to offer clients a multinational design presence and service.

As 1992 approaches, the words "pan-European" are repeated like a mantra. All the major consultancies have European clients and just a few examples will be sufficient to suggest their range. Wolff Olins has created corporate identities for Repsol in Spain and Akzo in Holland. Addison provides packaging for CCF Friesland in Holland and is a consultant for the Commerical Bank of Greece. Minale Tattersfield works for Carlsberg in Sweden. Many of these consultancies have opened European offices to serve their existing clients and develop new business. Even a relatively small, if highly regarded, company such as Banks & Miles now has outposts in Brussels and Hamburg. But real competition at this level would seem, to many companies, to require an even more aggressive strategy. The last two years have witnessed a number of mergers and alliances designed to assist the European penetration of London design groups. In 1989, Minale Tattersfield merged with Design Strategy in Paris, adding Bull, Spontex and Rhone-Poulenc to its client list. In March 1990, Landor Associates (American-owned but with a strong base in London) linked up with Beautiful Design House, the Paris-based packaging and corporate identity specialists. In November, Siegal & Gale, owned by advertising magnates Saatchi & Saatchi, formed an association with Ove Engstrom Communications in Stockholm. In the case of the Conran Design Group, the process worked in reverse. Sir Terence Conran's company was bought in summer 1990 by the French communications group Roux Seguela Cayzac & Goudard. Forty-three job losses followed, but according to Sir Terence, chairman of the newly named RSCG Conran Design, the emphasis will once again fall on design creativity rather than marketing issues. He professes himself very pleased at the prospect.

Sir Terence's remarks point up the dilemma now facing the monster design groups. The 1980s saw an unprecedented explosion of design activity. During the boom years, when the money was flowing, the opportunities seemed limitless. For a while, the designer was a kind of hero and, at least in his own eyes, the man (it was usually a man) with all the answers. The boom was intoxicating while it lasted, but there was little time to ask whether the feverish repackaging of every product, shop or service in sight was, ultimately, of any great durability, benefit or value.

It took a financial slump to bring the British design community to its senses. Now, style is supposed to be out and substance is in. Humanism is back. From Neville Brody at one end of the business, to Michael Peters at the other, the talk is of designers' responsibility. The key question for the 1990s is whether British designers will be able to reconcile their new social consciences with vast global empires and the relentless demands of big business.

Industrieel ontwerpen, April 1991

A POINT OF VIEW

JOHN HEGARTY

It's impossible not to like John Hegarty. Levi's, Audi and the *Independent* like him.
His colleagues in advertising like him. Television producers looking for a spokesman
like him. And the signs are that the public, when it gets to know him a little better, will
be very fond of him too.

Hegarty is telegenic. The chiselled features look good on the small screen and the
manner is unfailingly matey. Hegarty is on the viewer's side. He knows that 90 per cent
of advertising is junk and he's the first to admit it. It's hard to rattle Hegarty. They tried
him out on *Wogan* and Hegarty pulled it off. Michael Ignatieff lined him up for a
roasting on *3 Minute Culture* and Hegarty walked through it. The programme was one
long commercial for his agency, Bartle Bogle Hegarty. Even Hegarty was surprised.

The BBC like Hegarty. They've asked him to chair the graphic design panel of the
1990 BBC Design Awards, in the company of Norman Foster and Sir Terence Conran.
But wait a minute. Hegarty's achievements as a creative director of commercials are
considerable ... but graphic design? "He's there because he is a very distinguished end-
user and a good performer in his own right," says Keith Alexander, executive producer
of the awards. And the BBC do need a good performer. The monosyllabic graphics panel
for the first awards didn't exactly set the screen on fire.

Still, Hegarty was perplexed by this latest appointment, though his year as president
of D&AD means that he is no stranger to the role of industry representative. He even
voices regret that he's got to do the job. "I think it's a great shame that design, when it
impacts so much on our lives, hasn't thrown up somebody who the BBC could turn to
to represent the industry and a point of view that's exciting and different. It's not
something that I in any way actively sought. I was actually quite taken aback when the
BBC asked me and I said, 'But I'm in advertising ...' And they said, 'No, no, we'd like you
to do it. We think that the observations you make could be quite valuable to the debate'."

Hegarty's observations are rarely less than notable. It was Hegarty who said that his
almost mystical-sounding quest was to establish "the truth of the product", Hegarty
whose brochure declared "We don't sell. We make people want to buy" – a truly subtle
distinction. Last year, summing up the decade, he informed a Sunday newspaper, "If the
commodity of the Eighties was style, it will be integrity in the Nineties." Integrity
a "commodity"? Surely this wasn't the most apt choice of word? "Absolutely," Hegarty
agrees. "It was totally wrong." He was talking to the journalist, he now explains, in a
language more appropriate for clients.

Hegarty doesn't mince words when it comes to designers. He thinks they should get
out more. "They are very insular people, terribly insular people. The first thing they do
is to build walls around themselves and pretend they live in a nice little world of their

own. They don't mix with other designers – there's no integration. I think one of the great lessons they could learn from advertising is that advertising as an industry is integrated incredibly well."

The trouble with graphic designers, says Hegarty, is that they worry too much about the choice of typeface and the colour of paper. They forget about the idea. Hegarty should know – before joining Benton and Bowles in 1965, where he partnered Charles Saatchi, he studied graphic design at the London College of Printing. "I found the whole thing so precious that it just bored me. Nobody was having fun. It was all incredibly intense. Everybody was worried about redesigning the tax form. I thought the tax form was the most appalling thing you could ever want to look at anyway – whatever you did it was going to be appalling. I wanted to put jokes in it and make it funny. People didn't understand what I was going on about."

So what is he going on about? As Hegarty explains it, design's tendency to impose order is fundamentally at odds with the "destructive" tendencies of real creativity. The kind of creativity you find in the better class of commercial, presumably – all those ones about beating the Germans to the beach in your Audi. Where this leaves the tax form, the telephone directory, textbooks, dictionaries, maps, manuals or public sign systems isn't clear. Hegarty isn't saying that these things shouldn't be orderly, but nor does his undeniably inspiring call for "radicalism" and constant reinvention suggest a very close understanding of the problems involved in the less glamorous forms of graphic design. Even Tango, the BBH-affiliated design consultancy on whose board he serves, concentrates on image-making exercises for wealthy clients like Liberty, Levi's and TAG-Heuer.

Instead, Hegarty talks in vague yet insistent generalities. What graphic design needs is the right "tone of voice". What most designers lack is a proper "point of view". Most designers are not being individuals – "they are following a crowd, they are being sheep". Which, if any, graphic designers does Hegarty admire? He lists Neville Brody (he should – BBH, founded in 1982, learned a lesson or two from *The Face*), Mary Lewis, Newell and Sorrell, Martin Lambie-Nairn ("a very exciting point of view") and Pentagram ("very, very clever, but I think they are terribly insular as people").

Hegarty's own point of view is unequivocally self-serving. It puts advertising right at the centre of the social and philosophical picture. "Our whole structure of life is about selling something," he says. The function of design, much like the function of advertising, is to create an appropriate "atmosphere" around objects, so that people will want to buy them. The sooner designers stop fooling themselves that it can be otherwise and face up to this simple truth, the better. Hegarty is so convinced of his life-is-a-commercial thesis that he thinks the main dictionary definition of "to sell" is "to persuade someone of another point of view".

Hegarty should make an excellent chairman of the BBC's graphic design panel. He has plenty to say, a fully developed point of view and the camera likes him. Of course it might be, despite BBC assurances to the contrary, that a few viewers will derive the mistaken impression from Hegarty's prominence that advertising and graphic design are in some way synonymous. But in the very unlikely event that this should happen, those insular, sheep-like, uncommunicative graphic designers will have only themselves to blame.

Blueprint, March 1990

THE TWO CULTURES

There are now two cultures in British graphic design and each, in recent years, has experienced a defining moment – a point at which it burst into the public consciousness and the usually unremarked activities of the profession became a national talking point. The first occurred in 1988 when, at the precociously youthful age of 31, Neville Brody was granted a retrospective exhibition within the hallowed halls of the Victoria and Albert Museum. Here, if you wanted it, was final proof that the graphic designer, too, could be a figure of glamour – a star! – and achieve all this by operating within a subculture, refusing to play the professional game, and going it alone.

The second, more lugubrious moment came three years later when the national telephone company, British Telecom, introduced a new corporate identity designed by the consultants Wolff Olins. BT's new logo, leaked to the press before its official launch, provoked a furore that continued to rumble long after it had started to appear on the sides of phone booths and trucks. Hardly anyone had a good word to say about the poorly drawn, prancing pipe player. The newspapers, predictably, were outraged that so little (to their way of thinking) should cost so much. Wally Olins, the company's charismatic chairman, was able to offer excellent reasons why this now privatised national resource should abandon its existing identity and rearm itself with one better suited to the cut and thrust of international competition, but this did nothing to shake the conviction of many of his colleagues that the new design was, quite simply, bad.

The episode left a sour taste in the profession's collective mouth. In style the logo resembled nothing so much as the flimsy retail identities that had swamped the high streets of Britain in the 1980s. The few designers who leapt to Wolff Olins's defence argued that the profession was doing incalculable damage to its own credibility by turning so publicly on itself. More common was the view that it was the BT identity itself that had done the harm.

To nonconformists like Brody, the project provided a classic example of the way in which many of the larger firms had allowed business and marketing considerations to dominate all others. These conflicting viewpoints are now enshrined at the deepest levels of the profession. Increasingly, British graphic design divides between smaller, younger teams dedicated to the pursuit of creative freedom above all other goals and the larger, mainstream companies who see design primarily as a business and subordinate creative goals to the imperatives of commerce. This status-conscious mainstream (or at least its élite) dominates the professional awards, while the publicity-hungry marginals monopolise the pages of the design press. The mainstream wins the accounts of the corporate heavy-hitters, while the marginals have the fun. There are very few points, either socially or stylistically, at which these two groups overlap.

There are, however, a handful of youngish companies who have succeeded in carving out a middle ground, and it is here, perhaps, that the best hopes of British graphic design now lie. These designers are successors to an earlier generation of rebels – Brody, Peter Saville and Malcolm Garrett – who made their names in the early 1980s, working for style magazines, record labels and fashion companies. The difference with outfits like 8vo, Why Not Associates, Siobhan Keaney, Cartlidge Levene and one or two others is that they aimed, from the start, to attract serious, big-spending, corporate clients. They saw no reason why it should not be possible to serve commerce with work that by the conservative norms of the profession counts as riskily experimental, and by and large, they have had their way.

Few members of this later group will concede an explicit debt to the example of Brody (who has suffered the inevitable backlash experienced in Britain by the prematurely successful), but their approach is founded on similar assumptions. These designers are unashamed products of a decade in which the look was everything. They take it as an article of faith that in a culture of the image graphic design must work twice as hard to capture and hold its audience's attention. Their objection to the orthodoxy of British conceptual graphics, from Pentagram to The Partners, is that it provides a strictly "one-take" solution: once you have grasped the visual pun or got the joke, there is nothing much left to look at (or think about). This has led critics to dismiss their work for its supposed preoccupation with superficial styling – both typographic and photographic – at the expense of "ideas". But this is as much a caricature of how their designs operate at their best, by playing a knowing, postmodern game with familiar visual codes, as is their own blanket dismissal of the continuing validity, on the right occasions, of the conceptual approach.

This new generation of designers poses a challenge that their longer-established colleagues have yet to acknowledge properly, let alone address. The mainstream of graphic design in Britain is not distinguished by the plurality of approaches familiar in America. Sitting on an awards jury while working on this article, I was struck by the remarkable stylistic conformity among even the best submissions. The work was elegant, professional, tasteful, decorous – but almost entirely lacking in the daring, imagination and vigour we take for granted in British television, music, or advertising. Perhaps, to be charitable, we were witnessing some form of recessionary ennui and loss of confidence. It would be depressing news for the country's graphic design culture if it had told anything like the whole story. In fact, many of the most interesting designers had once again declined to submit their projects. For anyone who cares about the future of British graphics, reuniting its divided factions and reinvigorating its tired mainstream should now be a matter of priority.

AIGA Journal of Graphic Design, vol. 11 no. 1, 1993

THE DESIGNER AS AUTHOR

For the British graphic design companies who have come to expect to return from the D&AD awards dinner with a silver or two for the meeting room wall, the evening of 10 April 1991 will have proved a disappointment. While some of the household names – The Partners, Pentagram, Trickett & Webb – earned commendations in the categories of corporate identity and direct mail, the coveted yellow pencils proved persistently elusive in the main graphics section. Of the longer established consultancies, only Smith & Milton won the undivided admiration of the jury with a silver for their Tate & Lyle design manual.

This year, the shift in taste signalled in 1990 by the two graphics silvers given to Siobhan Keaney (one with Karen Wilks) began to look like a trend. There was a remarkable uniformity of style and intention to the work that the jury was prepared to allow into the next D&AD annual, to be published in November – never mind honour with a nomination or award. As always, the composition of the jury had everything to do with it. Last year, Keaney promised in an interview that "we're the ones who'll take over". This year, as a member of D&AD's executive committee, she helped to select a jury (myself included) in which, for the first time, it wasn't the "token newcomers" who were in the minority, but the token old-timers.

Doubtless some will say D&AD chairman Edward Booth-Clibborn and his committee have gone too far. They would have a very good point if it wasn't for the fact that the work favoured by the graphics jury is some of the most compelling and representative new design being created in Britain. The truth is that this work has been happening for some time – its deepest roots go back to the early 1980s. Yet, despite the repeated complaints from younger designers that the old guard kept tossing out their submissions, it has taken until now for the institutional machinery of D&AD to acknowledge its presence fully.

For older designers, much of this new work is deeply problematic. Once, communication used to seem like a relatively straightforward affair. You found out what your client wanted to say and you expressed that message as forcefully, wittily and persuasively as possible. This being Britain, where an undogmatic, eclectic sensibility held sway, you chose whatever formal and stylistic solution seemed most "appropriate" to the client's needs. Of course, the better you were, the more your own creative personality would shine through the project. Secretly, this might be your primary motivation (it was certainly why you liked to receive all those awards). But you never lost sight of the fact that it was the client, at the end of the day, who was paying the bill.

The new wave of designers pay at least lip-service to these principles. Unlike the first wave of rebels – Neville Brody, Malcolm Garrett, Peter Saville, who steered clear of the

The Written Image. Poster for an exhibition of visual work by thesis students. Designer: Jonathan Barnbrook. Royal College of Art, Great Britain, 1990

mainstream by working for the style magazines and independent record labels – many of the new generation cut their teeth at the serious end of the business. Siobhan Keaney did stints at Smith & Milton, Robinson Lambie-Nairn and David Davies; members of Cartlidge Levene, winners of this year's other graphic design silver, put in time at Conran, Trickett & Webb, Peter Leonard Associates and The Design Solution. Experience of dealing with demanding corporate clients gave the new wavers a head start when they came to set up their own businesses at the end of the 1980s.

Yet the designs that Keaney, Cartlidge Levene, Why Not Associates and others produce for oil companies, fashion retailers, property developers and TV facilities houses appear to fly in the face of British graphic design's most cherished beliefs. There is nothing straightforward about the "communication" occurring here. The undecorated, amusing, graphically direct ideas beloved by designers from Fletcher/Forbes/Gill to The Partners have been cast aside. In their place come multi-layered text zones and image-fields of mind-boggling complexity and doubtful legibility. The crisp one-liner is lost in a babble of competing voices. The unambiguous statement has been transformed into an annotated visual text.

The culprits, of course, are the Europeans, if only indirectly. "We would like to be thought of as European designers," stresses Ian Cartlidge of Cartlidge Levene. "That's very important because, to me, British design still has that nostalgic ring about it."

Gert Dumbar's brief installation as professor of graphic design at the Royal College of Art from 1985 to 1987 had a profound and, it would now seem, lasting effect. Keaney, who did not study with him, owes Dumbar an acknowledged debt. Students who did sign up with Dumbar, such as Russell Warren-Fisher, Sean Perkins of Cartlidge Levene, and the members of Why Not Associates, continue to carry the torch. The Thunder Jockeys, now working on advertising campaigns for Volkswagen, were regular visitors to Dumbar's department.

If one faction of the British new wave absorbed its anarchism from Dumbar, then another turned to Switzerland – by way of Peter Saville's album covers and 8vo's *Octavo* magazine, first published in 1986 – for its typographic structure. Suddenly, and improbably, small sizes of Helvetica set against acres of white space looked about as fashionable as you could get. The decade wound down in a short-lived burst of enthusiasm for Weingartian stepping effects. But the sanserif aesthetic has proved, in its latest incarnation, to be remarkably durable, whether used undiluted (Roundel, Williams and Phoa), or as part of a more complex assemblage of image and text (8vo, Cartlidge Levene).

For some, who had read their Müller-Brockmann in the 1960s, it was second time round. Mike Dempsey of Carroll Dempsey Thirkell, showing a sensitivity to the prevailing mood that few of his contemporaries could match, designed a series of album covers for the London Chamber Orchestra which remains one of the high points of the reborn style.

Common to all camps, though, is a renewed emphasis on the power of the photographic image, an inevitable reaction, perhaps, to the torrent of meaningless illustration that clogged the arteries of British design in the 1980s. "It's as if the designers were handing the problem over to the illustrators and saying, 'Here, you solve it, then we'll put a bit of centred typography underneath it and that will be fine'," says Keaney. Now Keaney and others are taking a new look at the Dutch tradition of staged photography and the typophotography of Moholy-Nagy. Working with sympathetic photographers such as Robert Shackleton, Trevor Key and Richard J. Burbridge allows a much greater degree of firsthand involvement and conceptual control.

What critics dislike most about the new graphic design is what they claim to be its relentless insistence on style. Last year's D&AD graphics jury complained about the triumph of "style over content" in the work submitted and there were those on this year's jury (admittedly a minority) who echoed their lament. It's a criticism which came to dog the design, and the design heroes, of the 1980s. Joining Pentagram in October 1990, Peter Saville was at pains to distance himself from the style graphics of the last decade.

When the issue is put to them, new wavers invariably affirm their own commitment to ideas, but always with qualifications. "I'm not against ideas," says Kia Boon Phoa, who used to be at Pentagram. "At one time, witty or obvious ideas were very good. You won an award because it was so obvious. I actually don't like that any more. You smile the first time you see it, but six months later you don't smile any more." Phoa provides a striking example of the way in which the new aesthetic has taken hold. Four recent brochures for the architect Peter Foggo are strict enough to satisfy the most doctrinaire Swiss typographer. Phoa used to vary his style according to the client, like the textbook said you should. Now he believes it is possible to solve the client's problems while retaining a recognisable style. He wants the use of black and white to become a personal trademark.

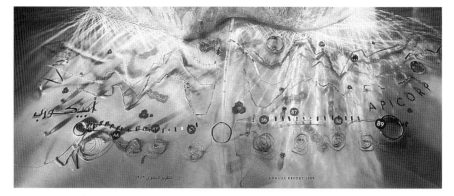

Annual Report 1989.
Front and back covers.
Designer: Siobhan Keaney.
Photographer: Robert
Shackleton. Apicorp,
Great Britain, 1989

This emphasis on visual styling and the precise detail of the way something looks characterises all of the new wave designers. "I think the problem with [the earlier generation] is that the idea takes precedence over what it looks like," says Keaney. "What I object to is people who have a strong idea and then don't give any attention to how they design it," Cartlidge agrees.

The assumption here is that the viewer will share the designer's aesthetic pleasure and that the pleasure will compensate for any difficulty in deciphering the text. "If the type is laid out in an intriguing, playful and entertaining way, the reader may be immediately stimulated and then begin to break down the type until the message is received," Andy Altmann of Why Not Associates told an audience of typographers at a Chartered Society of Designers debate on legibility. Altmann and his colleagues advance the familiar but undeniably self-serving argument that the public is more sophisticated than ever in the way that it filters and interprets visual signs. Make the presentation of the message too simple or obvious and the audience will only yawn.

The new wavers also make a much larger assumption. They take it for granted that graphic design can function as a kind of private language, with its own vocabulary and its own set of meanings. After all, the best-selling graphic design book of the 1980s was called *The Graphic Language of Neville Brody*. Most writers would hope to have their own personal style; very few would claim, as Brody did, to be communicating in their own personal language. At the very least, Brody seemed to be presenting himself as a new sort of author, on an equal footing with whoever it was that happened to be writing the text.

Who could blame *Face*-reading graphic designers, particularly those at college in the 1980s, for finding this heady stuff? Brody's fame, his book, his exhibition, his visibility, confirmed everything that the culture at large was saying: design, graphic design, is not simply a channel, it's a crucial part of the message, and the graphic designer can be a star in his own right.

It would be wrong, however, to accuse new wave designers of treating their clients simply as a pretext for self-expression. That would imply that the clients are being short-changed in some way. Most aren't – or no more so than usual. They are willing accomplices with an acute understanding of the way in which graphic design and its audience have changed. Next might be taking a risk when they commission Why Not Associates and type designer Jon Barnbrook to produce pages for the Next Directory, but they know the results will look state of the art. "Clients are quite prepared to have a subversive element if it adds interest to a mundane product," says Barnbrook, fully aware of the degree of "popstarism" involved in which designer gets chosen.

Only a year out of the Royal College of Art, Barnbrook already sounds disillusioned. His experiments with traditional letterforms (stone carving, black letter) and Macintosh technology have been widely published and admired. If you were to judge Barnbrook's work as an exercise in style alone, it is some of the most startling and beautiful British graphic design of the last few years. If, on the other hand, you were to judge it as a putative "graphic language", then it has a syntactical complexity and a visual intensity out of all proportion to the "mundane" content Barnbrook is being asked by most clients to express.

Barnbrook is perfectly aware of this disjunction. "Maybe we should discuss whether the message is worth reading anyway," he suggested at the CSD legibility debate. But Barnbrook's argument that the designer's "positive or negative visual associations can say more about the subject than the best written 'legible' copy" does not sound convincing. What are these messages going to say – that the product or service isn't any good? Few British designers, Barnbrook included, would claim that they are consciously applying the tenets of the deconstructionist critics who argue that stable meanings can no longer be held to exist (though at Cranbrook Academy of Art in the US, some designers claim to be doing this). Yet the fugitive meanings of the deconstructionists do seem to have infiltrated the graphics avant-garde at some deep intuitive level.

Barnbrook's willingness to address these issues of meaning, like Brody's before him, is commendable. They are issues which the new wave designers will sooner or later have to confront. Barnbrook and Brody find alternative outlets for their ideas in projects of their own. How much personal expression or additional commentary can a commercial medium sustain? At what point do the codes, layers and legibility games contaminate the message beyond retrieval? New wave designers tend to justify their interventions in terms of professional creativity and originality, but for the rest of us, clients and consumers, is that finally enough?

Perhaps there are occasions when graphic design can become a "language" in the sense that Brody meant. The problem now is for designers who are working to enlarge the vocabulary of British graphic design in the 1990s to decide what exactly they are trying to say.

Blueprint, May 1991

ABCDEF
GHIJK
L MNOPQ
RST
UVWXYZ

Typeface Six. Originally
designed for *The Face* in 1986
and later digitised. Designer:
Neville Brody. FontShop
International, Great Britain, 1991

SIGN LANGUAGE
NEVILLE BRODY

Among younger contemporary British graphic designers, Neville Brody enjoys an eminence without precedent. In April 1988, he will be honoured, at the tender age of 31, with a retrospective of his work in the Victoria and Albert Museum's Twentieth-Century Gallery – where previous exhibitions have cast backward glances at the much longer careers of Irving Penn, Zika Ascher, Alvar Aalto and Salvatore Ferragamo. And as if this early acclaim were not enough, April also sees the publication, on the back of the exhibition, of *The Graphic Language of Neville Brody*, a lavish volume devoted to his work and ideas.

Brody's rapid elevation to the status of graphics guru is, of course, one index among many of the importance design has assumed in the 1980s. British design needs its inspirational figures, its rebel heroes, and Brody, an articulate product of 1970s subculture, fitted the bill. No one could deny that Brody has talent and originality – he has them in abundance – but like many fast-risers before him he has also had the good fortune to find himself in the right place at the right time: in this case, Nick Logan's seminal style magazine, *The Face*.

There, after a slow start, the man who "had never in my wildest dreams intended working on magazines" transformed himself into the most talked-about magazine designer of the decade. Brody proved to be an able proponent of his own work, with an ability to deliver a telling quote that was bound to endear him to the journalists who started to call him in 1985. Brody wasn't brattish or boastful, but he was gently insistent on his significance in a way that his peers never were. Barney Bubbles, whom Brody often cites, modestly declined even to sign his work, while Malcolm Garrett, whose graphic experiments with *New Sounds New Styles* in early 1982 prefigure Brody's at *The Face*, seems temperamentally incapable of PR.

It's as well to keep these names in mind when considering Brody's familiar claim that his inventions have been appropriated by fellow designers and "kidnapped" by advertising. Undeniably they have – this is, after all, as *The Face* itself reminded us in 1983, "The age of plunder" – but Bubbles (were he still alive), Garrett, Jamie Reid and Terry Jones, to name only the most obvious figures, could make the same claim. It is not just Brody who has been obliged to retreat into typographic orthodoxy or an "anti-design" aesthetic in an attempt to elude the insatiable copyists in hot pursuit. Terry Jones's *i-D* magazine is also looking considerably less scrambled these days.

For Brody, however, it has been the greater loss. As he points out in *The Graphic Language*: "The style evolved from a breakdown of the traditional structure." By renouncing his logos, symbols and hand-drawn letterforms, his painterly freedom with image and text, Brody has weakened his ability to comment on editorial content in the process of articulating it. Spreads such as his masterly opener for a Dieter Rams profile in *Arena*, designed like an advert as a commentary on the marketing of design, are now the exception rather than the rule as they were in *The Face*. Yet never has the need for Brody's ironic intervention seemed greater, especially since the late 1980s materialism of this lifestyle magazine for men, where Brody is art director, does not always square with his principles. There are spreads, he admits, that he would prefer not to lay out.

Brody's strength as a "commercial artist", pursuing his own highly personal concerns, is also, paradoxically, his limitation as a designer in the familiar problem-solving sense of the word. The "graphic language" he devised, principally though his work at *The Face*, is something of a misnomer. Far from being the stuff of mass communication, Brody's visual codes were readily intelligible only to initiates. That, surely, was the point. *The Face* in its heyday, from 1983 to 1985, was an unashamedly élitist publication, offering privileged meanings to a narrow, self-defined audience in exactly the same way that Brody's enigmatic liveries for experimental rock groups like 23 Skidoo and Cabaret Voltaire provided their fans with tribal markings impenetrable to the outsider. Brody has always been at his most original when mediating a culture, a *cult*, in which he was also a participant.

Given his need for radical commitment, his desire to "internalise" a project, it is perhaps not surprising that Brody has gravitated towards sympathetic causes in his work outside *The Face* and *Arena* – redesigns for *City Limits* and *New Socialist*; logos for Red Wedge, Artists Against Apartheid and CND (the latter rejected). Most recently, he has produced a brochure for The Body Shop, doyen of socially acceptable retailers. Worthy as these projects are, none of them has shown the convention-breaking *élan* of the work that made his name.

Brody's brushes with mainstream publishing have been less happy. Democratic by nature, he is restless within the rigid hierarchies of large organisations. *Vive*, a fashion magazine project which promised much, was shelved by IPC after the company failed, in Brody's view, to show the necessary commitment. Working on a redesign of *Mademoiselle* for Condé Nast in the US, Brody clashed with the company's worldwide editorial director, Alexander Liberman. In 1986 Brody abandoned the *Tatler* after a single issue as art director.

As he emerges from the shower of plaudits that can be expected to greet his show and his book, Brody will surely be wondering where to find the clients who can fully accommodate his singular and uncompromising vision.

Blueprint, April 1988

RUB OUT THE WORD
NEVILLE BRODY

It must be just a little unsettling to be crowned "the first graphic design superstar", to achieve a degree of recognition by the age of 30 that most designers will not be granted in a lifetime, to be the subject of a book, a crowd-pulling retrospective in one of the world's great museums and an avalanche of admiring publicity, only to find – when you quite naturally assume you have well and truly arrived – that you have been written off as a "stylist", that fellow designers are publicly questioning whether you merit such treatment and, worst of all perhaps, that most of your clients have vanished so that within only a few months of your triumph you are on the brink of bankruptcy with no choice but to start all over again.

Such has been the remarkable career of Neville Brody. In the period immediately after he published *The Graphic Language of Neville Brody* in 1988 he entered a kind of limbo from which he is only now, six years later, beginning to emerge. Once a continuous, monthly presence in the pages of *The Face* and *Arena,* Brody is these days effectively invisible to many of his British colleagues. "I couldn't actually tell you what he's been doing with his life for the last five years," says a Pentagram London partner. It is not that he has not been busy. As his new book, *The Graphic Language of Neville Brody 2*, shows – it is sixteen pages bigger than the first – he has been busier than most.

Brody leads a curious, binary life. He is the rebel with boardroom access, a potentially mainstream talent who prefers creative life in the margins, an aloof and glamorous figure who doesn't return calls with the soft-spoken, easy-going, genuinely likeable manner of the boy next door. "On one level he's the international star who travels everywhere club class," says collaborator Jon Wozencroft. "On the other he's a north London lad who wants to go home and watch a video with his girlfriend." Brody gets short shrift from British colleagues. "He's an interesting sideline," one corporate-identity specialist told me; "A fashion designer who works in graphics," says another; "He never figured for me personally," says a third. Yet he is judged by more historically minded and perhaps less partisan observers to be one of the most notable designers of the last ten years. When Philip Meggs published his revised history of graphic design in 1992, Brody was the only recent non-American addition. Richard Hollis's *Graphic Design: A Concise History* singles out Brody over many of his detractors – only to damn him with faint praise. Brody, writes Hollis, "tamed punk into the consumer graphic idiom of the 1980s".

Was it really no more than this? While Brody would be the first to suggest otherwise, he knows there is a problem. He is remembered (and in some quarters blamed) as much for the paper mountain of advertising and retail graphics inspired by his work for *The Face* as for the pages of the magazine itself. "Essentially, I think I failed," he told me in 1990. "My ideas were weakened into styles. The very thing I used in order to get the ideas across – a strong personal style – was the thing that defeated reception of the ideas." His switch to stylistically neutral Helvetica for *Arena* headlines was an act of both atonement and self-denial ("I hate Helvetica"), but it did no good. They copied that, too: for the last eight years in Britain a spotlessly white, drip-dry neo-modernism has been the dominant graphic style. When, as a juror at last year's American Center for Design "100 Show", Brody came across a Pentagram Prize poster that looked like one of his *Arena* spreads c. 1987, he selected it only to give it a public dressing down: "This is, to me, a perfect example of getting it totally wrong," he fumed. "This sort of thing shouldn't happen."

As if this were not enough, Brody has sustained damage in more sensitive areas. He believes he has something important to tell us, wants to be taken seriously and in numberless interviews, culminating in the text of his first book, urges us to consider the substance of his ideas. But his critics, like his imitators, have a tendency to linger on the seductive surfaces where, they argue, the true meaning lies; and this meaning is never quite what Brody intended. In a superb essay on *The Face*, Dick Hebdige, now dean of critical studies at CalArts, argues that the magazine's use of advertising rhetoric, its urge to compress and condense – most pronounced in Brody's "sometimes barely legible typefaces" – creates "an absolute homology of form and meaning which cannot be assimilated but can only be copied". The exact opposite, in fact, of what Brody set out to do.

In December 1988, following the success of *Graphic Language*, a British newspaper gave Brody and Wozencroft an unprecedented opportunity to state their case against "the set up" of contemporary design and explain their desire to call a halt. Casting aside the *Guardian*'s usual grid and typeface, they filled the page with tall columns of tiny Helvetica, huge, arbitrary arrows and meandering pontification rendered in fathomless prose. Unfortunately, as readers pointed out, these strategies embodied precisely the qualities of "designerism" that the authors claimed to deplore. "The biggest contradiction is between the 'designed' form it takes, and its criticism of the role of design," ran one tightly argued riposte. "Significance has been sacrificed on the altar of style."

For Brody the manifesto was a turning point. He had mounted the pulpit, delivered his most withering sermon on what he saw as the Iniquities of Design and the audience had merely shrugged and turned its back. "At some point after the article there was a commonly held agreement not to talk about me any more," he told me a year later. "My name and my work were almost unmentionable." Even his status as a professional communicator was now being challenged. "Is Brody a designer?" concluded one sceptical letter to the *Guardian*. "I don't think so."

Brody quietly regrouped. In 1988, he moved to a new top-floor studio under the exposed rafters of an old furniture warehouse in east London. He became a partner in FontWorks, the British arm of FontShop, the international font distributor started by Erik Spiekermann. "I don't want to have to rely on the whim of the client," he says. In the 1990s Brody went digital with a vengeance. Through the Macintosh he has found his way back to the painterliness that is the basis of his talent. The halting angularity of his earliest experiments has been superseded by a sensuous organicism. In 1991, he launched the quarterly experimental type magazine *Fuse*, with Wozencroft as editor.

No longer fashionable in Britain, Brody found new clients in Europe and Japan. He

Freeform. Abstract digital
fonts. Designer: Neville Brody.
Fuse, Great Britain, 1994

redesigned and art directed the men's magazine *Per Lui* and redesigned the fashion title *Lei* for Italian Condé Nast. Then, in 1991, he put in a hectic year as airborne art director for *Actuel*, the Parisian news magazine – some of his most un-Brody-like and, it has to be said, ordinary work to date. Assisted by the Neville Brody Studio, a collection of freelancers who work for him as projects arise, he has undertaken cultural commissions in Germany (where his stock remains high), an on-screen identity for ORF (the Austrian state broadcasting company) and a signing project in Tokyo. He is currently setting up an office in Miami with Spanish fashion and industrial designer Chu Oroz.

This is the fourth time I have interviewed Brody and, hoping for some environmental clues to his character, I ask if we can meet at his home. I am politely but firmly rebuffed. One phone call too many at three in the morning from devoted fans who have somehow obtained his phone number has left Brody with a horror of invasion and a determination to keep his home life off limits. There is no computer, he says (and in his case this is saying something – he's an obsessive game-player), and the phone number is only known to four or five people.

So we meet at Brody's new north London office, a small, purpose-built block in muted high-tech that looks, unlike his previous offices, as though it is inhabited by designers. For the first time he has a reception area with regulation-issue black leather sofa, a secretary with a telephone manner and something resembling a meeting area occupied (let's not get too corporate) by a dart board, pool table and an electric racetrack that the studio bought itself for Christmas. This is where we sit down to talk.

Brody looked boyish well into his 30s. These days, at 37, he sports a beatnik beard and goes easier on the hair gel. He talks fluently, with conviction, but there is nothing messianic or overbearing about him. He makes the improbable sound reasonable, inevitable. Brody has got it all worked out – up to a point, and that point is where the contradictions start. Some of his analysis makes sense. But he cannot resist the provocative soundbite – "If [graphic design] was a truly honest means of communicating ideas," he once said on TV, "then there would only ever be a need for one typeface in the world" – and such loopy pronouncements do little for the gravitas of someone who made his name "painting" with type and now distributes fonts (9,000 at last count). "He's a wind-up artist, Neville," says Wozencroft. "He courts the media in an Andy Warhol-like fashion. Sometimes it's very witty and sometimes it's just . . . gulp!"

Language. It's a word that recurs throughout our conversation. "Language is a kind of hypnosis," Brody begins. "When language stops evolving and changing, it's because people have stopped thinking and evolving." At first, I assume he is talking about verbal or written language; there may be other kinds of language, but its primary meaning, clearly, is the formation of words. I find myself wondering why Brody should presume to step in where an army of writers, poets, lexicographers and linguists already treads. "Language," it soon emerges, is his own shorthand – so thoroughly internalised that he forgets it might need to be explained – for "visual language". It's an inversion that, once again, gives precedence to appearance over content.

"We've now got the opportunity in language to do what William Burroughs did in text," Brody continues. "What Burroughs did was extremely important, necessary and intellectual." He suddenly turns inquisitor. "Would you question that statement?" "Well, no," I reply. "Within a well-defined area of literary research he was important. But his innovations have yet to be applied to the airport best-seller."

"They never will be," says Brody. "*Fuse* will never be applied to the *Daily Mirror*. But we've never had the opportunity to experiment with visual language and I think that process of experimentation is necessary in itself because our world and the way we communicate are changing. Language is formed by social needs and philosophies. I'm talking about visual language almost strictly in the sense of the letterform and what happens after we've written something. I'm divorcing the look of the word from what the word says."

Since the late 1980s, Brody has been talking about making "a typography devoid of words", an organised set of abstract digital marks that carry no linguistic meaning and bear only a passing resemblance to the alphabets we know. *Fuse* is his decidedly non-commercial attempt to force the pace. Brody's own typeface, State, introduced in *Fuse* 1, though still just about readable, was a step in this direction. Other *Fuse* contributors have clung stubbornly to the notion of typography as a vessel of language, however clouded or chipped the goblet. Barry Deck resisted pressure to push Caustic Biomorph any further toward illegibility. Jeffery Keedy also declined to go the full distance with his goth-metal typeface LushUS. "I had a long series of discourses with Jeff Keedy when I met him in Chicago," says Brody. "He didn't get it." Not many people do, so Brody and Wozencroft are upping the ante. Issue 10, entitled "Freeform", makes the commitment to abstraction explicit.

"But language implies a common understanding," I suggest. "These private visual languages you're exploring can't have a wider application because the rest of us don't speak the language."

This is the closest Brody comes to losing his patience. "What you're saying is an exact echo of what journalists would have said when the first Dada exhibition was put on, or when they saw the first Paul Klee painting, or Cézanne. They would have said, 'This makes no sense, we've got a set of modular objects with very little relationship to realistic representation, I don't understand it, it's not important.' Would you have said the same thing to Cézanne?" Another appeal to a higher authority. Then he realises what he has said. "I'm not comparing myself with Cézanne," he adds hastily. "I'm not saying that. What would you have said to Jackson Pollock?"

"It's not the same, though. As painters, Cézanne and Pollock worked with wordless visual form. As a designer, whose medium is words, you are talking about draining off linguistic content so that only design remains."

"No, we're talking about representation. It's moving from representational to expressive typography. I think the parallel with what happened in painting is absolutely precise. Until the arrival of photography, painting was understood as a way of representing either fantasy or the real world. It had a very specific role just as typography has a specific role in western society as a carrier of words."

"But why would you want to take representation out of language? It's a contradiction in terms. What, ultimately, is the point?"

Brody replies at some length, but circles the question. Developing the analogy with photography and painting, he argues that putting desktop technology in the hands of the non-designer liberates the designer from the necessity of representation in the same way that the camera liberated the artist. The project of design, he seems to believe, is almost complete. The sign systems and identities are now largely in place. In-house staff equipped with digital templates can take care of implementation, freeing designers such as Brody to pursue other, more painterly ends. The digital future, he suggests, will be "more to do with art than with design communication as we knew it". He doesn't explain the point of such private "languages" – why do we need them? How will we use them? – or why we should want, *Ray Gun* style, to "treat printed media as painting". Why bother with text at all? Why not simply set up as a digital artist with a palette of pixels?

Returning to art history, Brody concludes with a question of his own. "The main point about Dadaism was a question mark. Why art? Why painting? And I think we are at the same junction in design and graphics. Why design? Why graphic designers?" What is his own answer? I ask. "Well, I've got no idea," he says, "and to be honest, graphic design is dead."

A couple of weeks later, still wondering what the point is, I call Jon Wozencroft. As co-founder of the audio-visual publishing company Touch, Wozencroft has been exploring the edges of print and performance since the early 1980s. A designer by training, he attempts feats of synthesis (drawing on art, design, literature, philosophy, sociology) in his heavily footnoted writings that would make even subject specialists think twice. They don't always come off. He has produced the text for two Brody books, collaborated on the manifesto and assorted commercial projects, talks like Brody's conscience ("I try to un-soundbite him"; "I'm always trying to improve his politeness"), but stresses his "distance" from the studio. He is in most days, though, according to Brody and it is clearly a relationship that benefits them both. Through Brody, Wozencroft gains immediate access to client areas it would take him "ages of attrition" to reach. Brody, in turn, enjoys the services of his own resident theorist and gets taken seriously by the hip subculturalists who converge on Touch.

Wozencroft, with little prompting, spells out things that Brody only hints at, or implies. "They need to take more drugs!" Brody had joked at one point, as I described the difficulties even experimental typographers have with his ideas. Later he says: "I'm excited by the computer as a tool for exploring a mental reality. It's the biggest LSD drug ever invented." But these are off-the-cuff remarks, not statements of a coherent programme. Wozencroft comes right out and tells me that *Fuse* is an attempt to apply "psychotropic, narcotic elements in a purposeful way to the visual realm".

"We're trying to reinvest a kind of magic and indeterminate meaning in what we are doing and at the same time to make it clearer," continues Wozencroft of the *Fuse* collaboration. The two aims don't seem particularly compatible. The problem for Wozencroft, as for Brody, seems to lie in the nature of language itself, the difficulty in stepping back from its mediations, and there is the same ambiguity about what kind of "language" he means. "I strongly disagree with the title [of the new book]," he says. "This one is not about graphic language. Both of us in the best of all possible worlds would like to call it *Language* period." Like the historical sources he cites in support of *Fuse* – Kandinsky's spiritual abstraction, the automatic writing of the Surrealists, Burroughs and Brion Gysin's cut-ups – he wants to break free from "the trap of words". As so often with theories of this kind, it takes an awful lot of words to prise open the trap.

A great deal rests on *The Graphic Language of Neville Brody 2*, though it isn't as it happens, the book we were promised. Brody was already talking about his projected follow-up, to be called *The Death of Typography*, even as the first book began to fly from the shops. Why, I ask him some way into the interview, does he feel the need to produce another book so soon after the first?

His reply is uncharacteristically short. "Because I felt I had to. It's very simple."

I press him. "Because the first book was such a . . . " He can't quite say it. "Because people still assumed the work coming out of the studio was . . . All they'd seen was the first book and, as you know, very little since then. The purpose of the second book is to kill the preconceptions that the first book created."

There, he's said it. And he is right. The first book, like all such books, was a kind of ending. At the age of just 31, a mere ten years into his working life, it froze him, labelled him, in the public mind. It was one of the best-selling design books of the 1980s. Every studio has a copy. The only way to erase its memory, or at least to counteract it, and reassert his centrality to graphic design in the 1990s, is with another equally commanding book. Brody said at the time he wanted *Graphic Language* to open a dialogue (he said the same thing about *The Face*), and he says it again about *Graphic Language 2*. He seems genuinely unaware that it might appear presumptuous to glorify yourself in this way every six years.

"Do you see yourself as a leader?"

"No, no, no." He seems really taken aback. "It's not a case of leading. The group of people who work here have come together because we're all interested in, as I said, research and exploration and pushing and challenging things. This book focuses much more on the work. I'm almost loath to do portraits or interviews for this at all, but the publisher expects it. People should be able to look at the book and get what they need, because it's about the work, it's not about me."

There will be another book, says Brody, in a couple of years. But, perhaps because his mood is less apocalyptic than it was immediately after *The Face*, the death of typography has been indefinitely postponed. "In fact," he says, "I think we've missed the point." The new title is in any case much cleverer: it both affirms and negates. Brody plans to call it *Beyond Typography*.

"Are you a Net user?" I ask Brody at one point, convinced his answer will be yes.

"I'm not. I'm not."

"Why not, given your interest in computers?"

"I don't know. That's something that I've never been fascinated with."

Then, just as the tape is about to run out, he says something completely unexpected, making me wonder if I have misheard him – just lets it slip and moves on to something else, an admission that seems, the more I think about it, to crystallise everything, the last thing he probably should say and the most revealing thing he could. Brody says "*I enjoy creating modes of communication, but I don't enjoy communicating,*" and I begin to see why he finds the thought of a typeface with which you can say nothing quite as exciting as he does.

I.D., September/October 1994*

Power, Corruption & Lies.
Album cover for New Order.
Designer: Peter Saville.
Painting by Fantin-Latour,
National Gallery, London.
Factory, Great Britain, 1983

A PENTAGRAM FOR THE NINETIES
PETER SAVILLE

The union of Peter Saville and Pentagram is not, on first hearing, the most obvious
of marriages. The prince of the 1980s stylists welcomed as an equal partner in the
stronghold of graphic ideas: five years ago the notion would have been unthinkable.
A year ago it might, at a pinch, have been thinkable, but few would have believed it
likely to happen.

The first thing Saville's Pentagram partnership points up is just how completely
the design decade is over. One by one the proselytes of style have recanted, repented
and re-dedicated themselves to the pursuit of content and the responsibilities of
communication. Saville, famous from the beginning for his Anthony Price suits, Rolex
and BMW, is no exception. "We are trying to understand ideas now," he says, "because
styling doesn't mean anything any more. You used to be able to say an awful lot with
how you styled something; it would position it culturally. That doesn't work now. You
aren't communicating much with the look of something, because it gets appropriated
so quickly."

Yet, despite his apparent about-face, there has always been more to Saville's graphic
design work than style alone. "His work clearly comes from a different generation,"
says Pentagram partner John McConnell, "but it wasn't so style-directed. There seemed
to us to be an intelligence there that meant it wasn't solely a style game. In the end,
with any partner, you want intelligence. If you look at the range of Peter's solutions,
it's very wide."

It was McConnell who first suggested Saville's name to the other partners after Saville,
struggling with his ailing six-year-old business, PSA, had called on him for advice. In the
course of their conversation, McConnell asked him if there were any other design
groups he would consider joining. Saville said "Pentagram", assuming the question was
purely hypothetical, and the seed was sown. (He had, in fact, already considered forming
a "Pentagram for the 1990s" with Neville Brody and Malcolm Garrett.) When, after many
meetings, David Hillman presented a selection of Saville's work to the thirteen other
partners, who had flown to France for the occasion, there wasn't a single dissenting
voice: Saville was in, bringing his own partner, Brett Wickens, and two other designers
with him.

The British partners will be hoping he stays. The London office has had the
misfortune to lose two partners in the last decade; to lose any more would look like
carelessness. David Pelham stormed out in 1984, still only a year into the two-year
probationary period (new partners must buy equity in Pentagram at the end of this
time), while Howard Brown, appointed in 1987, lasted a matter of months. With its
founding partners (Crosby, Grange, Fletcher and Kurlansky) now in their 50s or 60s,

Pentagram urgently needs to refresh itself with younger blood. Saville joins John Rushworth, also in his 30s, who was promoted to partner from the position of associate in 1990.

The question of the company's profile and direction is naturally an issue of some sensitivity. Pentagram is universally admired by its peers, not least for its unique system of internal organisation – with each partner in effect running his own business – which has proved to be not only workable, but conducive to design of the highest standard. Yet the very soundness of the Pentagram philosophy, the stability of its organisation and its refusal to play costly games in the City, made it seem less vital, and less relevant, in the style-obsessed, stockmarket-watching, go-getting 1980s. Immune to the parochial temptations of style, and sustained by its formidable international reputation, Pentagram preferred to pursue its ideal of "timeless", ideas-based design. This meant, in practice – at least to the jaded younger observer – solutions not so very different in kind from the solutions of the 1970s, when Pentagram really had seemed hip, vital and relevant.

So it's easy to sympathise with Saville when he observes, as tactfully as he can, that he is part of a generation "a little bit out of sync with the Pentagram generation". Or when he ventures less cautiously: "We have to make Pentagram a bit funkier again. We have to get it how it was in the early 1970s, because when it started they were all these groovy guys, among the best-known names in their fields."

Saville arrived, at the end of the 1970s, with a bit of fanfare himself. He was still a graphic design student at Manchester Polytechnic, in the company of fellow designer Malcolm Garrett, when he became involved in the founding of Factory Records with Tony Wilson. Saville's posters and record sleeves – for Factory, Dindisc and Chrysalis – made an immediate mark. By 1981, Saville had been recognised with a trio of D&AD silver awards. Ten years later, many of the early covers still stand out as among the most impressive graphics of their period.

Saville cut through the noise, amateurishness and squandered energy of punk graphics with images of striking simplicity. From the beginning, he was out to anticipate new trends in type. Philip Johnson's drawings of the AT&T building gave him the idea that a classical revival was coming, so he used Roman lapidary letters on the cover of Joy Division's *Closer* above a photograph of a French cemetery. On the surface there wasn't a great deal to it – with Saville it has always been a matter of sensibility as much as substance – but the resonance of the design, for fans of the music, was large.

For the first half of the 1980s, Saville treated his prolific commissions as an extension of his education. His borrowings from the history books and type manuals were legion. Saville, like the artists of the period, called it "appropriation". Jan Tschichold had got him started, but he rapidly moved on to Berthold Wolpe's typeface Albertus (for New Order), Herbert Bayer and the Bauhaus (for Orchestral Manoeuvres in the Dark), and a more or less wholesale lift of two pieces of Futurist graphics by Fortunato Depero (again for New Order) for which he was arraigned in *The Face* as a participant in "The age of plunder". He was himself appropriated when Julian Schnabel employed a detail from the cover of *Closer* in the painting *Ornamental Despair*.

As recently as 1988, Saville resurrected Wim Crouwel's 1967 New Alphabet for a couple of posters – superbly, it must be said – but since the mid-1980s he has been concerned to evolve a more personal style. Saville surprised everyone when he rejected oblique imagery for a portrait photograph on the cover of New Order's *Low-life* (the choice of a sanserif typeface pre-*Arena*, pre-*Octavo*, was, as usual, prescient). But this opened the way for designs such as the sleeves for Peter Gabriel and catalogues for Yohji Yamamoto, where the framing of the few compositional elements is even more rigorously controlled. It's this editorial rigour which is arguably Saville's greatest gift as a designer and art director, and it is certainly an essential part of his appeal to the equally unsparing partners at Pentagram. "He's intelligent enough," says John McConnell, "to leave things out, which is the hallmark of work that is truly classic, as opposed to work that is just passing through."

Saville's problem in recent years has been the same one that faces any designer, however talented, who comes up through the music business. "If you can package records … you can package anything," Saville insisted in 1981, in the first flush of success. It's a reasonable theory, spoilt only by the fact that clients are a literal-minded breed hungry for previous experience. And as Saville now admits, with an honesty that speaks much for his present self-confidence, he did indeed lack experience. "Somebody might have paid me a vast amount of money to do a record cover, but I actually didn't know much about doing a letterheading, or producing a catalogue, or laying out a page of text. You're this infamous designer for only one thing, and the truth is that you are not much good at anything else."

His saviour came in the form of Nick Serota, then director of the Whitechapel Art Gallery. "He was one of the most important people we ever met, because he was prepared to look at what we'd done and say, 'Okay, you do record covers, I think you can do a gallery identity.'" Serota, by Saville's account, was an exceptionally patient man. It took a month for Saville to realise that he could simply drop the words "art gallery" to leave the single name "Whitechapel".

However protracted the birth, the project was a turning point for Saville and Wickens. Thought at first by some observers to be too low key, boring even, the Whitechapel identity has worn well and won friends. In France it led to a commission to design the identity for the "Magiciens de la Terre" exhibition at the Pompidou Centre, which in turn brought them an identity proposal for Jack Lang's Ministry of Culture. Suddenly Saville was on the brink of a full-scale identity programme. "I was terrified by the idea of that one materialising because, if it had, I don't think we would have been able to do it at that point."

He no longer has to worry. At Pentagram, Saville and his team will have the resources to undertake projects on this scale. They will have a structured, tested framework in which to operate, long-term financial targets to meet, monthly progress reviews, and a financial advisor on hand. The prospect of so much support clearly enraptures Saville, who speaks of timesheets with the zeal of the newly converted, and of the Pentagram partners' "forgiving toughness" with an almost filial pride. Saville has wrestled with the problems of running his own company, made mistakes which he freely admits, and finally accepted that he just isn't the managing director type.

As for the work we can expect to see, it appears unlikely that Saville's essential concerns will change that much. There will be fewer record covers: "I'm 35. The things I think about are not that appropriate to fifteen- or twenty-year-olds buying a record." But his stop-at-nothing perfectionism is not likely to falter. (One former staff member speaks of three-day marathons spent deciding how to space a block of type, and still having to put all the pencils back in the drawers before they could go home at two in the morning.) Saville has not lost his touch for what he would once have called "aspirational" graphics. The lessons of album cover design could be applied he believes, to the packaging of perfume and luxury cosmetics.

"In some ways it's not that unlike packaging a band. If I did a New Order cover, I never actually packaged the record: it was an ongoing process of presentation. And to some extent selling a perfume or cosmetic is similar. You are selling a concept."

At school with Saville in the early 1970s, Malcolm Garrett used to chide him: "You always use your paint straight from the tube." But it is no longer enough, says Saville, simply to choose an exotic typeface and rely on that for effect, as he and so many other stylists did in the 1980s. There are dozens of designers who "do Peter Saville" better than he does himself, so why not leave them to it? When everybody knows all the references, and everybody can make graphics look good, the only way left for designers to distinguish themselves is in the regard that they pay to the content. But wait a minute: isn't that precisely Pentagram's point?

Blueprint, November 1990

POST-MODERNISM, POST-DESIGN
PETER SAVILLE

You returned to London last summer after an abortive year at Frankfurt Balkind in Los Angeles. What went wrong?

I think it was partly that my commitment to being in Los Angeles was questionable. It would have been much healthier to have been in LA for twelve months as an individual, and if I wanted to stay then having discussions with a company. Even though I was familiar with LA, I completely underestimated what it meant to live there and how far away it is, and I began to realise that there weren't so many people in LA that I actually wanted to work for.

Presumably the company found your notorious working habits – the late starts, non-arrivals and all-nighters – pretty baffling.

It baffled Pentagram when I was there, it baffles me actually, and of course in America, with the American work ethic, it's just unheard of. I have a real problem with going to work for the sake of going to work. When I have to produce something, I do it. When I don't have work to realise, I'm looking for what to do. In a way, I work all the time, but I've never disciplined myself or been in a situation that disciplined me into going to an office at 9.30 in the morning and staying there until six o'clock and then going home.

But there were some mitigating circumstances. There was little for me to do at Frankfurt Balkind. I was there pursuing an almost intangible concept. I hadn't thought through who the clients were going to be.

Many people say to me, "Well, you're better off out of Pentagram." And I am better off – so are Pentagram. And with the things that have happened since leaving Frankfurt Balkind, I can only say that I'm better off out of Los Angeles too. Perhaps I should have had the sense not to get involved in the first place, but it seemed worth a try, just as it seemed worth a try at Pentagram. But neither situation was right for me. It's better for me to be an independent consultant and leave implementation and back-up to people who enjoy it and cause less trouble for the system.

Like your contemporaries, Neville Brody and Malcolm Garrett, you have received a great deal of recognition and by this stage in your career you might have expected to become, if not the new establishment, then certainly a more central figure. But somehow it hasn't happened. What are your feelings about that?

That's absolutely right and it's something I've thought about many times. In some ways we are an establishment – though I didn't realise it until recently. You work away through your 20s and into your 30s thinking, "My contemporaries and I will never get our break." And then, interestingly, something happens, which I don't think you can imagine when you're younger, and that is that the previous generation, who are the establishment, finally fall off the top and purely by this process of elimination you do eventually become the establishment. It was comforting to realise that when you're in your late 40s or 50s you will be one of the few who are deemed "suitable and appropriate". It's just the natural process of evolution.

The more critical point you are touching on is, I think, a circumstance of the design business as it has developed over the last ten years. In some ways, graphic design is still a young profession. The 1980s came only a decade or two after graphic design as we now think of it gained recognition in Britain. The 1960s generation became the establishment of a profession that they invented. They wrote the rules as they went along and led the clients with them. As ever, another generation came through which was in some ways radical compared to the previous one. But there was no new "corporate" client-base for the next generation. I was among this group and we were full of alternative ideas, but these were raw thoughts – not mature philosophies – and by the time the mainstream was in sync with our thinking, our ideas had been absorbed into the culture of the existing design establishment and assimilated into their strategies. By virtue of being the first "established" consultancy generation, this was an impediment that our predecessors had not confronted. Our commercial viability and visibility, and what we intrinsically had to offer through our understanding of our generation, were later hijacked by all those younger new design groups who were really just a splinter division of that establishment. Almost every week though the 1980s you would hear about a company that had just been set up by designers from Michael Peters with an account executive from Fitch – and they were already working for W. H. Smith. Well, they always had been . . . probably always will be.

How have these insights affected your own relationships with more mainstream clients?

Well, I think it's important not to feel bitter about reality. You can't help but wise up as you get older. I have recently been working with a major television station in Germany on a review of their identity. There was a feeling – implied, not stated – that anything was possible. But of course it wasn't. The latitude for change was terribly limited. As a high-rating station they have an investment in their identity. Who in their right

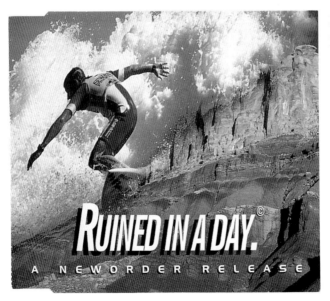

Ruined in a Day. CD insert for New Order. Art director: Peter Saville. Designers: Howard Wakefield and James Adams, Icon. Centredate, Great Britain, 1993

mind is prepared to gamble with that? All you can possibly do is try to solve any
practical problems, subtly enhance the identity and nudge its image towards the future.
You realise why the men in suits say they're not interested in innovative creativity.
It's because they can't afford to be. They can't afford to change the identity of the station
overnight unless they're prepared to invest heavily in supporting that change and in
the media campaign to accompany it.

**But are you nevertheless still primarily looking for situations which will allow for, as you put it,
innovative creativity?**

If somebody asked me to consider incremental improvements to the packaging
of Spaghetti Hoops, the implementation is unlikely ever to appeal to me, but the
thinking involved would intrigue me. I'm very happy to apply my mind to all kinds
of communications and visual problems, but I find the carrying out of a lot of the work
tedious. I was completely spoilt by my first five years working and only wanted to do
things that I enjoyed doing and that would provide incredible freedom.

How important was the music to you during those early years?

It was massively important – in the abstract sense – in that pop music is something you
wish to be associated with when you're young. It's the single most powerful form of
popular culture. So it's an incredible stimulus, an opportunity you must grasp. That said,
it's important – I'll use some marketing-speak now – in a branding sense to know how
you feel about each particular band you're working for. If it's a kind of music, a brand,
that you personally love, that helps. It may be a brand that you hate, but you have to be
detached and professional. You have to understand a Peter Gabriel customer whether or
not you are a Gabriel customer yourself. These days it's harder than it was fifteen years
ago. There are more scenes than anybody can know – it was relatively simple back
in 1980.

But I never used to base my work literally on the music. Because of lead times, the first
chance you had to hear the finished music was six to eight weeks after you should have
started the design. I based the work on my knowledge of the client and the category their
music fell into, but more importantly, on what I felt the visual aspirations of the group's
audience to be. Those covers were very carefully positioned – they were "pitched" at
a perceived audience.

**Sometimes in the early days you said you were using the covers as a way of learning about the
history of graphic design, but more recently you have described them as acts of "appropriation"
parallel to what was happening in the art world. Which was it?**

Both. I've found myself accounting for the work in different ways at different times,
depending on what people were able to appreciate. Appropriation – in the postmodern
sense – has never really been understood by the journalists of the music or graphics
press who wrote about the work. I find myself talking to people now who seem to
understand it, but between 1980 and 1985 they didn't understand it at all. You would
say things that didn't go into print. People just glazed over.

So what was the thinking behind your use of appropriation?

You have to remember the design climate back in the 1970s. In British popular graphics,
music and fashion there was a spirit of revivalism, recycling and retro-chic – dressing up
in 1950s clothes, having your hair cut short, buying Bakelite radios. My feeling is that
the twentieth-century *fin de siècle* started in the early 1970s as a reaction to contemporary
culture having finally run out of steam – the 1960s being to my mind the last bright
burst of modern spirit. From a young person's point of view, the things that were in

a way avant-garde in the early 1970s were David Bowie, Roxy Music and movies like *Bonnie and Clyde*. When you lose confidence in your own time you seek comfort in another time. The cutting-edge graphic designers in London at the time were George Hardie, Bush Hollyhead and Dan Fern, the airbrush illustrators Mick Brownfield and Philip Castle and art directors such as Nick de Ville who did the Roxy covers.

As a chronically groovy wannabe, I was desperately keen to know what was going on in music and fashion and graphics and art. I had a wonderful art teacher at school who said "You should do graphics." Many times afterwards I've thought, "Maybe I should have done photography. Maybe I should have been a fashion designer." At college, one thing that made me different from the other graphics students was that I was more interested in what was going on in the other departments – in fashion, photography, product design and architecture. Around 1974, Roxy were the single biggest influence in my life – from hairdressing to fine art all points were covered. I had a good grasp of Pop and they were the quintessential living expression of Pop Art.

I had – and to some extent still have – more a fashion designer's or stylist's sensibility than a graphic designer's. The fashion world has a readier understanding of what's happening. Fashion's existence is dependent on reference and reinterpretation, season after season. You see a radically new look perhaps once every ten years, usually accompanying real sociological change or technological development. The rest of the time, in between those major changes, everybody's going through little changes just for entertainment.

And for your generation, punk was a moment of radical change?

Punk itself, as a look, was really only a moment's aberration. For six months, punk was like the parting of the Red Sea and anybody who was fit and ready enough could run through. By association with certain people in Manchester I got pulled through the gap. But the look of punk didn't offer much hope for a fresh graphic language – this is where Malcolm [Garrett] was to be invaluable. Malcolm had a copy of [Herbert Spencer's] *Pioneers of Modern Typography*. The one chapter that he hadn't reinterpreted in his own work was the cool, disciplined "New Typography" of Tschichold and its subtlety appealed to me. I found a parallel in it for the new wave that was evolving out of punk. In this, as it seemed at the time, obscure byway of graphic design history, I saw a look for the new, cold mood of 1977–78.

Of course, the whole point with appropriation is knowing what to do, and when. Try to find the graphic design house that didn't have a Bauhaus book on its coffee table by the mid-1980s – you wouldn't have found one in 1978 or 1979. In 1983, when I put flowers on the cover of *Power, Corruption & Lies*, we hadn't seen flowers in pop culture since the 1960s. But [fashion designer] Scott Crolla was buying Sanderson fabric and Georgina [Godley] was running it up into dresses and there was this buzz about Flower Power coming back.

So for me, the door to graphic enlightenment was this book, *Pioneers of Modern Typography*. My entire education about the art and design movements of the twentieth century, other than Pop, began at that point. Every time I found something that really touched me, I was eager to express it.

Apart from fans of the music, the art community seems to have understood this work more readily than other designers.

Well, they pick up the references and they don't have a problem with the idea of appropriation. In the postmodern era, the notion of plagiarism didn't come into it.

If Jeff Koons took a photograph of a Nike ad and put it in a gallery, at the time nobody
called it plagiarism. He was obviously making a statement about Nike and the art
market. To me, it was better to quote Futurism verbatim, for example, than to parody it
ineptly – it was a more honest, more intellectual and in a way more artistic approach.
It was so literal and so obvious that it never crossed my mind that people would think
that I had invented this work. But some did. People were shocked because they thought
I had created an original and were disappointed to discover that it was reinterpreting
a previous work. I think they were missing the point.

At what stage did you become aware of postmodernism as a cultural idea?

In 1978, while working on the second Factory poster. On a trip to London I picked up
a book of Philip Johnson's proposals for the AT&T building in New York. On the cover
was the broken pediment. It made me think that maybe I wasn't wrong in wanting to
use Tschichold's later work – that and a John Foxx album cover for Ultravox [*Systems of
Romance*] with serif type on a black background. Within twelve months, neo-classicism
and the influence of architectural postmodernism were everywhere. People in New
York were buying columns to put in their apartments. My contribution was the graphic
equivalent. It was always an emotive feeling and after a year or so I began to trust in
my senses. I didn't need to wait for supportive signals and became brave enough to take
a step myself, but nearly always informed by some historical reference.

Did you ever read much of the theory?

I've never read much of it because I always find art criticism gets too heavy to read
through. The funny thing is that the art world didn't really speed up until the early
1980s. The fascinating thing was then seeing what that school of early 1980s artists
in New York did with the thinking.

**When did you first see Julian Schnabel's 1980 painting *Ornamental Despair*, with the detail from
your cover for Joy Division's album *Closer*?**

Robert Longo told me to look at it. I didn't know it was happening at the time. I met
Robert around 1983. He said "What you've been doing for the last five years has been
an influence on me and a lot of my New York contemporaries." Robert told me about
Schnabel's velvet *Closer* painting and said that the music of Joy Division was a major
inspiration. They were interpreting the same themes, as art. I found that all the way
through the 1980s I could predict the phases of New York's art. Neo-Geo was particularly
obvious. I wish I'd had the confidence to go and do it, but I was not brave enough.

Do you view your work as a kind of art?

Yes, it is in certain examples where the innovation was the appropriation. But I'm
happier with the pieces where I created a genuinely new image or a new combination
of things, as in *Power, Corruption & Lies* where I began to mix A and B, instead of just
presenting A or B. Then the whole period around New Order's *Substance* in 1986–87,
because that was when I felt really compelled to produce something new. Reference
and retrievalism were no longer appropriate.

You have to remember there was never a brief, never a problem to solve, and clients
who had no time to make any input and were confident that I would come up with the
input anyway. Given those circumstances, what can you do except your own thing?
And my own thing happens to be a synthesis of what's going on at the time expressed
through the graphic medium. I can't paint it, I can't sculpt it and I have great difficulty
turning it into three dimensions. I'm dependent on the methodology of graphics to
realise my ideas.

So it is a kind of art and that body of work in particular motivated some people to say "Peter, why aren't you making this as art?" And 1988 onwards was a very sobering learning process about what made something art. It may be art, but defining it and ultimately selling it as art is another thing altogether. I spent a couple of years tentatively considering the art market and came to the conclusion that with art, it doesn't really matter what you do. As long as you're prepared to give up your day job to do it, it will be your art. But if you only do it at the weekends, it's a hobby.

So one of the things I've been doing over the last few months is reassessing who I am in the scheme of things, and I've tried not to burden myself with the demands of a studio or staff or company or business. And some interesting questions have occurred to me: the outside world may see a distinction between being an artist and being an art director, but do I see a distinction? Why do you have to do it the way it's always been done? Do you have to fit into a known category? If I made art I would use the same media that I always use.

What are the sources of your recent designs, based on photo library shots, for the New Order singles and the album *Republic*?

Immediately prior to this had been the longest period I had ever spent in Los Angeles – six weeks doing the identity for Channel 1. In 1992, the idea was circulating that perhaps the mass media had become our new avant-garde. American art had run out of energy and the really interesting new European art, which was going to come out of London, had yet to impact. For twelve months there was this curious fascination with Hollywood. And I was thrilled to be there soaking up the influences, but there was nowhere much for them to go because I was at Pentagram, with few outlets for freeform activity.

Then I found myself with a New Order campaign. It was a commercial album and I knew that visual "entertainment" would be a requirement. I showed the group perhaps 200 visual references – things cut from magazines, bits of type, photographs, written pieces, cartoons, digital things, anything that said "1992/1993". One particularly LA category I called "PCH" – "Pacific Coast Hi-way". Just one image from "PCH" was all that they could agree on, out of 200 possibilities. The only context in which I could imagine using the image was in juxtaposition with others, as in [Dan Friedman's] *Artificial Nature*, creating some kind of narrative.

For the first time I had a tape of the tracks, so over Christmas I drove to a beach, listening to one track a day. I played word association – feelings, moods, anything – and wrote them down. The result was a list of almost 100 topics which were despatched to the photo libraries. Every day was like Christmas! I'd go into Pentagram and there would be this stack of images to look at. Out of every 50 pictures there would be one or two. I wanted cowboys and along came these guys. I wanted burning buildings and I got this one. We had no idea at this point how they would go together, but what was evolving in my mind was a post-LA experience: television culture, mass-media overload, the irony and wild juxtapositions of channel-surfing, where you flip from CNN to MTV to the Shopping Channel to something really quite horrific on the news. Brett [Wickens] scanned a few into Photoshop to try out the "blend" function and suddenly a narrative had entered our project. It's LA, it's a riot, it's Nero fiddling while Rome burns, and the juxtaposition of two images – fire and water – becomes the Los Angeles experience.

What was the American response to this work? One American admirer of your early covers I spoke to didn't like them at all.

They are more likely to get it in the art world than they are in the design world, where they are still nostalgically in love with design. This is a post-design era. It's deliberately embracing the photo library and it's going against all those precious things that were canonised in the 1980s and are now exhausted. This is like plastic clothing. It's a sort of coming to terms with the trashy realities of our time and saying, OK, there is an aesthetic here, let's work with it. Let's stop pretending that our world is antique papers and woodblock type. The real world is a Whoopi Goldberg movie. So what can we find there to talk about and work with?

Are you still as enthusiastic about the Hollywoodisation of the information business as you seemed to be a while back?

I'm not so enthusiastic about Hollywood from an image point of view. *Republic* was styled in a way that was both a parody and also a tribute to that look. I've worked through that and I think some more interesting threads have emerged from popular culture since the early 1990s.

My professional theory was that as communication design becomes increasingly screen-based, Hollywood – where there is a deep pool of talent in filming, lighting, editing, mixing, casting and so on – would become involved in multimedia production. In practice, nothing has changed to alter that theory, except that multimedia is in a much longer development stage and implementation cycle than anybody was facing up to. Everyone was excited about it and wanted to believe that multimedia and interactive television would be the normal course of events within 18 months. If it had happened that quickly you probably would have found more communications design going on in LA as a response. But because it is taking so much longer it's probably fair to say that other places, which have the same kind of talents but perhaps not the same depth, will become equally competitive.

So where do you see yourself fitting in?

I really don't know. To be horribly honest, as a graphic designer the one period of my life when everything felt right and fell into place was from 1978 to perhaps 1986, the period during which I was doing record covers and happy to be doing record covers. I had the benefit of being considered successful at it and I had some recognition. But in 1986 I was 31 and that is a fairly critical age. The time had come to go somewhere else.

There is no shortage of things for me to do with my life, but what should you be doing to be happy? In order to answer that I think you have to find out who you are. Over the last ten years there has been a lot of asking myself, "What is it that I do?"

Eye, no. 17 vol. 5, 1995*

Come on Pilgrim. Album cover
for the Pixies. Designer:
Vaughan Oliver. Photographer:
Simon Larbalestier. 4AD,
Great Britain, 1987

SURREALIST OF THE SUBURBS
VAUGHAN OLIVER

Inaugurating new French galleries is getting to be a habit with Vaughan Oliver. Last year, the Espace Graslin announced its arrival in Nantes with a Brody-at-the-V&A-sized retrospective of Oliver's graphics of the 1980s. This month, an expanded version of the same exhibition opens in Paris, in the recently completed Oscar Tusquets pavilion at the Parc de la Villette.

If Nantes is anything to go by, not everyone will be pleased. *Liberation*'s critic demanded to know what a public gallery was doing mounting a show of commercial record covers and music posters as though they were some kind of art. Even Oliver's French admirers were confused. If these cover photographs were taken by someone else, then why was he getting the credit? To anyone outside the design business – and Oliver enthusiasts, by and large, are rock fans – the role of the art director is hard to fathom.

Not that "art director" comes anywhere near to summarising what it is that Oliver actually does. At different times, he is also designer, typographer and image-maker, equally at home with the process camera and the digital paintbox. Oliver himself is ambivalent about terminology. "I would hate to be described at a dinner party, or on a passport, as a graphic designer," he says, though most of the discussion about his work to date has, in fact, been framed in these terms. Yet, while he can't have minded when *Art Line* compared him (favourably) with John Heartfield and Max Ernst, Oliver does not regard himself as an artist either.

It's this descriptive uncertainty that makes Oliver's work so interesting. It confronts us with a form of cultural activity for which we have no entirely satisfactory label. The work has a consistency and a coherence that has as much to do with Oliver as with his clients, the bands. The designs are aesthetically compelling – a lot more compelling than much of what passes for gallery art. They are motivated by strong personal concerns, even obsessions. They demonstrate the development of themes over time. And, as the exhibition proves, they retain their meaning as images in the absence of the products they package.

Clearly, the old culture barriers are coming down. Artists know it, the audience knows it, and postmodernist TV producers have come to depend on it. But nobody seems quite sure where, for the purposes of description, to locate the new barriers, or whether we really need them at all. The critics, set in the aspic of the arts pages, continue to write as though culture can easily be divided into neat little containers that don't even touch at the edges, while work such as Oliver's slips away through the gaps.

In some ways, Oliver has not helped his own cause. Although his name has been belatedly tacked on to the end of the Brody–Garrett–Saville triumvirate, he has received nothing like as much attention. For the best part of a decade he has worked for a single company, 4AD, record label of the Cocteau Twins, This Mortal Coil, the Pixies and Ultra Vivid Scene. In the early 1980s, Oliver and his then partner, photographer Nigel Grierson, opted for enigmatic anonymity by signing their designs "23 Envelope". It worked too well. By the time Oliver's close-cropped head emerged into the limelight, the triumvirate were post-punk legends with their best album covers some way behind them. It was 1987 before a design magazine got round to profiling him.

Oliver, now 33, claims not to regret this. "I've always believed that early popularity would have only put extra pressure on me and led to my adopting formulas for the work. Anonymity allowed me to develop personally."

While his famous contemporaries designed for a wide range of clients, Oliver concentrated on 4AD – with occasional excursions for Virgin, Picador books, Ron Arad and fashion designer John Galliano. Not since Reid Miles and Blue Note in the 1960s had there been a working relationship between an in-house designer and an independent record company quite as sustained, intense and productive as this. It limited Oliver's audience to fans of the music, but it maximised his awareness of their interests and tastes.

The owner and founder of 4AD, Ivo Watts-Russell, allowed Oliver to do much as he liked. An obsession with the music had brought them together and enlightened independence remains the governing ethic. Watts-Russell sometimes complained about the size of his print bills, but the importance of quality was never in doubt. From the outset, cover boards were heavier than standard, fifth colours and metallic inks almost routine. 4AD reinforced its identity with postcard and poster sets, lyric booklets and calendars. The limited edition *Lonely is an Eyesore* compilation, released in 1987, came in a box made of American beech, containing record, cassette, CD, a video by Grierson, and two prints. It looks like a reliquary designed by Donald Judd.

If projects like this have an air of designer hubris, then a meeting with Oliver obliges you to rethink. Britain's most lavishly packaged record label is located in a residential street in Wandsworth, south London, and Oliver, despite his big frame, shaven head and collection of photographs by Joel-Peter Witken, master of the perverse, is equally self-effacing. "People are surprised how unassuming I am," concedes the soft-spoken Geordie. 4AD bands have always been free to choose other designers and many have done so. Couldn't Watts-Russell simply tell them who they were going to work with? "He could do that, but he still holds to the independent idea that the band must be happy with their sleeves. I'm working with people who also have huge personal obsessions. It's not as easy a job as it seems." You can see what he means. One of Oliver's more bizarre exploits, for the cover of *Pod* by the Breeders, involved dressing up in a belt of skinned eels and a loin cloth, then dancing like a dervish for the camera.

Asked to explain his intentions, Oliver observes, reasonably enough, that he could hardly ask anyone else to do it. He leaves the larger question – why do it in the first place? – unanswered. Oliver never probes or intellectualises his work; he isn't at all comfortable talking about it. In his exhibition catalogue, he quotes Robert Doisneau's dictum "to suggest is to create ... to describe is to destroy" and – lest this disclaimer should sound too formulated and humourless – he punctures it with Tommy Cooper's "glass, bottle ... bottle, glass". A natural and guiltless surrealist, Oliver cheerfully submits to the direction of his unconscious. The frisson he wants an image to generate sounds a lot like André Breton's idea of convulsive beauty. The methods he uses – chance, word association, serendipity – are textbook procedures of Surrealism. His favourite symbols (hair, teeth, knives, eels) would give a psychoanalyst a field day.

It's no surprise then to find that Oliver's grasp of art history is intuitive rather than analytical, and that design history barely figures. As a graphic design student, Oliver neglected typography, concentrating on illustration. "It was only when I came to design whisky labels at Michael Peters that I realised how many typefaces you could put together and what that could feel like." At 4AD, Oliver began to blend typefaces with untutored freedom. He piled up capitals and italics, serif and sanserif, brush scripts and box rules into panels of type as haunting and melancholy as an East European shop front, one of his admitted inspirations. Bold, condensed letterforms became a virtual trademark.

There was too much emotion here for the work to be dismissed as postmodern or pastiche, though it was certainly a highly specialised taste. The cover designs from 1983 to 1986 were a kind of late-flowering romanticism, as peculiarly English and ethereal as the music of the Cocteau Twins, whose records they often adorned. The frisson came from the tension between the photographic image (during this period by Grierson) and the placement of the type. The art was in the assembly: neither photograph nor

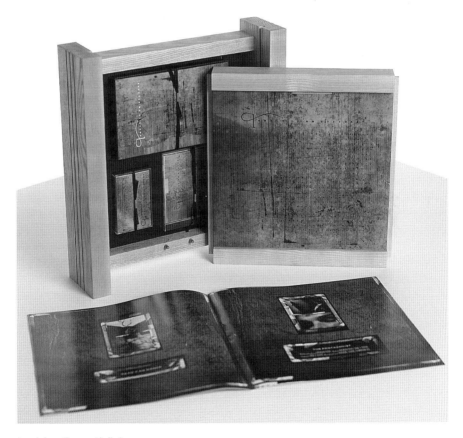

Lonely is an Eyesore. Limited
edition (100) boxed set,
containing compilation album,
CD, cassette and video.
Designer: Vaughan Oliver.
4AD, Great Britain, 1987

type on their own would be enough.

Since the dissolution of 23 Envelope in 1988 and Oliver's re-emergence under the name v23, with assistant Christopher Bigg, his art has broadened and changed. The concepts are more elaborate, the typographic detailing of individual projects less intensive. "I get fulfilment now from the year's work and seeing the development," he says. Oliver's covers for the American band the Pixies, working with photographer Simon Larbalestier, pursue a darkly surreal and freakish iconography of stuffed monkeys, screaming babies and hairy-backed men, though the vision is beginning to brighten. The Ultra Vivid Scene series, on the other hand, provides Oliver with an opportunity for Paintbox-generated, junk culture automatism. "*Joy 1967–1990*, with the tyre that could be a crown of thorns, the hand, the drill and the madonna – that happened in the space of a day."

As his better-known contemporaries bail out of pop culture, Oliver, too, must be wondering "what next?" Brody, these days, does little in this area; Garrett is making painful public statements about entering the "real world"; and Saville has renounced sleeves as a task for the under-30s. Oliver acknowledges ruefully that his principal canvas is about to disappear with the vinyl it clad. "But that doesn't frighten me." And when it happens? More TV work, perhaps – he did the graphics for the last series of the rock show *Snub*; book covers; a personal print-making project.

In the meantime, Oliver's work for 4AD goes from strength to strength. Graphic design or graphic art? Someone should bring this remarkable exhibition to Britain soon.

Blueprint, June 1991*

TYPE AS ENTERTAINMENT
WHY NOT ASSOCIATES

In less than five years as a formal partnership, Why Not Associates have come to occupy a pivotal position on the experimental wing of British graphic design. They are leading figures among a handful of London-based companies increasingly perceived on the larger international stage to represent a new wave of energy and invention in British typography and graphics. While the most obvious point of comparison, 8vo, produce a progressively more mutated version of Swiss Style, which stands out in the British context but offers fewer surprises to Europe and the US, Why Not's inspirations are more firmly rooted in local traditions and culture.

The question Why Not's three partners – Andy Altmann, David Ellis and Howard Greenhalgh – are most often asked is how they get away with it. Altmann and Ellis, the team's graphic designers, routinely pull off visual stunts that more cautious contemporaries assume would send their own clients into shock. Why Not designs are constructed from frantic scribbles, arbitrarily chosen images and weird typographic mechanisms that look like something Jean Tinguely might have dreamed up on a day off from making auto-destructive sculptures. As a result, Why Not have a reputation for craziness and pleasing themselves that is not wholly borne out by more recent projects, or by the statements of the designers themselves. In that sense, their choice of name – a jibe from their student days that doggedly stuck – is already coming back to haunt them. It is undeniably memorable and, as Altmann says, "one of the few graphic design company names that professes an attitude". But it also sounds jokey and glib. "What it really means," says Ellis, "is that you shouldn't have to account for every single little mark you make."

Why Not's willingness to trust their own instincts, and quietly insist that their clients do the same, has distinguished their work from the start. They moved from St Martin's to the Royal College of Art – Ellis in 1984, Altmann in 1985 – because they wanted to test the limits of their craft. "At St Martin's, at that point," remembers Altmann, "the type was the line you put under the idea. A 'joke'. Bob Gill. People were still doing that kind of stuff."

Herbert Spencer's *Pioneers of Modern Typography*, on the other hand, confronted them with an alternative tradition of heroic experiment. From Piet Zwart in *Pioneers* to Gert Dumbar, their new professor at the RCA (whose freewheeling creativity had first impressed them at a lecture at St Martin's) the emphasis lay on the expressive integration of image and type.

By the time they graduated in 1987, Ellis and Altmann had convinced themselves they were unemployable. "We certainly didn't want to work for anybody else," says Ellis, "and I couldn't think of any London studio that would let us do the kind of work we wanted."

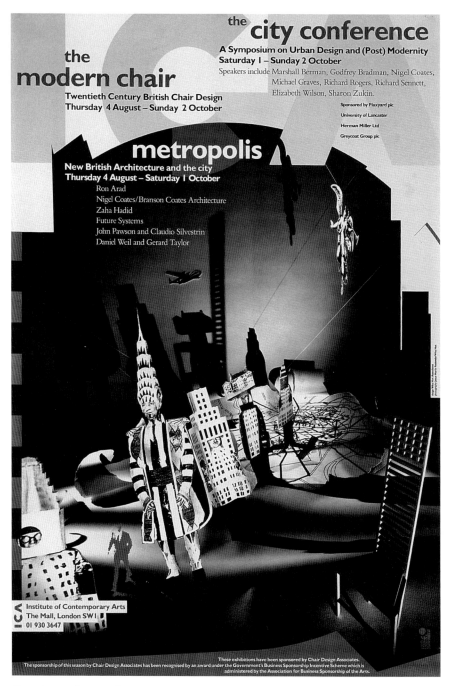

The Modern Chair/Metropolis/
The City Conference.
Exhibition and conference
poster. Designers: Why Not
Associates. Photographers:
Jesus Maria Redondo/Why
Not. Institute of Contemporary
Arts, Great Britain, 1988

Luck intervened when Greenhalgh, a fellow student, came to them with a magazine project for the US cosmetics company Sebastian. Other commissions followed and within six months the decision was taken – "It just sort of happened," says Altmann – to form a partnership. Greenhalgh later set up the film side of the enterprise.

Their clients since then have embraced both commerce (the clothing retailer Next, Smirnoff vodka) and culture (exhibitions on the Situationists at the Pompidou Centre, Paris, and on avant-garde Japanese architecture). Unlike an earlier wave of British designers reacting against the mainstream, Why Not have shunned the potential ghetto of the record sleeve; it is an outlet they hardly need when their existing projects have proven so rich in opportunities for self-expression. They resist the suspicion, though, that this is their primary motivation. "We wanted to produce work that was self-expressive, but also solved the client's problem," says Altmann. "You might as well be a painter if you are not solving the client's problem."

In common with other members of their generation, Altmann and Ellis argue that many of the conventions of conceptual graphics, however successful in the past, are no longer enough. They believe that a visually sophisticated audience needs, and expects, rather more. The painterly quality of Why Not's work is their way of drawing viewers into the message and holding attention: a retinal reward. In the case of the Next mail-order directories, the "message" was more a matter of lyrical image than literal communication. These chaotic covers and volatile divider pages, which appeared to be in the grip of a typographic Big Bang, were their most notorious example to date of what Altmann calls "type as entertainment".

As Why Not develop, the essential Englishness of their design – a quality shared by some of their closest associates – is becoming clearer. As with Phil Baines (their contemporary at the RCA) and Jonathan Barnbrook (who worked with them on a Next directory) there is a love of ornamental complexity that throws out echoes of Gothic architecture, illuminated manuscripts, even the Arts & Crafts tradition. Why Not's two most significant projects to date, both remarkable instances of their assimilation into the professional mainstream, enshrine fundamental polarities of English cultural life – individualistic rebellion and a love of pomp and circumstance – that the social commentator Peter York once summarised as "Punk and Pageantry". In their postage stamps commemorating the 40th anniversary of the Queen's accession, and their identity for the Hull 1992 Festival, their existing graphic repertoire found a perfect, though improbable, match in the deep traditionalism of the subject matter.

Why Not confess to having been "flabbergasted" when they received a call from the Royal Mail asking them go ahead with their invited proposals for five first-class stamps. Yet the overriding impression of regal dignity and human warmth was a keenly judged answer to the brief. The expected Why Not-isms take the form of broken silver borders with steps and curves, and a network of filigree rules that links typographic elements within the stamps and connects them when seen as part of a sheet. These elements combine with heraldic devices carefully muted on the Quantel Paintbox to create a jewellery box-like setting that vividly conveys the Queen's status as national treasure.

With the Hull Festival project, Why Not had another unexpected chance to apply the graphic language they have developed in earlier projects to a more precisely defined set of problems. Their clients were fifteen bluff Yorkshire councillors with a reputation, among local designers, for conservative taste. At the core of the festival's graphic programme, the council hoped to find an identity that the city could use after the festival was over. "The last thing they wanted was a single logo to be slapped on everything," says Ellis. "It needed to be adaptable and malleable."

The starting point for the programme is an "H" (for Hull) with the bar replaced by five arrow-tipped vertical strokes – a stylised portcullis that evokes the city's past and symbolises the council's conception of both city and festival as a "gateway to Europe". These few simple elements provide the graphic vocabulary and typographic framework for the festival's posters, brochures, maps, shopping bags, street signs, invitations and stationery. Even when they are used in their most exploded or dissected forms, it is still easy to recognise the festival's identity, reinforced by the bold use of turquoise, a reference to the verdigris on the copper roofs of the city's buildings. The typography itself, Eric Gill's Perpetua with a smattering of Gill Sans, like the project as a whole, is both traditionally English in mood and austerely modern in its asymmetry.

Why Not won the Hull project, one of the councillors told them, by being the most "down to earth" designers in the way they presented their ideas and work. Here, it seems certain, lies one of the reasons for their commercial survival against the odds. Not only are they blessed with the popular touch, but they genuinely believe it should be possible to have their creative cake and eat well on it, too. Unlike the American deconstructionists, with whom they are sometimes bracketed on stylistic grounds, Why Not adhere to no discernible theoretical programme. Disjointed and strange as their solutions might look to some eyes, Why Not justify their visual strategies (though only up to a point, of course) in the most conventional, and modest, of professional terms.

"I think our work is funny," says Altmann, and perhaps it is, in a Monty Pythonish way. Lurking beneath the surface, and occasionally breaking through in more personal projects, is a taste for daft music hall song lyrics and word-play, and the surreal catch phrases of stand-up comedians like Tommy Cooper, and Morecambe and Wise. From this unlikely stew of schoolboy influences, and their later experiences at college, Why Not have forged a graphic attitude and method that looks utterly contemporary, while retaining its ties with the past.

"Our work is going to date," concedes Altmann. "My god, it's going to date!" "But that's one of the nicest things about graphic design," counters Ellis. "You pick up a piece of 1950s graphics and you marvel at it because it represents a whole other language."

Eye, no. 7 vol. 2, 1993

RULES ARE THERE TO BE BROKEN
CARTLIDGE LEVENE

Cartlidge Levene's collective résumé reads like a roll-call of design groups in the 1980s. Conran, Peters, Leonard, Olins, Lambie-Nairn, Davies, Trickett & Webb ... they have served time in the graphic design studios of some of London's finest, learned their craft, and bade a not particularly fond or regretful farewell. Nobody could ever accuse them of turning their backs on something they never tried.

The company's founders, Ian Cartlidge and Adam Levene, joined forces on the rebound from The Design Solution in 1987. They were convinced they could do better. Two promotional brochures issued in 1989 show that it took them a while to discover how. One was dour, precise, a prayerbook clothed (like the designers) in black; the other was a riot of photographic games and colour in a fun-packed shrinkwrap bag. Their logo symbolised the aesthetic rift in a *Guardian* masthead-style fusion of italic Bembo and sanserif Grot, and the company's projects for Boots, property developer Stanhope and Sutherlands restaurant showed a similar eclecticism.

One year later, Cartlidge Levene had experienced a typographic purge. Their identity had narrowed and hardened. They had found their own voice – though their new logo was a single weight of Helvetica so small on the letterhead it amounted to little more than a whisper. Yet the effect of using a typeface lovingly described by one of them as "void of personality" has undoubtedly been liberating. This was the point at which their studied exercises in typographic cool started to get noticed. Their notorious experimental pieces – the giant conceptual "Christmas card" and the crazily expensive sheets of aluminium stamps for a show at the Design Museum – all date from this time.

"If we were buying a flat I think we would all live in a Japanese concrete bunker," says Simon Browning, who joined in 1989. Cartlidge Levene's most recent recruit, Yumi Matote, comes from Kyoto, and Browning will shortly depart for a six-month sabbatical in Japan. But while the group's tastes, especially in typefaces, are strikingly homogeneous, their method is based on confrontation and a broad mix of skills. Cartlidge and Levene, who run the business, are the main client-handlers and the most cautious in their comments. Browning, the oldest at 33, is by collective agreement the "antagonist" of the team. "He's the guy who at the end of the day slaps on the brakes and says 'this is getting too corporate'," says Sean Perkins, inducted in 1990.

Browning returns the favour by calling Perkins (Dumbar-trained, ex-RCA) a "fanatic" in matters of type. "I know I piss everybody off because of my attitude," concedes Perkins, "sticking my head over people's shoulders and pointing out things I don't like." In fact, it is a process of self-criticism in which all five designers take part. No one's boards are sacred. Layouts are reworked and refined long after client approval, until the printer finally takes them away.

The method might be abrasive, but the printed and varnished results are as smooth as a glacier. Cartlidge Levene's designs are formally lovely and icily exact. The underlying grids are made manifest (deconstructed, to use the jargon) in the rules and boxes used to define zones of activity and to demarcate the page. The rules act as wires and braces holding their elaborate constructions in a state of dynamic tension. All of the elements – text, photographs, display type, page numbers – are slotted into the compositional scheme with the precision of mechanical parts.

The risk, of course, is that such icy perfection will daunt, if not wholly deter, the reader – and in the latest edition of *Issue*, the Design Museum's magazine, one might argue that it does. Pull-quotes, a standard magazine device for attracting attention to the text, are set in a tiny point size rendered even more unreadable by being printed in a delicate shade of grey; columns of Helvetica are turned on their side to form a jagged fringe across the top of the page. In each case, the text is treated as a unit in a composition, rather than writing that demands to be read.

"We try very hard to design interesting spreads and there is perhaps inevitably a conflict between that and accessibility to the reader," admits Cartlidge. "You can't avoid it. We don't try to design exercises in illegibility as perhaps some design groups do. But we don't let the pure galleys of type in its basic form detract from the overall interest of the layouts."

This might sound like a diplomatic way of saying "we please ourselves", but Cartlidge Levene do acknowledge the need to ease back and let the information breathe, even in their more experimental projects. Two posters for the printer First Impression caused heated debate. Perkins envisaged an effect as densely layered and encrusted with detail as their earlier poster for *Eye*. "I like to have a lot happening. I can't help it. Every time I look at it I want to see something else – a different configuration, or another level of information." Browning, encouraged by their regular photographer, Richard J. Burbridge – "It hasn't got the rules in again, has it?" – argued for simplicity.

The rules survive, but in a much abbreviated form. They intersect with blocks of text letter-spaced to suggest the crude typography of an engineering manual and Burbridge's photographs of iron filings magnetised into arbitrary shapes. The ostensible purpose is to describe and demonstrate the capabilities of the printer, but the images, further abstracted by the use of colour, have a peculiarity, an air of self-contained enigma, that breaks the boundaries of graphic design and propels them uncertainly towards the autonomous language and territory of art. What the clumsy typography and blue boxes most recall, in fact, are the posters of American conceptual artist Lawrence Weiner – a suspicion confirmed by the two Weiner catalogues, one with marked pages, on their shelves. The same iconography of rules, boxes and diagonal bars features in a recent letterhead for the designers Johnson Naylor and in a self-promotional advert showing the tops of their heads.

By any standards – elevated or trivial – this is highly personal work. It seems to promise an ingenious rationale, but Cartlidge Levene skirt the central issue. They make no particular claims for the artistic content of their output, though it is clearly an issue they have pondered. Browning, the guiding vision and colour-sense behind the First Impression posters, goes so far as to say that an artist's approach never transfers wholesale into graphics: "It just doesn't live there." Well obviously not without a degree of translation. Cartlidge, Perkins and Levene are concerned to establish the responsibility of the "thought processes" behind their much more sober work for organisations like

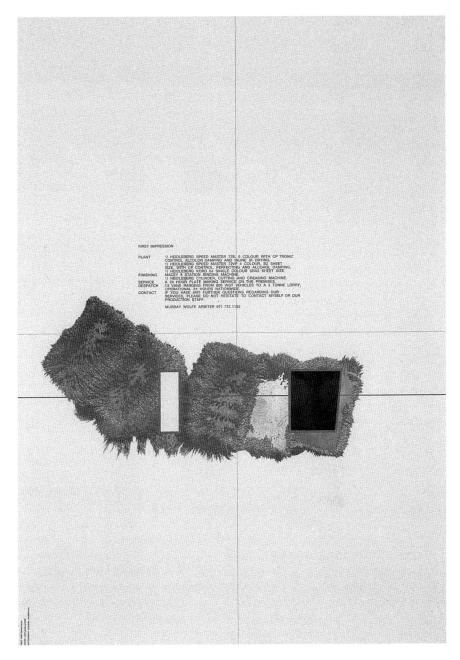

Promotional poster. Designer:
Simon Browning, Cartlidge
Levene. Photographer:
Richard J. Burbridge. First
Impression Printers, Great
Britain, 1991

the security company ADT, or the property developer London & Edinburgh Trust.

"I think the two sides of our business are equally important," says Levene. "If this [he indicates the posters] tips the balance we would never get another corporate client again. We mustn't be seen just to be producing designs like that because it isn't a true reflection of the way we work."

But the tensions in the group between commerce and art are apparent enough. They have felt the pain of the recession as sharply as anyone else. Should a studio that prides itself on the sophistication of its ideas, that slams the "crass blatancy" of the old guard, and fears, in Browning's words, that it is becoming "The Partners of 1993", compromise for the sake of essential revenue? The answer is an agonised "yes". "There is a tendency during a recession to be not quite as brave as you ought to be," concedes Cartlidge. "We've been guilty of designing completely over people's heads and losing jobs we wanted to do," says Perkins, "and we've lost them to appalling design groups who've done appalling jobs. Then at other times we've known that the client would kick us out, and we've gone down a bit, and that's really upset you." This last remark is to Browning.

"The point is, you should never design down," counters Browning. "That's what saddens me the most." Recession is the time to take risks, he argues. On the other hand, he prefers to have as little contact with clients as possible, daring to say what many designers secretly believe, but few will admit: "My overriding desire is to satisfy myself before the client. The client is going to take all your satisfaction and filch it away."

Cartlidge tries some hasty damage limitation. "To balance that argument – and it's a very valid point – I think the best work often comes from designers who are selfish and design for themselves almost without considering the client. But the fact is, we don't just do that, though that might be the basis for starting something. I believe the client gets the best out of you when you design something you are incredibly proud of and excited by." Which is essentially the same argument, rephrased in client-friendly terms. The years in the mainstream have not been in vain.

Blueprint, May 1992

INFORMATION SCULPTURE
TOMATO

So far 1994 has been Tomato's year. Need a talking head for the BBC Design Awards? Call Tomato. A design team with a difference for the lifestyle pages of *Arena*? Think red. In the nightclubs an album by two of the team is a dancefloor hit. On the college lecture circuit their gospel of self-expression has bemused tutors accusing them of irresponsibility. The students love it. Colleagues are taking notice. On the afternoon set for our first interview, Peter Saville, ex-Pentagram, ex-Frankfurt Balkind, drops by their Soho offices to check them out. From Saville himself to Why Not Associates, the cult names of British design in the 1990s are by and large the cult names of the 1980s. Tomato, whatever else they might have achieved, are the first home team of the new decade to equal this impact.

In many ways they are natural successors to Britain's earlier wave of graphic pioneers. But Tomato go a crucial step further. There has always been an uneasy match between what the more corporate-minded experimentalists say they are doing in their work and what they actually do. The rhetoric they use to explain their intentions when pressed is no different in essence from the rhetoric employed by the more traditional competitors they affect to despise. They claim to offer their clients "solutions" specially tailored, just as the textbook says, to fit the "problem" at hand. Self-expression, they will argue, in the face of all evidence to the contrary, is always subordinated to the client's communication needs.

Tomato abandon any such pretence. "You can't 'solve' a problem," says Simon Taylor. "You can only respond to it for that moment in time . . . When we are doing what we do best it's not about doing it for the client, it's not about business, it's about making the images." They draw no functional distinction between commercial work and their ambitious extracurricular projects. They are all part of the same continuing process and this process – a word they use constantly – is the key. "They are not by-products," says Graham Wood of his explorations in typo-video. "They are the main thing."

This openness about their real motivation is invigorating. Many will reject Tomato's approach, but at least it can be seen for what it is. If the much-needed debate in British graphic design has yet to take place it is partly because the new guard still claims to be performing substantially the same service as the old guard. So the discussion becomes bogged down, simplistically, in a dispute over matters of taste: do you like your graphics garnished with "ideas" or "style"? Tomato's challenge is much more fundamental than this. Rejecting conventional categories as limiting, they roundly dismiss the very idea of professional graphic design. "What does 'graphics' mean?" asks John Warwicker, professing to be none the wiser after fourteen years in the business. "I have no idea."

Faces of Funk. Blueprint/
dyeline promotional images
for a Japanese nightclub.
Designers: Dirk van Dooren
and Simon Taylor, Tomato.
Strive, Great Britain, 1994

Tomato emerged three years ago from the collapse of Warwicker's previous venture, Vivid I.D., the print wing of pop promo-maker Luc Roeg's production company. Collectively dedicated to the idea of creative cross-pollination, its eight members are linked by friendship, shared office space and the loosest of financial arrangements. Four – Warwicker, Wood, Taylor and illustrator Dirk van Dooren – have a background in graphics. Karl Hyde and Richard Smith are two-thirds of the techno band Underworld and there is a film-maker now based in New Zealand. Everyone stresses the lack of hierarchy in the group, but Warwicker, the oldest designer at 38, is clearly a pivotal figure. "He taught me a hell of a lot," says Taylor, and Wood, who met Warwicker as a student and then went to work at Vivid, agrees.

For Warwicker more than any of the others, Tomato provided a chance to take stock and start again. After studying graphics in the mid-1970s, he spent two years at Birmingham Polytechnic researching electronic interactive media. The technology was in its infancy and he concentrated on the philosophical and linguistic dimensions of the changes to come. In the early 1980s, as a member of the CBS-signed rock group Freur with Hyde and Smith, he operated computers and video on stage. His early conviction as a student that "there are no borders – the definitions are ridiculous" has become Tomato's operating principle.

In the 1980s, before Vivid, he put in stints as creative director of design studio da Gama and at A&M Records, where he was art director and head of video. He learned a great deal, but it was hard to produce truly personal work for stars like Janet Jackson or Chris de Burgh, whose music he did not even like. "Those years were not wasted," he says now, "but misplaced maybe." After Tomato started, it took another two years of tough collective criticism and "cleansing the system" before he was happy with his new portfolio.

"We are all on a journey," says Warwicker. "All your work is just experience. What you are drawing is maps of your experience and Tomato is the place where we go to compare experiences through these maps. We often take our reference points from areas outside the medium we are using – to enrich it. We bring a map from one territory and overlay it with another to see what happens."

Typography is treated filmically; video is reconceived, in accordance with film-maker Andrei Tarkovsky's dictum, as a kind of sculpture in time. Hyde, a former environmental artist, reworks graphic notations from Warwicker, who edits and rewrites words generated by Hyde that will be used in songs for a CD or in a book that may combine with the mutating graphics to become the shooting script for a collectively made film. The common platform that makes these interactions so fluid is the Macintosh. It is rare for a piece of work with only one author to emerge from the flux of the studio.

Language is another shared preoccupation. "The reason I like type is because I read," says Wood. "I like paintings with words in. I like films with words in. I like title sequences." His MA thesis, completed in 1992, is less a conventional dissertation than a piece of compressed and elliptical creative writing. Hanging on the studio wall is a quotation used in the thesis taken from *The Enigma of Kaspar Hauser*, Werner Herzog's film about the acquisition of language and the making of personal identity. Kaspar sows his name with cress seeds. Somebody comes into the garden and steps on them. He plans to sow his name again.

Next to it is another typographically treated extract from the thesis that begins with the first line of Wittgenstein's *Tractatus Logico-Philosophicus*: "The world is all that is the case." Wittgenstein, it emerges, is the patron saint of the team; three out of four of them mention his name. "The last thing he wrote, two days before he died, was 'outside I can hear the rain on the window'," says Wood. "And that's what it's about: it's about life. For me, the last line of the *Tractatus*, 'Whereof one cannot speak, thereof one must be silent' is just about the most beautiful thing I have ever read."

Conversations with members of Tomato have a way of circling inevitably back to this point. What is this intensely personal work about? On the face of it the answer is always vague. It is about "experience". It is about "life". It is about the "process" of doing it and this process, says Wood, "is as much about breathing and heartbeat as about the things that you do". We may not be able to enter or understand or say anything useful about Wittgenstein's silence ("the mystical", as he termed it) but we can make work about the fact that it is there.

"We're sculpting information," says Warwicker, "and the process goes through various media and you cut that media at a certain point and that becomes your piece of work." Taylor likens the process to a road movie: "It doesn't matter where you came from or where you end up. Anything can happen en route and it's not restricted by its beginning or its end. In design terms I like the same approach."

Tomato's work is not so much about ideas, though it is richly informed by them, as about emotion and expression, an attempt to snatch and log the fleeting multiple details and momentary atmospheric sensations of daily experience. In literature this tradition has stretched from Joyce and Woolf's stream of consciousness to the transcribed-as-they-came-to-me typewriter confessions of Kerouac and the Beats. Tomato's exaltation of the moment leads to imagery whose natural state seems to be one of digital transition – next time you see it it might look entirely different – or that is "finished", in the sense that no more work will be done on it, without being definitively resolved or complete.

Nowhere is this essential instability clearer than in a 200-page book made by Warwicker and Hyde evoking a "typographic journey" through New York. Titled *mmm... skyscraper i love you*, it emerged from their collaboration on the sleeve of Underworld's first album *dubnobasswithmyheadman*. While there is no single Tomato "style", the sleeve's graphics ("Art by Tomato") come closest to encapsulating the dominant mood of their printed work. The spirit of New York Abstract Expressionist Franz Kline – "a vast influence on our typography" according to Warwicker – animates the huge hovering blocks and impacted shards of typographic matter. Kline too rendered the city as a brutal rhapsody in black and white.

In the book, assembled from their joint output, the sense of typographic collapse and renewal takes on greater complexity. "When you walk along the street you are assailed by noises, textures, smells," explains Warwicker. "The atmosphere and emotion of walking through the city forms the content and description." Randomly spliced together by Hyde, *skyscraper*'s pages are a subjective documentary seen one moment in overpowering close-up, then in long shot so that only mass and outline remain. Hyde and Warwicker's texts, bizarre and disjointed urban narratives based on conversations Hyde overhears in the street, move in and out of frame. In Tomato's imaginary paper Manhattan, as in Archigram's instant cities of the 1960s, the parts can be removed, replaced and recombined. The printed book represents just one possible version of events.

The next step, using the book as screenplay, is to make *skyscraper* into an hour-long film for television. They are talking to potential backers. "We're going to New York with a blank canvas in all the different media," says Warwicker. What do they want it to communicate? "That's for the viewer to decide." Again the final outcome seems less important than the process itself – and here, perhaps, they may run into the limits of their improvisational method. Holding a channel-zapping audience's attention for 60 minutes is an altogether tougher challenge than "jamming" for your own pleasure and "sending secret codes to each other" – as Warwicker puts it – with the Macintosh.

Like much recent graphic design, Tomato's work seems to aspire to the condition of film – or if not film exactly, then some still more plastic and permeable synthesis of media. Warwicker cut his teeth directing promos for rock stars at A&M Records. Taylor and Van Dooren also have projects on the showreel. It is Wood, though, who has emerged in the last year as arguably the most original and Zeitgeist-attuned typographer working for British advertising, with commercials for the *Guardian*, Nike and MTV and a string of other moving-image projects. For six months he was in-house typographer at London agency Leagas Delaney, before coming to the conclusion it was not for him. "I don't know what my opinion is of advertising *per se*," he says. "But I've come to understand it over the last year and sympathise with it in a way."

The long hours Wood puts in at The Mill, one of Europe's best-equipped and most expensive TV and video facilities houses, qualify him for free studio time. "You've got to put manure on a rose to make it grow," he says bluntly. In other words, the advertising pays for the art. The roses in this case are two experimental videos which exploit the same reverse-order, print-to-video production techniques and low-res textures as his commercials. Wood generates ordinary flat black and white artwork with the Macintosh, then cuts it together with live-action footage, treats, blurs and roughens it up. Soundtrack and image clatter along in sync. "I always had problems with pop videos because I thought, why aren't people cutting to the rhythm? It's so obvious it's almost stupid, otherwise what's the point of making a piece of film to the music? Most of the things I do are the wrong way of doing it, or the most obvious way that everyone seems to have forgotten about."

What Wood has created is a kind of ambient typography comparable to the ambient music and ambient video of artist-musicians such as Brian Eno, David Sylvian and David Cunningham. The earliest experiments in ambience in the 1970s were characterised by their deliberate, calming slowness. They gave a reduced quantity of musical or visual information relative to their length. You could dip in and out while doing other things because you would miss nothing crucial. The point was the way they coloured the atmosphere.

In its most stroboscopic form ambient typography insists on your attention, speeds you up rather than slows you down, prefers ultra-compression to the theoretically endless continuum postulated by Eno – this is advertising, after all – and bombards you with more typographic information per screen-second than you can possibly absorb. But in one crucial sense the effect is the same. The meaning lies as much in the atmosphere generated by the flashing wordshapes as in their particular linguistic content, as much in the pattern as in the solitary particle.

There is no reason, though, why ambient typography has to be so fast. In Wood's video for the Underworld dancetrack "Cowgirl" there is less information and a higher degree of repetition, with the words on screen sometimes supplementing or contradicting what is said. A metallic voice sings "everything, everything, everything . . ." Wood expands it with Wittgenstein's "The world is all that is the case." The voice sings "I'm invisible". Wood amends it to "indivisible" – as good a description as any of his own method. Cutting words and phrases to the beat and echoing, or not quite echoing, the verbal with the visual turns screen typography into a medium of almost physical sensation. The effect is compelling. In a more recent video for Estonian composer Arvo Pärt's inherently ambient "Festina Lente" ("make haste slowly"), for strings and harp, Wood achieves something even closer to the original slowed-time conception of ambient video. Brief poetic phrases written by Wood himself emerge in a leisurely cycle from the tinted mist of the abstract background.

Is Tomato's work art, graphic design, or some new as yet improperly understood communication hybrid – "information sculpture" to use Warwicker's term – somewhere in between? Tomato recognise the existence of the categories, but they waste no time wondering where they fit. "To categorise something is to put it in a box," says Wood, "to build barriers, walls. Process is about evolution and development. Categories and process are anathema to each other."

Tomato would be much less significant if they were alone. Among British designers working in this area they stand out for being unusually clear about their aims. But their attempt to inject personal art into commerce is part of a wider Euro-American tendency which, though bitterly resented in some quarters, is transforming our conception of graphics.

If potential clients feel Tomato's aims are compatible with their communication needs they can buy into the process, but the team will not suppress, distort, disguise or otherwise change its approach to fit the brief. To date they have worked for advertising, publishing and the music business, electronics giant Philips (a 350-page multimedia strategy report), the BBC (an identity for the corporation's entry into the Internet is in progress), a Japanese footwear retailer and architect Richard Rogers. As for solving their clients' problems, here is that rare phenomenon: a successful, sought-after design team that makes no claim to have solved any problems at all.

Eye, no. 13 vol. 4, 1994

DESIGN IS A VIRUS
JONATHAN BARNBROOK

Any designer who took as much time to complete a product brochure as Jonathan Barnbrook has spent designing his own typefoundry catalogue would have filed for bankruptcy by now. With an obsessive commitment that makes "loving care" seem like a wild understatement, the British designer has been crafting his sixteen intricate pages, building them up layer by layer, stripping them back and refining them for the last three years. Now, finally, the catalogue is printed and Barnbrook's nine idiosyncratic, commentary-laden Virus Foundry typefaces are officially for sale.

Whatever the speed of its production, Barnbrook's design work has a spectacular fluency on the page or screen. It develops the post-Brody assumption that design can be a personal "language", though it is closer in form and spirit to recent American experimentation than it is to the muted typography and "street style" of so much British graphic design. Barnbrook has a reputation for sharp thinking, but he isn't a master of the soundbite and his choice of words to explain himself doesn't always match the eloquence of his design. At his studio, in London's Soho, he holds court to a never-ending stream of student admirers and he is a frequent speaker at design events, yet it is obvious, despite all his experience, that our interview is an effort. At moments of conversational stress his voice drops so low that the tape recorder barely registers it. He covers his eyes with his hand as if to block out distractions to the framing of his thoughts.

Beneath the hesitant exterior is a designer of sinew driven by a sense of personal purpose that few of his London contemporaries can match. Even by the accelerated standards of 1980s design stardom, Barnbrook's ascension was rapid. Within two or three months of his graduation in July 1990, his Royal College of Art student projects were being fêted by an excitable profile in a British trade monthly and a four-page, self-designed layout in one of Tokyo's trendiest visual arts magazines.

Barnbrook, now 30, kept his head and has gone on to carve out a high-profile position in Europe and the Far East. There have been innovative book designs, a notorious typeface for *Emigre* – Manson – which drew comment in *Time*, and a string of television commercials, sometimes as director, for Nike, Mazda, Guinness, Bank of America and fashion designer Nina Ricci. Recently, he collaborated with Damien Hirst, the British artist who pickled a twelve-foot tiger shark in a tank full of formaldehyde, on the monumentally ambitious monograph *I want to spend the rest of my life everywhere, with everyone, one to one, always, forever, now*. Personal projects, such as the Virus Foundry, are fitted in as often as a demanding schedule allows.

"Design, for me, is a cathartic exercise," says Barnbrook. "When I've expressed a point of view about society, then I'm released from it. I've never seen the point of just doing work. I try to see the work in its broader social context, but I do it for myself as well. I want to get intellectual satisfaction out of it, but I also want it to function. I'm very different from the Tomato idea that you buy into their process."

In early projects, his compulsion to question the sophisticated assumptions of his own design practice revealed itself in a cynical interior commentary perversely at odds with his lush visual frameworks. "It's a funny old world/you can say that again/said the actress to the bishop," reads a Royal College of Art poster in which he explores the compositional possibilities of his typeface Bastard, now released by the Virus Foundry. And a similiar conceptual tension, a contradictory gap between aesthetic form and linguistic content, can be found in the aggressive but humorous nomenclature of his black-letter family: Spindly Bastard, Fat Bastard, and Even Fatter Bastard.

Barnbrook hopes that when we look at his designs we will be made aware of paradoxes, contradictions and "the stupid dichotomies we're faced with". His recurrent targets include consumerism, multinational corporations, production for profit rather than need, and the western alliance's war machine. If the seductive forms of Barnbrook's typographic weaponry are a far cry from the crude visual languages of protest and agitprop, and seem at times to undermine the sincerity of his often quite basic political messages, that uncertainty is precisely their point. Real weapons, after all, carry an even more disturbing charge of ambivalence. For Barnbrook, the coexistence of beauty and ugliness is a perpetually absorbing theme.

The Virus Foundry catalogue is the most complete summation to date of his acerbic worldview. Here is Nixon, "the typeface to tell lies in", Prozac to "simplify meaning with" and Drone "for text without content". An opening statement establishes the terrain of Barnbrook's concerns, but declines to offer a clearly drawn map: ". . . Virus is right-wing paranoia. Virus is a social stigma. Virus is not responsible for its own actions. Virus is the language you use to speak to others. Virus is in league with the CIA. Virus is the end of the millennium. Virus is a small being which downs a huge organism or organisation . . ."

Apocalypso, the collection's spikiest piece of satire, is a font of 75 pictograms and 55 crosses "to be used in the event of the apocalypse". Barnbrook nukes the glib conventions of corporate communication with symbols announcing "Arms for sale", "Genuine Messiah", "I'm with this hostage" and "Your son was killed by friendly fire. Thanks." The pre-millennial anxieties that haunt a culture learning to live with media overload, terrorist outrage, gun-crazy militias, rampant fundamentalism and looming ecological disaster are compressed into a semiotic system for private desktop manipulation and T-shirt display (special licences available from the designer on request). In the age of 24-hour news, mega design consultancies and globe-spanning PR, Apocalypso dares to suggest that even our worst nightmares could be "repositioned" as desirable brands.

Barnbrook first met Damien Hirst when he supplied the type for a never-shown commercial directed by the artist for Tony Kaye & Partners. He was the natural choice of both artist and publisher to design Hirst's first monograph. The project was expected to take them three months; in the end this overwhelming, large-format, 300-page shark of a production, equipped with pull-tabs and pop-ups, took much longer to complete and publication was delayed for a year.

The individual visions of artist and designer proved to be highly compatible. Works like *Mother and Child Divided*, a cow and her calf sawn in half and suspended in tanks of

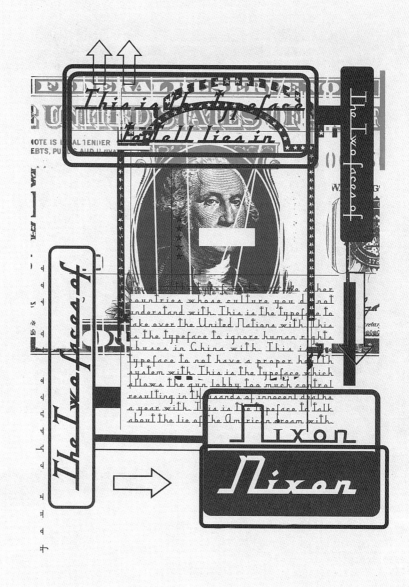

Welcome to the Cult of Virus.
Catalogue page showing
the typeface Nixon. Designer:
Jonathan Barnbrook.
The Virus Foundry, Great
Britain, 1997

formaldehyde, have made Hirst internationally notorious beyond the world of art. Almost everything he creates – installations in which flies hatch, live, procreate and die; cabinets full of surgical instruments and pharmaceutical supplies; exquisite butterfly paintings – reveals an unflinching awareness of the physical body's frailty and the closeness of death. "There's only ever been one idea in art," Hirst says bluntly. "What the hell are we doing here, and what's it all about?" Barnbrook's intense fascination with beauty and ugliness is echoed by the artist's statements in the book: "Butterflies are beautiful, but it's a shame that they have the disgusting hairy bodies in the middle . . . Butterflies still look beautiful even when dead."

I want to spend the rest of my life . . . busts the stuffy art monograph mould in ways that seem certain to irritate as many people as they excite. "It's trying to address a lot of things that have happened in graphic design that haven't affected art books," says Barnbrook. "With most art books, you get large pictures on white pages and a piece of academic text which, unless you are writing a thesis, most people don't bother to read. We were trying to make an art book entertaining and a bit more populist." Hirst takes up the theme. "The book to me is like a night in watching TV and channel-surfing. All this stuff exists at the same time. It works like that rather than having a beginning and an end."

The book's governing conceit, though it's not programmatically applied, is the medical textbook. The dust jacket, instead of playing safe by showing the artist or his work, is a montage of hospital scenes, while the letters that make up the title are treated as elements in the periodic table. The leatherette binding is a parody of a reference work on *Biochemicals, Organic Compounds for Research and Diagnostic Regents*. Photographs chosen to augment the clinical mood are spliced into the flow of projects: an ambulance interior, a surgical close-up, an old person walking with a Zimmer frame, painfully objective images of suicide by throat-cutting and shotgun. "Death is an unacceptable idea," advises Hirst in one of the many quotations. "So the only way to deal with it is to be detached or amused." Later in the book, a section devoted to his pharmaceutical works lays them out on gridded paper like specimens prepared for analysis.

The antiseptic tone finds reinforcement in Barnbrook's unexpectedly low-key, sanserif typography. "Damien did quiet me down on the quotation pages," he says. "There was a lot more Gothic type in it originally, but then I realised it wasn't quite right. The main typeface is Din, but it's still my work because what I do is a process of collage. The sanserifs are referencing something else. It's not actual modernism, it's in quotation marks. Modernism is this hostile, sterile environment that you go into when you are in hospital."

Barnbrook confesses to "moments of difficulty" with the anything but punctual artist, but rates Hirst one of the most open-minded of collaborators. Hirst is equally enthusiastic about a creative partnership that eventually saw the pair spending two weeks together in Hong Kong, checking the book on press. "He isn't precious about his ideas," says Hirst, "which is great. He'll say to me, 'What are you trying to achieve with this? What kind of feeling do you want?' We'll have a lot of silly ideas, a lot of good ideas, but it's definitely a collaboration. A lot of the things I didn't agree with and still don't agree with, but I left them in because he convinced me."

For Barnbrook, the book is one of the projects that most pleases him, but it is also a reminder of a concern that nags at many a designer in his position. "It made me not want to be a graphic designer again," he reveals, "which is the idea I keep going back to all the time and never quite manage to achieve." Barnbrook speaks admiringly of Hirst's freedom as an artist to "instigate" projects, but these projects are central to his work and livelihood and there is a gallery support system to ensure they happen. Barnbrook's Virus project, by contrast, has allowed him to do what he wants, without constraint, but it had to be accommodated on the side, and it is supported by compromises – as he himself admits – that sit rather uneasily with his socio-political views. "My primary motivation for doing advertising is money," he says, "and nothing else. Sometimes I wish I were able not to do it, but it is very difficult to survive without it."

Designers, says Barnbrook, should stop seeing themselves as second-class citizens. Graphic design has a visual sophistication, an understanding of how to use media to communicate and a closeness to society's concerns that makes plenty of contemporary art look flat-footed and dull. "I think art should take on a lot of what graphic design has come up with over the last few years," he says, "rather than designers always looking to art. I don't think it's acceptable for graphic designers to copy artists. They should value what they do themselves."

Let's put it to the test, then, with an artist who has found his way deeper into the design process than most. Does Damien Hirst think graphic design can be art? "Yes," he says at once, "it's a language. As an artist, I'd love to design a typeface. Does that mean a typeface can be art? Yeah. When you start a typeface you set up rules for yourself and it's obvious to anyone looking at it whether you've succeeded or failed. And if you succeed, then I'd say you are an artist . . . if you succeed in a big way." But observe that final pause and additional note of qualification. It is going to take quite a typeface to compete in the public imagination with a bisected heifer or a twelve-foot shark.

I.D., May 1997*

4. IMAGE-MAKERS

OPEN TO INTERPRETATION

In Christopher Frayling's book celebrating 150 years of art and design at the Royal College of Art, the illustration department barely gets a mention. When at last it does, just a few pages from the end, it is little more than a brief roll-call of the names and achievements of some of the department's more famous students. Considering the impact that illustrators from the RCA have had on the look of British graphics in the last ten years, this is a surprisingly casual dismissal. An extensive exhibition at the college of printed work plus selected originals provides a much-needed opportunity for the department to set the public record straight.

The treatment of illustration in the RCA's official catalogue of its own achievements is particularly odd, since in many ways the department is the very model of the college's changing brief under its present rector, Jocelyn Stevens. The number of students who have passed through the department since it was founded in 1963 may be small, not much more than 250 (a rate of ten or so a year), but the vast majority – to make a properly Thatcherite assessment of return on investment – have found work in the profession for which they were trained. The same could hardly be said of the ceramicists or the textile and product designers, let alone the painters and sculptors.

It could be that the short shrift given to the illustrators in the RCA book merely reflects the stigma of "commercial art" that has always attached in some degree to illustration. Even now, it's not unusual to hear a representational artist of Edward Burra's stature dismissed as an "illustrator" by snobbish students of fine art. Illustration, Francis Bacon has repeatedly insisted, is what he strives to avoid. And this lingering stigma of shallowness and commercial impurity is compounded by imprecision as to what "illustration" is, since there are as many different types of material to illustrate – books, magazines, brochures, advertising, packaging, reportage, film and video animation, technical literature and natural history – as there are types of illustration. One reason that illustration lacks status in the eyes of the fine art community is that it is viewed as subordinate to the texts it serves, standing in a similar relation to art as film scores stand in relation to music.

Of course, most illustration is secondary in this way; it would be misguided, given a crunchy bar label or a magazine wine page illustration, to argue otherwise. As Dan Fern, head of illustration at the RCA and organiser of the exhibition, points out, there is an enormous difference in "the scale of intention" between an illustrator's typical commission and an artist's highly personal concerns. What such a formulation leaves out, though, is the illustration that challenges the limitations of the craft and through the intensity of its vision becomes as interesting as, or more interesting than, the purpose that inspired it. Editorial projects inevitably provide the arena in which such work is most likely to occur.

By the start of the 1970s, RCA illustrators were reacting against the day-glo psychedelia and airbrush fantasies of the *Yellow Submarine* period with a darker, more disquieting vision. For inspiration, they looked outside the home-spun world of illustration to Dada, Surrealism, Constructivism, Flemish art and the Renaissance. Stewart Mackinnon, a brilliant draughtsman, produced drawings for underground *Oz* and mainstream *Nova* that looked as if they had been conceived in loathing and inscribed with acid. Terry Dowling, now head of graphics at Newcastle Polytechnic, combined quirky, almost autistic drawings with proto-punk, taped-down collages – devices so widely plundered in the 1980s that Dowling has rarely received the credit he deserves. Less easy to assimilate was the art of Sue Coe, whose stern political convictions issued forth in savage expressionist paintings.

The influence of these pioneers was most keenly felt in the mid-1970s, when a second, loose-knit group of students began to challenge conventional assumptions about the role of illustration. Robert Mason, Ian Pollock, Robert Ellis, Russell Mills and Anne Howeson, among others, responded to the dislocated sounds of punk rock and the bleakness of the recessionary 1970s with work that was by turns personal and obsessive, socially aware and political. Because the work so accurately caught the mood of the times, it found sympathetic outlets, as the 1970s drew to a close, in the pages of *Radio Times, The Listener, New Scientist* and, most improbable of all, in *Esquire*, where expat British art editors Robert Priest and Derek Ungless had recently arrived.

What gave this work its energy and conviction was its origin in the private investigations of the illustrators. The worn-out distinction between commissioned and personal work was being overturned. It was possible, these illustrators suggested, to move from one area to the other, just as "fine artists", crossing over from the other side, had always done. Russell Mills's series of mixed-media "interpretations" of the songs of Brian Eno, eventually published in 1986 as *More Dark Than Shark*, was the most complex and intensive demonstration of these possibilities, the book *How to Commit Suicide in South Africa* by Sue Coe the most committed, but work by Ian Pollock (on drunks) and Robert Mason and Anne Howeson (on prostitution) also showed a high level of ambition. The tendency reached a high point of cohesion – and self-consciousness – with the 1981 "Radical Illustrators" issue of the Association of Illustrators' house journal.

To make their case, it was probably necessary for the radical illustrators to overstate it, and these days the temperature of illustration at the RCA is much cooler. "What the radical group did was to break open a whole new series of possibilities, which other people can follow or not as they choose," says Fern. Naturally, there had always been dissenters, such as Glynn Boyd Harte and Lawrence Mynott, who regarded the attempt to broaden illustration's programme as insufferably pretentious. Mainly, though, radical illustration was killed by kindness, at least as a banner to rally under. In the 1980s, RCA illustrators have absorbed the stylistic innovations of the earlier wave and regurgitated them without the politics or conviction that gave them their meaning.

It's no surprise, then, that the general standard of editorial illustration in magazines has declined, though this has run in parallel, it must be said, with a decline in opportunity. *The Listener*'s switch, under new editor Alan Coren, to largely photographic covers is symptomatic. During his time at *The Face*, Neville Brody, himself an illustrator of considerable ability, avoided commissioning illustration, saying that he preferred to operate within the more certain constraints of photography. Other magazine art directors have continued to use illustration, but find themselves disappointed by the lack of "journalistic" bite on offer, and by the inability of illustrators to formulate strong visual ideas, as opposed to painting pretty pictures. Roland Schenk, group art director at Haymarket, recently looked through the portfolios of an entire class of RCA illustrators. There was no one, he says, whom he wanted to commission – a worrying sign, even allowing for the vagaries of an art director's personal taste.

New sources of magazine work have arisen in the 1980s, most notably at *Elle* and *Business*, but here a glossy, decorative style, rather than a questioning, journalistic one, predominates. It signals the most remarkable development of all, the wholesale taking up of illustrators by the design groups, and subsequently by the advertising agencies, a process accelerated by the commercially astute portfolio peddling practised by the new breed of illustrators' agents. Some excellent work has certainly resulted from this tendency – think of Pentagram's IRM computer journal for Ericsson, virtually a handbook of 1980s illustrator talent, with work by Bush Hollyhead, George Hardie, Huntley and Muir, Robin Harris, Ralph Steadman, Russell Mills and Dan Fern (not all RCA), or of The Partners' brochures for Hewlett Packard – but far too often the use of illustration on endless bank hand-outs and building society brochures hardens into empty decorative formula.

What British graphics perennially lacks, in marked contrast to the better Dutch and Swiss examples, or some of the work coming out of Cranbrook and California, or the great days of the 1920s and the 1930s almost anywhere, is a sense that typography and image should be inseparable elements, fused dynamically together, of the same graphic conception. Or, indeed, that typography, treated in the manner of a Wolfgang Weingart, or his hard-line English protégés 8vo, might be illustration enough. So often in Britain, it's a crudely assembled case, as Fern points out, of "typography to show the cool, rational approach and illustration as a bit of a rough". In other words, you could remove the pictures and put something equally beguiling and vacuous next to the exquisitely balanced typography and it wouldn't make the slightest difference to the composition of the image or to the meaning of the design.

Perhaps what British graphics needs now is fewer illustrators and more image-makers with an ability to reconcile imagery and type in properly integrated designs. The problem, as Fern himself concedes, is that few illustrators know anything about typographic design (just as few designers are able to produce imagery of their own). "Typography on BA courses is taught as a cold, hard, clean discipline," says Fern, "and that is anathema to the way a lot of illustrators work. They get put off early."

Fern, whose first degree was in graphic design, is a notable exception. A trademark of his collages is the wit with which he incorporates letterforms as an illustrative element, harking back to the punk period's rediscovery of Dadaist typography. Andrzej Klimowski, who teaches at the RCA, is another illustrator whose power comes from his graphic sensibility and training, though typically, since he returned to Britain from Poland, he has hardly ever been given the opportunity to use his typographic skill. Another all too rare example is Russell Mills, whose frustration with the way designers treated his images – a common complaint among illustrators – led him to try, wherever possible, to control his own typography.

Recognising these problems, Fern's department will introduce, from next term, a typography course geared to meet the needs of its illustration students. Beyond that, he would like to see a return to simplicity and clarity, and verges on departmental heresy by citing Bob Gill's 1960s dictum that good graphic design is something you can describe over the phone. At the very least, the self-expressive tendency of the artist needs to be modified by the analytical tools of the designer. "It's comparatively easy to do a picture with a hundred different elements," insists Fern, "and very difficult to do one with two or three."

But his concern is understandable. Every era has its stylistic tics, and in the lesser hands of imitators, the highly textured abstract treatments developed for particular uses by Russell Mills and Vaughan Oliver are fast becoming a cliché, a kind of voodoo graphics applied willy-nilly, whether appropriate or not.

Fern squares up to the task ahead. "We need to stand back and rethink illustration," he says robustly. "I'll want to cast a hard and critical eye over the work to see if it's progressing." The exhibition should provide a fine opportunity to plot the way forward.

Blueprint, October 1988

COMPLETE CONTROL
RUSSELL MILLS

Outside the pages of the professional creative magazines, which tend to be undemanding and celebratory, the work of British illustrators has received little critical attention. There is a general acknowledgement of their impact, a broad consensus among insiders as to which artists are carrying out the most interesting work, but little discussion of the nature and potential of the medium. In Britain, exhibitions of illustrators' work, even those at national galleries, are ignored by the art critics. Despite the ubiquity and commercial importance of their work, British illustrators enjoy very little power. Responsible almost by definition for just one stage in the design process, the making of the actual image, they remain subordinate to the art directors who commission them.

The work of the British artist Russell Mills is interesting precisely because of the way it challenges these practices and assumptions. Seeing the visual arts as a continuum, Mills refuses to acknowlege any distinction between painting, sculpture and illustration. He blames the lack of interdisciplinary studies for the way that different media have become compartmentalised. Drawn towards the editorial uses of illustration rather than more constrained commercial applications, Mills rejects the idea that the role of the medium is simply to function as passive decoration. The best illustration, he argues, is an act of interpretation, an opening up or extension of its subject, with results as complex and as unexpected as the subject itself. Mills brings the same intense commitment to his commissioned projects that he brings to his personal work. One nourishes the other and in his one-man shows the two are exhibited side by side. If anything, there are times when his determination to create an artwork that can stand in its own right, independent of the context for which it is commissioned, leads to imagery that is overdetailed for its purpose. Many illustrators, lacking typographic training, shy away from involvement in the broader considerations of design. Mills has made it his business to learn about typography and, increasingly, has argued for and achieved control of the way in which his images are assembled and used. He doesn't have an agent, he doesn't make portfolio visits, he doesn't submit roughs for approval, and if he is asked to repeat himself, he turns the job down. Until he moved to the Lake District in 1992, art directors who wanted to look at his work were encouraged to visit his south London studio. Mills believes that collaborations are more likely to flourish where art directors have a first-hand understanding of his methods.

Although he is by no means the only British illustrator to adopt such an assertive, uncompromising stance, Mills is virtually alone among those who seek recognition as fine artists in his refusal to distinguish between private and commissioned work. Mills doesn't see himself as an illustrator at all, but rather as an artist who happens, as artists always have done, to work to commission. The American artist Marshall Arisman, with whom he has much in common, has said, "I see illustration simply as another outlet for the work I do. I think the publishing industry is using me, and I am using the publishing industry. It seems a fair exchange most of the time." Mills would undoubtedly second that.

Many of Mills's attitudes were shaped during his time at the Royal College of Art, where he studied for a Masters degree in illustration from 1974 to 1977. He had been attracted to the course by the work of an earlier wave of RCA illustrators – Sue Coe, Terry Dowling, Stewart Mackinnon and the Brothers Quay – which he had seen in the underground press and other magazines. Menacing, aggressive and strange, their art was a reaction against the kid's book colouring, toytown Surrealism and airbrush overkill of so much 1960s illustration. Equally inspirational were the thinking of Marcel Duchamp and the collages of Max Ernst and Kurt Schwitters, and their influence – Duchamp's desire "to put painting once again at the service of the mind", Ernst's Victorian juxtapositions and Schwitters's torn-edge, garbage-can aesthetic – pervades his student work. Mills's early collages had a dislocated, obsessional quality perfectly in sync with the punk energies of mid-1970s London, but it was not until his final year at the RCA that he developed an approach and an iconography entirely his own.

Mills was a fan of the music of former Roxy Music synthesist Brian Eno, and for his final year project he decided to illustrate a number of Eno's quirky, surrealist songs. Later, following discussions with Eno, he continued the series, producing by 1979 interpretations for all 38 of Eno's songs (they were eventually published in 1986 as the book *More Dark Than Shark*). Mills took the lyrics not as a programme to be followed to the letter, but as clues or pointers for researches of his own. Composed using a range of non-musicianly methods (verbal instructions, directed chance, random collaborations), the songs provided an opportunity to experiment with a vast range of found, non-art materials – sewing needles, artificial eyes, computer punch cards and shattered windscreen fragments among them. "Why not use broken glass rather than trying to draw shards of broken glass?" Mills explained later. Chance factors, too, were allowed to play their part in the development of the imagery, much as Eno would accept happy accidents in the recording studio, and images were layered and then stripped back in the same way that sounds are assembled on multi-track tape. Representational fragments combined with more abstract, grid-like or "musical" passages to create a fractured, non-naturalistic pictorial space. Some of the interpretations, like the disturbing "Baby's on fire", follow Eno's text more closely than others, but even here Mills turns "Baby" into an adult and supplies imagery not present in the lyrics – a thermometer and a measuring scale – to bring out the documentary quality of the song.

During this period and into the early 1980s, Mills produced many illustrations in a similar style for British magazines such as *Radio Times*, *New Society* and *New Scientist*. With the arrival of British art editors Robert Priest and Derek Ungless, *Esquire*, too, proved to be an unexpected haven for Mills and other ex-RCA radicals. He quickly realised, however, that he was being pigeonholed by art directors for his enigmatic, science fiction imagery. Tiring of his earlier, more figurative work, but reluctant to change his approach so completely that it would alienate potential employers, he began to incorporate a higher degree of abstraction in his images. In typical transitional works such as the *New Scientist* "evolution" cover of 1983, with its meticulously hand-painted

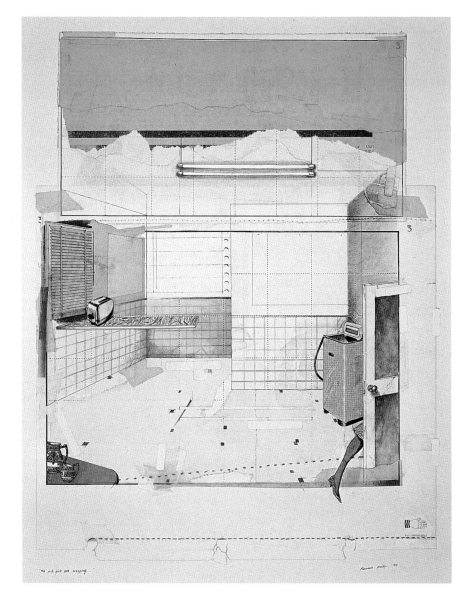

Cindy Tells Me ... the rich girls are weeping. Mixed media interpretation of a song by Brian Eno. Artist: Russell Mills. Great Britain, 1977

lizards, foreground elements are played off against thickly textured backgrounds.

New Scientist continued, under the inspired art editorship of Chris Jones, to be an outlet for his work. In the main, though, Mills has preferred to concentrate on posters and covers for books and records, with occasional excursions into corporate work, since they provide more opportunities to experiment. A series of five covers commissioned by Gary Day-Ellison for Pan Book's literary Picador imprint in 1982–83 gave him an opportunity to explore another personal obsession: the work of Samuel Beckett. Mills's bare-bones designs in collaboration with Day-Ellison place stark, simple, graphic elements – painted images, some pebbles and a slate, a clump of masonry nails – against pure white backgrounds and freely placed, black type. A 1984 cover for *The Pearl*, an album by Brian Eno and Harold Budd, was approached in the same oblique manner, though, in this case, with sensual rather than cerebral results. Experimenting with washes of watercolour on a Japanese rag paper, Mills discovered on lifting the paper that it had left a patterned residue on his Formica work surface. Repeated applications of the same technique, combined with some poppy seeds to simulate gravel, produced an aquatic, river-bed effect.

In cases like these the "artwork" is fragile to say the least and it has become Mills's habit to present art directors with five- by four-inch colour transparencies to work from. This allows him the additional freedom of being able to make adjustments to the artwork at the photography stage and to control the precise way in which his three-dimensional surfaces are lit. The most striking example of this process to date is the series of covers for books by the British novelist Ian McEwan which Mills produced for Picador in 1985. Given a week and a half to complete the assignment, Mills elected to make a single painting, four foot square, which he divided into five distinct zones, one for each cover. His choice of imagery, based on a close reading of the texts, was an attempt to evoke a range of moods without resorting to figuration or narrative. (In two cases, the composite approach was also a way of resolving the perennial problem of how to suggest the multiple narratives of a short story collection in a single cover image.) On a bed of cement and plaster treated with acrylic paint and pearlised nail varnish, Mills arranged fishing flies, a chain, fragments of broken glass, several star fish, and a razor blade. Many of these elements only found their final position in the image under the lights in photographer David Buckland's studio.

The finished covers crop tightly into Mills's imagery, giving them a cohesion that the complete painting, titled *Fringe of Memory Tinged*, might be said to lack. The continuity of the images, the sense, even if you don't know as much, that they are fragments of a larger, more complex picture helps to suggest the continuity of the author's own worldview from book to book. Delicate typographic variations by Vaughan Oliver, so recessive that they take on the quality of pictorial elements, also play an important part. It is no surprise then, given their originality, that the covers have been widely admired by the graphic design community and continue to bring Mills commissions; or that the more conventional forces of publishing have found them difficult to accommodate. Picador's sales force was never convinced that the typography had sufficient impact in the bookshops, and the audacious vertical-reading titles of three of the covers won little favour. The treatment of Mills's last McEwan cover, for *The Child in Time* (1988), was thus an almost inevitable step backwards, with Picador taking control of the typography. The type might be more immediately noticeable on the book shelves, but it is much less sympathetic to the mood of the imagery and, for that matter, to the tone of the novel itself.

Implicit in all of Mills's activities is a challenge to the idea that an "illustrator", or any kind of artist, is good for only one thing. He sees no reason, for instance, why a visual artist should not also design stage sets and points to historical precedents from Picasso to Hockney in support. By and large he has encountered professional resistance ("stage designers design stage sets") but persistence has paid off in a few cases. Without exception, though, these opportunities have come about through his contacts in the music world, which continues to be a primary source of inspiration to him. Indeed, the more overtly "musical" aspects of his work – the explorations of notation and abstraction, his often-stated longing for music's emotional force – can be explained by the fact that he is, in a sense, a frustrated musician. "I know that if I wasn't doing this, if I wasn't making statements in vision, then I would be involved in music more than I am," he has said.

In 1980, Mills designed a stage set for the experimental rock musicians Graham Lewis and Bruce Gilbert of Wire, which was constructed during a London performance by the Japanese artist Shinro Ohtake, while Mills himself played synthesizer. Other collaborations followed, including *MU:ZE:UM/Traces*, an audio-visual installation at the Museum of Modern Art, Oxford, in 1982–83. In 1986, Mills (with David Buckland) constructed a gigantic backdrop for *The Run to Earth*, a dance piece by the British choreographer Siobhan Davies of the London Contemporary Dance Theatre. As the dance unfolded to the rumbling, ambient music of Brian Eno's *On Land*, a vast painted tarpaulin, suggestive of rock faces and caverns, descended with glacial slowness to the stage. Designs for a second Davies production, *Wyoming*, followed in 1989. Mills's other stage projects, for the "Opal Evening" concerts mounted by Eno's management company, and for David Sylvian's "In Praise of Shamans" world tour in 1988, have consisted of elaborate "light sculptures", in which controlled lighting or slide material is projected onto elements hanging above the stage in a 1980s update of the 1960s lightshow.

In both of these cases, the stage designs form part of a wider programme of design activity undertaken on behalf of the musicians. David Sylvian first approached Mills in 1984 because he admired the cover of *The Pearl* and wanted something comparably atmospheric for *Exorcising Ghosts*, a retrospective compilation of songs by his group, Japan. A second collaboration followed in 1986 with a gatefold sleeve for Sylvian's double-album, *Gone to Earth*. Once again Mills was responsible not only for painting the main cover image, but for all typography and subsidiary design elements: the inner sleeve, labels, and adaptations for cassette and compact disc. Subsequently, for the "Shamans" tour, Mills and his regular design partner, Dave Coppenhall, undertook all merchandising design, including a tour booklet of considerable sophistication (ornate typography, images on trace overlays, spot varnishing). Mills has achieved a similar degree of involvement in the design process in his long-standing relationship with Brian Eno, producing a stream of posters and covers for artists represented by Eno's management company, Opal, and since 1988, for Eno's Land record label.

As Mills's understanding of reprographic processes grows, an increasing number of these images exist only as flat artwork with specifications to the colour house, or as photographic elements marked up for scanning. He continues, however, to produce painterly objects conceived for the gallery wall as much as for reproduction. A 1988 cover for the album *Between Tides* by Roger Eno provides a particularly compelling example of Mills's ability to make the two sides of his work correspond. (Significantly, he went on to use the painting on a poster advertising a London exhibition of largely personal work.) In the publication *Opal Information*, Mills supplies a detailed explanation of the approach that underpins the picture and his work in general:

"I am not an 'abstractionist' in the recognised sense, in that I've never felt mentally or physically comfortable or honest in applying paint, texture, etc. with total abandon (the visual equivalent of 'free'/improvised music and 'squeaky gate'/avant-garde music). Although chance is an important procedural tool, a trigger, it is always employed in tandem with reason, whether conscious or intuitive. Rigour and discernment governs the use of chance thereby leading me to work in a reductive rather than an additive way; as with fashion (and all the arts) I don't believe in redundancy of materials. I always use colour for associative or perceptual reasons, never arbitrarily, and the same is true of the integration of objects and of compositional decisions . . ."

According to Mills, the front and back cover images stem from a preoccupation, shared by Roger Eno at the time of recording, with Europe's historical transition from the Dark to the Middle Ages and from ignorance to enlightenment. The cover combines references to alchemy (the use of gold leaf and lead) with Christian allusion (the cross-shaped composition) and other elements are also accounted for by Mills in precise historio-symbolic terms. The trail of aniline dyes and the root dusted with black sand represent the coming of gunpowder and mankind's increasing command of nature; a book cover fragment suggests Gutenberg and the dissemination of printed knowledge; clock parts embody the acceptance of Arab mathematics and the growing sophistication of science; and the red thread cross which binds this cluster of objects together stands for religion's dominion. Of course, little if any of this will be obvious to the casual record store browser and much of it is likely to remain permanently opaque. But that in no way lessens the mysterious intensity, the sought after "strength of presence", with which he has endowed the painting. It is better therefore to think of Mills's symbolism

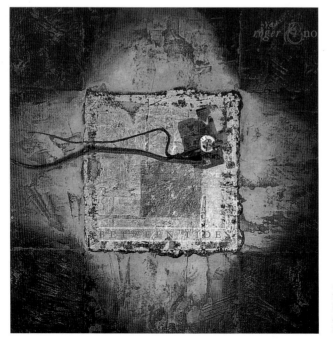

Between Tides. Album cover for Roger Eno. Artist: Russell Mills. Designers: Russell Mills and Dave Coppenhall. Land Records, Great Britain, 1988

not so much as a hidden programme in need of literal interpretation as a set of strategies which he uses to generate and order the image. Literal interpretation would in any case be contrary to the spirit of his aims.

Dense, allusive works like these place Mills in the vanguard of British and world illustration, but the position is not without its difficulties. Mills's quest for ever greater freedom has led him to pick assignments where the brief is as open as possible. But in moving away from magazine work he has largely abandoned a medium for which his early mordant style was particularly well suited. (His withdrawal has coincided, too, with a general slide, in Britain, back into less demanding forms of editorial illustration. In contrast, Americans of similar temperament, such as Brad Holland and Marshall Arisman, continue to produce their most challenging illustration as visual journalists.) On the other hand, in Britain at least, opportunities to illustrate book and record covers are increasing all the time with a correspondingly fast turnover of styles. In the last couple of years, Mills's innovations have been seized on and diluted by a wave of imitators. The price he has paid for being a cult figure in the art colleges is to see his style reduced to dozens of interchangeable images in which a few collage elements are scattered on murky backgrounds. Meanwhile, illustration as a specialism is no nearer achieving conceptual, aesthetic or critical parity with fine art, obliging one to conclude that Mills, himself an exceptional talent, is placing self-expressive demands on an applied medium which it simply is not equipped to satisfy most of the time. The example of an earlier innovator, the American Robert Weaver, certainly points up the contradictions inherent in his position. Still producing remarkable personal work in his 60s but receiving few commissions, Weaver seemed unfairly stranded between the worlds of fine art and illustration.

Given the specialised nature of art and design today, desirable or not, the courses open to Mills do not, after all, seem especially compatible. He could disengage himself from the applied arts in a bid to win acceptance as a fine artist (and the gesture would need to be decisive) but this might well require a fundamental reorientation of his art to be successful; and there is always a risk that work which looks stunning in its applied uses might seem less vital in the pages of *Artforum* in the context of current debates. Alternatively, Mills could continue as he is, gradually consolidating his control of the design and image-making process. This, too, has its limitations: access to corporate projects, for example, comes to him at present mainly through the agency of design consultancies. The chances of their surrendering the right to art direct are slim. It might be, of course, that Mills's work will continue to thrive in such collaborative ventures. The drift of his career, though, has been towards autonomy, achievable or not.

Mills's interpretive talents suggest that it is the second course that is most likely to continue to produce challenging results. The great strength of his art is that it does not simply reflect on, or temporarily colonise, the processes of communication from a detached fine art perspective, for a knowing audience of media theorists (like, say, the work of Jenny Holzer and Barbara Kruger). Rather, it is the process of communication: part of ordinary people's lives; subject to commercial pressures and responsive to market needs, though never determined by them; pushing always at the boundaries of the possible; and carried out with the highest degree of intelligence and artistic integrity.

1989

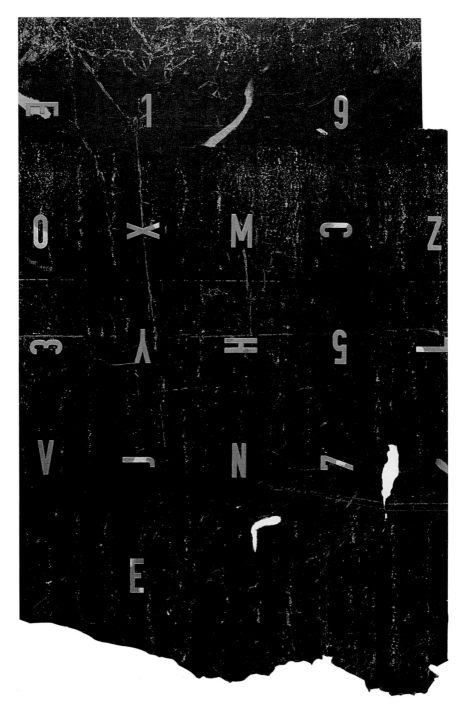

Type Construction. Collage on
tarred paper. Artist: Dan Fern.
Great Britain, 1984-85

AT THE IMAGE'S EDGE
DAN FERN

For better or worse, the split between typography and image-making is one of the most striking characteristics of British graphic design. The orderly separation of elements apparent in so many designs is a reflection of the way that the disciplines themselves are taught. Designers and illustrators might be compelled to collaborate by their shared commitment to the medium of print, but their art school training does little to foster mutual sympathy or understanding. It contrives, if anything, to keep them apart. Designers learn to solve problems, to be rational and logical, to subordinate self-expression to the demands of the brief. Illustrators, on the other hand, are encouraged to look inside themselves for the answers, to develop a highly personal style, to become artists. Neither can exist without the other, but the illustrator suffers the greater loss. Without a grounding in typography, or a proper understanding of the design process, the illustrator will always play second fiddle to the art director. The average art director, meanwhile, knows very little of art. So long as the illustration fills the prescribed space on the page to decorative effect the job has been done.

What sets Dan Fern apart from most other British illustrators and gives his work its particular interest is that he has been through a training that encompasses both disciplines. Fern studied graphic design before moving on to study illustration. "My aim since then has been to try to find a fusion of typography and graphics with image-making, which would not only be satisfying to my individual needs as an artist, but which would enable me to work across a wide spectrum of commercial outlets," he has said. To a considerable extent he has succeeded. Fern is Professor of Illustration at the Royal College of Art; he works as a commercial illustrator, creating posters, stamps, magazine covers, record sleeves, corporate identities and packaging, as well as teaching the subject; he produces personal non-commissioned pieces for exhibition; yet his illustration reveals a tutored grasp of design principles and issues. If Fern has a recurring subject as an artist it is the language of graphics itself. Printed letterforms, numbers, symbols, diagrams and grids are the raw material of his collages, and collage, his preferred medium, allows him to combine papers of different weights, colours, textures, age and provenance in endless permutations. At the end of the 1980s, a vogue for collage swept through British design, much of it poorly considered, but Fern's work remained distinctive for the purity, simplicity and discipline of its graphic forms. The process of picture-making, for Fern, is a process of elimination rather than accretion, a stripping away of superfluous material until only the essential remains. Although figurative elements are sometimes imposed on him by clients, they are a distraction from the formal issues he prefers to explore. Fern's personal pieces are noticeably more sensual and abstract, allowing the structural tensions within the images, the sense of order, disruption, resolution and harmony, to be perceived more clearly.

In childhood, Fern believes, lies the source of adult originality. In his own case there is a remarkable continuity between boyhood interests and his later art. Fern is a tireless collector of the tin toys and colouring books he loved as a child. He enjoyed making model aeroplanes and remembers admiring the graphics of a Messerschmidt 109; echoes of the plane's markings and camouflage survive in Fern's graphic collisions of number and shape. The pages of a stamp album he laid out as a seven-year-old show the same concern for meticulous arrangement now seen in his collages. Fern was fascinated by the regularity of the album's grid and the combination of imagery, type and numbers on the stamps themselves. Today the plan chests of his north London studio overflow with stamps from Turkey, Afghanistan and India, as well as more complex examples of postal history from around the world: envelopes covered by franking marks, stamps and seals to form accidental designs of great subtlety; ancient letters written in flowing scripts on paper as brittle as dried-out leaves, or etched by corrosive inks into a fragile tracery of apertures. The habits of the stamp collector live on in the Chinese notebooks lined for calligraphy practice in which Fern mounts examples of the printed ephemera that fascinate him – tickets, matchbox graphics and luggage labels. Other drawers in his studio contain wood type, prize tickets from nineteenth-century agricultural shows, children's alphabet books, letters from a Czechoslovakian stationer (a form of primitive Letraset), "Kan-U-Go" game cards, "Econasign" stencils, post-war ration books, ink rubbings of Chinese tombstones, and fragments of Islamic papyrus. Fern is constantly adding to his collection, selecting each item with inordinate care, and he spends much time sifting meditatively through his plan chests, inspired as much by the grain and texture of the pieces in his hands as by their delicacy or beauty. Some of this material, particularly the letterforms, finds its way into his collages. Much of it exerts a subtler influence. Marks made on envelopes by official hands, edges eaten away by the passage of time, the criss-cross of handwriting glimpsed through paper, or the accidental overlap of two items in a pile, can suggest unfamiliar approaches to composition and colour. In much the same spirit, Fern leaves cardboard frames in the drawers where he keeps his work to isolate by chance details that might prove to be stronger than the whole.

From an early age Fern expected to go to art school. His father, a Labour councillor from a large mining family, made detailed drawings of buildings and landscapes using a mapping pen, and the family would spend evenings in the days before television making pictures at the table. As a teenager, living in Gainsborough, Lincolnshire during the late 1950s, Fern travelled to nearby churches, renovating tombstones and memorials, and he hand-lettered certificates for the local music competition. After grammar school he went to Manchester College of Art in 1964 to take a diploma in graphic design. Fern studied typography and made posters using a combination of collage, printing and figurative drawing in a decorative, surrealistic style typical of the *Yellow Submarine* era. Increasingly, he was drawn to picture-making rather than to graphics. In his degree show in 1967, he showed two illustrated children's books and it was largely on the strength of these that he was given a place on the Royal College of Art postgraduate illustration course run by Brian Robb. The relationship Fern formed with another tutor, Quentin Blake, was to prove particularly significant. "He'd just been brought in and right from the start I hit it off with him – I'd simply never met anyone with his depth of knowledge about illustration, literature, theatre, art history and so on – and the way he talked about making pictures, criticised our work and later on ran the course was the way that I learned to do it".

At the RCA, Fern continued to work on ideas for children's books; one he wrote and illustrated, titled *Wandering Albert Ross*, attracted the interest of a publisher, but Quentin Blake was unenthusiastic, and by the time of his degree show in 1970 Fern knew this was not the direction he wanted to take. The show, which also contained a number of posters, was well received. On the strength of it, Tommy Roberts, founder of Mr Freedom, the King's Road fashion shop, asked Fern to design a number of posters and he also received a poster commission from Shell. In 1970, Fern responded to the invitation of a designer friend, Keith McEwan, and moved with his wife, Kate, to Amsterdam, where he worked in a studio of expatriates. The next three years were a time to experiment and develop professional skills. Fern made an animated film, drew a strip cartoon for a bank and designed magazine advertisements, usually handling the type himself. The Dutch regarded the studio as a bunch of "crazy, over-the-top, freaky Englishmen", but gave them work anyway because their output was fresh and innovative. Fern, meanwhile, was discovering the pioneering designs of Piet Zwart, Hendrik Nicolaas Werkman and the De Stijl typographers, a purist aesthetic that would, in time, combine with his admiration for the Russian Constructivists to have a determining influence on his art. When he returned to London in 1973, Fern put together a portfolio of work that reflected his new preoccupations. Pentagram partner David Hillman, then art director of *Nova* magazine, gave him work, as did Clive Crook at the *Sunday Times Magazine*; three intensely worked and rather lush full-page illustrations for the magazine's cookery pages typify Fern's approach at this point. Elements of the image were drawn or airbrushed separately, then cut out and mounted in highly formalised, even symmetrical arrangements, sometimes combined with type.

In 1974, Quentin Blake asked Fern if he would like to share his teaching commitment at the RCA, which meant taking on a day a week for a term. Fern agreed and found himself cast in the role of tutor to an impressive line-up of final-term students: Sue Coe, Su Huntley, Paul Leith, Glynn Boyd Harte. The following year, Brian Robb invited Fern to return and he has remained with the department ever since, teaching for one day a week, then two, then three, and finally replacing Blake as full-time head of illustration in 1986. Fern's involvement in the department has proved to be of decisive importance to his own development as an artist. The art teacher's position is a particularly exposed one, requiring a high degree of self-awareness and self-criticism if he is to maintain credibility with the students. Showing personal work to the group forces the teacher to see its shortcomings through their eyes. To survive what could have been a destructive experience, Fern had to subject his art and ideas to the same process of continual review that he applied to the students. Fern does not regard himself as naturally articulate, but teaching has forced him to develop the language and confidence to account for and defend his own intuitions.

He quickly became his own harshest critic. The mid-1970s was a time of upheaval in the college's illustration department. A new wave of artists, inspired by an earlier generation of RCA illustrators (Stewart Mackinnon, Terry Dowling, Sue Coe) and the political radicalism and anger of punk, was bringing fierce commitment, shocking subject matter and innovative techniques to the once sedate and bookish world of British illustration. For Fern, tutor of Robert Mason, Russell Mills, Ian Pollock and other spiky newcomers, this period provided a "salutary experience". Dissatisfied with much of his own output, and viewing himself as a late-starter and insufficiently purist to boot, Fern burned the earlier pieces he no longer liked. What he did admire was the "thrown-together" look of punk graphics and in the late 1970s, the bright, simple, silk-screen images composed of colouring-book grids began to be replaced by more or less abstract pieces, full of bold shapes and torn edges, which anticipated the mature work of the 1980s.

It is virtually a truism to say that the most challenging illustration occurs where the artist has a reservoir of experience accumulated through personal work to draw on for commissions. The speed of commercial projects, the use of supplied subject matter, the physical nature of print, and the other inevitable constraints of the brief allow much less scope for experiment than work undertaken at a less forced pace in the artist's own time. Personal projects give the illustrator a chance to return obsessively to the same highly personal themes and motifs, to pursue an idea through a series of pictures with the freedom of the fine artist. Throughout the 1980s, Fern has combined commercial work for a broad range of clients with personal projects undertaken for their own sake and sometimes with a view to exhibition. The surprising thing, in some ways, is the closeness of the relationship between the two strands. Given the almost complete abstraction of his self-generated pieces, this is a measure of the formal originality and daring of Fern's work as an illustrator. Very few British illustrators, even now, have the experience or confidence to carry off a suite of images such as the one Fern produced for the Art Directors Club Nederland's *Annual of Dutch Advertising* in 1986. The collages draw on a handful of dislocated representational elements – a torn diagram of a saw, a line drawing of a cockerel, the corner of a Union Jack – but these are transformed by their abstract settings into visual ciphers stripped of anything other than a coded meaning. The precision of their placement in these deceptively random images forces the viewer to consider them as compositional units, no more or less significant than this mauve rectangle or that strip of masking tape. A certificate Fern created for the BBC Design Awards in 1987 shows his method of typographic integration at its most articulate. The sacrosanct letters "BBC" are irreverently sliced and truncated by diagonal slabs of torn and straight-edged paper, but they still emerge clearly from the testcard intricacy of the background, so carefully is the collage composed. Even the authenticating rubber stamps in the margins are treated as components of the image.

Similar compositional concerns were evident in the collages, prints and type constructions Fern showed in 1985 at London's Curwen Gallery. It is impossible to take in one of Fern's collages at a single glance and this is entirely deliberate. Fern has a fondness for pushing events out to the edges of his pictures, drawing the eye on a journey across the image, leading it by correspondences, inversions and contrasts, blocking its progress by ruptures and gaps, or deflecting its path so that something new comes to light. The pictures are scattered with symbols that imply the presence of language, or at least some structured system of signification, while specifying nothing: crosses, zig-zags, dotted lines, oriental characters (as a mountain climber, Fern particularly likes *yama*, the Japanese symbol for mountain) and fragments of letterforms turned on their side so that they read as code or notation. Sometimes, as in the triangular works, the image's shape is itself a symbol. "It's important that I don't understand it," Fern says of the ephemera he collects. "As soon as I do it's a barrier to seeing it clearly." Much the same taste for uncertainty and suggestion is at work in his pictures. From music, which he invokes as often as he does the visual arts, Fern has learned the importance of rhythm and the repeated phrase, and the power of introducing moments of discordance into a grand harmonic structure.

Such images are intended to stand in their own right, but Fern is cautious when discussing their relationship to the mainstream of gallery art. The radical illustrators he taught in the mid-1970s argued that illustration had been short-changed by the fine art world for too long, and that it was indeed possible for some kinds of commissioned work to attain a level of self-expressive intensity and conviction equal to fine art. There was a time, they pointed out, when all art was commissioned by a patron: why should this in itself be seen as a damning limitation? Illustrators were, moreover, just as capable of originating images of their own as so-called fine artists. Whatever the quality of the evidence, it is fair to say that the art establishment has not heard these complaints. Very few commercial illustrators, Warhol apart, have succeeded in breaking into the art world on equal terms with fine artists. Hardly any exhibitions are ever devoted to the subject of illustration and the professional art journals keep their distance, despite the fact that the visual landscape is flooded with illustrated imagery in obvious need of intelligent assessment. Fern's own view of the matter is typically realistic. Trained illustrators might draw on the discoveries of the major artists – Fern himself takes inspiration from Matisse, Rothko, Motherwell and the Californian painter Richard Diebenkorn, while owing an obvious debt to Kurt Schwitters – but their chances of joining those ranks are slim. It has always been far easier for artists such as Picasso, Miro or Hockney to move in the other direction.

"My concern is that these restraints shouldn't reduce our level of intent," Fern noted in a lecture in 1988. "Our aim should be to retain the highest possible level of artistic expression within the framework of whatever we happen to be working on. Ephemera it may be, but it is reproduced by the tens of thousands and seen by a far wider audience than most fine artists could ever hope to reach. This fact alone provides us with a terrific responsibility to produce work of quality . . . In my own work I've found it invaluable to

Shostakovich Symphony no. 4. CD insert. Artist/designer: Dan Fern. Art director: Ann Bradbeer. Decca, Great Britain, 1990

set time aside to make pictures for their own sake. I've found time after time that this has had the effect of revitalising my commercial work. It is in effect an area of research where I can explore new ideas and media, while at the same time trying to produce pictures which can stand in their own right, and might just transcend the level of ephemera. It's important, though, that this area of work is not regarded as something fundamentally different from applied work."

Equally important to Fern as a teacher and artist is the idea that an illustrator's art, like that of a painter or sculptor, should develop. Too many talented illustrators, he believes, lock themselves into a single, highly recognisable style, which, though at first original and much in demand, rapidly becomes *passé* and eventually turns into a prison. To avoid the same mistake, Fern watches his own work, with the mixture of spontaneity and detachment he has learned from teaching, for indications of the possible directions he might take in the future. His observations of the stylistic evolution of artists he admires – Mondrian's move from figuration to formalist abstraction; Rothko's rejection of Surrealism for abstract expressionism – reveal how dramatic some of these changes might be. Fern recognises in retrospect, though he could not have anticipated it at the time, that his concerns of the 1980s were foreshadowed by a couple of small abstract collages he produced during his final year in Amsterdam in the early 1970s. For a number of years Fern has been making drawings by using erasers to create lines against pencil backgrounds; more recently he has started to paint over old printed work using bold, gestural brushstrokes. None of these experiments is entirely resolved, and it is far too early to draw any firm conclusions about the paintings in particular, but the experiments are evidence that this highly sensitive artist could before long be producing work as different from his recent pieces as they are from his designs of two decades ago.

From: *Dan Fern: Works With Paper,* 1990*

THEATRE OF DREAMS
ANDRZEJ KLIMOWSKI

As the history of graphic design repeatedly demonstrates, the émigré occupies a special position in art and design. Liberated, voluntarily or not, from the constraints of their original culture and uninhibited by the conventions of their new home, émigrés are unusually free to innovate. The émigré artist, almost by definition, is expected to travel with a suitcase full of challenging new ideas.

Born in 1949 in London of Polish émigré parents, Andrzej Klimowski belongs to an even rarer breed. In British design at least he is probably one of a kind. For Klimowski is a three-times émigré, an émigré in reverse. Searching for possibilities he felt that British culture could not provide, he made his way as a student to Warsaw, where he rapidly built a career for himself as one of the leading young Polish poster artists of the 1970s. Then, in 1980, just before the imposition of martial law and at the height of his success, he saw what seemed to be a well-mapped future opening up ahead of him, took fright at the certainty of it all ("when you've passed 30 I think biologically and sociologically it's the last moment to change"), began to worry about the obligations to the Polish state that a permanent card of residence might entail, and decided to return with his family to Britain.

Klimowski's career since then has had its fair share of ups and downs. Like many an émigré he had to start all over again – this time, frustratingly, in the country in which he had grown up. Unable to rely on commissions alone, he was obliged to spend much of the 1980s teaching (he is still a part-time tutor at the Royal College of Art). Moreover, as Klimowski was slowly to discover, the rules of engagement had changed. In Poland he had enjoyed the status of *grafik* or graphic artist, a professional description on a par with doctor or architect, supported by the apparatus of understanding clients, appreciative public and a benevolent state. In Britain such a role might somehow be achievable, but it could not be taken for granted because it was not built into the system. The career choices, then as now, were graphic designer or illustrator, and rarely was it possible to be both.

At least part of the fascination of Klimowski's career lies in the way he has struggled to reconcile himself to these changes while remaining true to the essential core of his vision. It is clear, looking at eighteen years of Polish and British work, that "graphic artist" is the only fully adequate way of describing Klimowski, even though he is now mainly employed as an illustrator and sometimes dabbles in typography and design. He is an artist whose medium is the mass-produced, printed, graphic image. The dark theatre of his later Polish posters is just as apparent on the much smaller stage of his 1980s and 1990s book covers. Klimowski doesn't have a manner – surface in the painterly sense has never particularly mattered to him – so much as a mental library of obsessional images to which he must endlessly return: eyes, faces, hands, the naked torso, angels and demons, snakes, flames, pens, pencils and cameras. The strongest and most memorable Klimowskis are always the most personal and least compromised. The best commissions are those that come in series. The most acute commissioners – Pentagram for literary publisher Faber and Faber; the *Guardian* newspaper – are those who know when to leave well alone.

Klimowski's parents came to England after the Second World War. His father, a career officer in the Polish army, was a member of the resistance who fought in the Warsaw uprising. Klimowski's first language was Polish; he did not learn English until he was five and his accent still bears a trace of the latecomer. His first visit to Poland with family friends at the age of eleven revealed an unsuspected world of steam trains, lazy month-long summer holidays and fine living on a shoestring. An elegantly attired uncle with a shaven head showed him around. "When we went in the 1970s to live there," he remembers, "Poland was like the 1950s in England. Even the cars were rounded and slightly old-fashioned. You had wood panelling and chrome lights and radios with valves." This sense of pleasurable dislocation, of being out-of-time and adrift in a world of archetypes, has become one of the defining characteristics of his work.

From 1968 to 1973, Klimowski studied sculpture, painting and graphics at St Martin's School of Art. He did not plan to become a graphic artist, but he was drawn to the posters he saw in the jazz clubs on his trips to Poland. His interests shifted towards photography

The Book of Laughter and Forgetting. Book covers for Milan Kundera. Artist: Andrzej Klimowski. Penguin Books, Great Britain, 1983; Faber and Faber, Great Britain, 1992

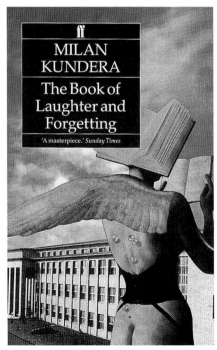

and European film-makers such as Jean-Pierre Melville, Chris Marker and the Polish
director Jerzy Skolimowksi. In his final year at St Martin's, as a postgraduate, he made
a 16mm short, *19 bis. Dreamstrasse* (a single copy survives in a Warsaw aunt's cellar).
Earlier, he helped to make a documentary for Polish television about photocollagist
Roman Cieslewicz, who was to become an influence on his own early work.

In the course of this research, Klimowski visited Henryk Tomaszewski, professor of
graphics at the Warsaw Academy, and showed him his portfolio. Tomaszewski offered
him a place and in 1973, with a British Council grant, Klimowski began his studies.
A brilliant *grafik* in his own right, Tomaszewski was a demanding, autocratic but gifted
teacher dedicated to the elimination of all ambiguity from a student's work. "He could
cut your stuff up completely with a pair of scissors and tell you to give up art and that
you were hopeless and crap," says Klimowski. "In one year I did just four posters. If he
liked something, he said, 'right, that's it' and you had to do the poster the same size as it
would be printed. I did one poster for him which he loved and after all these bollockings
he gave me a great kiss."

Klimowski began working professionally while still a student at the academy. With
a letter of recommendation to the ministry of culture from the irascible Tomaszewski
("it was almost a pleasure teaching him") he was able to join the artists' union.
He designed books and worked for the satirical magazine *Szpilki* ("Pins"), a sort of
Polish *Private Eye*. In 1974 he married Danusia Schejbal, also a child of émigré parents,

Four Stories and *Mrs Caliban*.
Book covers for Rachel
Ingalls. Artist: Andrzej
Klimowski. Art directors:
Pentagram. Faber and Faber,
Great Britain, 1987 and 1993

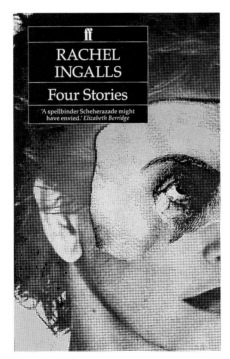

and she joined him at the academy to study set design. Klimowski asked to stay on for another year and spent much of the time working on stop-frame animations.

In the mid-1970s, after many fruitless visits to the central film distributors' building, where graphic artists gathered for screenings, Klimowski was assigned a poster for Costa-Gavras's wartime melodrama about the Vichy government, *Special Section*. This was followed by posters for Polanski's *Chinatown* and Altman's *Nashville*, which won him a bonus payment, a prize from the *Hollywood Reporter* and Polish newspaper coverage. "Suddenly I got masses of posters and I was one of these big poster designers. It was a big thing for a graphic artist because everybody saw them."

It was the theatre poster, however, that was to provide Klimowski with his ideal canvas. Theatre posters had smaller editions of 1,000–2,000 at most, compared with a run of perhaps 13,000 for a nationally distributed film poster. They were better printed on higher-quality paper, often to a larger format, and by the 1970s tended to attract the most accomplished artists. Polish film posters carried little enough information; theatre posters gave away even less: only title, playwright and theatre. For Klimowski, there was an even more fundamental difference: "Films have their own visual look and iconography, which is part of the director's vision. You could find a metaphor for something, a symbol which was nothing to do with any image from the film, but on the whole you had to adhere to that vision, or so I thought. With the theatre, all you were given was the manuscript, or the published play, and it didn't matter what the director was going to do with it because the poster would be printed way ahead of rehearsals. So you could give your own interpretation."

With his 1977 poster for the horror film *The Omen*, Klimowski began to find his own intensely dramatic and anachronistically Catholic iconography: a winged demon is substituted for young Damien's head. Similar substitutions occur in theatre posters for Schönberg's unfinished opera *Moses and Aaron* – a dragon – and Polish playwright Tadeusz Rózewicz's *Birth Rate* (*Przyrost Naturalny*) – an angel. "I like that melodramatic scenario of good fighting evil," he says. "That excites me a lot." Around the same time he began to explore another lasting visual theme. Zooming in cinematically on the heads of his protagonists, he mimicked that most elemental of film shots, the full-face close-up, and used the eye as a piercing transmitter of emotion. In a poster for *The Removalists* (*Przeprowadzka*) by David Williamson eyes bulge with the pressure of male rage and female fear. For Brecht and Weill's *Threepenny Opera*, eyes from three separate faces fuse to form the grainy features of a composite head.

"I was interested in an image without surface," explains Klimowski, "an illusion, which is like the projected image in the movies, or a printed image, not fine print like lithography or etching, but offset litho for the masses." Photocollage allowed him to cut into reality, sometimes crudely so the cut-lines show, manipulate it, and reassemble it with a degree of verisimilitude – "a deposit of the real world" – that the paintbrushes preferred by his fellow Polish poster artists could not achieve. Montages made from his own photographs and other elements were transferred to lith film, the film image was traced on to paper, colour (crayon, paint or pastel) and other textures were applied, then the two layers were taped together so the colour shone through from inside.

Klimowski continued to use much the same technique after his return to Britain. Later, he switched to the colour copier with some loss of graphic force. He began with posters for the Royal Court Theatre and independent film distributor Artificial Eye, but England has a limited taste for poster art, with few outlets, and these quickly tailed off.

It was his series of four images for books by Czech author Milan Kundera, quite unlike other British book covers of the period (1983–85), that first began to impress his vision on a wider consciousness. "To read Kundera without a Klimowski cover is to read a different book," writes British art critic Andrew Brighton. "The images invade the text. They share the syntax of the novels, the connection and relation of disparate elements – events, things and desires, the syntax of montage." The Kundera covers also introduced British readers to a figure who has had a central role in Klimowski's art from the beginning: Danusia, his wife.

Questioned about his use of Schejbal's naked or partially clad image, Klimowski always seems slightly perplexed. He appeared genuinely taken aback when, following a lecture, a woman design history student asked him whether he did not think he was exploiting his wife (and children) by showing them in his work. He did not. Partly, he says, it is a matter of expediency: models are expensive and Schejbal, by training and temperament, has a strong sense of theatre. It is also a public and very un-English celebration of desire. But irrespective of whom the images show, they have also been criticised for their content. In an essay on what she identifies as Milan Kundera's misogyny, British feminist Joan Smith notes the concealed or missing faces, the "female muteness" of these cover designs (she did not mention that a man's face – Klimowski's as it happens – is treated in the same way). "These are clever images," writes Smith, "grainy, slightly perplexing (why has the woman on the cover of *The Book of Laughter and Forgetting* been given wings in place of her left arm?), and therefore conveying the message that the subject matter of the books is the intellectually acceptable one of sexuality rather than common-or-garden sex."

Smith's line of attack points up one of the difficulties faced by any artist trying to work within a commercial medium with priorities of its own. Smith does not name Klimowski, or speculate about his intentions, preferring to talk about the publishers' agency in bringing these images to the commercial domain ("the publisher chose a female torso"; "no wonder Kundera's publishers flaunt [breasts] on his covers"). This might imply, wrongly, that the publishers told Klimowski what to put on the covers, but it comes to the same thing. They chose a certain kind of artist and having received his images they published them. The problem for Klimowski is that the meaning these images have within the context of his developing *oeuvre*, which is invisible to the casual viewer, is not necessarily the meaning they will have when encountered individually on the books.

A larger view, for those prepared to take it, suggests that Klimowski's interest in themes of possession and domination is much less one-sided than Smith's analysis implies. The facelessness, Smith's "muteness", may be less a matter of denying his protagonists speech than of rendering them symbolic, general rather than particular. "Sometimes a face is too specifically of an individual," he says, "so I have to put something in front of it – a flying pearl, a flame, a hand – so that we know it refers to a person, but not to a specific person." Most of these images are violent only in verbal description: the "Danusias" who confront these intrusive, disembodied male hands are sensual, self-possessed, untroubled. "In a couple," Klimowski once told me, "I am interested in who is the stronger of the two." And this is simply to acknowledge a fundamental truth about human relationships; it isn't to say that Klimowski believes either sex will be, or should be, always the stronger, and it applies equally to same-sex relationships of whatever kind. In a 1983 screenprint self-portrait of Andrzej and

Danusia, which may be a key image in the evolution of this private drama, it is her presence that dominates.

Such continuity of theme and image suggests narrative connection, and for the last few years Klimowski has spoken about making this explicit. In 1980 he completed the short film *Dead Shadow* and he might have made others had he not returned to Britain. He has written a number of unfilmed screenplays with Schejbal – in one a sphinx turns into a woman and a man becomes an obelisk and shatters. But the book, at this point, presents the most promising arena for his vision. In 1994, Faber and Faber, which has consistently understood and supported his work, published *The Depository: A Dream Book*, a wordless novel in the tradition of Ernst and Masereel, composed of 250 brush and ink drawings and described by Klimowski as "a contemporary silent movie". It is an intriguing but flawed book, which bears signs of haste in execution, but a brave and original venture in a country with little tradition for such publishing. Set in a mysterious modernist city, Klimowski's strange tale of a dreaming artist, an abduction, a sinister collector and flying spirits with book-leaf wings suggests a significant new chapter has opened for this unusually literary graphic artist.

Eye, no. 14 vol. 4, 1994

TWO HIT THE ROAD
SU HUNTLEY & DONNA MUIR

Historically, Su Huntley and Donna Muir fall into the middle period of a tendency that has lately become a trend. They weren't the first British image-makers to merge their artistic differences in a shared identity. That distinction goes to Gilbert and George (still the most hair-shirted example of creative self-denial) and cult twin film-makers the Brothers Quay. But Huntley and Muir's public partnership, formed in 1980, certainly predates the Duvet Brothers (video), the Douglas Brothers (photography) and Archer/Quinnell (illustration), though the last trumped everyone in 1988 by demanding that their Royal College degree be jointly assessed.

Of course, there is nothing at all remarkable about the idea of collective creativity in a design group or a firm of architects. A building, or even a shop-fitting exercise, provides plenty of pickings to go round. What happens, though, when the outcome is a single image? It is only natural to wonder exactly whose hand held the paintbrush or clicked the shutter and whose artistic vision is being expressed.

In Huntley and Muir's case, the vision – sustained with persuasive conviction – is quite clearly shared. For ten years their universe has been peopled by moody, cigar-chomping Latinos, muscle-bound sports jocks and solid-gone jazzmen honking on saxes of liquefied gold. Huntley/Muir events transpire in nocturnal cityscapes pulsing with energy and light, or at the wheels of huge convertibles driven by good-timers in sunglasses out for a cross-town cruise. It's a big-city, high-octane version of the (usually American) good life that's periodically refuelled by their trips to Los Angeles.

They've applied it with equal vigour to magazines, posters, paintings, book covers, pop videos, TV commercials, a mural (for the Border Grill restaurant in Santa Monica) and, in June 1991, to an issue of stamps. They started out separately, in the early 1970s as illustrators, but long ago outgrew such a restricting description. Huntley is a member of the highly talented generation trained at the RCA, which includes Dan Fern, Sue Coe and the Brothers Quay, for whom the discipline was simply a means to a larger end. Muir, a teenage painter of promise, put in a year at a Toronto art school, before dropping out at seventeen. "When I think back, it's embarrassing not to have had enough conviction. I needed to earn money and I didn't know about getting grants and the stuff you do when you want to be a painter. I went into illustration because it was the easiest option."

Muir came to London and despite a fabled reluctance to take calls – "Whoever it is, I'm not here" – rapidly established her anarchic hand-lettered style. By the end of the decade she had Pentagram and Pearce Marchbank for clients and shared a studio with George Hardie and Bush Hollyhead, where her desk was a spectacular crow's nest in a desert of masculine neatness. "She always looked really crazy," recalls Huntley. "Instead of buttons, she'd have all these different badges for doing up her clothes."

Huntley, meanwhile, had taken a wrong turning. Dissatisfied with the way that she had become typecast for tightly drawn foodie still-lifes – "I'd been fairly anarchic myself at college" – she took a position at Wolff Olins as art director and talent scout. Although she had always regarded Muir with suspicion and perhaps envy, even persuading her then-husband Clive Crook not to commission Muir for the *Sunday Times Magazine*, Huntley decided to call her in. With a great show of reluctance, Muir agreed. "She showed off like mad. She came waltzing in with this huge portfolio and upended it on the floor."

Huntley and Muir never took a firm policy decision to become partners; they just slid into it. It took a year or two of working on and off, while still producing illustrations under their separate names, before the decision was taken in late 1980, after a summer in the US, to amalgamate. Henceforth they would show a single portfolio and sign everything "Huntley/Muir". "It just seemed to be much better for both of us to work together," explains Huntley, who tends in interviews to do most of the talking. "It took a lot of the burden off Donna, I think. It stopped her having to go to the art director with a bag full of scraps and have him help her sort it out. Instead, I would help her sort it out."

This, broadly, is how they have continued, with Huntley acting as *in situ* art director for Muir's inspired but undisciplined digressions. Huntley supplies the concepts and organisational skill – "I would say that 90 per cent, 99 per cent of the ideas come from Su" – and Muir (modest to a fault) makes the marks. Muir dashes off the lettering and Huntley pastes the best examples, letter by letter, into words. The tension between their roles (and one suspects that the division of labour and thought is not nearly so clear-cut as the needs of an interview make it seem) leads to finished artwork with an engagingly provisional air.

The more timorous art directors find it hard to take. "Too strong, too aggressive," they say, when what they really mean is "too assertive". "People who want to control every aspect of the thing themselves wouldn't be attracted to us," admits Huntley. "We want to hog the action." Perhaps so, but it is still a flat-footed complaint. Huntley and Muir's open pictorial frameworks, through which the black paper they favour is plainly visible, are superbly graphic. Their integration of word and image is rich in expressive possibility, given a sufficiently sensitive, hands-off approach. These are qualities exploited with real finesse by Peter Dyer, formerly art director at Secker & Warburg, later with Jonathan Cape. And, for Dyer and those others who aren't scared away, the process is more open-ended than it sounds. "We've reached the point," says Huntley, "where even if we send out three bits of artwork, we would be happy to have any of them used."

In the mid-1980s, Huntley/Muir struck out on a second phase of their career. A widely praised but finally undeveloped animatic for Pernod ("too aggressive" as usual) led to a pop promo for Pat Metheny and then a commercial for Barclays. Before long Huntley and Muir were in Paris at a Sting concert struggling with a hand-held camera they didn't know how to use because their cameraman had been barred at the door. The resulting promo (1986) is arguably their most ambitious exercise in the now-flagging genre, with Sting and his entourage almost entirely obscured by Huntley/Muir's graphic interventions.

Huntley and Muir look back on this period ruefully. Once they had high hopes of transferring full-time to video, but it is two years since they have made a promo. They recognise that the integration of live-action and animation – the perennial problem of a medium that is more often a branch of advertising than art – was rarely achieved.

Faggots. Book cover for Larry
Kramer. Artists: Su Huntley
and Donna Muir. Art director:
Peter Dyer. Minerva, Great
Britain, late 1980s

They would only be interested now if they could work with musicians as visually receptive as Peter "Sledgehammer" Gabriel or Talking Heads. They recognise, too that their insistence on complete directorial control before they would so much as thumb through a proposal may not have helped. They have an impressive showreel, but they could have done four times as much in the same period if they had done more networking and been less hard to please.

This matters to Huntley and Muir because they still harbour ambitions to direct. Their most recent video project is a back-projected animation drawn in jumpy black and white, with the familiar flying lipstick collage elements kept to a minimum, for William Forsythe, the American director of the Frankfurt Ballet. They would like to translate their enthusiasm for cities and buildings into a series of short TV "sketch-books" – "We make no apology for the fact that they would be extremely personal" – on atmospheric but less visited centres like Munich, Bilbao, Marseilles and The Hague.

Architecture, street art and the urban environment remain their most consistent sources of inspiration. Huntley and Muir's visits to Los Angeles, where they designed print material for LA Eyeworks, reinvigorated their work with a new set of exuberant Spanish-American forms seen last year in their murals, ceiling paintings and graphics for the Border Grill restaurant designed by Josh Schweitzer. "A lot of the things that we try to do in our work – the captured energy and humour – are already there in Mexican art. Modern Spanish street artists do those wonderful signs for hairdressers and fruit stalls, where they don't just draw an apple, they do a couple of people dancing holding an apple and an orange."

Although they claim not to like architects as much as they admire their buildings, Huntley and Muir clicked with Schweitzer from the start. Like them, they say, he is "interested in the way that drawing and architecture seem to be too far apart". Now Schweitzer has asked them to apply their drafting skills to two Japanese bar projects, in Tokyo and Fukuoka, which he is designing through the agency of regular Nigel Coates collaborator Shi Yu Chen. The theme – it couldn't be more appropriate – is sport.

Huntley and Muir got their fingers badly burnt in Seville, where a planned five-storey, hand-painted mural for the British Expo pavilion based on two enormous "communicating" heads, along with the matching postage stamp designs, was scrapped after months of discussion and work. The precise reasons remain unclear, but it can hardly have helped that there was no consultation at any stage of the Department of Trade and Industry-managed project between the architect, Nick Grimshaw, and the artists. "It was a bad idea to give this to the architect after the event," says Huntley. "I don't know how I would react." Brought in at the beginning of a major architectural project, as they will be on a smaller scale in Japan, there is no telling what this highly ambitious team might design.

Blueprint, December/January 1992

DANGEROUS TOYS
MILTON GLASER

For a designer who has found himself all but written out of the history of American graphic design, at least as narrated by a recent exhibition in Minneapolis and New York, Milton Glaser looked and sounded entirely unruffled on a visit to London in March 1990. Glaser was speaking at the Design Museum to a sell-out audience of 300 who seemed in no doubt about his position as an elder statesman of American graphics, and his lecture and the accompanying display of posters might almost have been intended as a pre-emptive strike. In August, the museum will host the very exhibition – "Graphic Design in America: A Visual Language History" – in which Glaser has been relegated to the sidelines of history, four decades of achievement reduced to a couple of magazine covers.

Glaser says nothing of this during the lecture, but the following morning it becomes clear that the exclusion is still very much on his mind, and he is the first to raise it. "I think the show is basically an attempt to organise the material into a coherent presentation, but it has a very significant curatorial bias, which is that the work that is worthy of being shown is work that still has its roots in European modernism. So the romantic side is reduced, the decorative side is reduced, the illustrative side is reduced ... I just find it a mean-spirited way to look at the world. I wouldn't mind if that show were titled 'The history of American graphic design as an extension of the modernist tradition'. But for something that purports to be the history of what happened it seems to me that it is irresponsible."

It is clear, at any rate, that Glaser, along with a number of others, including his former partner in Push Pin, Seymour Chwast, has borne the brunt of a critical mood-swing as unpredictable and unanswerable as the weather. Bluntly put, Glaser's work isn't fashionable any more. This isn't to deny its prodigious facility and inventiveness, or to say that some future re-evaluation won't laugh in the face of contemporary judgement. But for the time being, precisely because it answered the visual needs of an earlier period so closely, much of Glaser's work looks dated. Taste in the last decade has passed it by. What could be more sixties than his Dylan poster, or more seventies than 'I♥NY'? His images have a largeness of spirit and, at times, a sentimentality, which is only now beginning to come back into favour.

Then again, at a time of modernist resurgence in graphic design, Glaser's postmodernism is a problem. When Glaser, Chwast and the others at Push Pin began to turn to art history for inspiration, to quote popular culture and vernacular sources, to use humour, parody and narration, it was an attempt, subsequently shadowed by Venturi's lessons in Las Vegas, to break free of the aesthetic arm-lock of modernism. "We didn't believe in eating vegetarian food all the time," Glaser noted in the catalogue of the US graphics exhibition. "Sometimes you want a greasy burger." For a while, the visual promiscuity of the hugely influential Push Pin method made it the most culturally and commercially radical – if not respectable – approach a graphic designer could adopt. By 1970, the studio's brand of decorative revivalism had been so thoroughly assimilated, had become so safe, that it was given a retrospective at the Musée des Arts Décoratifs in Paris. Four years later, Glaser decided he was becoming over-identified with this type of illustration and left.

Glaser's work since Push Pin has been a triumphant assertion that he is very much more than an illustrator, though there are times, you feel, when he protests too much. After a shaky start as art director of *New York* magazine, which he co-founded, Glaser went on to design a string of publications with Walter Bernard, his partner in WBMG. *L'Express*, a project for James Goldsmith, brought a further commission to design the Grand Union chain of supermarkets, which Glaser proceeded to visualise, using both semantic and organisational logic, as three-dimensional magazines (*magasin*, he liked to point out, is French for store). Glaser's company, Milton Glaser Inc, has created a graphics programme for the World Trade Center, and the former "Underground Gourmet" and cheap dining columnist has applied his culinary enthusiasm to a number of restaurant interiors, most recently the Trattoria Dell-Arte in New York. There have been projects for Olivetti, Alessi and New York's School of Visual Arts, where Glaser's legendary class is a Wednesday evening fixture.

These days Glaser's advice to anyone planning to become an illustrator is: don't bother unless your gift is remarkable – become a designer instead. In the US, he says, there are too many illustrators pursuing too few projects of interest. The profession of illustrator, which Glaser, Chwast and Push Pin colleagues like Edward Sorel and Reynold Ruffins practised with the highest intelligence, has been turned into a "second-class activity" by the rise of the art director, since it is the art director who conceptualises, commissions and ultimately controls the image. On the other hand, says Glaser, an ability to draw (by no means the same process as illustration, which is always inflected by the brief and context) has to be the starting point for design. "A designer who must rely on cut-outs and rearranging to create effects, who cannot achieve the specific image or idea he wants by drawing, is in trouble," he once observed, apparently reacting against the contemporary prevalence of collage techniques. Much of Glaser's Design Museum lecture was devoted to the subject of drawing, to the uses of light and the problem of likeness, "narrative" devices that he claims modernism has banished.

As co-chairman of the AIGA's "Dangerous Ideas" graphic design conference in San Antonio, Texas, in 1989, Glaser incensed some participants by announcing that there were computer rooms for those designers who needed them. Similarly slighting comments in response to a question at the Design Museum about new technology caused a ripple of dissent in the audience. Glaser knows he is fighting a neo-Luddite battle he cannot possibly win, but he is more than happy to enlarge on his views in conversation. The computer is a "frightfully dangerous toy" and an "incredibly clumsy instrument" . . . Designers' fears that they will be left behind unless they switch to the new technology are the result of "brainwashing" by the hardware and software companies . . . Students faced with a choice between painstaking classes in drawing and computer studies which allow them to "simulate reality in twenty minutes" will obviously pick the latter.

"One of the computer's great problems is that it pre-empts all the other stuff which seems fuddy-duddy and old-fashioned, but which is fundamental to understanding what form is, what light is, what colour is, what the world is made out of. I don't care if somebody learns how to draw and then they never draw again – that's different from never having learned how to draw. And there are other fundamental differences. Typography cannot begin with computer typography. Unless you have a sense of what classical form is, you can't deviate from it. There's a difference between deviating without knowing history and deviating wilfully."

Glaser's own understanding of history remains, along with drawing, the cornerstone of his work. After graduating from the Cooper Union in 1951 he spent two years studying etching with Giorgio Morandi at the Academy of Art in Bologna; Morandi hardly mentioned art during Glaser's stay, but Glaser's passionate devotion to art history nevertheless dates from that time. In *Graphic Design*, the book he published about his work in 1973, Glaser speaks of his intense personal identification with Piero della Francesca. Nearly two decades later, Glaser is about to begin work on a series of twenty to 30 drawings and paintings about Piero's life for a 500th anniversary exhibition in Borgo San Sepolchro, the painter's native town and site of his *Resurrection*. "I don't know how to begin that project," he says. As with the stage set he is designing for the opera *Falstaff* – his first – or his earlier, potentially risky excursions into industrial design and interiors, Glaser relishes the scale and complexity of the task.

It is the sheer scale of his ambition, in fact, which continues to set Glaser apart. Whether his work is fashionable or not, he brings an ethical seriousness to design which has been sorely lacking in the last decade. At the Design Museum he began a lecture that proved to be remarkably varied in subject and tone with a lucid restatement of the differences between the ethoses of business and art. "What's happening in design," he went on to say, "has to do with a loss of conviction, a loss of faith. There isn't a centre of belief. Things are floating in an off-centre and evasive way."

The next day Glaser insists that he does not want to tell other designers how to conduct their lives, but argues the need for clearsightedness about one's place on the continuum between commerce and culture. Unwilling to work with any client he doesn't personally like or respect, Glaser directs his scorn at the recent irresponsibilities of the business community. "In the United States this rampage of self-interest going on for the last ten years, with the leverage buy-outs and unmitigated greed of incredible proportions, has produced a terrible, dog-eat-dog atmosphere. It's the worst kind of thing that can happen to a society, this relentless selfishness." Design's most pressing task now, as Glaser conceives it, is to encourage the world of business to think beyond the airless confines of the bottom line.

Blueprint, June 1990

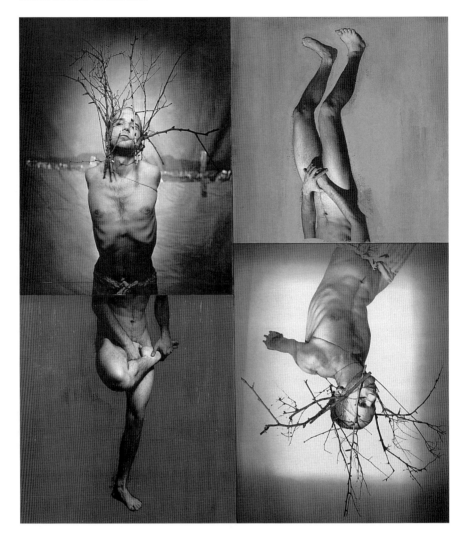

Portrait of the DJ/musician
Moby. Artist: Amy Guip.
Designer: Jodi Peckman.
Rolling Stone, USA, 1995

THE CLIENT SAYS HE WANTS IT IN GREEN

There is a peculiar irony, possibly unintended, in a recent release from the Emigre font library. The Californian company's latest font, Big Cheese, is not a typeface – at least as we used to understand the term – but a set of 126 illustrations in two weights, light and dark, which can be accessed like a visual alphabet from the keyboard. Designed by Bob Aufuldish and Eric Donelan, it is quite a character set: a goofy catalogue of heads, hands, hats, dogs, fish, talking cars and walking bombs that look more like the kind of stylised pictogram you would expect to find on the restroom door in a Barcelona nightclub than a serious offering from the nerve centre of typographic cool.

The irony? Simply that a once flourishing graphic medium, illustration, should now find itself subsumed by the organisational framework and borrowing the delivery system of the very phenomenon – digital type – that has supplanted it in the affections of trend-conscious designers.

For illustration, it must be said, has been looking rather sick of late. Fine work is, needless to say, still being done. The great names of the medium did not somehow cease to be good just because the computer arrived, though they may have been given fewer opportunities to perform at their best. But in the age of digital type, in a medium that is driven, whether we like to acknowledge it or not, by fashion and fad, even the best illustrators' work has suffered from the no doubt superficial but still unavoidable sense of looking less urgent, exciting or timely.

In Europe, there can be no sharper demonstration of this process in action than the annual *Illustration Now* (previously published as *European Illustration*). The book contains much that is derivative and dull – alongside such reliable contributors as Brad Holland, David Hughes, Caroyln Goudy and Peter Till – but its overriding problem is that its design by digital typographer Jonathan Barnbrook is far more imaginative and, yes, contemporary-looking than most of the supposedly fresh illustration it contains. Barnbrook's front matter and section divider pages are hard-edged montages of type, image and blocks of shrill colour that conceal a more serious message; they are, in fact, illustrations in their own right. But their very toughness makes many of the "real" hand-crafted illustrations in the book look twee.

Tweeness, indeed, has become the illustrator's curse. If European illustration is in difficulty now, it is not only because the arrival of the computer has recalibrated our aesthetic expectations. It is also because, as the 1980s wore on, illustrators and art directors seemed increasingly unsure what illustration was for. In Britain, there was simply too much of it to retain a sense of conceptual focus. The booming design business' insatiable need for acres of anodyne imagery to fill brochures, annual reports, financial services leaflets and point-of-sale displays was fuelled by an explosion of new courses in the art schools dedicated to the training of full-time professional illustrators – a concept which had barely existed before the 1970s.

If many of the finest illustrators of an earlier generation concentrated on editorial or culture-related projects – books, magazines, newspapers, film and theatre posters – to which they brought personal vision and a degree of bite, too many of the newer illustrators have evolved signature styles that are no more than the blandest of selling tools. The cumulative effect is of a nursery world in which people caper about like bendy dolls, the sun never fails to shine, and there are enough cut-outs to make Matisse throw away his scissors in disgust. It is Stanley Spencer, or Thomas Hart Benton, for the under-fives. And this, inevitably, became the kind of work favoured by the agents who sprang up to market illustrators' services to design groups and advertising agencies. Image-makers of less pliant or tameable vision found themselves rather less often in demand.

Using the design business' own well-worn rhetoric, the agencies attempt to sell illustration as a "problem-solving" tool. This is the approach taken in *Illuminations* (1993), a book jointly produced by the London agency Sharp Practice and the Edinburgh design group McIlroy Coates. Uncertainly pitched between seriousness (it has a hardback cover and is written by a journalist) and selling brochure, the book presents a series of fictitious design briefs with their illustration-led solutions. The agency represents some exceptional artists – Andrzej Dudzinksi, Liz Pyle, Richard Parent, Christopher Corr – but the effect is cloying and contrived. As is typical with work of this kind, word and image are not tightly integrated, with the type all too often pushed out to the margins as the illustration expands in a cloud of colour to fill the available space.

This is not for one moment to suggest that illustration can never be used successfully as a design tool. We know that it can. But designers and art directors who reach for the illustration annuals and agency portfolios as a kind of reflex should remember that many of the best-integrated and hence most satisfying examples of problem-solving illustration come from individuals with the ability to carry out both illustration and design: figures such as Edward Bawden, Ben Shahn, Milton Glaser, Seymour Chwast, Alan Fletcher and Bob Gill. As Chwast himself once put it, establishing the order of priorities: "I'm a designer who illustrates."

The art director, by comparison, starts with a distinct disadvantage. It takes rare talent, sound artistic judgement and great intuitive sympathy to recognise and harness the talents of others. Many try. How many truly succeed? There are worrying signs, too, that the relationship is breaking down – that art direction today is a less well practised, if not declining, art. Certainly it is a process that many illustrators seem to view with a mixture of disillusion and dread. The complaints are legion: art directors don't know what they want, fail to give a proper brief, or rethink the brief half-way through. Art directors meekly allow their clients to practise design by committee and to specify pointless changes. Art directors present clients with a mock-up cobbled together from the illustrator's previous work, turning the creative task into a depressing act of self-parody.

To which, if you are an illustrator, must be added a final note of woe: the ascendency of the photographer. Ever since Neville Brody – himself an illustrator of some talent – rejected the use of illustration in *The Face* in favour of photography, which he found more malleable and easier to integrate with type, many of Britain's most creative designers have preferred photographic emulsion to the crayon or brush. Companies such as Why Not Associates, Cartlidge Levene and Siobhan Keaney went on to establish

lasting relationships with individual photographers, while the most consistent
mainstream award-winners, Carroll Dempsey Thirkell, consolidated their reputation
with photography-based design. As with the new digital typography, the effect of the
continuing preference for photography within this influential group is to make most
design based on illustration look decidedly old hat.

In illustration, meanwhile, it is the work based on collage and montage that has
looked most convincing for several years, and this too allows the photographic image
to flourish. A tendency that began in Britain in the early 1980s with the texture-collages
of Russell Mills and others, and continues in the work of photographer–illustrators
such as Simon Larbalestier and the Douglas Brothers, is now well established in the
US, as for instance in the solarised photo-paintings of Amy Guip. Larbalestier's book
The Art and Craft of Montage (1993) is, incidentally, by far the most stimulating guide
to recent illustration.

There are those contemplating this trend who argue that what we need now is
a rejection of montage and image manipulation and a return to drawing and the skills
of the hand. They should not hold their breath. Designers now have the ability, using
desktop computers, colour copiers and CD-ROM, to manipulate photographic imagery
with greater freedom than ever before. As these systems become cheaper and more
accessible, the likeliest development is that the collage impulse will migrate from paper
illustration to the more fluid and dynamic screen. Designers will then become type
and image constructors in the fullest sense of the term. This will not make illustrators
redundant, but it may well force a reassessment of their role. If it leads to less but better
illustration, then it will be no bad thing.

Eye, no. 10 vol. 3, 1993

5. MAGAZINES

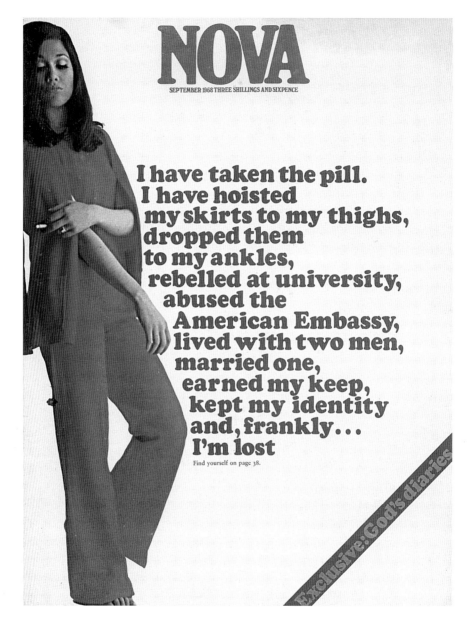

Nova. Magazine cover. Editor:
Dennis Hackett. Art director:
Derek Birdsall. IPC Magazines,
Great Britain, September 1968

WHITE HEAT
NOVA

Nova magazine has all the qualities of a contemporary legend. It burnt brightly – too brightly perhaps for its own good – tumbled into messy decline and expired tragically young. As the years pass, it looms larger, maybe larger than it was, in the memories of those who were there at the time. For a new media-obsessed generation, tracking down old copies and discovering its trail-blazing approach to fashion, it enjoys an unlikely afterlife as an icon of 1970s cool. The truth, as always, is more complicated than the legend.

Published between 1965 and 1975, *Nova* spans two eras. It was born in the white heat of Wilsonian optimism and wealth and brought low by the recessionary, utilitarian, new decade. As a piece of publishing it looks in two directions. Many of its innovations – certainly those that relate to its design – were inspired by great American magazines of the 1950s and early 1960s, such as *Esquire*, *Harper's Bazaar* and *McCall's*, and by continental titles like *Elle* and *Twen*. In its editorial preoccupations *Nova* anticipated today's more commercial, more rigorously targeted magazines.

To look through *Nova* from first issue to last is to realise that, despite the legend, the magazine's achievement is uneven – there are superb issues and dull ones. Consumer magazines of this kind are more even now, but rarely strive for, or achieve, such highs. They no longer take the risks. *Nova* veered this way and that with the enthusiasms of its editors. At its best, it contrived a fusion of editorial content and design that has been equalled by few other British magazines.

Nova's arrival in March 1965 was brash, but unfocused. It was, announced the cover, "A new kind of magazine for the new kind of woman". "This is a magazine for women who make up their own minds," wrote editor Harry Fieldhouse. "It's dedicated to the startling proposition that women have more to think about than what to do about dinner." Fieldhouse's *Nova* was worthy and well-intentioned – no knitting patterns or slushy love stories here – but lacked excitement. Despite enthusiasm in the postbag ("*Nova* – Supa, Winna!" wrote one reader. "We need this magazine," wrote another) sales declined by the issue.

From September, Fieldhouse was replaced by Dennis Hackett, hot from the editor's chair at Jocelyn Stevens's *Queen*. Hackett, drafted in by corporate headquarters, was a man in a hurry. He knew exactly what he wanted and he was not about to brook much argument. "I wanted to do a glossy that was not for chinless wonders," he says. "I took off the 'new kind of woman' slogan, which I thought was patronising. I wanted to use the kind of material adults would talk about over the dinner table. My objective was to put the sale up. In September it went up from 117,000 to 134,000." Under Hackett, the changes came thick and fast. He knew the last thing the publishing company, George

Newnes, could afford at this point was to sack him, and he played his cards for all they were worth. In a coup that would be all but unthinkable now, he banished advertising from the centre of the magazine, creating an uninterrupted editorial well of 36 to 40 pages. He overrode designer Harri Peccinotti and threw out the eye-glazing sanserif text typeface. By January 1966, the new editorial and design mix was in place, the two departments pulling as one. *Nova* had a consistent masthead, headline typeface and coverline style – Windsor, a Pop period-piece based on an old wood type discovered by Peccinotti in Ralph Steadman's garage. "I wanted a typeface that was the same throughout," says Hackett. "Sometimes we used it very large and stacked it, sometimes quite small with a lot of white space."

Nova's finest covers were classics of economy and wit. By concentrating on a single issue, rather than the now obligatory menu of contents, they left readers in no doubt about the magazine's priorities. The coverlines were miniature masterpieces of confession and provocation: "Yes, we're living in sin. No, we're not getting married. Why? It's out of date." The "I have taken the pill . . . and, frankly . . . I'm lost" cover of September 1968 encapsulated a generation's experience in a brief disillusioned paragraph. Hackett's best-known cover – "You may think I look cute but would you live next door to my mummy and daddy?" – strips the editorial message down to a single compelling challenge, while Peccinotti's aggressive use of white space around the little black girl intensifies the sense of unease.

And so Hackett continued. In April he became editorial director with a seat on the board. For a while, almost anything seemed possible. For one article on confession, illustrated with puppets by Roger Law (later to co-found *Spitting Image*), Hackett had a hole cut in the page to represent the screen between penitent and priest. Being a Catholic himself didn't stop him running an article on contraception: "Six Catholics say yes". One cover story, "They consent in private", by Irma Kurtz, examined attitudes to homosexuality. "The homosexuals on the cover – they tried to kill that," says Hackett, who got up from his sickbed to beat them off. "What they did do, which I didn't think of, was to cut the print. In fact, it sold out. How stupid can you get? Hugh Cudlipp – and I have Cudlipp's letter – wrote to IPC [the parent company] saying: 'Do we have to show buggery in full colour?' And I wrote back and said: 'Most people see in colour.'"

So who was the typical *Nova* reader? Its perverse strength was that, during its early years, if it wasn't for the nail polish and girdle ads, you would be hard pressed to tell. "If you look at Hackett's issues," says David Hillman, art director from June 1969, "you are never quite sure who he's aiming at." The magazine may have announced itself as a women's title, but its editor and staff saw it in more general terms. Says Hackett: "I didn't think of it as a women's magazine. Only in the service area. I talked to women as I would to anybody else." Forty-two per cent of his readership, he insists, was male – "nobody has come near that". "We didn't think in terms of reader profile," says Margaret Pringle, who joined as a feature writer in 1968, became fiction editor, and stayed until the end. "We did what we thought was interesting."

In Hackett's sympathetic hands young talent flourished. "Part of his genius was to develop unknown writers," says Pringle. Irma Kurtz, now agony aunt with *Cosmopolitan*, was taken on over the phone on the strength of two pieces of copy. Hackett signed up Molly Parkin, a painter without a fashion spread to her name, as fashion editor and encouraged her to write. Under his stewardship, *Nova* regulars such as Kurtz, Peter Martin, Michael Wynn-Jones and John Sandilands turned in long, personal, sharply observed reports and profiles that put the magazine in a class of its own. "I didn't ever tell them how to write," says Hackett. "Nor did I ever tell them how much to write. They'd say to me, how long? And I'd say, whatever is adequate!"

It was combustible fuel. In *Nova*'s Southampton Street offices, above old Covent Garden, there were slammed doors and broken glass. Parkin was fired with the same dispatch with which she had been hired. "Every feature was a row," remembers Peccinotti. *Nova*'s brilliance lay in the way it reconciled editorial and design, but for the designer at least its effects were hard won. "I don't think I did anything with disregard for the text," says Peccinotti, "but they always said I did. You'd set a big wide column of type and they'd say people can't read it, and you'd say – 'have you got a novel with you?'"

Nova insiders have strong views about the point at which the magazine started to lose its edge. Many say it was never the same after Hackett's last issue in April 1969. A self-congratulatory radio profile ended the story at this point, as though the next six years never happened. Kurtz says simply: "It was Dennis's magazine." Peccinotti, who left after just a year and a half but continued to shoot its fashion, puts the turning point even earlier. "It was already softening. At the start it was an adventure. It should have evolved, but it didn't." But he takes issue with Hackett's dismissal of the later *Nova*. "Hackett's a little unfair. He seems to think that after he left *Nova* was dead. It survived, but on a more level basis."

For a while, though, *Nova* wandered. Hackett's replacement, Peter Crookston, had been features editor at the *Sunday Times Magazine*. He brought with him as art director an old *ST* colleague, David Hillman. "Crookston loved famous names," says Margaret Pringle. "As soon as he came in he had these rather grandiose literary figures. It did get more *New Yorkery*." For Hillman, struggling to design pace and variety into the pages, it was a frustrating eighteen months.

Nova's last, and longest-serving editor, Gillian Cooke, happily installed as editor of IPC's successful teenage title *Honey*, returned from holiday to learn of her new job. On *Nova* she found few supporters. There were bitchy stories in *Private Eye*. "When she joined it was with a certain amount of animosity on the part of most of the staff, including myself," says Hillman. "But she was the one who really encouraged me to go off and do things that weren't perceived to be the norm. And I think she had a very clear view of the reader she was aiming for."

"I found *Nova* very intimidating as a reader and I was the sort of person who should have been reading it," says Cooke. "You can't read type in that quantity, not on your lap on a train, which means you just look at the pictures. The writing was superb, but it was difficult to get at." Cooke was the magazine's fifth editor, but she was the first woman to be entrusted with it. "There were some good women associated with it in the early days," she says, "but it was still essentially a man's view of women."

Under Cooke, the magazine became more focused. She published articles on single mothers, adoption, rape, baby snatchers, house husbands, abortion, cot death, transsexuals, women terrorists, "vaginal politics" and latch-key kids. Years before Neil Lyndon or the hairy-manism of *Iron John*, assistant editor David Jenkins set down: "The men's liberation manifesto", while Germaine Greer anticipated the top-shelf title for women by asking: "What do we want from male pin-ups?" The sexual content, always a feature, now became blatant eroticism.

Hillman used tough conceptual illustration as a way of pulling readers into the text.

Whole pages were devoted to unforgettable images. Contributors included Roger Law, John Holmes, Edda Kochl, Sue Coe, Celestino Valenti and Stewart Mackinnon. For an article on impotence by psychiatric health writer Catherine Storr in February 1972, Hillman brought in Mike McInnerny, who had designed the cover of the Who's *Tommy*, to create a wince-making metaphor in which two huge screws tie themselves in knots.

Nova's directors didn't much care for it. For Cooke and Hillman, by then deputy editor as well as art director, it was a battle every column inch of the way. "We had a lot of opposition to probably the best material that's ever been done on breast cancer," says Cooke. "Doctors were sending for copies of that. A lot of them had no idea that women were losing breasts without biopsies; it was absolutely scandalous. That was immensely important, but very unpopular with management. One of the problems was it was one of the magazines their wives, or their friends' wives, looked at, so if we did something that upset one of them they felt it personally. Every director had his oar in. Everything was up for analysing, criticising and post-mortems."

They were on a collision course and eventually it happened. The "Ted weds" wife-for-Heath issue, conceived to blow *Cosmopolitan*'s March 1972 launch out of the water, should have been a triumphant restatement of everything *Nova* was best at: controversy, satire, irreverence, stop-at-nothing art direction and visuals. Instead, thanks to management nerves, it was a disaster. The idea was to find a wife for the bachelor Prime Minister. A computer dating agency was given Heath's characteristics and one of the shortlisted women agreed to take part. "We asked her to redesign the bedroom of 10 Downing Street," says Hillman, "to plan her first dinner party, to think about where the wedding was going to be, and also about how she would change him." The cover, inspired by the bride-to-be's lack of enthusiasm for sailing, was a spoof of the *Daily Mirror*. On the eve of publication the woman revealed that she was wanted on drug-smuggling charges and that she was about to turn herself in. She was later cleared of all charges, but IPC panicked.

"The whole print-run was fed into the boilers at Battersea Power Station," says Hillman. "We came out three weeks late and *Cosmopolitan* had a trouble-free launch. As far as I am concerned, that was when it all started to go wrong. It took us a long time to get over the killing of that issue."

In the long run they never really did. *Nova* never looked quite so confident or coherent again. The recession deepened, paper prices soared, advertising declined, readers fell away and, in May 1974, *Nova*'s page size was reduced. In May 1975, it was reduced again. Talk of making it as thick as French *Elle* came to nothing. A shadow of itself, *Nova* seemed to have lost all direction: six pages of Willie Rushton stripping down to his Y-fronts, a cover story on male baldness and, most damning of all, a knitting pattern. In October 1975, IPC shut it down.

Nova deserved a kinder fate. Clive Irving, executive editor of magazines at IPC in the 1960s, casts its demise in almost tragic terms. For him, *Nova* was an "aesthetic insurrection finally snuffed out by the blockheaded regime it violated". Its legacy is a considerable one. *Nova*'s fearless social and sexual controversies are now the currency of the mainstream. In magazine publishing there was nothing remotely like it for catching the contemporary mood until the arrival, in 1980, of *The Face*. But it would be wrong to press the comparison too far. You need a great deal of money to fuel editorial ambitions on the scale of Hackett's *Nova*, and *The Face* never had the resources or, perhaps, the vision. "I think it was more intellectual than *The Face*," says Peccinotti. "There, the design was more important than the content. They were reinforcing the popular saleable image."

And in women's magazines? "I don't wish to be rude to any of them," says Hackett, "but, apart from *Marie Claire*, who is doing anything different?" He might have been much ruder, for today formula is everything. Look at that gallery of glossy faces and babble of competing coverlines on the newsstands. When was the last time you saw a cover that expressed any message other than "this issue is much like the last"? If those old copies of *Nova* are worth digging out and looking at and reading again – and they are – it is because they bring back a time when the point of the exercise was the excitement and conviction of the message itself.

The *Guardian*, 16 October 1993*

THE MAGAZINE AS THEATRE OF EXPERIMENT

OZ

"As a freelance writer and instructor in Magazine Journalism, may I say that rarely have I seen a more confused, confusing, botched-looking, noxious, sloppy, tasteless or incoherent magazine than yours." So wrote an admiring reader from the University of Iowa in the ninth issue of *Oz*, and lest anyone take his words without the required pinch of salt, he ended his letter: "Keep up the good work!"

Oz was one of the most remarkable magazines ever published in Britain. It sputtered into life almost by accident in February 1967, discovered a role as the house journal of the psychedelic counterculture, and gasped its last, after just 48 issues, in November 1973. There were many other British underground magazines and newspapers – 1960s veterans may remember some of them: *IT, Friends, Ink* – but none looks so interesting today as *Oz*. As a result of an absurd and unnecessary obscenity trial in 1971, precipitated by the notorious "School Kids" issue, *Oz* entered British folklore (the trial was even restaged on television in 1991) and its impact as social history has tended to eclipse its achievements as an experiment in publishing and design. Some issues, admittedly, were "appalling messes", as their editors and designers are the first to point out. It is also true that *Oz*'s use of sexual and violent imagery as a means of goading the establishment now

Oz. Spreads from issue 16,
"The Magic Theatre".
Editor: Richard Neville.
Artist/designer: Martin Sharp.
Oz Publications Ink, Great
Britain, 1969

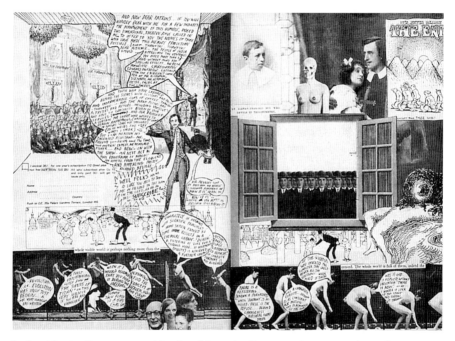

looks at best naïve, at worst objectionably sexist. But many issues remain, at the very least, editorially intriguing, and some are graphically superb.

From 1967 to 1970, *Oz* was designed mainly by Jon Goodchild, with Martin Sharp (an Australian émigré, like the magazine's editor, Richard Neville) contributing illustrations and art. Other issues were designed or co-designed by David Wills, Richard Adams, Barney Bubbles, and Pearce Marchbank (who brought an art director's sense of structure to the magazine), but the process was far more collaborative than a roll-call makes it sound. Adams describes it memorably as "the artroom as theatre of experiment". Almost any passing visitor was invited to get involved. "It was genuinely anarchic," he says. "The only time there was a coming together of editorial and design was when the issue was flat-planned. Nothing was etched in stone. If something came in at that point that was better than something else, then the original was either reallocated or put back on the shelf."

In its format, too, *Oz* was a publication in a constant state of flux. It could be portrait one issue, landscape the next; a slimline magazine, or a fold-out newspaper. One audacious cover (no. 11), printed black on day-glo orange, took the form of a sheet of perforated stickers carrying provocative slogans ("We are lepers, give us bells, not degrees"). In his memoir of the 1960s underground, *Hippie Hippie Shake*, Richard Neville recalls the night that Martin Sharp, high on hash, proposed to take charge of the next issue. It would, Sharp said, be entirely visual, and working away on the project, night after night, assisted by film-maker Philippe Mora, the designer was true to his word. Sharp's "Magic Theatre" issue (no. 16, 1969) was recognised at the time as outstanding and holds up in retrospect as one of the most extraordinary visual artefacts of the period. Sharp cast aside the conventional journalistic apparatus of discrete articles, headlines, supporting pictures and captions for a writhing 48-page collage-fusion of images and text. "Price of admittance your mind," his cover announces. "All men are madmen." And for much of its length Sharp's theatre feels more absurdist than magical, closer to an asylum than an auditorium, a tragi-comic inferno of babbling media and human craziness that alternates between acidhead deathwish and occasional flashes of a more optimistic vision.

Flouting copyright as a matter of principle, the "Magic Theatre" works by associative juxtaposition: a skull with copy from a Coty Dew Fresh lipstick ad; a crucifixion scene opposite DC's *Justice League of America* comic; a jailbreak headline above lines about the expulsion from Paradise. Panels from Winsor McCay's *Little Nemo in Slumberland* and the underground comix of Robert Crumb collide with images of John and Yoko, Hitler and the Queen, famine victims, human freaks, and the paintings of René Magritte. Running

Oz. Cover of issue 11. Editor: Richard Neville. Designers: Jon Goodchild with Virginia Clive-Smith. Oz Publications Ink, Great Britain, 1968

along the foot of each page to form a continuous ribbon from beginning to end are Eadweard Muybridge's locomotion photographs, their silent naked figures brought to life by speech bubbles. "[O]ne of the richest banks of images that has ever appeared in a magazine," enthused art critic Robert Hughes. "Martin Sharp pushed the art of psychedelia almost further than anyone," observed writer and *Oz* contributor David Widgery in 1988. "The 'Magic Theatre' issue is the one thing created by the psychedelic era which might be looked at with interest in 100 years' time . . . [Sharp] was a critical influence on *Oz*'s visual extremism."

Two other factors made these freedoms possible and, as with the Macintosh in our present era, both have to do with technology. The IBM golfball typewriter gave on-the-premises access to inexpensive typesetting ("Anyone with two fingers could learn how to use it," says Adams) and facilitated the ranged-left aesthetic that looked so progressive compared to most British design. At the same time, offset litho printing meant that literally any kind of mark – even a thumbprint – could now be transferred from artwork to printed page. *Oz* was one of the first British magazines to use web offset and certainly the most experimental. "So many of the *Oz* innovations occurred as a result of getting the printing guys interested in doing something they would never be able to do again," recalled one of the editors, Felix Dennis. "We used colour washes, silver ink, gold ink . . ."

The colour freakouts led to some famous disasters – Germaine Greer, for one, was unamused to see an extract from *The Female Eunuch* all but expunged – but *Oz*'s reputation for illegibility is exaggerated. Nor should it overshadow the magazine's use of illustration as surreal marginalia or full-page psychedelic fantasy, which did so much to establish its incisive, bourgeois-baiting visual style. The example of Jim Leon, Peter Till, Stewart Mackinnon and many others, as well as the incomparable Martin Sharp, was to have a decisive influence on the next generation of British punk illustrators.

And graphic design? "A lot of it certainly wouldn't stand up alongside the work of Glaser and Chwast and Lubalin," concedes Richard Adams. "They were much purer and dedicated to the whole idea of the graphic arts, whereas the underground press tried to achieve a blend of image and word in which there was a complete free-for-all. If there were rules, they were there to be broken." Many of *Oz*'s inventions, like some of its personnel, flowed out into the music press, where they were subject to inevitable dilution. Something of its samizdat spirit (though little of the panache) resurfaced in the punk fanzines of the late 1970s. Today, the most obvious genetic link – in the use of colour, variations of format, and a fierce anti-formalism – can be seen in the energetic pages of the long-running British style magazine *i-D*.

AIGA Journal of Graphic Design, vol. 11 no. 1, 1993/*Eye*, no. 24 vol. 6, 1997

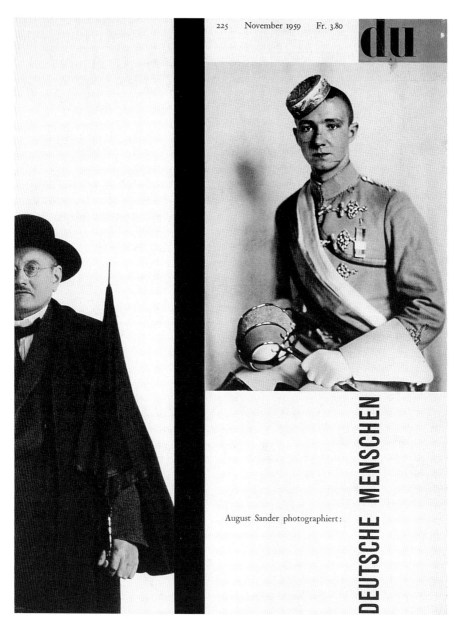

225   November 1959   Fr. 3.80   **du**

August Sander photographiert:

DEUTSCHE MENSCHEN

Du. Cover of issue 225.
Designer: Roland Schenk.
Photographer: August Sander.
Verlag Conzett & Hüber,
Switzerland, November 1959

PAPER ENGINEER
ROLAND SCHENK

Roland Schenk designs the tightest magazine layouts in the business. He assembles pages with the precision of an engineer, calculating loads and stresses. Words and pictures are clamped together by the hidden structural grid, cantilevered headlines swing out into white space, and captions are cut into photographs or recessed into text with the care and authority of a Mies van der Rohe. Generous supplies of air circulate round Schenk's modernist constructions, but there are times when it is almost too pure to breathe.

The formal language, best seen in the revitalised pages of *Management Today*, brooks no argument and, according to reputation, neither does the man. For twenty years Schenk has presided over the visual identity of Management Publications, a subsidiary of Haymarket, the publishing company founded by Michael Heseltine. He has designed most of its business titles, an achievement in itself, but more that this, he has succeeded in imposing a uniformity of approach (he would probably take issue with the notion of a "house style") on a body of trade publications that might otherwise have been visually chaotic. If the standard of trade press design has been raised at all in the intervening years, it is largely thanks to the influence of Schenk's designs for such titles as the ad world's bible, *Campaign* (which has survived two decades virtually unchanged), *Accountancy Age*, the doctors' magazine *MIMS*, *Medeconomics* and *Computing*.

It's not an achievement, however, that Schenk seems at all anxious to play up. "I think the trade press is still very badly handled actually," is as much as he is prepared to say.

The first time we meet, at Haymarket's Lancaster Gate base in London, Schenk has recently moved offices. He doesn't like his new room and, although we have agreed to begin the interview by looking through his portfolio (actually a briefcase), he is eager to get out to Bibendum, one of the South Kensington restaurants where it's his habit to take his lunches and entertain guests. He leafs through the laminated pages quickly, as though these precious glimpses of his history could only be of passing interest.

The subject of Haymarket in the 1980s also excites little enthusiasm. Schenk, not, one suspects, a man much inclined to nostalgic reflection, looks back to the early days. "In the 1960s it wasn't a very hierarchically organised structure. There was more improvisation and freedom, more interaction with people. When Lindsay Masters was vice-chairman, he talked to everybody. Since he became chairman he has become a remote figure. I speak to him occasionally, but it's not the same. You get the in-betweeners. It's the big company syndrome."

The only magazine that Schenk still designs on a day-to-day basis is *Management Today*, the first title he worked on when he joined Haymarket in 1968. Its subsequent attrition in the 1970s and 1980s is the subject that rankles with him most. The page size was reduced twice, the second time to A4, and the art budget was cut until the magazine, in theory the company's most prestigious title, looked uncared-for and undernourished. In 1987, however, in a belated response to the arrival of Kevin Kelly's plushly upholstered *Business* magazine, *Management Today* was overhauled by Schenk and its new editor Lance Knobel.

"The redesign, which I quite like, took place in an interregnum when there was no editorial director," says Schenk. "We didn't have these bureaucratic intermediaries. We had a more entrepreneurial approach again – that's the word to use. At the beginning it was an entrepreneurial climate. Then it became a corporate climate. *Management Today* was killed in the process. It was resurrected by some temporary chaos."

Schenk laughs. His conversation, mumbled in delivery but every bit as precise as his page layouts, is punctuated by these ironic ellipses. It's not a mirthless laugh, but it isn't a belly laugh either. It's a sound that originates in the throat, almost willed and slightly cerebral – it could be a warning. You have a reputation for being difficult, I suggest to Schenk at one point (one disgruntled illustrator had described him to me as a "Swiss watch"). "In what way?" Schenk asks. Demanding of others. "Oh, yes," he agrees, "I think that's a good thing. If I wasn't demanding, I wouldn't be doing my job, heh, heh, heh."

After a false start as a painter, Schenk, now 55, studied graphic design at the Basel Kunstgewerbeschule from 1948 to 1951. His professor, the modernist poster designer Armin Hofmann, remains his greatest influence, though Schenk, who is given to decisive gestures (when he abandoned painting he burnt his pictures) did not finish the course. On holiday in Paris, he heard that there were Swiss designers working at the American embassy. He presented himself, was given a try-out assignment, bought some equipment and set to work in his hotel room. He ended up staying in Paris for eight years.

Schenk returned to Switzerland to become art director of *Du* in 1959. The magazine, which is now regarded as a classic, covered everything from art and artists to English eccentricity. But it was Schenk's brilliant handling of the photographic issues, featuring such subjects as the portraits of August Sander or Robert Frank's portrayal of American life, that was most vital to his development. The other essential ingredient was supplied by the German weekly *Quick*, a scandal sheet full of crashing cars and nubile actresses that Schenk worked on for about a year in 1966. He still recoils at the "vulgarity" of the magazine, but it did at least teach him how to use pictures and words in a journalistic way to seize the reader's attention.

Schenk came to swinging London the following year, attracted by its cosmopolitan atmosphere and, he insists without a trace of embarrassment, the mini-skirts. Haymarket's *Town*, the *Arena* of its day, gave him a chance to explore the approaches suggested by *Quick* – "Last Ditch of the Very Rich", an exposé of the Marbella set, was typical – but the opportunities for probing journalistic photography there and at *Management Today*, in particular, were limited. Schenk responded by encouraging photographers to develop highly "aesthetic", rather than naturalistic, styles of portraiture and still life, and he splashed the stylised results across double-page spreads and ran them in series through features with a confidence that rivalled, and often outdid, that of the colour supplements. Some photographers, such as Lester Bookbinder, he drew in from advertising, which in turn incorporated his innovations; others, such as Rolph Gobits and Brian Griffin, a later collaborator, he discovered himself.

Griffin, more than anyone, has helped to define the photographic look of the redesigned magazine. In one extraordinary example of facial sadism, the features of prominent trade unionists were blown up to several times life size and emblazoned menacingly across the page. The message to management – can it possibly not have been intentional? – was plain: these are the monsters from your worst nightmares. "Each time Griffin does a job, it's a challenge," says Schenk. "He gets quite tense, he gets in a trauma, and to me this is evidence of a creative person, because he starts afresh. I'm in a similar situation. If I start to design a magazine, I don't apply X, Y, Z like a formula. If that does happen, it's because Haymarket or some other client wants it."

Yet certain stylistic traits, as well as structural principles, do recur. Schenk has been shunting the letters of sanserif headlines to within a hair's breadth of each other since *Du*. Columns of type are leaded as tightly as possible, while still preserving legibility, and text butts up to within a point or two of the pictures. Headlines are offbeam, asymmetrical, as though Schenk feared that to introduce an element of stability or certainty into the design might encourage complacency in the reader. The effect is reinforced by their occasionally massive proportions, a tradition that goes back to the work of Willy Fleckhaus (whom Schenk admires) on *Twen* magazine in the early 1960s, and to some of Herb Lubalin's magazine designs of the same period. Colour values are assessed and matched with spectrographic accuracy – too dark a black can ruin a spread for Schenk. Rigour, formalism and austerity are the constants of his typography; "graphic integration" is the effect that he aims to achieve.

"Maybe that's the weakness of my versatility, which I don't see myself – which somebody has to point out to me," concedes Schenk reluctantly, though qualities like these can hardly be constituted a weakness. "I don't believe in change for change's sake, but I think one should start from scratch, throw everything out when there is a new problem to solve."

In recent years, however, there have been rather fewer new problems to solve – at least of a design nature. What surprises most observers about Schenk's career is that he should have stayed at Haymarket for so long (although he only does three days a week and for a while it was down to two). He is certainly no admirer of trade journalists. Had he moved outside the narrow purview of the trade press back in the 1970s, his impact on mainstream publication design could have been much greater.

"I did have some spells outside on *Vogue* and *Marie France*," he says, "and I indulged in intellectual hobbies that took up more than 50 per cent of my time. This was an easy way to earn my living and I enjoyed easy-going relations here for a long time." He laughs

Management Today. Magazine spread. Art director: Roland Schenk. Photographer: Stuart Redler. Haymarket Publishing Group, Great Britain, March 1988

ironically. "I've never looked at it as a career – that's maybe a bad thing. In Germany, they have an expression *Privatgelehrter*, someone who carries on respectable studies on his own without being part of an academic system. I neglected my career possibly because of that."

But Schenk, who says he had read two-thirds of Nietzsche by the age of fourteen, is no dilettante. He has a degree in linguistic philosophy from the University of London, taken while he was art director on *Town* and early *Management Today*, and he followed this up with a diploma in computer science at Imperial College. He carries reader's tickets like other people carry credit cards. "I discovered the material they used for *The Holy Blood and the Holy Grail* two years before they wrote it," he claims. "It was a microfiche file in the Bibliothèque Nationale. I photocopied all the stuff. I had it all." The higher reaches of freemasonry are a speciality. For Schenk, one gathers, design simply isn't intellectual nourishment enough. "I'm one of those nutcases," he says, "who has got more or less equally weighted intellectual and aesthetic interests."

Creative satisfaction and a climate of cooperation and discussion therefore remain important to him. To foster this, Schenk has started his own consultancy with a former assistant at Haymarket, Stephen Cary. "I can't realise enough of my ideas within the framework of my job," he says; he would very possibly "die creatively" if he were to live solely on the opportunities presented by Haymarket. An exclusion clause in his contract with Haymarket will prevent him from designing marketing titles for other companies that would be in competition.

Schenk's most recent project, a redesign of the French advertising magazine *Création* – a chaotic cross between Haymarket's *Campaign* and *Direction* – for the publisher Stratégies, suggests that a rough ride could lie ahead of him. "They made so many errors I didn't want my name on it," he says of the September issue. "But it looks miles better than the crap they had before." Imperfect or not, there could be no mistaking the much clarified design for the work of anyone other than Schenk; it even has the same Franklin Gothic headlines, with key words accented in red, as the latest incarnation of *Management Today*. Schenk's next project for Stratégies is a *Marketing*-style news magazine called *Le Journal des Médias*. He spends several days a month in Paris.

With a fine sense of timing and irony, or maybe because he is just relaxed by the lunch, Schenk keeps his most unexpected revelation until the end of the interview. It suggests that his regrets might run deeper than he otherwise lets on. "One thing I haven't mentioned to you, if you are interested, is the biggest mistake in my career." That laugh again. "I once had the opportunity in the 1960s for [film producer] David Puttnam to become my agent. He proposed his services. I stupidly enough consulted Robert Heller [then editor of *Management Today*] and Heller said: 'Stay away from it, you're going to be exploited.' I think it was the stupidest thing I ever did."

But what does Schenk imagine might have resulted – surely not a career in the movies? "Well, I would be a self-supporting man, which I'm now trying to achieve. I find that compromising is quite a stressful experience – and my work involves a fair amount of compromise. The older I get the more difficult the process becomes."

You've been very frank, I tell him. "It's a bad habit," says Schenk. "If you are a Continental it's okay, but over here, it's very bad."

Blueprint, November 1988

MANIFESTO OF A RADICAL CONSERVATIVE
MODERN PAINTERS

Slumped in an armchair in his living room, the self-appointed scourge of the art establishment, and latterly of the design world, is not exactly the picture of truculence. On the eve of the launch of his new art quarterly, *Modern Painters*, Peter Fuller entertains visitors to his home in Bath with surly civility. Only the occasional irascible phrase hints at the vast and implacable depths of Fuller's scorn for the new orthodoxy: "post-structuralist, neo-Marxist drivel" ... "this thing called postmodernism" ... "everyone's whining on about postmodernism". They tumble, like depth charges waiting to go off, into the conversation.

It's only February and already Fuller has fallen out – cataclysmically – with his friend and mentor John Berger. On 29 January, *New Society* published a scathing attack in which Fuller accused Berger of being "ethically and intellectually dishonest" in his treatment of Kenneth Clark. Berger, Fuller claimed, had pillaged Clark's ideas for use in *Ways of Seeing* and elsewhere, while publicly writing him off. Moreover, the arguments that Berger presented as radical alternatives to bourgeois aesthetics have, in the 1980s, "turned out to be almost identical to the philistine attitudes to the arts espoused by Margaret Thatcher's government". Gilbert and George, Fuller argues, are the living embodiments of this trend.

Two weeks later *New Society* published Berger's devastatingly ironic "confession" to Fuller's charges. "I would like to pay tribute to the courage and patience of the modern sleuth who has unmasked me totally," Berger begins. By the end of the piece one can almost feel Fuller wilting under the onslaught. Recounting the tale, he certainly looks rattled: "Berger's reply was more like murder, I should say. Or attempted murder ... Outrageous lies!" Fuller goes on to stretch credibility by insisting that he had not been criticising Berger personally, just his influence on the armies of art students who have taken *Ways of Seeing* as gospel. Yet here he is accused by Berger of "treachery and worse"! Clearly the biter does not much like to be bitten.

What, one wonders, does Fuller expect? It's never the pieces he writes praising late Rothko and minor landscape painters that linger in the memory. Demolition jobs are his speciality. Scorched by his "vitriol and hate" (Fuller's own words, lightly used), his victims and scandalised onlookers are bound to fight back. *Time Out*'s art critic, Sarah Kent, responded to the arrival of *Modern Painters* with a counterblast so voluble – "pompously opinionated prose", "born-again sense of certainty" – that the publisher of *Time Out*, who also happens to be a backer of *Modern Painters*, felt obliged to tack a signed disclaimer on to the end of the article.

Fuller certainly dishes it out in the first issue of *Modern Painters*. Julian Schnabel, Gilbert and George, Francis Bacon, The Turner Prize, *Artscribe*, Nicholas Serota, Joanna

Drew and the Arts Council all take a battering – if not from the pen of Fuller himself, then from one of his like-minded contributors. The gang includes Robert Hughes, art critic of *Time*; former Arts Minister, Lord Gowrie; Brian Sewell, hatchet man for the *Evening Standard*; ex-secretary-general of the Arts Council, Sir Roy Shaw; and Roger Scruton, apologist of the New Right, who puts the boot into Gilbert and George.

Hughes one can understand (his piece is the most entertaining in the issue), but Scruton, in particular, seems a curious soul mate for Fuller, a sometime Marxist. "I've often said that I disagree with Scruton on politics, but there is a wide area of agreement on aesthetics," counters Fuller. "There was nothing in that article that I didn't personally agree with." Fair enough. To some observers, though, it still looks as though Fuller is playing into the enemy's hands.

More controversial still is *Modern Painters'* single-minded – some suggest myopic – concentration on British art. Fuller believes this is undergoing a "renaissance" at the moment. "There's a lot of critical neglect because the existing art magazines have felt it their duty for whatever reason to chase international art world fashion," says Fuller. "Only the tip of the iceberg of what's going on in British art gets covered." Asked for examples of what is going on, he points, predictably, to the public and critical interest generated by the Lucian Freud exhibition at the Hayward Gallery. Pressed for further examples, he mentions Therese Oulton and Dennis Creffield (both, like Freud, covered in his first issue) and "a host of others" who he doesn't specify. The theory is offered up more readily.

"One of the things that is happening in painting and sculpture is that people are beginning to ask: 'Can something be gained from returning to nature and developing some new imaginative view of the natural world?' – which may be a very complicated one, involving computers or whatever. It certainly isn't necessarily nostalgic. In that situation people come to see the British tradition as peculiarly valuable because it's always been one of the strengths of our painters and poets, and our culture as a whole, that we have this tradition of an imaginative, and at times romantic, response to the natural world. That is at the centre, I think, of why British art is beginning to matter again."

Fuller's themes are signalled – noisily – by his choice of title, which is at once contemporary-seeming and backward-looking. Like Ruskin, who he is writing a book on, Fuller will range widely. "Ruskin's *Modern Painters* is about everything under the sun. It's about architecture, religion, politics, crafts – it's all there." Fuller has already done his bit for conservation by reprinting the Prince of Wales's Mansion House speech. In future issues we can expect to see Roger Scruton on the Classical revival; a piece posing the vital question "Is there a modern Gothic?"; and an examination of the architectural ideas of Adrian Stokes. Fuller doesn't rule out the possibility of reviewing an exhibition like Nick Grimshaw's recent show at the RIBA, although he "can't guarantee that our review would be reverential". It's an odds-on certainty that it wouldn't be.

"I don't want you to get the idea that the magazine is narrow," Fuller confides. "As you saw in the first issue we allowed Matthew Collings [sacked editor of *Artscribe*], at the polar extreme of art publishing, to have his say. I've got people like Stephen Bayley, than whom you cannot get more modernist and high-tech, reviewing for me. But I think that they realise what they are doing when they agree to review for me, just as I used to when I wrote for ultra-modernist magazines."

Modern Painters is a magazine with a mission and certain aspects of that mission make considerable sense. The international art journals that Fuller despises are given to far too much navel-gazing. The editor of *Artforum*'s extraordinary statement, quoted by Sir Roy Shaw, that "quality is a dangerous word" does have disturbing implications. It should be possible, as Fuller argues, for artists, and those who write about them to address a wider public. Indeed, the commercial success of *Modern Painters*, which will attract at best only 4,000 "core" art world readers, depends on the assumption that a further 3,000–4,000 interested non-specialists can be persuaded to buy.

Whether Fuller's parochial views of art are an adequate response to the complexity of the international art scene is less certain. Reading Fuller's writings, which are never less than forceful and provoking, it is hard to escape the feeling that his dogmatism leads him, on too many occasions, to throw out the baby with the bath water. The art world according to Fuller permits no place for collage, mixed media, photography, performance, video or conceptual art. Fuller might relish "the collapse of modernism", yet its ideas are not, as he seems to believe, either intrinsically pernicious or wholly outworn.

Blueprint, April 1988

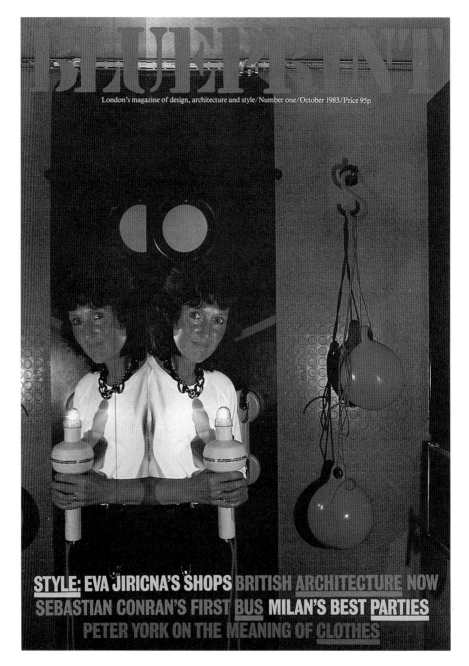

Blueprint. Cover of issue 1.
Editor: Deyan Sudjic. Art
director: Simon Esterson.
Photographer: Phil Sayer.
Wordsearch, Great Britain,
October 1983

LONDON'S BOOMING
BLUEPRINT

The first thing that strikes you, delving into the first issue of *Blueprint* a decade later, is its convivial, almost parochial tone. The magazine's world was much smaller then. The "moonlighters' cooperative" of journalists who launched it were by no means certain they would find an audience at all. *Blueprint* set out, modestly enough, to be "London's magazine of design, architecture and style" and its first issue reads as though it has been written by and for a small group of design insiders about a cast of characters the reader can be presumed to know well. There is Eleanor Murray, the "tall stalwart secretary of the grand Georgian Group", "debonair furniture designer" Rodney Kinsman, and Stephen Bayley, "dapper director" of the Boilerhouse.

Blueprint's aims, as laid out in its first editorial, seem equally modest in retrospect. The magazine hoped to "look at design without wanting to preach, talk about architecture without using gobbledegook, and to keep a sharp eye on styles and trends". It would profile the taste-makers and talk to designers and architects in a way that was happening in neither the professional nor lay media. It would be a medium for communicating ideas on buildings and artefacts: "what they look like, how they work, what they could be like and what they should be like."

Today's *Blueprint*, indeed the *Blueprint* I joined myself nearly six years ago, is there in embryo, and this consistency of growth is by no means as inevitable as it sounds. While most of its rivals continue to confine themselves to either design or architecture, *Blueprint* has always treated the two camps as one. It is a delicate balance – the perception that it is at root an architecture magazine remains strong among some readers (and non-readers) to this day – and you can see this tension in the first issue. The six features, on architecture, fashion, interiors, transport, furniture and taste, are genuinely varied. The publisher and editor were architects by training, however, and of the eight associate editors, seven specialised in architecture and only one, James Woudhuysen, exclusively in design. The news pages, too, have an architectural bias, confirmed by the inclusion of a "new readers start here" glossary of architectural "isms".

The architectural message is also, I would argue, a powerful function of *Blueprint*'s own design. In this sense, too, the first issue is a template for the rest. The eye-bruising all-cap headlines, the tough contrasts of picture and text, and the tidy framework of rules and boxes add up to the kind of graphics that architects like best: bold, forceful, precise, well engineered, cleanly articulated. It is revealing to compare the first *Blueprint* with the October 1983 issue of *The Face*. Neville Brody's stylised graphics date it almost to the year; *Blueprint*'s design by Simon Esterson is less time-bound, more objective and measured. It comes from a tradition of visual journalism that embraces *Town* and *Twen* in the 1960s, mid-1970s *Time Out* and *Blueprint*'s most obvious precursor, the New York design and architecture title *Skyline*, designed in 1978 by Massimo Vignelli. What it lost in contemporaneity, though, it gained in authority, and as the magazine developed it became clear that Esterson's structure allowed a use of photography that for sheer visual impact was virtually unbeatable.

Here the tabloid page size made all the difference. *Blueprint* was printed A3 from issues one to 21, after which it slimmed down. It used fewer pictures than other magazines, but it used them three times bigger. In the first issue, a towering shot by Phil Sayer of the Joseph store in Sloane Street sucks the reader down the staircase and into the shop. Ian Dobbie's grainy full-pager of Scott Crolla's Dover Street outpost is a richly detailed portrait of both the fashion designer and his interior.

But the format served another function. *Blueprint*'s very confidence and expansiveness helped to make the subject seem not just important, but heroic. It looked like the product of a boom even before, properly speaking, there was one; it didn't just embody the emerging mood, it helped to drive it along. The cover portrait and black and white personality shots were much cheaper to produce than full sets of colour transparencies of every tiny glowing detail of a project. But their real effect was to glamourise the designer, to transform him (less often her) into a cultural player. Now that designer types throng the ads and colour supps, it is easy to lose sight of just how fresh and original this seemed in 1983.

Yet it was an approach that always ran the risk of élitism. Despite the stated open-house policy, there is a feeling of incipient exclusiveness in the first issue which many still identify as a failing of the magazine. "We don't want just anybody coming through the door," says Zeev Aram of Designers' Saturday. "This is Design World Headquarters, and everybody who is anybody is here," says Deyan Sudjic in a piece on Milan. "Paul Smith is a simple little name for a person," notes Peter York (all the more devastating, this one, for not apparently being intended as a put-down).

This was the price you paid, though, for writing that was fluent, clear and jargon-free; but also, at its best, stylish, knowing and semiotically sharp: writing that assumed you had the references to keep up. Here is York again on the clothes of Scott Crolla: "the men square-cut, top-heavy glamour thugs, space cadets; the women tall, thin, but big-breasted Movie Queens. Tom of Finland meets Cobra Woman." Or rather more down to earth, but no less pointed, James Woudhuysen on the need for manufacturers to study the users of design: "*Woman* [magazine] has suggested that thousands of its readers make love on sofas and in the bath. Have upholstered furniture designers and designers of sanitaryware considered this? It seems unlikely."

Woudhuysen, one notes, is still saying much the same thing (about users, not sanitaryware) and well he might, because this was not the turning that design, or for that matter *Blueprint*, chose to take at this point. "What people do seem to want . . . is a touch of glamour to take their mind off things," wrote Maurice Cooper in the first issue's Eva Jiricna profile. "Nightclubs, limousines, cabaret and proper clothes are back." And at the end of 1983, in the first glimmerings of the design boom, when it was still possible for *Blueprint* to refer to Margaret Thatcher almost affectionately as "Mrs T", such a prospect felt like the most startling and welcome of novelties.

More than equal to the task, *Blueprint*'s correspondents wryly submitted themselves to a hectic round of restaurant openings, designer hotels, ritzy new shops and nightclubs, and jetset conferences with the powerbrokers of international architecture. I know. I was one. Showering colour on these seductive confections, the magazine forgot, perhaps, that it had also set out to show the bad alongside the good, but then, in truth, whatever the text might say, celebration is written into the very bones of its design. (Who in their right mind, after all, would use up a huge double-page spread to show junk?) *Blueprint*'s dilemma and challenge, at a time when personalities are widely deemed to be *passé*, and collective attention has turned, we are regularly assured, to the more vital subject of issues in design, is that it still looks like a monument built in praise of heroes. For its next 100 issues *Blueprint* needs a new direction, and speaking here as a reader, which is how I started out, I'm looking forward to the ride.

Blueprint, September 1993*

Starting From Zero

KEITH ROBERTSON

Zero

The will to eradicate the past with a new set of values and establish a new age is the Modernist mythology we inherit in the art books. The Modernists were political ideologues who rewrote history with a new brush. It was the Bauhaus groupies and Constructivists who designed a radical new workers' paradise and these movements helped create a new age; a future where the past would no longer be recycled because the new theory exposed the past as corrupt and outmoded. Theory was above all a belief that justified action. Theory WAS ideology. Starting from zero was not the obsession of the Dada anarchists nor the naive optimism of the Futurists. "Starting from zero" was the catch-phrase of one of the most influential, opinionated and ultimately conservative groups of architects and designers who were ideologically working out theories of functionalism in design. Here was design governed by an idea.

Much of the nineteenth century had to do with coming to terms with the Machine Age. John Ruskin and William Morris criticized nineteenth century British design and manufacture for their obsession with the materials of manufacture and utilitarianism. Reeling after the death and destruction of the First World War, it is not surprising that the next generation should take a harder line, apply the Modernist theory to their art, and be supermen creating a bold new future. They, after all, created the new Modernism and called it the "International Style" - it was international because it transcended the parochial national styles and traditions. It was the new art that expressed that which was universal in the world - the new technology of mass production and standardization. In the past, it had been claimed that the machine was used to express the foibles of fashion victims who chose historical motif for ornament. A truly utilitarian art, they argued, would be based on an accurate appraisal of mechanical production in order to develop the truest, purest mechanical aesthetic. Standardization and streamlining were the key to this approach.

Towards a new order

Walter Gropius is the best known ideologue of the International Style, but he was only one of a phalanx of artists espousing the new art. He promoted a new unity where architecture became the center. Here, the fine arts served the crafts, which furnished the building with all its fittings and ornament. Theo van Doesburg was an important theorist. Neo-plasticism was concerned with the hard-line geometric truth behind all human production - both artistic and industrial. El Lissitzky and Laszlo Moholy-Nagy were two of the major practitioners of the new Neo-plasticism or Constructivism. What they shared was the desire to transcend national styles, a response to a new technology through their art. Early in the Modern movement, these artists were still developing what can be identified as parochial styles. But their theory was well ahead of their practice. They were working towards a new order even through the anarchy of Dada and the concrete poets.

In 1928, which was early in the development of Modernism, the first major manifesto on modern design was published by Jan Tschichold, called *Die Neue Typographie*. As with most radical movements, the more extreme ideas emerged first only to be watered down in practice. In Tschichold's case, he was to become one of the finest classical designers, overturning nearly all of his early theories. His propaganda for the International Style, however, was to remain influential in Europe and even the USA long after the war.

Die Neue Typographie advocated a new approach to typographic design, because modern designers were working in a new age. Tschichold rejected the printed tradition from the position of style, however, not of function, which was the flaw in his early argument that he was himself later to identify. So what was the new typography according to Tschichold?

1. It was essentially simple and pure design in harmony with the modern world.
2. Asymmetry replaced symmetry because it was more functional, reflecting the more complex rhythms of the modern age.
3. Only sans serif typefaces were efficient communicators of modern information. Serifs were relegated to the historians' scrap heap.
4. Where greater emphasis was needed, he insisted on using different weights of type (e.g. bold, demi-bold, light) rather than different faces and even point sizes.

There was also emerging a new emphasis on "objective" and "scientific" approaches to the page grid - one planned less by tradition (the golden section) and more by mathematics. The mathematical grid can be most clearly identified in the early designs of Theo Ballmer. The radical beginnings of the Modern movement started with the mad fruit salads of point sizes and faces of Dada and the bold asymmetry of Tschichold, Bayer and Moholy-Nagy. Slowly, however, there was a formalization and ossification of the Modern movement, culminating in Switzerland after the war.

Helvetica Hel-

Emigre. Spread from issue 19.
Editor/designer: Rudy
VanderLans. Emigre Graphics,
USA, 1991

INTO THE DIGITAL REALM
EMIGRE

It's a peculiar convention of design publishing, and of the designer monograph in particular, that the commonest way of getting a book into print is to write it yourself. Perhaps, as a designer used to seeing and buying such books, and maybe even producing one of your own, you don't think this is so odd. Well, try substituting a name from some other area of culture. What would we think if the sole book about the novels of Ernest Hemingway, the paintings of Jackson Pollock, or the films of John Ford had been written, published, and even financed by the artists themselves?

It's a mark of the artist's essential seriousness and of public interest that other people initiate the book because they think your work is admirable, or damnable, but in some way significant. You, as *éminence grise*, grant the necessary access, interview time, and permissions, and then sit back, while other people do all the running, and bask in the critical glow. Of course, there are many subtle ways in which you can seek to influence this process, but your critics, if they have any integrity, will diplomatically resist these manoeuvres every step of the way. And besides, you are, or should be, bigger than that. You can have your say in your three-volume autobiography or the elegant production diary published to celebrate your eco-epic in the Amazon.

Books such as these represent clearly defined genres. They supplement the critical task without pretending to act as substitutes for it. Not so the designer monograph, which stands glossily alone, since there will rarely be a market for more than one monograph at a time on the same subject. It's an all-too-familiar pattern. The designer, relishing the chance to create the ultimate extension of his or her oeuvre, proposes the book; the publisher receives a heavily subsidised, ready-made self-panegyric; and graphic design criticism (assuming you believe we need it) advances not an inch.

With the publication of *Emigre: Graphic Design into the Digital Realm*, some of these problems are especially acute. For one thing, *Emigre* really matters. Whether you are passionately committed to it, militantly opposed, or just slightly bemused by all the fuss, there can be no denying that this fusion of magazine and typefoundry is one of the most significant phenomena in recent American graphic design. The debate about the future of graphic design and typography ignited within its pages has travelled to the farthest outposts of the profession, and the landscape would look very different without it.

An exceptional phenomenon cries out for analysis and a sense of its context. But this is not an analysis that the book – as an *Emigre* project and product – can possibly supply. Yet *Digital Realm* does appear to acknowledge the need for a more objective viewpoint and tone. Although the main text is written by Rudy VanderLans and Zuzana Licko (with one "Mary E. Gray"), about their own activities, it is narrated in the third person, giving the illusion if not the substance of external authority. Using

"I" and "we" and possibly assigning separate texts to each writer would not have supplied the missing perspective, but it might have led the writing toward a more personal and anecdotal style.

It would also have presented a structural problem (hence, perhaps, the decision to write as they did), since *Digital Realm* features a series of first-person extracts from writings and lectures by VanderLans and Licko. Addressing such themes as Aims, Criticisms, Conventions, and Change, these are by far the most engaging and revealing parts of the book. VanderLans's dissection of the external forces – advertisers, printers, distributors, and even the post office – that conspire to restrict the format of most American magazines to a narrow range of unimaginative norms is particularly pointed. "It is easy to ignore all of these restrictions," he notes, "but it will always end up costing you money." In this case, eventually, it paid off. One of the main reasons *Emigre* has survived and prospered is because they took the decision to distribute it themselves.

Such discussion of editorial policy as there is is embedded in these small-print quotations. Can *Emigre*'s policy really be as freewheeling and unexamined as VanderLans – who did not officially appoint himself editor until issue 16 – makes it sound? *Emigre* sets out to show work overlooked by the "major design magazines and design competitions" with the aim of providing a "more complete picture of the state of graphic design". But surely he can't mean it when he says, "There is no rhyme or reason in our selection process."

VanderLans gives his contributors a free rein and work is never rejected on aesthetic grounds. This makes the magazine exciting and unpredictable; it also makes it tremendously variable. There are excellent issues that open up territory for debate that other magazines have barely even noticed (I would nominate 15, 17 and 19, to name but three); and there are others that are disjointed, indulgent, or wildly overstate the case (a whole issue, for instance, given over to a young British designer right at the start of his career). These issues might have been stronger if VanderLans did not take the limiting view that to edit is in some way to interfere with and compromise the material. What about the idea that editing – both textual and visual – is about helping to focus the material and ensuring that the parts mesh together coherently?

Regrettably, some of this uncertainty of purpose found its way into the book. In the acknowledgements, the designers note how the publisher accepted practically everything they submitted without making any changes. "Had we known this beforehand," they write, "this book would have looked quite different." This is passed off as a joke, but the suggestion of self-repression has the ring of truth since the design is not at all what you would expect from a team which has challenged, rejected and constructively refashioned the conventions of magazine typography and page layout with every new step. In its typography and organisation, the book is suprisingly conventional and static. The typographic specifications of the various text elements are constant, even down to placement on the page, and there are no attempts at visual interpretation, emphasis, or even plain whimsy. The pages are clear, accessible and easy to read – virtues all – but they lack the engaging freedoms and restless, let's-try-something-new intelligence of the magazine, which at its best gives us both.

VanderLans and Licko's book does, in fact, carry a one-page commentary by a voice from outside, though *Emigre* contributor and typeface designer Jeffery Keedy is not the most impartial of witnesses. Its title, "Graphic Designers Probably Won't Read This . . . But," embodies all the ambivalence and hesitancy that surrounds graphic design publishing projects like this. No one seems entirely sure what the books are for, beyond celebrating the oeuvre, and even the authors have their doubts that anyone is reading.

Richly illustrated, *Emigre: Graphic Design into the Digital Realm* is a worthy enough companion for *The Graphic Language of Neville Brody* or April Greiman's *Hybrid Imagery*, books that were also initiated and/or assembled by the designers. But at this point in the discipline's development, I would argue, these are not really what we need. Graphic design will not become a significant area for cultural criticism until graphic designers surrender their work to the kind of critical appraisal given to art, architecture, literature, or film, until properly independent studies are published as a matter of course, and until designers show their commitment to the growth of such criticism by buying the books.

AIGA Journal of Graphic Design, vol. 12 no. 1, 1994/*Eye*, no. 12 vol. 3, 1994*

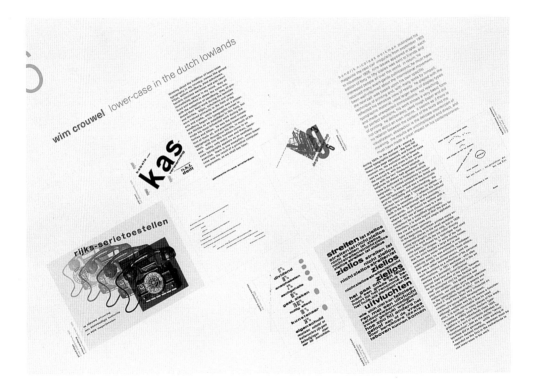

Octavo. Spread from issue 5.
Editors/designers: Simon
Johnston, Mark Holt, Michael
Burke, Hamish Muir, 8vo. Eight
Five Zero, Great Britain, 1988

IS ANYBODY OUT THERE READING?
OCTAVO

One of the features of *Octavo* magazine that made it so appealing to anyone who encountered the first issue, published in the summer of 1986, was the finite nature of the enterprise. Its publishers, the London design company 8vo, planned to produce just eight issues of their sixteen-page journal of typography, at a rate of one every six months. By the end of 1989, the mission would be complete and *Octavo* would dissolve.

If such a schedule suggested seriousness of purpose and a precise agenda of ideas, this was more than confirmed by the early issues. Two members of the team had studied with Wolfgang Weingart in Basel and *Octavo* had a high-mindedness and purity that set it apart intellectually and aesthetically from both the commercial and "style" wings of contemporary British graphics. *Octavo* was sternly opposed to typographic mediocrity, nostalgia, fashion, decoration, symmetry, centred type and the hated serif. It was for a semantically determined use of structure and the infinite possibilities of typographic experimentation. "We take an international, modernist stance," the first editorial concluded. "This is necessary in England."

The first three issues fall into a natural trilogy: the white issues. There is a beautifully sure sense of exposition to the page designs and, in articles on Anthony Froshaug, Ian Hamilton Finlay and Geoff White, great care in the matching of pictures to text. The format changes from issue to issue, but the designers' hands working the levers of the grids are relatively unseen.

Judged as magazines, these issues (and perhaps issue 5 on lowercase) remain the most conceptually rounded and interesting. It has taken three years longer than originally planned to complete the series, but despite the time lag the magazine has not really developed. Most significantly, it has not engaged critically with new developments in typography (digital or otherwise), or with the challenge to modernist assumptions such work poses. *Octavo*'s heroes, even when they are still alive and working, are all figures from an earlier phase of typographic thinking – Weingart, Greiman, Willi Kunz – selected for their conformance to 8vo's modernist ideals. Not until its article on Philippe Apeloig in issue 7 (1990) did *Octavo* venture into less familiar territory, though even Apeloig, whose work permits a high degree of distinctly frivolous non-structural decoration, has clear links to modernism.

This is not to say that 8vo should like postmodernist developments. Quite possibly they detest them, but by ignoring work from what, for the sake of shorthand, we might call the *Emigre* school the magazine has cut itself off from the main lines of Euro-American debate. A modernist rebuttal of *Emigre*'s position would certainly have been possible, perhaps desirable, but *Octavo* has not attempted this. Yet strangely, while it fails to analyse deconstructionist tendencies that one might have supposed would be anathema to it, it displays them like symptoms in its own electronically generated pages.

All too often in the later issues, the structural conceits overwhelm the content. *Octavo* was heading this way by issue 5, where the grid is rotated so that everything – headlines, pictures, text – reads on the slant. In issue 6, an editorial on visual pollution is buried alive under slabs of backwards-reading type. In issue 7, bright yellow grids like gingham tablecloths swamp the pages, while picture captions are given as grid references which must be looked up at the back.

By this stage there is a feeling of aesthetic surfeit and exhaustion about *Octavo*, especially when compared with the confidence and clarity of its debut. For the first time production quality becomes an end in itself. Five pages of issue 6 are given over to embossed car number plates, an idea that would have occupied only one or two pages at the start. There is an inescapable sense that the editors doubt whether anyone is reading and have stopped trying to ensure that they do. They give us tiny type, dauntingly wide measures, a chronology tipped unusably on its side. In issue 7, these doubts are declared. "Most people who buy *Octavo* do not read it," writes Bridget Wilkins in the magazine's most notorious experiment, a brief essay on "Type and Image" shattered into several dozen impenetrable word-bites.

As it turned out, this spread proved to be more prophetic than it knew. The final issue, published at the end of 1992, takes the form of a CD-ROM on the theme of multimedia and the future of non-linear communication. It is a move both brave and frustrating, which denies *Octavo* physical unity as a set of objects and robs it of a proper sense of ending, while undeniably opening up an important new topic for discussion (for the minority of readers with the drive to play it on at this point). For its long-awaited final act, *Octavo* has ceased to be a journal of record and become the manifesto it always threatened to be. In my view it is a mistake. Imagine the book dealers selling second-hand copies in twenty years' time: issue 8 will be the not-quite-*Octavo* and nine times out of ten, I would guess, the missing part of the set.

For me, the editors had it about right in issue 1 when they quoted Jan Tschichold: "Simplicity of form is never a poverty, it is a great virtue." Somehow, in the seven years it has taken them to complete this audacious and memorable project, it is a truism they slowly forgot.

Eye, no. 9 vol. 3, 1993

GRAPHIC WEAPONS
RAY GUN

I came across *Ray Gun* a couple of hours after arriving in New York. The first issue had only just hit the newsstands, but over the next few days it seemed that every other graphic designer I ran into had seen a copy. The magazine was a talking point and it was already travelling at speed along the graphic design grapevine.

Ray Gun, I had better explain, is the latest project from the team that brought you *Beach Culture*. Beach – what? Well might you ask. This paean to avant-garde surfing lasted only a handful of issues before it was sucked back out by the tide. In design terms, though, it made more of a splash, in the US at least, than any other youth culture magazine since *The Face*. In America the awards rolled in like the ultimate wave. Its designer, David Carson, became a star.

Does any of this matter? It matters because *Beach Culture* and now *Ray Gun* exemplify everything that an older generation of graphic designers in the US, and less vociferously in Britain, thinks is currently wrong with graphic design – and everything that an impressionable younger generation finds influential and exciting. *Ray Gun*'s tagline, "(the bible of) music + style", might seem to date it c. 1982, but its graphic treatments are typical 1990s mayhem: fractured layouts, strange mutant letterforms, and an assumption that the reader will be prepared to meet its complexities more than half-way.

It's the kind of design that Massimo Vignelli, high priest of New York modernism, might anathematise as "disgraceful", "garbage", or an "aberration of culture". Actually he hasn't (it's hard to imagine him even noticing *Ray Gun*, let alone buying a copy), but he did publicly use the very same words about another experimental magazine, *Emigre*. No less a figure than Paul Rand has also been getting incensed. In *Design, Form and Chaos*, a book-in-progress which has already been excerpted in Britain and in the US, he thunders: "The absence of restraint, the equation of simplicity with shallowness, complexity with depth of understanding, and obscurity with innovation, distinguishes the work of these times."

Leaving aside the rights and wrongs of all this for a moment, such outbursts from the established heroes of graphic design make it clear that a profound shift is taking place – and the great names know it. It has been under way for at least a decade, but it is only recently, in these public attacks on younger designers, that the full bitterness of the situation has become apparent. After brilliant careers, during which their genius went unquestioned, the greats now find themselves on the defensive. People are daring to suggest – often no more than implicitly through the kind of work they do – that these earlier approaches no longer look right for the times. And it hurts.

The battlegrounds on which these struggles are most overtly waged are the design awards. In *Print* magazine (the source of his other remarks) Massimo Vignelli recalled his experiences on an American jury: "I was in the minority all the time. These two girls [sic] turned down Paul Rand, Milton Glaser, Seymour Chwast." In recent years, D&AD juries have been the site of similar generation-gap conflicts.

It is the American recession, though, that has really brought things to a head. There are too many graphic designers chasing too little work. On a visit to Milton Glaser's 32nd Street studio, I saw empty desks and boards. The jobs are going to one-person-and-a-computer outfits who can work on the cheap. The market is glutted with new graduates, fees have taken a nose-dive and standards are on the slide. In such desperate circumstances, designers with 30, 40 or more years invested in their art can perhaps be forgiven for talking as though the barbarians were at the gate. But are they right to denounce work that ranks, at its best, as some of the most interesting and timely now being done?

One thread that runs through all their rhetoric is a tendency to invoke a single, idealised, unitary past. Back in London, Marcello Minale told me what was wrong with graphic design was that there were no universally observed "rules" any more, as there had been, supposedly, when his company started out in the 1960s. He didn't explain what these rules were, but he did say that the 1980s had seen a succession of "false messiahs" – he named Neville Brody and Memphis – who had led their followers astray. What we need now, Minale said, is a new messiah to bring us a new set of rules (presumably much the same as the old ones we lost).

Here, and in the complaints of Vignelli, Rand and others, you can't avoid sensing an almost nostalgic longing for a set of certainties (in an ephemeral medium of all places!) that society itself can no longer provide. The old guard talk as though graphic designers on their own could somehow slay the dragon of postmodernism – for this is what they really mean – and turn back the clock. But young designers, like artists, or writers, or politicians, are shaped by their times. Their role is to interpret. If a magazine like *Ray Gun* panders to the cult of personality, embodies extreme subjectivity of viewpoint, and reflects an obsession with surface and a suspicion of determinate readings, and even of the validity of the message or product itself – and does all this with the utmost brio, invention and wit – it's because these are symptoms of the culture we are obliged to inhabit. This, and not their younger colleagues, is what graphic design's old guard should be tilting at, though it is unlikely to do any good.

Blueprint, December/January 1993*

PAGANINI UNPLUGGED
DAVID CARSON

With the publication of his book, *The End of Print*, David Carson attained a level of personal celebrity and influence that many designers will dream about, but only the rarest will achieve. Constantly on the move between lectures and workshops all over the world, rarely out of the design magazines, and increasingly the subject of wide media interest in glossy magazines and on television, Carson is now, unquestionably, the most famous graphic designer to have emerged in the 1990s.

In his laid-back, genial way, he has shown a talent for putting himself about that verges on genius. Everyone you talk to about him singles out his knack for publicity in tones close to awe. "He can promote himself like nobody else I've ever met," says *Emigre* magazine editor Rudy VanderLans, no slouch himself in the promotions department. Acutely sensitive to criticism and hungry – even by design business standards – for awards and acclaim, Carson is the most advanced model to date of a comparatively recent invention: the graphic designer as pop star. In his work, attitude and wanderlust he is, in the words of his New York collaborator Mike Jurkovac, a "rock and roll typographer".

Carson's résumé unfolds in a series of exemplary subcultural moves. In the late 1970s, he was a pro surfer, achieving a top ranking of eighth in the world. After four years as part-time designer at the "glorified fanzine" *Transworld Skateboarding* (by day he taught high school sociology) and a brief interlude at *Musician*, he caught the wave in 1989 as art director of the thinking sand jock's surfing magazine, *Beach Culture*. Six little-seen issues and some 150 relentlessly press-released design awards later, Carson was firmly established among colleagues as the 1990s art director most likely to succeed. *Ray Gun*, Marvin Scott Jarrett's "alternative" music magazine, launched in November 1992, became Carson's most visible platform to date and won him a following among disaffected young designers the world over.

Along the way Carson has made some important friends. For David Byrne, who wrote the foreword to *The End of Print*, Carson's work "communicates on a level that bypasses the logical, rational centres of the brain and goes straight to the part that understands without thinking". Albert Watson, who agreed to Carson's type-only front cover for his photography book, *Cyclops*, is equally certain of his status as a fellow artist. They have already collaborated on a number of advertising projects, including a Superbowl spot for Budweiser, and more are planned through two newly launched companies – David Carson Design (partners Carson and Jurkovac) and Cyclops Productions (partners Jurkovac and Watson) – sharing the same building and floor in New York's Flatiron district. Jurkovac says roughly half of Carson's time will be spent in the city.

Carson resists any suggestion that he consciously sets out to appeal to Generation

X-ers, but whatever the intention, his way with youth codes is manna for American advertisers. "David has tapped into an area of communication that a lot of people have been trying to figure out," explains Jurkovac, formerly of the ad agency Foote, Cone & Belding. "Younger America, people who are looking at multiple options and choices, or different ways of interpreting things from past generations – the MTV-quick-cut-barraged-by-information-all-at-the-same-time society." With projects in his portfolio for such high-profile companies as Nike, Pepsi, Levi's, Vans, Citibank, and American Express, Carson is already a significant ad-world player. His growing ambition to do work for television and his New York support system mean he is poised to get even bigger.

For anyone who has followed the development of experimental design over the last ten or more years, David Carson is a fascinating – and pivotal – figure. He has produced some of the most striking and era-defining designs of the decade. I once flew from London to Philadelphia to debate the "new typography" with him at an AIGA evening event and had looked forward to talking to him again with a view to writing about his work in depth. I had many questions – questions that have still, even with the publication of his book, not been fully addressed. But Carson declined on three separate occasions to be interviewed for this article. He doesn't like the few things I have written about him previously and he didn't think this would be an "objective" piece. "I think you are going to put your own spin on the thing regardless of my input," he told me. It seemed a slightly curious objection coming from a designer who has often stressed the personal and emotional nature of his design method and has urged other designers to do the same.

One of the most striking aspects of *The End of Print* is its unabashed attempt to uproot Carson from the surrounding terrain and, in the process, rewrite recent history. Carson, the British edition's jacket blurb claims, has "single-handedly changed the course of graphic design". Given that the book has been produced with Carson's full cooperation – his design for it uses a battery of *Ray Gun*-esque type treatments – this presumably represents the designer's current view of himself. The text by Lewis Blackwell, editor of the British magazine *Creative Review*, lionises him as a transcendent originator whose work somehow eludes the theoretical frameworks and categorical definitions that, according to Blackwell, bedevil and constrain other less popular forms of experimental design. It is misleading, Blackwell writes, to associate Carson with the "deconstruction" graphics of Cranbrook. At one point, in an interview, he raises the question of Cranbrook and CalArts. "The focus of my work has become quite dissimilar in theory and practice to those schools," replies Carson. "Perhaps in some of the small regular sections of *Ray Gun*, which are often done by an intern, the content is not explored as much and there is more of a style at work."

When I spoke to some of Carson's colleagues about the issue of influences, I received reactions ranging from wry amusement to fierce resentment. The more positive are glad to see their ideas vindicated by Carson's commercial success. Educators such as Lorraine Wild of CalArts have staked their reputations on the belief that the controversial experiments of the academy might some day find a home in the mainstream. "I think it needs to be stated," says Wild, "that it was accomplishment enough for him to figure out that [experimental] work was quite valuable and of interest." Barry Deck, who supplied Carson with prerelease versions of his typefaces for use in *Surfer* magazine

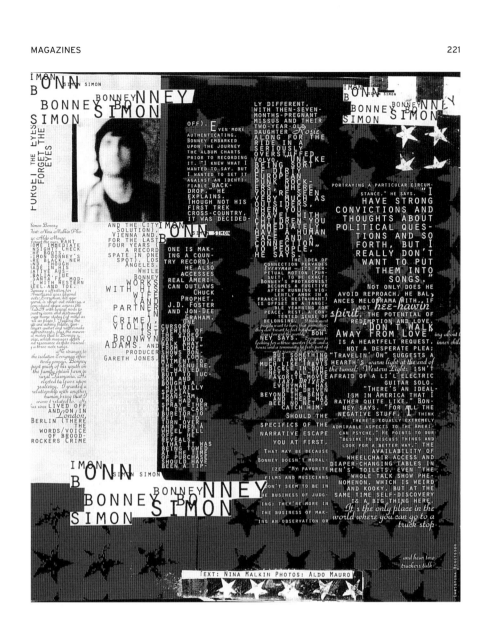

Ray Gun. Page from issue 24.
Editor: Marvin Scott Jarrett.
Art director: David Carson.
Ray Gun Publishing, USA,
March 1995

and *Ray Gun*, is more critical: "I think he's taken almost everything he does from the CalArts/Cranbrook community and sort of ripped out the heart – that is, de-ideologised it completely and delivered it to the masses."

While this is clearly a matter of personal interpretation, what can be said with certainty is that from *Beach Culture* onwards Carson's path has intersected with the experimental design community at many points. Christopher Vice, a graduate of North Carolina State University, designed a fragmented contents page for issue two of *Beach Culture* that inspired Carson (according to an article he wrote for *How* magazine) to go even further in his own dismantling of a next-issue announcement page. Many of the typefaces that were vital to *Ray Gun*'s abrasive texture and reader appeal were designed by students and alumni such as Deck and Susan LaPorte of CalArts, and Lisa Vorhees, Brian Schorn, David Shields and P. Scott Makela of Cranbrook. The names are listed in the front, but exactly who did what is not made clear to the annoyance of some. "He got so famous for work that included some of my work," says Deck, "that when people look at my work they sometimes think of him."

Many of *Ray Gun*'s single pages and later, as the magazine developed, whole spreads were the work of interns such as Cranbrook graduate Martin Venezky. A detail from a poster by CalArts professor Ed Fella was used as *Ray Gun*'s masthead. Carson seemed happy enough two or three years ago to acknowledge these connections. "Overall, the most interesting work, writing, and attitude I've seen from a grad school in the past year has come from Cranbrook," he told Rudy VanderLans in a notoriously prickly *Emigre* interview. "... And CalArts has such an amazing pool of talent..." He went on to say that he had spent three days at Cranbrook, giving a lecture and sitting in on critiques, and had considered going there himself.

For Ed Fella, who hand-lettered a page for *The End of Print*, Carson is best understood as "the Paganini of typographers". "Maybe Carson is the most virtuoso player of this kind of stuff," he explains. "The truth is, of course, he doesn't invent it all. He's not the Beethoven or the Mozart. He's the performer of these ideas that come from other sources." Some of the ideas that Carson presents as *aperçus* go back decades. Quite apart from the century-old artistic tradition of the found object or image, his use of the street for design inspiration has a recent Anglo-American lineage that stretches from Robert Brownjohn's early 1960s photographs of street typography to the well-documented vernacular reworkings of the 1980s. Similarly, the anti-design that he has built a career on was explicit in 1970s punk graphics, aggressively applied by the Dutch provocateurs Hard Werken in the early 1980s, theorised a few years later at Cranbrook, and brilliantly explored by Fella before *Beach Culture* was so much as a distant wave in its publisher's eye. This is not to invalidate such ideas in Carson's output, or to deny that he "performs" them with panache; it is simply to reintroduce a sense of context missing from much of the press and *The End of Print*.

Everyone I spoke to felt that Carson's real gift was for synthesis. "He's a great art director," says Rudy VanderLans. "He knows where to get the good talent. He has an incredible eye for what is hip, for what is cool, for what is current." As a designer, though – particularly of text – Carson has a more limited toolbox. While his opening spreads for *Ray Gun* can be stunningly unexpected and painterly patchworks of illustration, photography, splotches of broken type and scintillating rushes of white space, his treatment of the story that follows the initial flourish has rarely – even on its own idiosyncratic terms – been as convincingly resolved. "For the most part his designs are based on shock value," agrees VanderLans. "David is constantly thumbing his nose at typographic convention. For someone who's considered such a design wunderkind, it's disappointing there's been so little progress towards something a bit more challenging."

Even to the most casual reader of *Ray Gun* it will be obvious that Carson has enjoyed exceptional freedom. I learned exactly how much freedom when I caught up with the magazine's founder and publisher, Marvin Scott Jarrett, on a visit to London, where he lectured to the Typographic Circle. Jarrett clearly has enormous regard for Carson's talents; at the talk he calls him a "genius". But there is an undercurrent to what Jarrett tells me at his hotel that only makes sense some weeks later when he confirms that following a disagreement over the cover of the October issue he has let Carson go.

Carson and Jarrett have always worked at a distance – Carson in San Diego, Jarrett in LA – with few meetings, "not even once an issue," according to Jarrett. He and *Ray Gun*'s executive editor, Randy Bookasta, supplied Carson with edited copy on disk and most of the photography; Carson commissioned some of the photography and all of the illustration. From then on he was completely on his own. The editorial office did not insist on page proofs. Often Jarrett would not even see the magazine, except for the cover, until it was printed.

Magazines are by their nature team creations. Their best moments are often forged in the close collaboration between editors and designers. The unusual circumstances of *Ray Gun*'s production, with Carson's "interpretations" arriving as a *fait accompli*, meant these interactions could not occur. There could be no discussion, response, refinement, or rethinking. It was already clear, during our London conversation, that Jarrett missed this involvement; his other magazines, *Bikini* and *huH*, are produced in-house.

Does he now believe, following Carson's departure, that the previous arrangements represented – as some design world observers committed to graphic authorship might have hoped – a viable model for magazine publishing? "It was certainly an interesting test," Jarrett says. "It worked for me for a while, but then it just started to get old." What he now wants to achieve with *Ray Gun* is a "creative energy" between editors and designers. Portland design team Johnson & Wolverton have designed issue 31, with Bookasta working alongside them in their studio. "I am still giving my art directors more creative freedom than any other publisher on the planet," claims Jarrett, "and I'm a tremendous fan of great graphic design. But there comes a time when you've just got to say, 'Hey, wait a minute. This is a case of the tail wagging the dog.'"

Whatever its long-term viability, *Ray Gun*'s first incarnation has been a notable success. The magazine has a readership of 150,000 and rising, and you only have to scan its letter pages – "*Ray Gun* is me!" – to see how it thrills its young audience. Yet beyond offering a sophisticated outlet for ordinary teenage rebellion, what does *Ray Gun*'s much-vaunted visual "radicalism" actually stand for? "We still believe that music and the people who make it can change the world," spiels a 1960s-sounding paean to rock and roll in issue 1. Written by former *Beach Culture* editor Neil Feineman, who lasted four issues as *Ray Gun*'s editorial director, this is clearly not Carson's view. "Graphic design will save the world right after rock and roll does," he observes ironically in *The End of Print*. It doesn't appear to be Jarrett's view either.

Jarrett told his Typographic Circle audience that he and Carson were non-conformists and anti-authority. But when I ask him later what exactly he is rebelling against, he answers – as Carson tends to answer such questions – in purely inward-looking professional terms: "I'm rebelling against traditional publishing, constantly being challenged by my magazine distributors and consultants telling me I'm doing the wrong thing."

Feineman says that his own conception of *Ray Gun* – as with *Beach Culture* – "was all about giving disenfranchised people in the arts a voice". Still loyal to Carson, he seems wholly disenchanted with the magazine's routine music-biz content as it has developed. "What is amazing is that David has taken such standard fodder and at least put a new graphic spin on it," he says. "I can't think that without David, or at least somebody of David's ilk, that magazine would have lasted as long as it has, because it's certainly not worth reading." Carson himself expressed a similar point of view a little more diplomatically in an interview on British television: "I firmly believe if you had done *Ray Gun* traditionally it wouldn't have survived. It's not that unique in the writing and it's a pretty narrow scope – a lot of of band bios and things."

From the time of his earliest interviews, Carson has always insisted that his design approach is "conceptual". In other words, beneath the agitated surface lies a problem-solving response to the content of an article based on his close reading of the text: there is an explainable reason for what you see on the page. His famous "Surfing blind" spread in *Beach Culture* – two pages of solid black, with only the headline for text – is a quintessential "big idea". What is genuinely remarkable, and a credit to Feineman's vision too, is that Carson was able to realise such an idea, and others just as memorable, without compromise in the pages of a magazine; many editors would have balked.

Ray Gun, though, is less clear-cut. If Carson's later method really was a "conceptual" response to the editorial content, it would have been enlightening to learn from his book about the concepts behind familar spreads. But when it comes to the inside story, *The End of Print* doesn't get much hotter than such lukewarm revelations as: "The attitude of this design involves a quiet laugh at optimum line length." Perhaps David Byrne comes closer to the essence of Carson's *Ray Gun* work when he talks about a form of "understanding without thinking" and likens the design's communicational effects to music.

Carson says in the book that as well as being a graphic designer, he considers himself an artist; the ultimate source of a designer's work, he once suggested, must come from within. "I set out to do things in an emotional way. When I turn to a page in a book, to a magazine, to any graphic design, I want an emotional reaction. That's probably the basis for how I judge it." Artists, of course, are under no obligation to explain what they do.

Seen in this way, Carson's huge appeal to advertisers makes perfect sense. For a designer without ideological baggage, pursuing a path of design for design's sake, it is the obvious next step. Advertising targets the emotions. It bypasses the logical centres of the brain. It has no critical relationship to its own content (though as a strategy it sometimes pretends to). Mike Jurkovac worked with Carson on the launch of L2 worker jeans for Levi Strauss: "David came back to us with a phenomenal packaging programme that really helped reposition the brand. It was to appeal to the same target that David's *Ray Gun* magazine appeals to; the work he did was like a Rorschach collage. When we did the testing on it, the kids were saying this is exactly how I feel in terms of life."

Does Carson's work (and other work like it) herald some fundamental typographic shift in the way not just youth subcultures but all of us will soon be communicating? Jurkovac is sure that it does. He points to the usual technological factors, the Internet

and 500-channel TV. "If you are going to try to do marketing or communication, you
have to take that into account." Carson himself has often explained his typographic
operations in terms of a changing audience: "You can't give an eighteen-year-old a page
of solid grey type and expect him or her to read it." Yet any magazine worth its salt, for
any age group, proceeds from the starting point that unrelieved grey type looks dull,
that pages should be lively and varied, and that the uncommitted browser will need to
be seduced into reading. It's a gigantic conceptual and cultural leap from here to tangled
columns, mutilated type, and Carson's empirically untested claim in the *New York Times*
that making readers work to decipher text may mean they remember more of what they
read. It is certainly clear from *Ray Gun*'s letters that many of its readers do find it heavy
going, or even impossible to read on occasion. That is what they say they like about it.
As one of *Ray Gun*'s writers observed in a recent issue: "Just by opening this very
magazine, you've gained admittance to an exclusive club."

New York-based designer Bill Drenttel – well known for his commitment to
publishing and literature, and a *Ray Gun* admirer – speaks for many Carson watchers
when he suggests that the "eighteen-year-old reader" argument is cynical. "I'm not sure
I buy that. I don't think reading is a lost cause. Employing alternative strategies of
engaging people is great, but that doesn't necessarily lead to the conclusion that those
are the only strategies. Or that people won't read if you don't engage in strategies that
are only about new typography, as defined by people like David."

Excitingly iconoclastic as it seemed for a time, car-crash typography is now
everywhere. Jarrett is bored with it. Some of *Ray Gun*'s letter-writers are bored with
it. Carson may well be bored with it, too. Before his exit cut short any plans he might
have had, he had been talking about redesigning *Ray Gun* for more than a year. During
his London lecture, Jarrett refers to something he calls "the new simplicity". Issue 28
contained a story on Neil Young consisting – perhaps it was a joke – of tall columns
of solid grey type. With issue 29, Carson trashed the retinue of grunge-font suppliers
for just three contributing typeface designers and some low-key, largely sanserif fonts
arranged in orderly rows.

The End of Print, on the other hand, is very much in his established, convention-
busting style – a style which, despite the surprise value of seeing it within the
traditionally more reserved pages of a book, is beginning to look distinctly tired.
Is Carson, as Rudy VanderLans suggests, a "one-trick pony", whose lack of formal
education in typography will limit what he can accomplish, or does he have the
natural ability – the "genius" as some see it – to reinvent himself and retain his
vanguard position? The new simplicity? The new something else? Or more of the
same? All eyes are on him and it's his move.

I.D., November 1995*

^{6.} OLD MEDIA/ NEW MEDIA

A CURE FOR INFORMATION ANXIETY
RICHARD SAUL WURMAN

Richard Saul Wurman has been called the data doctor, the architect of information and the Barnum of the design and architectural world, but to himself he's "Johnny One-note". This isn't false modesty on the part of an architect and graphic designer who has established one of the most remarkable publishing operations in the US – Wurman is far too sure of himself for that. It's an honest admission of the essential simplicity and consistency of his message. Whatever project Wurman tackles, his aim is always the same. He wants to convert the "catastrophic" quantities of data that confront us every day into the tools of understanding.

Wurman's way of going about this is nothing if not audacious. Far from trying to present himself as an expert, he makes a point of coming clean and admitting his ignorance. He is a waiting sponge, he says, a blank slate. "It's not my ability to do things, but my desire to figure out how to do them that I sell, therefore I have an unlimited repertoire." Wurman produced his first Access Press guidebook to Los Angeles because he was new in town and couldn't find his way around. *Medical Access*, an illustrated guide to diagnostic tests and surgical procedures, came about when he was going to have a physical and didn't know what questions to ask. And 1989's *USAtlas* – "the smartest distance between two points" – was a response to the frustration he felt with existing road maps. In each case, Wurman's lack of preconceptions, his rare ability to stand in as designer for the typical reader, has led to publications of exceptional clarity.

Wurman studied under Louis Kahn at the University of Pennsylvania and practised as an architect for thirteen years. Kahn – "he was the youngest person I ever knew" – remains his great mentor. Wurman put together his first book, *Cities: A Comparison of Form and Scale*, at 26 and followed it with a stream of self-published projects in which he taught himself the skills of statistics, cartography and graphic design. He began Access Press in 1982 by selling books out of his own garage. Today, he has about 60 staff spread between the offices of The Understanding Business and Access Press in San Francisco and New York, but the atmosphere of his studio on SoHo's Wooster Street still suggests a cottage industry. Wurman receives visitors in a boarded loft dotted with big leather armchairs and cardboard tables designed by himself and Frank Gehry, which are covered with animal skulls and alabaster objects. It's the playpen, complete with paintings and a grand piano, of a self-styled intellectual hedonist and Wurman lives up to the part in sweat pants, training shoes and an open-necked shirt. Even if you are president of Pacific Bell, for whom Wurman redesigned the California yellow pages, this is how you would find him.

The architect of information likes to play down the scale of his activities and the scope of his influence. "I have no power base," he will say, "I'm not dean of a school,

I'm not head of a corporation … I'm just a little guy. When I'm in the bathroom, the place is closed." It's Wurman's way of making you understand that he is an independent, a maverick. He doesn't solicit the billion dollar clients – they come to him, or at least they have done since they found time in their overloaded schedules to read *Information Anxiety*, the book that has transformed Wurman from being a highly respected but not particularly famous designer into a best-selling self-help guru for the information age. Once it was colleagues such as Lou Dorfsman and Ivan Chermayeff who made the case for Wurman in the pages of *Graphis*; now he gets testimonials from John Sculley of Apple and Nicholas Negroponte of the Media Lab at MIT.

But there are also dissenters. It has always been legitimate to ask of Wurman: does the understanding problem he describes really exist? His reply was his books, and the books have consistently demonstrated that large quantities of information can be made more accessible and entertaining than we are accustomed to expect. Try going back to crusty old Baedeker after using one of Wurman's streetwise city guides. The traditional alphabetical organisation makes no sense next to Wurman's decision to arrange colour-coded entries by location, so that readers can see at a glance the museums, shops and restaurants in a particular area. Wurman's approach is grounded in the way we actually

15 Bessie Shonberg Theater Formerly a garage, this theater (named after a dancer and choreographer) is one of the most active dance, mime and poetry houses in the city. Famous clown/dancer/mime Bill Irwin has often played here. ♦ Seats 160. 219 W 19th St (7th-8th Aves) 924-0077

16 Cola's ★$$ You must bring your own wine to accompany Cola's casual mix of Northern and Southern Italian cuisine, but hand-painted, antiqued walls lend a gentle ambience to the room, where a lively downtown crowd come to take on the pasta. ♦ Italian ♦ M-F 11:30AM-3PM, 4-11PM; Sa 4-11:30PM; Su 4-11PM. 148 8th Ave (17th-18th Sts) No credit cards. 633-8020

17 Chelsea Place ★★$$ They bill this as the only speakeasy in America. You enter through the back door of an antique shop that leads to a crowded bar. The room behind it, which they call a garden because it has hanging plants, is quieter and more intimate. The upstairs bar offers jazz with a liberal sprinkling of Broadway tunes. ♦ Italian ♦ M-F noon-4AM; Sa-Su 5PM-4AM. 147 8th Ave (17th-18th Sts) 924-8413

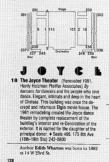

Chelsea

18 Man Ray ★★$$ Guided by a skilled chef, formerly at Quatorze, this bistro has attracted a following who appreciate well-cooked, authentic French food. ♦ French ♦ M-Th 5:30-11PM; F-Sa 5:30PM-12:30AM; Su noon-3:30PM, 5:30-11PM. 169 8th Ave (18th-19th Sts) 627-4220

18 The Joyce Theater (Renovated 1981, Hardy Holzman Pfeiffer Associates) By dancers for dancers and the people who love dance. Elegant, intimate and deep in the heart of Chelsea. This building was once the decrepit and infamous Elgin movie house. The 1981 remodeling created the Joyce dance theater by complete replacement of the building's interior and re-Decoization of the exterior. It is named for the daughter of the principal donor. ♦ Seats 496. 175 8th Ave (18th-19th Sts) 242-0800

Author Edith Wharton was born in 1862 at 14 W 23rd St.

128

19 La Luncheonette ★★$$ The homey bar and open kitchen in the bistro style seem familiar enough, but the free-range chicken with mustard, the lamb sausage with apple bé cognac and the gratinée trois poisson (lobster, crab and sea scallops) are interesting turns on an honored cuisine. ♦ French ♦ M-Th 11:30AM-3PM, 6:30PM-midnight; F-Sa 11:30AM-3PM, 6:30PM-1AM; Su 11:30AM-5PM, 6:30PM-midnight. 130 10th Ave (18th St) Reservations recommended. No credit cards. 675-0342

THE KITCHEN

20 The Kitchen This veteran institution for experimental performing and visual arts presents the works of young artists in dance, film, video, music and performance art. Programs are scheduled most evenings at 8:30. The video viewing room presents the works of avant-garde video artists. Call for current performance schedule. ♦ Video room free. Tu-Sa 1-6PM. 512 W 19th St (10th-11th Aves) 255-5793

21 Guardian Angel Church (1930, John Van Pelt) This little complex of Italian Romanesque buildings surrounds what is known as the Shrine Church of the Sea. The name reflects the one-time presence of the busiest piers in the Port of New York, a short walk to the west. The church's Renaissance interior is even more impressive than the red brick and limestone facade. The priest in charge of this Roman Catholic church is designated Chaplain of the Port, with duties that include assigning chaplains to ships based here. ♦ 193 10th Ave (21st St)

22 West 21st Street Almost all the 19th-century houses on this block follow Clement Clarke Moore's requirement of front gardens and street trees. In its earliest years as a residential community, all of Chelsea looked much like this. The building with the unusual peaked roof on the 9th Ave corner is the oldest house in the neighborhood. It was built in the 1820s by James N. Wells. ♦ 9th-10th Aves

23 Something Else There are dozens of antique shops scattered around this neighborhood, some authentic, some dubious, all of them browsers' delights. But this one is, indeed, something else. It's a collection of old toys, quilts, jewelry and, best of all, feathered masks. ♦ M-F 11AM-7:30PM; Sa-Su 1-6PM. 182 9th Ave (21st St) 924-0005

To celebrate King Kong's 50th birthday in 1981, a gigantic ape-shaped balloon was hung from the Observatory at the Empire State Building. The balloon version was approximately 80 feet tall; the real King Kong measured only 18 inches.

20 October 1896: *The New York Times* adopts the slogan, "All the News That's Fit to Print."

24 General Theological Seminary (1883-1900, Charles C. Haight; Library, 1960, O'Connor & Kilham) You're welcome to enter this oasis through the library building on 9th Ave during public hours or, in summer, to take the free *Grand Design* tour. Land for the Episcopal Seminary was donated by Clement Clarke Moore in 1830, on the condition that the seminary should always occupy the site. The West Building, built in 1835, is the oldest building on campus, as well as New York's oldest example of Gothic Revival architecture. It predates Haight's renovation, which includes all the other Gothic buildings. In the center is the Chapel of the Good Shepherd, with its outstanding bronze doors and 161ft-high square bell tower. Hoffman Hall, at the 10th Ave end, contains a Medieval-style dining hall complete with a barrel-vaulted ceiling, walk-in fireplaces and a gallery for musicians. The other end is dominated by the new and very much out-of-place St. Mark's Library, containing, along with one of the world's largest collections of bibles in Latin, some 170,000 volumes. ♦ M-F noon-3PM; Sa 11AM-4PM; Su 2-4PM. 175 W 20th St (9th-10th Aves) 243-5150

25 406-24 West 20th Street (1837, Don Alonzo Cushman) An extremely well-preserved row of Greek Revival homes built by a dry goods merchant who developed much of Chelsea and built these as rental units. The attic windows are circled with wreaths, the doorways framed in brownstone. Even the newel posts, topped with cast-iron pineapples, are still intact. ♦ 9th-10th Aves

26 St. Peter's Church (1838, Clement Clarke Moore and James W. Smith) This Episcopal church and its rectory and parish hall are outgrowths of Moore's plan to build them in the style of Greek temples. According to legend, the plan was changed on the advice of the vestrymen come back from England with tales of the Gothic buildings at Oxford. The congregation decided to switch styles, even though the foundations were already in place. The fence that surrounds this charming complex was brought here from Trinity Church on lower Broadway, where it had stood since 1790. ♦ 346 W 20th St (8th-9th Aves)

27 Chelsea Food Gorgeously designed modern store and café with many interesting, but expensive, prepared and packaged foods to go. ♦ Take-out ♦ M-F 9AM-9PM; Sa-Su 9AM-6PM. 198 8th Ave (20th St) 691-3948

The cast-iron pineapples in the Cushman Row are part of an iconography that began in New England in the days when merchant sea captains roamed the world in search of things to sell. After a voyage to the South Seas, it was customary for them to put pineapples outside their houses as a sign that they had returned and were receiving guests, who would be treated to exotic fruits and wild yarns. Eventually the pineapple became a symbol of hospitality, and was rendered in more permanent wood or iron.

28 Meriken ★★$$ New Wave Japanese served to a trendy crowd. Interesting Art Deco decor in celadon and pink. ♦ Japanese ♦ Daily noon-3PM, 6PM-midnight. 162 W 21st St (6th-7th Aves) Reservations recommended. 620-9684

29 Third Cemetery of the Spanish & Portuguese Synagogue (1829-1851) The third cemetery established by the first Jewish congregation in New York. The second cemetery is in Greenwich Village, the first on the Lower East Side. ♦ 21st St (6th-7th Aves)

30 Hotel Chelsea $$ (1884, Hubert, Pirson & Co.) Brendan Behan, who lived here during his New York years, said that there was more space in the Hotel Chelsea than in the whole of Staten Island. It has housed more writers, poets and musicians than any hotel in the five boroughs New York, Staten Island included. In the 1880s, Chelsea was the heart of the Theater District, attracting creative people as Greenwich Village would a decade later. In its early days the hotel was home to writers like William Dean Howells and O. Henry, and later to Thomas Wolfe, Arthur Miller, Mary McCarthy, Vladimir Nabokov and Yevgeny Yevtushenko. Sarah Bernhardt once lived here, and this is where Dylan Thomas spent his last days. In the 1960s and '70s, it was a

Chelsea

favorite stopping place for visiting rock stars (including the Sex Pistols), who shared the atmosphere with modern classical composers George Kleisinger and Virgil Thomson. The Chelsea was originally an apartment building, the first in New York with a penthouse. When it was converted to a hotel in 1905, each of its 12 floors became a single suite. The lobby has been altered, but the stairway, best seen from the 2nd floor, is intact. ♦ 222 W 23rd St (7th-8th Aves) 243-3700

129

New York City Access. Spread from guide book. Concept: Richard Saul Wurman. Design director: Stuart L. Silberman. Access Press/HarperCollins Publishers, USA, 1989

experience cities. A guidebook, like a city, should be inherently understandable through its structure, he says.

The drawback with *Information Anxiety*, on the other hand, is that it contributes to the very problem – "the black hole between data and knowledge" – that it affects to describe. To get the full benefit of its 350 pages you probably need to be chronically insecure, American, or both, and it seems likely that the book's British reception will be a good deal less rapturous when it is published by Pan. It's true, as Wurman claims, that you can enter *Information Anxiety* at any point, read forwards or backwards, or even dispense with the bulk of the book and digest the twenty-page table of contents instead. But the conclusion to all this non-linear huffing and puffing will seem blindingly obvious to many: concentrate on reading, watching and learning what is interesting and relevant to you and don't be distracted by the rest.

Perhaps the most significant aspect of the book will turn out to be its structure. Wurman claims that a number of American publishers have received proposals for books that make use of a similar approach. He has already shown how a subject as convoluted as Wall Street finance can be broken down into easily assimilated capsules of pictures and text – "that book could be used for a college course in economics," he insists – and many other subjects could be clarified, rather than simplified, in the same way. Steelcase certainly think so – they have asked Wurman to produce an office access book. Wurman is also working on television listings, a newspaper project, a new approach to weathermaps (they might look like information as in *USA Today* but they invariably fail to inform) and an enormous official guide to airlines. If anyone is rash enough to approach Wurman with a brief to design anything so frivolous as a brochure, he will turn them down flat. In the next few years, he predicts, emphasis will switch from beauty-driven graphics to information-driven graphics, a change that is long overdue.

"Graphic design has in it an enormous body of extraordinarily talented people who are totally irresponsible. There are many graphic designers who have, by several magnitudes, more talent that I will ever have, but content is not what drives them. The idea of graphic design is to make the world legible and they don't make it legible. They are a body of people who are fashion designers, who work in hair salons and cosmetics. They are the Michael Graveses of graphic design.

"Louis Kahn's definition of architecture was 'the thoughtful making of spaces' and there's a lot of meaning, in my mind, to the word 'thoughtful'. It wasn't the decorative making of buildings, which is what we've just been through for the last ten years. And when I say that good design makes things legible, I'm talking about thoughtfulness. I don't know any other way to think. Any other way seems so shallow."

Blueprint, March 1990

THE VISIONARY CONSUMER

Experience is one of the most idiosyncratic and intriguing design books to be published in the 1990s. It is also one of the most problematic. Its strength lies in the challenge it inventively poses to the still-relevant question: what makes a book? Its weakness is that having broken with the conventions of design book publishing in a number of constructive ways, *Experience* ducks the issues it raises. It is not that it doesn't want to pursue the implications of its own method and discoveries; it doesn't notice they are there.

Experience's first departure is to present art, architecture, advertising and design on apparently equal terms. Without batting an eyelid, compiler Sean Perkins's infinitely cool gaze pans from Japanese architect Tadao Ando's sublime Church on the Water in Hokkaido to the high-tech retail-theatre layerings of Nike Town; from the shock tactics of bad-boy British artist Damien Hirst, famous for pickling sawn-in-half animals in formaldehyde, to the career "re-engineering" of Australian cutie-pop singer Kylie Minogue; from a *Fuse* typeface made of buttons, bottle-tops and string to eight Bulgarian women in national costume singing on a beach.

What, if anything, links these seemingly unconnected phenomena? *Experience* leaves it, fashionably, for the viewer to decide. The Situationist Raoul Vaneigem is quoted approvingly: "Ideally a book would have no order to it and the reader would have to discover their own." *Experience*'s reluctance to connect the dots puts it – despite the compromise of its physical binding – in the anti-linear 1960s tradition of loose-leaf novels you can start reading at any point and works of art in boxes that can be opened and reshuffled as randomly as a pack of cards, so that the experience is different each time.

Experience contains very little text and its telegraphic assertions in 30-point caps raise more questions than answers. The book's at first sight straightforward purpose, flagged on its front cover, is to inspire and challenge its readers. Conventional communication, the authors declare, is no longer enough, though they don't explain what they mean by this, or how, why, and with whom it has failed. As they see it, the task now for commissioner and creative alike is the expression of "new experience". The projects featured are their answer to the form these new experiences might take. What they share, claim the authors, is the insight and imagination of their creators and a consistent quality of execution.

Somewhere behind the screen of convention-busting rhetoric and quotations from Paul Klee, Jean-Luc Godard and Marshall McLuhan, the main object of the exercise goes tastefully unremarked. The "communication" proposed by the authors boils down in most cases to nothing more mysterious than the transmission of the client's sales message. The shocking, confusing and entertaining experiences they seek to provide – however obliquely delivered – amount in the end to a routine encouragement to buy. While the book does include projects for public institutions such as the Dutch police force and parliament, at its heart lies the immense corporate power and tentacular marketing presence of Coca-Cola, Sony, BMW, Benetton, and Ford. "[These ideas] provide a visionary glimpse of a future that is already amongst us if we are brave enough to pursue it," claim the authors. Is being a consumer, even a cultured and tasteful one, really this avant-garde and heroic?

The once uneasy relationship of art and advertising may be collapsing into alliance, but this is hardly as unproblematic as *Experience* makes it seem. Here is Cindy Sherman doing her thing for Comme des Garçons, Barbara Kruger putting her weight behind *The Economist*, and an extraordinary land art project in the service of – what else? – Cable & Wireless's global digital highway. Is it misplaced nostalgia to wish that art might still provide a space where we can escape from the clamour, intrusion and false consciousness of so much commercial media into altogether different realms of experience? What *Experience* seems to offer is more of the same.

Sean Perkins, head of brand communication at London design consultancy Imagination, has engineered *Experience* with an exemplary eye. His project confirms that even in the electronic era the book has structural possibilities never fully explored. But in its unjournalistic eagerness to take on trust everything people say about their own work, it lacks detachment and irony. In one of the weirdest projects, two artists bottled a collection of weeds gathered from the borders of EuroDisney. The authors seem unaware that anything other than oddball celebration may be implied. A quote from the religious philosopher Simone Weil on the imperatives of the imagination is superimposed on a bank of pulsing TV screens at a motor show. It seems doubtful that a woman who lived a life of extreme self-denial had Ford's latest line-up in mind.

"Everybody experiences far more than he understands," said Marshall McLuhan. "Yet it is experience, rather than understanding, that influences behaviour." Quoted twice on the cover, once on the flap and again inside, this shrug of the shoulders would appear to be the book's credo. But *Experience* itself, handsome as it is, cannot hope to offer experience in the sense that the authors intend. You could only experience Tadao Ando's Church on the Water by going there, and most of us never will. But a book, by collecting such a diversity of material, organising it into patterns, explaining and analysing it, can offer understanding. *Experience* exhibits some remarkable evidence, but its commercial agenda prevents it from making much sense of the ambiguous new reality that the evidence suggests.

AIGA Journal of Graphic Design, vol. 13 no. 2, 1995*

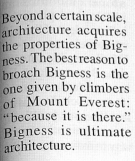

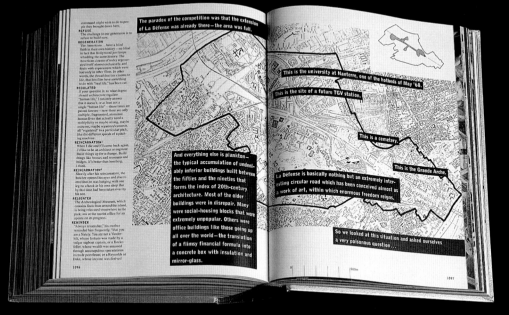

S,M,L,XL. Spreads from an
architectural monograph.
Authors: O.M.A., Rem
Koolhaas and Bruce Mau.
Designers: Bruce Mau
Design. The Monacelli Press,
USA/010 Publishers, The
Netherlands, 1995

AUTHORING A LABYRINTH

For a medium regularly pronounced by a small army of attending experts to be in its terminal stages, the printed book is maintaining a remarkable appearance of health. One paradoxical side-effect of multimedia's arrival may be to generate new editorial and structural approaches to the making of books; the form, it seems, has plenty of life in it yet.

S,M,L,XL, Rem Koolhaas and Bruce Mau's huge "novel about architecture", is certainly a publishing project that it would have been difficult to imagine ever reaching the printer before CD-ROMs encouraged us to expect nothing less than encyclopedic vastness. Heavier than the average Bible and running to almost 1,400 pages, it is daunting to contemplate and even harder to hold in the hand. It is a book you could easily reject on sight as a folly without ever opening its die-stamped silver cover. Architects, accustomed as a profession to monumentalising themselves in steel, glass and stone, have never been shy of celebrating their own virtues in print. *S,M,L,XL* is generic in that sense, but in most other respects it is out there on its own.

For one thing, Mau shares equal billing, as co-author, with Koolhaas and his team. Since the mid-1980s, the Canadian designer has argued for the right to be accepted on equal terms as an author capable of bringing his own research, commentary and point of view to a project. Mau wants to be involved from the earliest stages, not to arrive on the scene after all the key decisions have been taken and the writing has been done. In recent years, many have campaigned or just longed for the same authorial freedoms. The difference between wishing and doing, however, is the difference between unrealised "paper architecture" and built form. Mau has a formidable talent for winning over clients with publishing power and getting things done.

"Architecture," says *S,M,L,XL*'s introductory note, "is by definition a chaotic adventure." Resisting coherence as a denial of contemporary architecture's true condition and embracing contradiction, Koolhaas and Mau have turned this observation into the book's organisational principle. Projects are divided according to size into four sections – small, medium, large and extra-large – and texts punctuate them without attempting to act as explanatory glue. As with multimedia, you are encouraged by the structure to enter at any point, almost at whim, to pursue your own path forward or backward, and to establish your own connections.

While a doggedly linear reading of this chaotic mass of plans, photographs, drawings, diaries, essays and manifestos would miss the point, Mau's treatment of individual sequences is exhilaratingly cinematic. By eliminating text margins wherever possible and bleeding full-page and double-page images on all sides, he gives long stretches a screenlike impact that makes the page-turns fall with the precision of film cuts.

The most effective sequences are often almost wordless. A section on the Netherlands Dance Theater superimposes lone keywords on the images: "Transplant" (a void in the site where the building will be), "Innocence" (the first uncompromised drawings), "Panic" (showing the model to the client), "Battlefield" (the building site) and so on. This is followed by a four-page, month-by-month chronology printed on yellow and paced with the excitement of a soap opera: the client has a heart attack, money runs out, just about everyone, including the architects, is fired, but somehow the building still gets built.

In another more oblique sequence, dialogue from Samuel Beckett's absurdist masterpiece *Waiting for Godot* runs for 34 pages across images of the Rotterdam Kunsthal. The accompanying instructions for a tour of the building take on the quality of stage directions ("Walk down . . . Turn the corner"), emphasising the architecture's combination of theatricality and silence and the sense that the empty galleries, too, are zones of possibility waiting for something to happen.

If *S,M,L,XL* is a hybrid comprising many smaller books, then one of its most intriguing structural devices is the unexplained dictionary that runs from its copyright page to its close. It surfaces in the same left-hand column, seemingly at random, in the middle of a project or essay before disappearing again. Credited to Jennifer Sigler, the book's editor, it is presumably intended as a lexicon of Koolhaas's (and perhaps Mau's) concerns, defined using a collage of quotations from sources ranging from Umberto Eco to Ayn Rand. It belongs to a genre of Surrealist dictionary-making that includes Bataille's *Critical Dictionary* and J. G. Ballard's "Project for a Glossary of the Twentieth Century", published in a previous Mau-designed project, *Zone*. According to Koolhaas's own definition, Surrealism is "a rational method which does not pretend to be objective, through which analysis becomes identical to creation" and there could be few better descriptions of *S,M,L,XL*'s editorial and design methodology. While the book's restrained typography conforms to the convention of rigorous elegance in contemporary academic publishing that Mau himself helped to define, it is subverted at almost every turn in *S,M,L,XL* by the subjective uses to which it is put.

Years in the making, *S,M,L,XL* has been conceived on a scale and realised with a dedication that defeats adequate summary in a brief review. Its undoubted pretensions and deliberate lack of focus will put off some readers, but I found its labyrinths, chambers and occasional dead ends highly enjoyable to explore. *S,M,L,XL* arrives at a time when the calls for new kinds of collaboration and graphic authorship need to find fruition in ambitious, widely distributed projects if the point is to be convincingly made. Koolhaas and Mau's book deserves close attention from designers as a compelling example of design taken to the highest levels of engagement, an achievement not simply claimed by its designer, but acknowledged publicly by his co-author where it counts most – on the cover.

AIGA Journal of Graphic Design, vol. 14 no. 2, 1996*

XXXL

If Rem Koolhaas and Bruce Mau's 1,400-page *S,M,L,XL* was the most gargantuan publishing project of recent years, its hard-won record for size and endurance has now been eclipsed by the arrival of yet another leviathan. Irma Boom's astonishing centenary book for the Dutch multinational SHV Holdings – dubbed an "insane adventure in paper, ink and print" by one of the Netherlands' leading newspapers – threatens to break the scales at nearly eight pounds and a wrist-buckling 2,136 pages.

Boom, an Amsterdam-based designer, has established an international reputation in the 1990s for uncompromising reinterpretations of the book form in which aesthetic values sometimes take precedence over ease of reading. At a time when graphic designers are restating the possibilities of authorship through design, her 100-year history of SHV ups the ante with a spectacular demonstration of what can be accomplished by a designer entrusted not simply to give form to content, but to determine content itself.

Seen by Boom herself as a once-in-a-lifetime commission, the book has its unlikely seeds in her first project after going freelance, for SHV Holdings chairman Paul Fentener van Vlissingen. The philosophically inclined multimillionaire was so pleased with the limited-edition book that Boom and art historian Johan Pijnappel created to mark his 50th birthday that, in early 1991, he asked the pair to begin work on the centenary project. "He said he wanted to have an unusual book," Boom recalls. "Nothing more and nothing less."

SHV is a family-owned business, with profits in 1995 of $200 million and operations in Europe, South America and the Far East. SHV Energy sells liquefied petroleum gas; SHV Makro is a chain of wholesale centres serving restaurants, hotels, clubs and so on. To help them come to grips with the conglomerate's ethos and mentality, Boom and Pijnappel moved into an office in SHV's Utrecht headquarters, which later became Boom's design studio. They attended shareholders' meetings and company celebrations. At first they put in just a day or two a week; for the last two years, says Boom, the book occupied them "day and night".

Having chosen his collaborators, Fentener van Vlissingen gave them remarkable freedom. Budget was never an issue, says Boom – she has no idea what the book cost – and the visuals she showed him were basic. "We talked not so much about the format, more about the ideas. Another client would say, 'Show me the size of the book.' We didn't do that. We talked without paper, just like he does with his managers."

Boom and Pijnappel were allowed complete access to the company's files. Because SHV had no organised archive, they spent three and a half years sifting through the records of secretaries and managers and visiting archives in overseas affiliates

thinkbook. Spreads from
a book about the Dutch
multinational SHV. Authors:
Irma Boom and Johan
Pijnappel. Designer: Irma
Boom. SHV Holdings,
The Netherlands, 1996

such as Calor and Primagaz. Starting in the present and ending in 1896, the narrative
constructed by the designers from the fruits of this massive research effort is
a panoramic montage of primary source material: reports, speeches, interviews,
letters, memos, poems, advertising, and photographs of family members, company
occasions, employees and facilities, and historical events. "The human factor, that was
the most important thing," says Boom of the story-telling process. "Their doubts, their
mistakes, their own thinking." The book makes no secret of SHV's occasional business
failures – in the US, for instance – while its withdrawal from South Africa in 1987,
after three politically motivated arson attacks on its Dutch Makro stores, is explored
in unflinching detail.

   This openness is reflected in the book's structure and editorial devices. There are no
section headings; instead, the largest text type is used for 61 occasional questions that are
primarily the work of Fentener van Vlissingen – "Questions are often more interesting
than answers," he notes – with help from Boom and Pijnappel. Some are businesslike
("Why should profit always grow?"); some homely ("Do we feel better with a new pair
of socks?"); some Zen ("Can you hear dew falling?"). Least expected of all in a corporate
communication is the penultimate "Can death become a friend?" though reminders
of mortality run through the book, from the black-edged pages that announce family
bereavement, to Fentener van Vlissingen's private notes in 1980 after a serious illness:
"Particularly in the weeks before the results came through, I thought about death –
day and night."

   Boom has patterned the narrative into alternating sequences of text and image. Text
is evened out into a single point size and weight, while the 100 per cent cotton pages
make rich though unsystematic use of colour. Boom has reached similar conclusions to
Mau's in her treatment of photographs, which are given a full-bleed televisual intensity
of presence. A screen of fine horizontal lines, applied digitally to the image at the repro
stage, helps to unify disparate originals and makes even poor-quality pictures seem
aesthetically intriguing. "I'm really fond of video images," says Boom. "I put lines in
the image to give it a feeling of 1996 and the future." The pages' coloured edges – tulips
seen from one angle, a poem by Gerrit Achterberg seen from another – frame and
accentuate the imagery.

   Four thousand copies are being printed, with another 500 translated into Chinese –
reflecting SHV's developing interests in the region – but unlike *S,M,L,XL* the book is not
for sale and few outsiders will get to see and hold it. It will be consulted as inspiration,
education and example by SHV shareholders and managers, both now, as part of the
centenary celebrations, and in the future. "It's a special book," says Boom, "a learning
book, a thinking book, a working book." Corporate wisdom percolates from the very
watermarks of the paper – MOTIVATE, KEEP THINGS SIMPLE, LISTEN, LEARN AND
REACT – and its exhortatory purpose is subtly confirmed by the nine letters of its
hidden title, *thinkbook*, scattered randomly throughout its 2,000 pages.

   Would Boom have made the book differently for a different audience? "I didn't
think of the audience at all," she says without hesitation. "I thought if it's good for me,
it's good for them." By pursuing her own inclinations, she has defiantly reasserted
the design possibilities of the printed book in the digital era. But *thinkbook*, despite its
overwhelming confidence and presence, occupies an uneasy position as a publishing
project. It contributes in the most positive way to the culture of an unusual organisation
led by an unusual chairman, yet it remains an internal communication aimed at

a limited readership. To put it another way, although Boom's book would provide
a business historian with fascinating evidence, it does not, as a company product, achieve
the critical detachment to make it a piece of historical commentary in its own right.

After working on this scale, Boom is reluctant to take on commissions offering
anything other than total freedom. If she now turns to initiating her own projects,
she has the experience and vision to create some extraordinary books.

I.D., November 1996

PICTURES IN SEQUENCE

If you think you've got the hang of the high and low culture issue, why not try this simple test. Get out a graphic novel – any one will do – on a rush-hour train. How do you feel? Just the tiniest bit self-conscious? Maybe you would not consider reading such a thing in the first place. For despite all the press hype in the late 1980s about the emergence of the comic book, and in particular the graphic novel, as a fully adult genre, nothing much has changed. In Britain, the most typical reader is still the young male comics fan and the subject matter of many of these books, however "revisionist" in approach, is the usual tedious superhero stuff. As the promised graphic novel buyers failed to materialise, bookshops rapidly reassigned shelf space, publishers rethought ambitious launch plans and media interest fizzled out.

In many ways, the comic book industry has only itself to blame. Its products lacked the diversity of ordinary novels. The new readership was assumed rather than adequately courted. It was never going to be easy to overcome a deeply ingrained British resistance and persuade us to consume comic books with the avidity of the Japanese, Europeans, or even Americans. And yet I, for one, find it hard to give up on the medium. The comic book achieves an expressive integration of word and image in the service of narrative with a directness, complexity and, in the best examples, a sophistication that gives film a run for its money and has important lessons for the emerging multimedia.

Three recent books suggest that, with or without the hype, the comic continues to evolve. Scott McCloud's *Understanding Comics: The Invisible Art* is a brilliantly conceived treatise on the medium, self-reflexively cast in the form of a graphic novel, with the comic-book-artist author iconically present as roving lecturer. Beginning by defining comics, clumsily but completely, as "juxtaposed pictorial and other images in deliberate sequence", McCloud moves on to dissect their vocabulary (words, pictures, other icons), their grammar (identified as the "closure" that separates one panel from the next), their treatment of time (which must be rendered spatially); issues of line and colour; and the fundamental comic book problem of when and what to show and tell. One of the pleasures of the book, though it has a didactic purpose, is the effortlessness with which it integrates a wide range of fine art references into the comic book idiom – from *The Tortures of Saint Erasmus* (c. 1460) to Ernst's *Une Semaine de Bonté*. "There's a big gaping hole in the official history of art," complains McCloud with comic book peevishness, "and it's high time somebody filled it!"

In one of many illuminating passages, McCloud considers the nature of transitions between panels, concluding broadly that there are six main types: moment-to-moment, action-to-action, subject-to-subject, scene-to-scene, aspect-to-aspect (where the artist singles out atmospheric details within a scene) and the *non sequitur*. He then analyses

*Understanding Comics:
The Invisible Art.* Book page.
Author/artist: Scott McCloud.
Kitchen Sink Press/
HarperCollins Publishers,
USA, 1993

the proportion of each type in a random sample of American comics, including Marvel's *X-Men*, the Hernandez brothers' *Heartbreak Soup* and Art Spiegelman's *Maus*. Action-to-action is by far the most common type of transition, while subject-to-subject and scene-to-scene form the remainder, in equal proportions, the three other types being unrepresented. A comparative analysis of several Japanese *manga* reveals significant cultural differences. Moment-to-moment transitions are used in a high proportion of examples, giving the imagery a cinematic intensity, and there are a substantial number of aspect-to-aspect transitions, which encourage the reader to assemble a single moment from scattered fragments. "In Japan, more than anywhere else," McCloud concludes, "comics is an art . . . of intervals."

Western interest in *manga* seems likely to ensure that these and other Japanese techniques will become increasingly important to the graphic novel. Two recent examples, British and American, feature a high proportion of moment-to-moment transitions, while also pushing at the boundaries in other ways. In *The Tragical Comedy or Comical Tragedy of Mr Punch*, established stars of the medium Neil Gaiman and Dave McKean use the violence of the Punch & Judy show as a backdrop for a tale of childhood innocence and adult betrayal. McKean mixes photography (of his own model puppets and three-dimensional assemblages) with collage, drawing and painted elements and ties his densely worked panels together with a threatening tar-black frame. Visually a *tour de force*, the book possibly even justifies its publisher's claim that it is the most beautiful graphic novel ever to be published in Britain. But this degree of visual ambition puts the writing under pressure to compete or hang back, and the book feels, ultimately, too novelistic. Gaiman's captions are wordy and stilted, their rhythms erratically balanced against the lush technicolour flow of images.

City of Glass, an adaptation of a story from Paul Auster's *New York Trilogy* by writer Paul Karasik and artist David Mazzucchelli, is superficially less impressive; at a quick glance it looks like an ordinary black and white comic. But its unabashed readiness to refashion highbrow literature for a lowbrow medium makes it a landmark – "an almost inevitable development", according to *Newsweek*, which devoted a page to it. Karasik and Mazzucchelli have made a remarkable job of condensing Auster's already hard-boiled prose, dividing it up into panels without any loss of momentum or sense of strain, and have found convincing comic book correlatives for the narrative disjunctions and mood of unease that pervades the metaphysical thriller. In one virtuoso sequence, Mazzucchelli, faced with the problem of making visual a lengthy monologue from a man confined to a dark room as a child, combines moment-to-moment symbolism with an aptly disorientating use of the *non sequitur* – McCloud's rarely employed sixth type of transition. At moments like this it becomes clear that comics have an artistic potential – could we finally abandon our prejudices – that is only just beginning to be explored.

Frieze, January/February 1995*

VISUAL PROSE

Something funny is going on in the pages of contemporary fiction. Words are restless, on the move. While there is generally no reason to give the look of the printed page a second thought, readers have lately had no choice but to take notice. Once meekly quiescent, an unregarded window on the narrative within, type is showing marked exhibitionist tendencies; and not just in publishing's more marginal experiments, but in some of the 1990s' most fashionable novels.

In Jeff Noon's *Pollen*, a deadly airborne mutation descends on the streets of a future Manchester. The book opens with an attention-grabbing "aachoosh!" in which letters of all sizes are sprayed across three pages as though the computer printer itself has emitted a huge typographic sneeze. Other kinds of fictional type play are less literally illustrative and more convincingly sustained. In Irvine Welsh's violent and disturbing *Marabou Stork Nightmares* the typography itself is dysfunctional, speeding with barely controlled rage towards terminal breakdown. In the extreme effort of communication, type stutters and repeats itself, words are dismembered letter by letter, lines read up the page rather than down and parallel commentaries are crudely bashed into the broken body of the text.

More sophisticated still in its use of typography as an additional expressive layer is Douglas Coupland's witty dissection of life in computerland, *Microserfs*. In this concerted (and fitting) attempt to make the prose novel more consumably graphic, e-mail messages are shown in a computer-like typeface, their errors uncorrected, and whole spreads are given over to duplicated keywords, impenetrable exercises in vowel removal and wodges of binary code. *Microserfs* is further punctuated by frequent lists in headline-sized bold type, a technosphere stream-of-consciousness pieced together from random word-bites that more resemble the starting point for a conceptual artwork than the stuff of conventional narrative fiction:

fight
morphin mighty
VFX-1
colonize
thrust
boy game
64 bits
pods
Softimage
anti alias
BAR

Contemporary as all this will sound, such interventions are not particularly new. Visual prose, as it is sometimes called, has a history that can be traced from the visible graph lines plotting narrative development in Sterne's eighteenth-century *Life and Opinions of Tristram Shandy* to the meandering mouse's tail of type in *Alice's Adventures in Wonderland.* Hubert Selby Jr was hammering out passages of screaming demotic capitals for *Last Exit to Brooklyn* while Irvine Welsh was still in short trousers. B. S. Johnson's 1971 "geriatric comedy" *House Mother Normal,* though set in a single point size, makes highly original use of fractured typographical layouts as a metaphor for the psychological condition of its elderly subjects.

But as with concrete poetry, visual prose's close cousin, there has always been a problem of critical definition and ownership. The visual representation of language is a significant component of so much of this century's literature, demanding proper appraisal, but literary reviewing and criticism are not well equipped to probe or encourage this extra-literary dimension. Concrete poetry, as a result, found a more sympathetic audience within the pages of fine art journals and in gallery exhibitions. Inherently more literary, visual prose has remained in the perhaps reluctant care of the Word's official custodians and its implications and potential for mainstream publishing have, in both critical and commercial senses, been largely unexplored. In less rigidly

Nicky D. from L.I.C. Spread from a "narrative portrait" of Nicholas DeTommaso. Author/designer: Warren Lehrer. Bay Press, USA, 1995

defined circumstances, the French designer Massin's remarkable graphic interpretation in 1964 of absurdist playwright Eugène Ionesco's *The Bald Prima Donna* might have initiated a new genre of visual literature with a considerably wider audience than that for the limited edition artist's book.

Clearly, though, such a literature would also require a new kind of writing that could be more than intermittently sensitive to the parallel possibilities of visual language. The rudimentary typographic effects seen in the novels mentioned could be achieved by any writer with a word-processor and a little help later on from a publisher. *The Bald Prima Donna* involved a much greater degree of intervention by the designer and a willingness on the part of the writer to allow such changes to the text as the removal of all punctuation except for question and exclamation marks, and the creation, ultimately, of a hybrid work.

In four new publications by the American artist Warren Lehrer, the implications of Massin's work are at last being pursued. Lehrer studied graphic design at Yale University, going on to write, design and publish the books *versations, I mean you know* and *French Fries*, all complex transcriptions of recorded speech with each voice expressed on the page by a different typeface to form a typographical analogue of a musical score. Though they ran to editions of 1,000 copies and sold for as little as $35, these were in both production and appearance artists' books. By contrast, Lehrer's "Portrait Series" – first-person word and picture narratives of four eccentric male acquaintances – takes the form of ordinary, low-cost trade paperbacks published by Bay Press, their only unusual feature, at first sight, their tall and narrow proportions. "The monologues that make up this series," writes Lehrer, "are informed by the structure of supper talk, messages left on phone machines, ruminations of long walks, and reminiscences evoked by photo albums and rainy Sundays ... I've taken liberties that a painter or photographer might take when a subject sits for a portrait."

In *Nicky D. from L.I.C.*, Lehrer dispenses with punctuation and capitals, breaking the recollections of 72-year-old Long Island City dweller Nicholas DeTommaso into short, punchy, rhythmical lines. Nicky D. spins his alternately amusing and poignant yarns in Template Gothic, a typeface of pronounced vernacular energy; other characters speak in their own typographic voices. Indentation, size change, overlap, repetition and inset pictures help to animate Nicky D.'s tales of his war years as a longshoreman working with the Mafia and the miraculous fusion, when he was still a child, of his damaged spine. Pages that can look needlessly emphatic or even clumsy when scanned, prove when read to be articulated with enormous feeling and care by an author with an ear superbly attuned to the cadences of spoken language.

Lehrer, unlike so many contemporary graphic stylists, begins from a deep engagement with content he has created himself. There is a convincing expressive unity in these four books – four more portraits, this time of women, are in preparation – that challenges other artist–writers to explore this still largely overlooked publishing path.

Frieze, May 1996

INSTAMATICS OF THE FUTURE

Here it is, one of the most sophisticated pieces of technology ever marketed in the name of domestic leisure, and its status in design circles is not much higher than that of the shell suit or the satellite dish.

The trouble with camcorders is that it is impossible to forget how they are going to be used. This is an area of industrial design, like the television set, where the medium is so porous and engaging (whether you like it or not) that it diminishes any strong sense of the tool. You look at a camcorder and before you can say "I've been framed!" you think of mirthless television hosts, showing viewers' video clips of cats attacking their own reflections and dogs jumping up to pull off their owners' wigs. Your feelings about the camcorder as an artefact are unlikely to recover.

Most, as it happens, are not much to look at. They are far too complicated to become cult objects. For the design buff they lack that vital classic simplicity. They are all function and very little style. The full-sized ones bear some family resemblance to the old-fashioned cine camera, but the compact travel version, the regrettably named "palmcorder", is a brand new type. Some are boxy. Some have the raked, aerodynamic nose profiles of a high-speed train. Swivelling eye-pieces jut from their sides with the aggression of hot-rod tail-pipes. Their buttons are labelled with tough-sounding cam-concepts like "auto lock", "digital picture" and "zero mem".

The visual processing power these cameras confer on the ordinary user is awesome. Digital timecoding, stereo over-dubbing, broad bandwidth Hi8 tape technology, near broadcast quality pictures – hook Sony's top of the range CCD-V6000 camcorder to an editing deck and a professional would not sniff at the results. In fact, it would probably take a professional to milk anything like the full creative potential from equipment as over-specified as this.

Becoming a camcorder user is more than simply a pastime, more even than taking on "the greatest family hobby of the century", as one enthusiast was moved to eulogise it – it is an existential choice. Camcorders offer the unnerving prospect of being able to record everything that happens to us and truly matters to us, and the equal certainty that this is the last thing we want. The late Jo Spence, a former wedding photographer who turned the camera on herself, pointed out the way in which we use photographs to lie about our lives by confining them to a strictly affirmatory role. The camcorder, in theory a superb documentary tool, provides exactly the same camouflage, but in real time rather than snaps.

To be a camcorder user you need an unshakable faith that the banal is intrinsically fascinating. Other people's holiday snapshots are hellish enough. Their camcorder footage is infinitely worse. For one thing it lasts a whole lot longer. It holds you in its garbled spell. It has no aesthetic coherence or discernible point of view. It tells you nothing you didn't know or ever wanted to know about its subject. It exists only to say I was there, I saw this, I had a good time, I captured it on tape.

In the most profound way, camcorders play on the fear of missing out. Other people have their tapes, their audiovisual mementoes – where are yours? The camcorder makers are on to a winner here. The more people buy their handycams and palmcorders, the more it will seem socially peculiar not to join in the fun. Meanwhile, all those precious moments are cascading past unrecorded, unarchived, forgotten, lost! You may decide now not to acquire a camcorder, perhaps on grounds of taste, but will you still feel the same way in ten years' time? In twenty? Thirty? By then it will be too late and you will have only fallible memories and your mute, unmoving photographs to rely on.

"All photographs are memento mori," writes Susan Sontag in *On Photography*. "To take a photograph is to participate in another person's (or thing's) mortality, vulnerability, mutability." That is every bit as true of tape. The individual moment might not be frozen, sliced out of time, in the manner of a photograph, but the sequence as a whole is just as ruthlessly embalmed.

Video Camera magazine has some breezy advice on what to do with old cine footage: transfer it to video. "A fascinating *This is Your Life* sequence could show a certain member of the family at various stages, from being a baby to becoming an OAP." Such a sequence would be moving but commonplace in an album of photographs. On videotape, the compression of an evanescent life into a few brief minutes of living-room screen-time becomes an insensitive act of unbearable pathos.

But camcorder owners blunder on regardless, videotaping their children, their holidays, their weddings, their parties (and if they are Demi Moore, their parturitions). They use their camcorders in a doomed attempt to stave off the inevitable, while pretending to play it for laughs. They have an alibi now for carrying them everywhere: there is always the possibility that whatever they are taping might go deliciously wrong. Perhaps the cat will fall off the sofa. Perhaps the two plump ladies will collide by the pool. Maybe the mirthless host will cough up £200 to show their clip on the box.

It would be utterly vain at this point to suggest that what matters to us individuals does survive in the memory and that we have no real need of the rest. It would be pointless to call, as Susan Sontag does at the end of *On Photography*, for a self-imposed "ecology" of images (still or moving) as though it were remotely possible that people would spontaneously surrender customs and pleasures already so deeply entrenched. Camcorders are the Instamatics of the future. Everyone will have one. We will grow old, but our tapes will stay young.

Blueprint, October 1992*

NOTHING ON THE NEWS

The subject of this article is an illusion. Don't misunderstand me, though, it's real enough. You can touch it, or to be more accurate you can touch the image of it. Millions of Britons see it at least once and perhaps several times a day. And yet it isn't really there. Or perhaps some of it is there and some of it isn't. That's the nature of the illusion: it is impossible to tell.

I'm referring to the new identity of BBC news, introduced in April 1993, and the virtual set – the BBC's description – at its core. In some ways it is quite unremarkable, an averagely fancy studio with a long curved newsdesk and a strangely old-fashioned emblem. If the BBC hadn't told us that it was all – desk, floor, lighting grid, ceiling, and coat of arms etched into a huge pane of crystal – a figment of its computer's imagination, few would ever have suspected the truth.

Quite why the BBC should want to play up the virtual – that is, unreal – nature of its news studio is a mystery, since the studio's business could not be more brutally down to earth. "Virtual" is an exciting buzzword, with its immediate connotations of "virtual reality". But this is hardly a link you would expect a responsible news-gathering organisation to want to stress, especially when you remember that the most fervent and deluded proselytes of VR – a ragtag alliance of millenarian New Agers and born-again 1960s acidheads – talk of the VR wonderland as an escape from the dreary old "consensus reality" shared by you, me and the BBC's roving news crews.

It's strange to think the people we entrust to deliver our news aren't really there any more. It's stranger still once you start to think about what it is, flesh and blood presenters aside, you are actually looking at. For this is the "intangible electronic arena", a so-called cyberspace which, if it can be said to exist anywhere, lies somewhere in the unfathomable depths of a machine.

From the glass coat of arms through which we see the refracted image of the set, to the mirror-like panels with bevelled edges used for captions and charts, the graphics perfectly capture this sense of fluid transparency. You can watch and rewatch the title sequence, but even if you freeze-frame it, the image is still too detailed for the size of the screen to be grasped as a whole. The sense that you are looking at, well . . . nothing, is purest in the blue-tinted mist behind the breakfast newsreaders' heads, where there would once have been a solid partition. This space can't be described as flat, because that would imply the existence of a physical surface; nor does it convey a sensation of depth. It's just blank, like a digital tablet, waiting for someone to write on it. It's cyberspace with nothing in it.

What a long way we've come. Early television graphics were heavily influenced by the film titles of Saul Bass. Classic title sequences such as *Man with the Golden Arm* (1956) treated the cinema screen as though it were a kind of moving page. They were graphic in the most basic sense of the term: strong, flat, simple shapes expressively animated to music against plain-as-paper backgrounds. Early TV titles, too, retained a strong sense of their two dimensional origins as flat, filmed artwork.

Video is a fundamentally different medium from film, though, and it was entirely logical for TV designers to explore its possibilities as a generator of graphic effects. It is apt, perhaps, given the point we have now reached, that the best documented origins of the new approach should lie in a science-fiction programme. In 1963, for the titles of *Doctor Who*, Bernard Lodge pointed a video camera at a monitor, exploiting a well-known effect to create rushing clouds of electronic feedback. It was an epochal moment in retrospect, one of the earliest public glimpses in Britain of a new kind of self-referential electronic space.

The history of television and video graphics since then has been a slow climb from "pencil to pixel", as one writer put it, towards a seamlessness of process and result that make-do pioneers like Lodge could scarcely have imagined. It was the computer's arrival that made all the difference. As wonder succeeds wonder – Paintbox, Harry, Henry, Flash Harry and "morphing" – you have to ask whether "graphics" in the Saul Bass sense is really the right term, or at least sufficiently all-embracing, for the special effects-driven design we are now seeing. In the BBC news identity, the software used to conjure up the virtual studio also controls the graphic elements of the image. The graphics are just one fairly average element in what is in essence a branding exercise. Compared to the *Nine O'Clock News'* now abandoned TV-mast titles, a classic piece of late 1980s hoo-ha, the new news graphics aren't very graphic at all.

I have to confess I find the perfection rather off-putting. For me, at least part of the charm of a filmic illusion lies in its fallibility, in the once inevitable gap, however small, between intention and result. With the latest video technology there is no gap. The use of morphing in TV commercials is another case in point. In a paradoxical way, the very ease and plasticity of these transformations becomes a sign of artificiality and glibness, a kind of electro-kitsch. Your knowledge that it is a computer effect, rather than a mechanical process, changes your relationship to the image. The technology itself is enormously clever, yet its application feels like a cheat. You are supposed to marvel but despite the evidence of your own eyes, there is no dramatic justification for believing these curiously repellent images are true. Who cares if the morose comedian in the beer commercial turns into a ladybird? If only he would.

That's the trouble with technology, though. It's there, so it gets used. It's not the usual reason to find oneself siding with news-doubting conspiracy theorists, but the fact is, to watch the news these days requires a suspension of disbelief.

Blueprint, June 1993

LINEAR PROGRESSION

As you read them, try to savour these lines. These scraps of print, considered historically, are among the last of their kind, the final anachronistic moments of the revolution in human consciousness and communication that began in the fifteenth century with Gutenberg's invention of the mechanical printing press.

Since the coming of television, people have been telling us that print is not long for this world and the Book is already Dead. They never sound particularly sorry. This time, it seems, they might actually be right. We now have a half-way believable, commercially available alternative to space-wasting print. CDs for music are old hat. These days they come packed with dictionaries, typeface libraries, photo libraries, documentaries on art, lessons on how to use a camera, play golf or collect stamps.

This is a development, like virtual reality, that thrills the socks off the gurus and technobuffs. "Multimedia will become part of the fabric of our modern civilisation," announced multimedia producer Max Whitby in 1992. "Walk into any room and there'll be a flat panel on the wall where you can get information. You'll completely take it for granted that the information is interactive. There won't be any linear information except for those who want it."

Even graphic designers are catching up. The eighth and final issue of *Octavo*, the typography magazine from 8vo, is not the sixteen pages of immaculately varnished paper subscribers have come to expect, but a CD-ROM which amounts to nothing less than an electronic manifesto for the multimedia age. This is a provocative and intelligent piece of work that deserves to be widely seen and debated. Too bad that in 1993 so few designers own the CD-ROM drive needed to play it on the Macintosh.

8vo's essay (written by Deborah Marshall) comes with a battery of tricks. Using a mouse, you can click your way through its thematic sections in any order, delving as deep as you want into each. You can chase an argument into another section, or stick to your predetermined path. You can replay the sequences that interest you most, while giving others a miss. Some of the argument comes as a voiceover, some of it has to be read off screen. The typography, squeezed until the letters touch, is a treat.

And yet, having said all that, it doesn't really work. It is a clever illustration of its subject, but in the end there are only two compelling arguments for multimedia: cheapness and efficiency of communication. I will come back to the question of cost; suffice it to say that you pay the same as you would for a paper *Octavo* (that is not to assume that it wasn't cheaper to make). But efficiency? 8vo estimate that the disc contains perhaps 2,500 words. Presented as a magazine article, you could read that in ten minutes. It takes at least 40 minutes to finish *Octavo*. Do you absorb proportionately more? In this instance, I doubt it, but the answer probably depends on your efficiency as a reader in the first place. And this is a key point: multimedia is a tool for the reluctant reader, the reader daunted by columns of grey type, the reader (perhaps it is most of us now) who would rather be watching television.

To hear the prophets of multimedia talk you would think that some intrinsic quality of linearity itself creates a barrier to understanding. Non-linearity is touted as an unquestionable virtue, everyone's natural first choice. If we are to believe Max Whitby, old-fashioned linearity will persist only as a quaint and specialised taste. Yet non-linearity is not an idea that has enjoyed widespread success in the popular arts. The cut-ups of Brion Gysin and William Burroughs have yet to make much impact on the writing of bestsellers. Hollywood film-makers do not by and large consult the 1960s cinema of Jean-Luc Godard and Alain Resnais before deciding on a narrative approach. Even the simple flashback has become a rarity.

Does it help an argument to explode it into a hundred fragments and put them back together in no definite order, to throw the problem at the reader? It is one thing to present pure information in an interactive form. Sequence is less important (though not irrelevant) and you can take in as much, or as little, as you like. The logical links in an argument, though, are the argument. Take them away and all you have is a collection of soundbites, or viewbites: superficially impressive perhaps, but incoherent at the core.

8vo could not have chosen a more tightly sealed bottle for their message of cultural revolution. The talk may be of openness and access, of global compatibility, but the reality, at this point, is closure and silence. In a year or so many more of us – that is, the design community, not the wider public – will own the hardware needed to play *Octavo* (play seems the more natural verb here than read). In the meantime, the difficulty of viewing it highlights the most worrying aspect of this technology: information becomes the property of a select group wealthy enough to afford access. The thought bothers the democrats at 8vo. "When information is the currency of power," they insist, "access must be universal." Max Whitby, meanwhile, dreams of a future with a screen in every room.

Must be universal? In every room? I'm sorry to be linear about this, but is there any evidence to suggest that multinational corporations now view themselves as a branch of the social services? Quite the opposite. Look at the way they buy film studios and record companies to ensure a steady flow of product for their hardware. Look at the attempts of Sega and Nintendo to control the software developed for their consoles. Look at the inflated prices (in Britain) of computer games and music CDs. Look at the globalisation of culture, the relentless promotion of the bland, the mediocre and the moronic, the wholesale erosion of local difference. The linear and literary culture that some of our visionaries are so anxious to banish might just have been a way of resisting this process.

Blueprint, February 1993

BORN AFTER TELEVISION

I opened a magazine the other day to find myself stopped in my tracks by a logical absurdity. It was the first sentence of an article on magazine design. "Most likely," it said, "you're not reading this anyway." But if no one was reading, then why address this notional non-reader as though they were (actually, why bother to write at all?). For anyone who was reading, it was a daft thing to write because clearly it wasn't true.

It did, however, embody one idea very effectively, an idea that is now tantamount to publishing wisdom. I hear it so often these days that I am starting to feel seriously out of step with the times. I'm also wondering whether I should start looking for a new job. You see, apparently, *Nobody reads anymore.*

You're sceptical that anyone could sensibly claim this? After all, you are reading this; and that's two of us who still read. Well here is Roger Black, design director of the Hearst publishing empire, quoted in the same article: "Nobody 'reads' anymore." Okay, I admit there is a slight difference. Black reportedly said "reads" with inverted commas around it – perhaps he made those air marks with his fingers as he spoke.

Presumably what he meant was that although people buy magazines, leaf through them, look at the pictures, sample the odd intro and caption, dip in and out, they don't actually read articles in the old-fashioned, tediously linear, A-to-B sense of the word. If so, the quotation marks should, strictly speaking, be round this new kind of reading – the "reading" that is not really reading at all. Of course, to the "post-TV generation . . . conditioned to be visual" invoked by Black, such niceties will seem beside the point.

I'm going to come back to the assumptions routinely made about this post-TV generation. First, though, in case anyone doubts it, I want to emphasise that this issue – is anybody reading? – far from being a sideshow, is fundamental to the development of communication design. This is where the debates, such as they are, are taking place. This is where the battles should be fought.

The problem is that in the rhetoric that surrounds new media and which is increasingly coming to invade graphic design, there is a complete lack of proportion. The utopian proclamations start to look suspiciously like a cover-up for a power struggle, with one side preparing to seize the opportunity to wrest control of the means of communication from the other. For the self-appointed visionaries, you notice, everything must change. It is not enough to put reference books on to CD-ROM, the entire library must be digitised. It's this use of absolutes the whole time – "nobody reads", "the book is dead" – that is the surest sign that vested interests of one kind or another are doing the talking, and not common sense.

Listen to Jeffery Keedy, head of graphic design at California Institute of the Arts: "The dominant and repressive role of the text over the image is breaking down," he writes in *Fast Forward*, a selection of recent projects from the school. Sounds pretty momentous, but what on earth does it mean? Does "text" dominate in the movies pumped out by neighbouring Hollywood? In television? In pop videos? In computer games? Or are we just talking about the printed realm in which graphic design has (until now) mainly operated? And is all text, any kind of text, even his own text, really, as Keedy appears to be saying, somehow by its very nature repressive?

It is no use looking to Keedy's text to answer any of these questions. Keedy's essay (his word) is cast in the form of a digital painting in which words and phrases drift and meld and blur. It is readable enough, given a little patience, and it looks quite exciting, as though something is happening, but its text-bite approach to argument is no more substantial or convincing in the end than a puff of hot air. It touches on subjects of great interest and importance, whets your appetite, then floats off after 50 words to the next one. It is far too busy asserting the priority of word-image over textual content to explore any of the issues it raises in depth or with the clarity they require. Yet for all its superficiality, it will have influence. Keedy is a respected figure and students will parrot this stuff about repressive text to justify work that serves their own purposes if no one else's.

Which brings us back to the post-TV generation. I am "post-TV" myself – you probably are, too – in the sense that I was born after the invention of television and grew up with one in the house. I also grew up with plenty of print. I don't want one thing or the other, the verbal or the visual. I want both, the best of each, used and where appropriate combined, for whatever they do best. I'm with Keedy when he tells us that the "computer influences the creation of meaning". This is true, surely, of any communication medium. It is why, for instance, American television news gives such a circumscribed view of the world. And it is just as true of text, printed or electronic. Anyone who has tried to write anything at all knows that the amount of space allocated has a direct bearing on what you can say. Reduce the space and you reduce what can be said. Reduce what is said and before long you start to oversimplify. Oversimplify and you reduce understanding. Reduce understanding and you encourage ignorance. Now that's what I call repression.

The wisest counsel I have seen on this issue comes from the French theorist Gilles Deleuze. "The choice isn't between written literature and audiovisual media," he writes in *Zone 6: Incorporations*. "It's between creative forces (in audiovisual media as well as literature) and forces of domestication. It's highly unlikely that audiovisual media will find the conditions for creation, if they've been lost in literature." Exactly. For a healthy culture, we still need the words – information, analysis, debate, criticism – and if we fail to provide them the consequences will be dire. If no one is reading Roger Black's magazines it might just be not because people are post-TV, or sub-literate, or conditioned to respond only to visual stimuli, or oppressed by the dominance of text, but because these publications (the latest being *Esquire Gentleman*) have nothing of very great interest to say in the first place.

Blueprint, November 1993*

SENSORY SEDUCTION
BRIAN ENO

Brian Eno wears so many hats even he seems uncertain how best to describe himself.
Musician, record producer, video artist and installation maker are the easy ones. Then
there is the consultancy for a Parisian perfume company, the vase for Alessi, the lecture
to EC businessmen on "The Future of Culture", the study he sponsored on central
African pygmies, and his visiting professorship at the Royal College of Art. On *Desert
Island Discs* Sue Lawley suggested Eno was a bit of a dabbler and the accusation of
dilettantism has dogged him since his earliest days as Roxy Music's befeathered synth
man. Eno prefers to call it "inter-disciplinary research". He is "someone who deals in
ideas", a "frame-maker" who looks at the artificial boundaries we draw round an activity
and suggests ways of enlarging the frame to take in new things. "My whole career
can be seen as a continual redesigning of various accepted formats," he said recently.
"I think about design all the time, in that I think about the form of things and of their
other possibilities."

We meet at his London studio to discuss *Self Storage*, the installation that Eno, fellow
artist–musician Laurie Anderson and eighteen of Eno's RCA students are devising in
association with Artangel for a 650-unit storage depot next to Wembley Stadium. "It's
a very neutral, strange space and mysterious because you are always wondering what's
behind all these doors," says Eno. The team has 30 or so empty units, varying from
50 to 4,500 square feet in size, to fill with unexpected diversions, sonic interludes and
art stunts. A series of spoken stories by Anderson – "some of them abstracted so they
become almost pure sound" – are the starting points for these environments, but with
one month to go Eno is candid about how much remains to be done. "I've got 35 or 40
ideas of my own. I'll just go there, try them, think 'oh, that one looks good' and it might
suggest another idea I hadn't thought of before."

For British visitors it will provide a rare opportunity to take the measure of Eno as
an audiovisual artist. Since 1979, he has exhibited "vertical format" videos (*Mistaken
Memories of Mediaeval Manhattan* was one title), light paintings, light sculptures and
more recent slide-based work in New York, San Francisco, Amsterdam, Toronto, Tokyo,
Sydney, Berlin, Milan and Venice. But there has been only one substantial British show,
"Place #11" at the Riverside Studios in 1986. While most gallery art is consumed at a far
from contemplative clip, the darkened Riverside installation lives in the memory as
a remarkable fusion of ambient washes of sound and soothing prismatic light which
hijacked the metabolism and slowed the body to an almost involuntary stop (armchairs
and sitting areas were provided). Its effect was both calmative and invigorating.

For Eno, it is the nature of the viewer's perceptual experience, rather than the formal
qualities of these pieces, that counts. The object is no longer the principal aim of the

Speaker Flowers. Unit at the
storage depot installation,
Self Storage. Artist: Brian
Eno. Artangel, London, 1995

design process. "The classical idea is that the artist has an idea in their mind, this vision. They put it into the art work and you come along and look at it and that vision is then in your mind. This idea that there's a transmission process is the old idea, as far as I'm concerned, of how art works. Of course if that's the model you are using, all your attention goes into getting the object exactly right. Another way you can think of an artist is as someone who wants to make something happen inside the viewer. What I make is a generator; the output of it is intrinsically uninteresting unless it has some effect, whereas classical art always says the object is intrinsically interesting – the value is embedded in the thing. If you are lucky you will apprehend the value and some of it will communicate to you. But what I'm saying is that the value is in the interaction."

These preoccupations have taken a new turn in the 1990s. The interactive promise of hypertext and CD-ROMs made Eno a natural convert. There are two computers in his studio and we spend the afternoon moving back and forth between them as Eno demonstrates new software, calls up a file for reference, or stares as if mesmerised at the swirling patterns created by the screen-savers he cobbles together and modifies in his spare time. For Eno, writing in a recent *New Scientist*, the most interesting consequences of interactivity will be the "blurring of distinctions between artist and audience . . . the diffusion of authorship".

A studio wall is covered with cards inscribed with phrases such as "role blur", "acceptance of uncertainty" and "making the medium fail", working notes for a book to be published, if he ever finishes it, by Faber and Faber. For a while it was going to be a hypertext, but, as Eno discovered, the technology has yet to live up to the theory. In the 1970s, he made a virtue of malfunctioning synthesizers and shunned the latest upgrades. His attitude to new media, confronted by the reality, is equally critical and subversive:

"All this stuff is crap." He puts in a hypertext disk, a barrage of text boxes and criss-crossing lines. "Whatever the literary content of this, I maintain that the experience of reading off here is so off-putting that you would never do serious reading like this." What is missing, he says, is sensory seduction and narrative pull.

Heel-dragging CD-ROMs get equally short shrift. "People doing CD-ROMs are trying to occupy the space currently occupied by film or video, CD music and text. And it's a very unsuccessful medium in all those three respects. Interactivity only makes sense if it's happening at the speed you are happening at. You just don't want to be stuck waiting for days for the next silly decision to come up."

Most existing CD-ROMs are archival: they are ways of navigating through big chunks of pre-formed data which have to be loaded into the computer's RAM. Eno's experiments with screen-savers suggested a different model. "A screen-saver is a very small program that constantly generates material. It's not a playback of an existing block of data. It's a system for making new material using the computer as a generator. The future of CD-ROMs doesn't lie in stuffing them with huge blocks of data that you clumsily shovel around, which to me seems like trying to move huge forests. The future lies in using the CD-ROM as a system for carrying thousands of seeds. All you do is plant those seeds in your computer, which takes a fraction of a second because they are two or five kilobytes, and they tell the computer what to make."

The next generation of CD-ROMs, suggests Eno, will be a combination of data carrier and seed carrier. The data part of the disc would, for instance, store a foreground figure in a representational scene, while the seed part would generate the less complicated background against which the figure moved. Eno hopes to use these ideas in collaboration with David Bowie on a CD-ROM that will function as a "visual machine" for generating "paintings-in-motion". The user could either sit back and let the disc run without the tedious, point-and-click imperative to "interact", or cause reactions in the program just by moving the mouse, or touching the keyboard, or even by making sounds. Either way, you would never see exactly the same thing twice on screen. There would be two or three different mixes for each piece of music.

This idea of the self-generating system, capable in theory of an infinity of permutations, is the central idea in Eno's work. As he himself once observed, "a very small number of ideas can be permutated in a very large number of ways". The ambient loops that form the soundtrack to his installations will eventually turn full circle (even the one that lasts 168 weeks) but they will never coincide with exactly the same visual events generated by the concealed video monitors and desynchronised slide projectors Eno uses as light sources. His Alessi vase was manufactured according to a complicated system, involving the throwing of dice, which meant no two designs were the same. "What excites me," he once said, "is seeing the same few things reclustering and thrown together in different perspectives in relation to each other." While the process might sound random, or soullessly automatic, the quality of the musical and visual "inputs" is carefully controlled. Eno has learned from the Cageian process-art and process-music of the 1960s that inspired his first experiments as a student. Such work failed because it placed all the emphasis on the conceptual dimension, overlooking the sensory factors that make us return to it.

Watching Eno playing with his screen-savers, his capacity for unselfconscious and almost childlike absorption is clear. For Eno, the sensory level is the hook. He can lose himself in colour, go into a kind of dream. "I often sit here like this." He leans in towards the screen. "I try to make it fill my field of vision. What I would love is to be able to make wallpaper like this." When I ask him what effect his own slide shows have on him, he says "I'm totally hypnotised by them. I just sit there thinking 'God, that is so amazing. I've never seen anything like that in my life,'" Eno can spin an effortless web of words and theory around almost anything – art, music, technology, politics, perfume, defence – but in the throes of the art experience there is only a kind of wonder to be expressed.

Eno is best thought of, perhaps, as an environmental artist. He conceived ambient music in the 1970s as a darker-hued muzak for the artistically inclined. *Music for Airports* was installed – to disquieting effect – at La Guardia Airport and, in 1989, *Tropical Rainforest Sound Installation* brought a jungle ambience to the World Financial Center's Winter Garden (and subsequently to the Barbican Centre, London). But if Eno's interests once seemed to incline towards landscape, with vinyl "sound paintings" such as *On Land*, his concerns are more urban now. Since the early 1990s, he has been in discussion with Laurie Anderson, Peter Gabriel and the Barcelona authorities about the possibility of building a Real World Theme Park in the city. Recently the idea has been reactivated. Another theme park project, in collaboration with the Austrian artist André Heller, is for the depressed industrial city of Bochum in the Ruhr. (Heller has also commissioned Eno to create a permanent "quiet room" installation for a museum he has designed for the glass-maker Swarowski near Innsbruck.) The Bochum and Barcelona teams will participate in each other's projects.

"I'm always keen on things that are cheap and therefore disposable," says Eno. "If you build a $10 million ride and no one likes it very much, what are you going to do? A lot of theme parks have made this mistake. But if you have an idea for a singing tree and you hang it with 25 five-dollar speakers you can leave it up for two weeks and if nobody likes it you just get rid of it, no problem. But if people do like it, then you might do it with better quality speakers and people might start writing music for it. For me, these things must evolve, they must start from quite simple, improvisable routes."

Blueprint, April 1995*

MULTIMEDIARAMA

Multimedia has been hyped so heavily and unthinkingly in the 1990s that it comes as no surprise to find we are now on the cusp of a CD-ROM backlash. Among early adopters (as ad agency researchers like to put it) there is a growing mood of disenchantment and a feeling that CD-ROMs have failed to deliver. The technology is ploddingly slow, the interfaces clumsy, the mainstream product-line banal, and who really wants to spend large chunks of their leisure time gawping at computer screens?

CD-ROMs do, of course, have their uses. The makers of encyclopedias and other information products are rethinking the future of print with good reason. But art? A few months ago at the Royal College of Art I attended a packed screening of the Residents' *Freakshow*, regularly touted at that point by the computer press as one of the best CD-ROMs you could buy. Art and design students and teachers trooped into the viewing theatre with a real sense of anticipation, but the feeling afterwards was one of disappointment. The whole experience, from the stop-start momentum to the crudity of the animation compared to its cinematic equivalent, was deemed to be neither seductive nor compelling.

So far, despite the ballyhoo, very few visual artists have produced CD-ROMs. It is not possible to visit the ICA bookshop and come away with an armful of interesting experiments. The reviews pages of *Frieze* have featured only one, the highly recommended *Blam!* by the New York-based digital satirists Necro Enema Amalgamated. Defiantly low-tech and aggressively non-interactive, it shows what the technology can achieve in the hands of independent media artists with guerrilla sensibilities and a lack of preconceptions. Another early exponent is Los Angeles painter Bill Barminski, creator, in the 1980s, of the Situationist cartoon hero Tex Hitler. "The important thing about CD-ROMs is that they're cheap enough to keep in the hands of individuals," Barminski explained on Channel 4's *Once Upon a Time in Cyberville.* "It's important to keep corporations from taking control and basically making everything bland in order to sell more."

Barminski's *Consumer Product* CD-ROM (1994) takes the archival approach and in that sense relates to a disc like *Freakshow*, which packs in punter-friendly back-catalogue details and pop promo snippets. As well as browsing Bill's *catalogue raisonné* – imaginatively animated – we can see him in interview, listen to LA critics and collectors singing his praises, leaf through his entire comic book output, watch him hanging a show, drop by for the opening, and read his cuttings file. I had mixed feelings about Barminksi's rather obvious neo-Pop paintings full of car tyres, spark plugs, football stars, Elvis, Nixon, and smiling all-American faces with doubled-up eyes and mouths. A typical example, *Product Identification* (1991), shows Christ crowned with thorns, with the slogan "Time out for a refreshing Pepsi". But while *Consumer Product* told me more about Barminksi than I would ever have asked, it did it in a way that was engaging – on-screen icons take the form of bottles and packets – and nicely reflective of the popular culture that inspired him.

What Barminski's disc doesn't do, except in a rather clumsy animated sequence, is attempt to use the resources of the CD-ROM to create a new kind of art particular to the medium. Two recent discs tackle this problem in radically different ways. The aptly named *Headcandy* (1994) is a collaboration between American video whizzkids Christopher Juul and Douglas Jipson, with music by Brian Eno. The basic idea, presented here as a discovery though it's as old as the *Doctor Who* title sequence, is to point a video camera at a TV screen. The resulting feedback, used to extraordinary effect in *Headcandy*, is what *2001* would have looked like if it had only consisted of the "Star Gate" sequence. Cloudbursts of psychedelic colour rush towards you from some distant planetary horizon. Strange geometries replicate and fold in on themselves in feats of cosmic origami.

The only interaction involved in *Headcandy* lies in pulling down the blinds, donning a pair of prismatic spectacles (provided), selecting one of the five pieces for viewing, and keeping a straight face. Eno's track titles – "Beast", "Spunk Worship", "Manila Envelope" – are red herrings. There is nothing concrete here, no ideas, just overwhelming visual sensation. *Headcandy* is a disco for your desktop and the most notable thing about it, ultimately, is that it longs to dissolve the distracting division between the hardware frame of the monitor and the space around it: standing well back, wearing the glasses, causes the central image to multiply around the screen. The wallpaper version will be fabulous.

Equally playful, though it comes much closer to the mood and conventions of gallery art, is *The ToyBox* (1995), released in association with Video Positive 95. Inside the box are twenty "toys", each by a different artist. A few achieve real resonance. With Jon Thomson and Alison Craighead's *Thalamus* you use your mouse to tune a kind of spirit radio. "Do you know where you are going?" asks a medium. "Heading for the sea," replies a quiet voice. "Do you have friends?" "Dead." And yet, in a way that has no obvious solution at this stage, the computer tends to domesticate the experience. A similar idea, installed in gallery conditions, could achieve a much greater control of atmosphere. Some *ToyBox* contributors confront the delivery medium's limitations by building the computer into the piece. Janni Perton's *Squeezer* turns your display into a conceptual fruit machine with pay-out noises and ironic punchlines ("fondle blissful supplication"), while Robert Mettler's *System Decay* invades your desktop and bugs you by repeatedly calling on a telephone icon ("Sorry, incoming calls only").

As *The ToyBox*'s makers acknowledge, "no one piece could be said to be definitive". But the project offers enough imaginative variety to suggest that the CD-ROM has considerable untapped potential as a medium for artists. New ways of thinking about interface and content are exactly what is needed at this point to lift the medium from the doldrums and propel it to the next stage of development.

Frieze, summer 1995

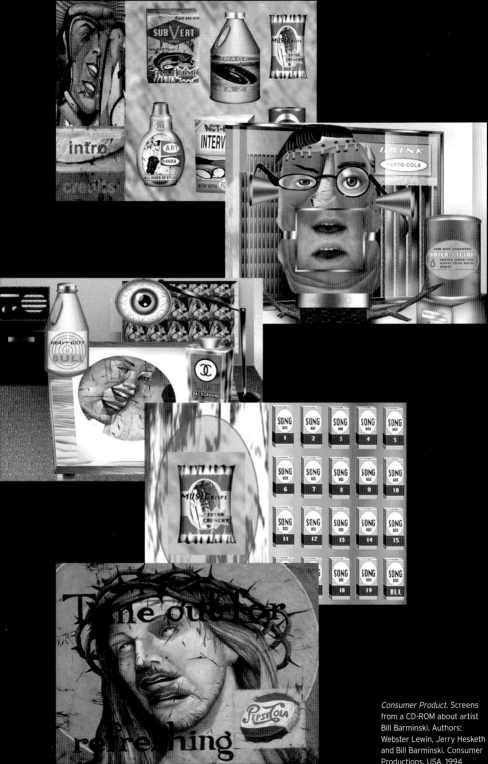

Consumer Product. Screens from a CD-ROM about artist Bill Barminski. Authors: Webster Lewin, Jerry Hesketh and Bill Barminski. Consumer Productions, USA, 1994

7. CROSSOVERS

CULTURAL APARTHEID

The received wisdom these days is that we are all moving effortlessly along a value-free expressway that connects high culture to low culture, the popular with the highbrow. Every so often dissenting voices are heard and the hoary old debate starts up again – is Keats better than Dylan? – on *The Late Show* and arts pages. The daily reality, though, in television and the press is that from opera to comic books, it's all equally valid. When the issues of quality and hierarchy do find their way back into the discussion, the progressive critical consensus seems to be that it is right to try to distinguish between good and bad within a particular art form, but misguided and pointless to rank one against the other, poetry against pop lyric.

On the face of it, this sounds like good news for design. In a climate with so few preconceptions and a willingness to embrace cultural activity in all its forms, we ought to see a new openness in the media to the many facets of a wide subject. Has this actually happened? Well yes, on the surface, over the last few years, there has been an increase in design coverage on the features, "living", "style" and business pages of our national press. In the average commissioning editor's mind, design is classified in a file marked "shopping (exotic)". But design as culture, in a quality broadsheet, given the same kind of prominence in the arts pages as art, film, theatre or music? That remains very much the exception to the rule.

A widely publicised exhibition at the Barbican Centre, London provides a telling instance of this peculiar cultural apartheid at work. "The Sixties Art Scene in London", and the accompanying book, are exceptional for the way they bring together examples of painting and sculpture with posters, photographs, catalogues, magazines, manifestos and satirical cartoons. As a visitor equally interested in both art and design, this seemed to me a more than usually engaging and revealing approach for its organiser, David Mellor of Sussex University, to take. The interconnections and crossovers formed one of the key arguments of the show.

You would hardly realise this, though, from reading the papers. Most of the art critics assigned to cover "The Sixties Art Scene in London" conveyed the pained impression of having visited an ordinary fine art exhibition with some regrettable omissions (Bacon, Moore, Auerbach etc.) and a certain amount of inconsequential and irritating ephemera thrown in. Of the seven broadsheet reviews I saw, only one gave anything more than a passing mention to this aspect of the show. Those they cold-shouldered included Ken Garland, Herbert Spencer, Robert Brownjohn, Archigram, Jock Kinneir and Margaret Calvert, Fletcher/Forbes/Gill, and Gordon House, active as both artist and design consultant, and designer of a complete graphic identity for the seminal Situation group. It took Bauhaus scholar Frank Whitford, writing in the *Sunday Times*, to make the self-evident point that the links between graphic design and the fine arts during this period were unusually close and productive.

These reviews are a particularly blatant example of the bias against design, but the fact is that design as visual culture is short-changed in the same way all the time. Does a newspaper have a regular critic, correspondent or column dedicated to design and located somewhere in the vicinity of its art and architecture coverage? If the answer is no, and it almost invariably will be, then it doesn't take the subject very seriously. So here at least, the conventional pecking order is very much intact: art is "high" and worthy, design is "low" and negligible, and rarely the two shall meet.

If the British media has difficulty in seeing design as culture, high or low, it could be because the design community and the magazines that speak for it have a similar problem. Most discussion of design within the design press is couched in terms of client briefs and business goals. Journalists and publishers seem happier with commerce than culture. It is hard for a specialist press to stand apart from the subjects it depends on for survival and speak truthfully about the wider implications, cultural or otherwise.

Designers are wary and defensive when the cultural aspect of their work comes under scrutiny, especially when the conclusions are unfavourable. The most notorious example of this in recent years was the introduction of the BT identity. Here, for once, in both design press and newspapers, much of the response was cultural in nature, with many designers also charging headlong into the debate. The identity was criticised as an example of bad design and as a lamentable contribution to national visual culture. The consultants, inevitably, were aggrieved. We were invited to reconsider the issue in terms of global market positioning and commercial necessity. We always are.

Graphic design remains, in many ways, the most difficult area of design to discuss in broader cultural terms. Outside American design journalism, which has strong ties with the universities, there are few useful precedents. In Britain, graphic design criticism is still at a rudimentary stage. Away from the big national stories such as BT, newspapers have problems with graphic design subjects because, by and large, there is nothing tangible for the reader to buy – so what's the angle? If there is something to buy, it will already be covered by some other area of the paper, though not specifically, or even at all, for its design content: books on the book pages, magazines on the media page, historical ephemera such as posters in the "collecting" column. It is far from enough.

I dwell on media coverage because it is probably the best index of public design awareness we have. If the papers can't see the point of thinking about material culture as a part of their regular arts coverage, then what chance their readers? Awareness won't improve until it is routine to send both an art critic and a design critic to an exhibition like "The Sixties Art Scene in London", or better still a single critic who can write even-handedly about both.

Blueprint, May 1993

KIT OF IMAGES

Pop Art began, at least to some extent, as an act of recovery – part homage, part analysis – of the graphic imagery of popular culture. But it ended by stimulating the design culture it had set out to map. Pop's distillation and framing of the disposable image was so graphically accomplished that it would have been astonishing if it had not influenced commercial designers and image-makers professionally attuned to the smallest changes of style in the fine arts. Long after the period of classic Pop had passed, its repercussions were still being felt in typography, book covers, magazine illustrations, posters, advertisements and album covers.

Some of the first British graphic designers to reflect the full impact of Pop were, not surprisingly given its provenance, those at the Royal College of Art. Throughout the late 1950s, the college magazine, *Ark*, had played an enthusiastic role in the debate on popular culture initiated by the exhibitions of the Independent Group. It published Peter and Alison Smithson's essay, "But Today We Collect Ads", with its notorious proposition that "advertising ... is beating the fine arts at their old game", and cast a tolerant eye on the (then) culturally dubious subjects of science fiction, comic books and the Hollywood musical.

In an article titled "New Readers Start Here" in issue 32 (summer 1962), the critic Richard Smith presented the work of three graduating college artists: David Hockney, Peter Phillips and Derek Boshier. But the magazine itself was a striking demonstration of the Pop graphics effect, from its orange, red and yellow cover illustration constructed from a fairground slot machine, joker playing card and Victorian moustaches, to the collage "Kit of Images" by art editor Brian Haynes that came inside. The iconography included targets (an obvious reference to Jasper Johns and Peter Blake), tin cars and robots, and a packet of Kellogg's Special K (Boshier had tackled the same theme in a painting the previous year).

Ark's graphic experimentation was to have a considerable influence on the consumer magazines and colour supplements of the early 1960s, as its student art editors moved into the world of commercial publishing. Writing in the catalogue that accompanied the "Graphics RCA" exhibition in 1963, Mark Boxer, editor of the *Sunday Times* colour section, acknowledged *Ark*'s impact and its central position, both drawing from Pop Art and also sending its messages back via magazines of the consumer society Pop was celebrating: "... it has exuberance, and at the same time style. The reason for this must surely not be unconnected with the Painting School. The pop art movement certainly owes a great deal to graphics. But in its turn it has enriched graphics and *Ark* in particular ... In these issues there is a spontaneous enjoyment of today, with a typographic and design style that has a wide future. The pop-graphic movement

Town. Magazine cover. Editor:
Nicholas Tomalin. Art director:
Thomas Wolsey. Artist: Barry
Fantoni. Haymarket Publishing
Group, Great Britain, May 1963

may be instant nostalgia, but this is the very stuff of visual magazines."

The speed with which Pop Art images became part of the visual currency of magazine graphics is well demonstrated by a *Town* cover from May 1963 (art director, Thomas Wolsey). Owing much to the colouring and compositional method of paintings by Peter Blake and Peter Phillips, Barry Fantoni's illustration unites the pop culture themes of the issue (love comics; singer Ray Charles) to form a wonderfully integrated collage in which even the titlepiece, cover price and date play a part. Inside, the stencil lettering used for the love comics headline recalls early pieces by Joe Tilson. Undoubtedly it is parody Pop – but carried off with exactly the right balance of affection, irreverence and wit.

As the decade progressed, the influence of Pop on British graphic design became more diffuse, the homages less literal. It was as much a question of attitude – Richard Hamilton's "popular, transient, expendable, low cost, mass produced, young, witty, sexy, gimmicky, glamorous, big business" – as of specific styles. Penguin Books took on 23-year-old Alan Aldridge (later to edit *The Beatles Illustrated Lyrics*) as art director of its fiction titles; his aim, he declared with youthful zeal, was to "reach the kids", to which end he employed airbrush illustration, photographic still lifes and shock-tactic cover lines ("who put Hopjoy in the acid bath?"). Alan Fletcher, co-founder in 1962 of the design group Fletcher/Forbes/Gill, also designed posters for Pirelli which are as "Pop" in conception and impact as any graphics of the period. One, a graphic spiral of rubber showing alternative tyre radials, anticipates Hamilton's *Five Tyres Remoulded*, not completed until 1970. Robert Brownjohn, another key exponent of Pop graphics, designed a poster for "Obsession and Fantasy" at the Robert Fraser Gallery, while Fraser himself was at the nexus of graphics, music and Pop.

It was pop music, in fact, which found the most apt uses for the new imagery. "Pop art borrowed from real pop and we're taking it back again," said Pete Townshend, former student at Ealing Art College and guitarist of the Who. Townshend and his manager Kit Lambert presented the Who as a self-consciously Pop Art act, draping the band in chevrons, arrows, Union Jack jackets (courtesy of Johns's and Blake's flag paintings) and, of course, the by now obligatory targets, and parodying advertising graphics on the cover of the album *The Who Sell Out*. The Beatles' manipulation of Pop codes and practices was equally sharp. A promising early exercise in Warholian repetition by the photographer Robert Freeman for the cover of *A Hard Day's Night* was followed, in 1967, by the definitive Pop/pop crossover, *Sgt Pepper's Lonely Hearts Club Band* – "not so much a sleeve," according to George Melly, writing in that heady year, "as an art object".

Its creators, Peter Blake and his then wife Jann Howarth (also a Pop artist), were the inspired suggestion of Robert Fraser. Blake had more than served his rock and roll dues with paintings of Elvis, the Everley Brothers and a loving transposition on to canvas of the cover of an album by the Lettermen (even the typography of the original was improved). Blake's intentions were unashamedly populist; his paintings of the late 1950s and early 1960s as tough and impersonal as jukebox vinyl. "I like to think my pictures can be enjoyed by young people who like pop music," he said in 1963, working on a portrait of the Liverpool moptops. *Sgt Pepper*, an icon of 1960s graphics so familiar that it needs little gloss, brought the cycle of influence full circle. Its cardboard insert of cut-out memorabilia, including the eponymous sergeant's stripes, moustache and portrait, is a painter's update of the "image kit" included in *Ark* number 32, which was itself, of course, a graphic designer's précis of Pop.

Although it might once have seemed to presage some ultimate fusion of graphics and Pop, *Sgt Pepper* did not lead to the spate of similar collaborations one might have expected. Richard Hamilton was commissioned to create the cover of the Beatles' next album, but signalled his conceptual purity and art world reserve by specifying a plain white sleeve marked only by an "edition" number for the first two million copies. Much later, in 1981, Peter Blake designed a sleeve for the Who's *Face Dances* using band portraits by Hamilton, Tom Phillips and others. Warhol, whose career had begun with jazz sleeves, did covers for the Velvet Underground and the Rolling Stones.

Mostly, though, it was the commercial designers and illustrators who took on the task of translating the artists' sensibility into pop. *Sgt Pepper* opened the floodgates of graphic ambition, and the album cover rapidly became, as George Melly put it, "the natural home of the Pop visual style". But the purest, most intense (and shortest-lived) medium for the new Pop graphics was the psychedelic poster, a deranged amalgam of brash screenprint colours, Aubrey Beardsley fantasy and typographic freakout – like Art Nouveau on Surrealist acid. Its most accomplished exponents in London were Michael English and Nigel Waymouth, working under the name Hapshash and the Coloured Coat, and the Australian Martin Sharp, designer of album covers by Cream and the early issues of *Oz*. The posters usually had some notional function – news of a concert at the Marquee or UFO – but legibility and linear sense were the last concerns on their designers' minds. Their real, LSD-soaked purpose was a revolution in consciousness.

The psychedelic posters took Pop out of the gallery and into the street. Their virtue was their authenticity. They didn't simply recycle Pop mannerisms as the earliest graphics had done; they transformed its spirit (popular, low cost, sexy, expendable) into something new. But commerce, in this case, had got there first. Long before the summer of love, Pop's classic motifs, the Union Jack and target, were surfacing as emblems of swinging London on mugs, shopping bags, sunglasses, T-shirts and knickers. Carnaby Street was awash with Pop graphics tat. By the end of the decade, even the makers of a breakfast cereal were giving away "Pop posters in brilliant psychedelic colours" – yours in return for a handful of packet tops. Filtered, diluted and ready for disposal, Pop as a graphic style had run its course.

RA, no. 32, 1991

THE PROPHET OF POP
RICHARD HAMILTON

Richard Hamilton is one of those rare artists whose work fixes with a sharp, documentary eye the artefacts, images and technological obsessions of his age. "I would like to think of my purpose as a search for what is epic in everyday objects and everyday attitudes," he wrote in 1962. Three decades later, he continues to make pictures which resonate, not always comfortably, with the spirit of the times.

Hamilton's output is famously various and sparse, his gestation period counted in years rather than months. "Every opus is ponderously contrived," he admits. Even Hamilton enthusiasts find this quicksilver stylist "maddeningly difficult" to place. Like his friend and similarly cerebral mentor Marcel Duchamp, he has made it an operating principle to do next the opposite of whatever he did last. Hamilton positively veers between media – printmaking, painting, photography, installation, industrial design – and has tried his hand at almost every genre of art, even landscape and flower painting.

The last few years have seen a resurgence of interest in his work. His central role in the Independent Group – "that loose association of unlike spirits", as he called it – was underscored by an exhibition at the ICA in 1990. In a letter to the Smithsons in 1957, Hamilton sketched out a working definition of Pop Art that still holds good: "popular, transient, expendable, low cost, mass produced, young, witty, sexy, gimmicky, glamorous, big business". In summer 1991, Anthony d'Offay put on his first major show in London for fifteen years, while the "Pop Art Show" at the Royal Academy provided a rare opportunity to assess Hamilton (and other British painters) against the more bombastic Pop of the Americans. Where many erstwhile icons now proved to be loud but empty vessels, Hamilton emerged with his reputation enhanced, every bit the old-style fine artist committed to traditional painterly values that he had always claimed himself to be.

Hamilton's genius, as 1992's Tate Gallery retrospective showed, was to have it both ways – to celebrate the glamour of the mass-produced advertising images he and his IG colleagues so enthusiastically clipped and filed, while preserving his aesthetic detachment and cultural poise. He is an artist who can graft contours derived from Praxiteles's classical *Hermes* on to the body parts of musclemen and call the hunk that results *Adonis in Y Fronts*. By comparison, American Pop artists such as Warhol and Lichtenstein stayed very much closer to the surface of their twentieth-century sources. Their transcriptions of commercial reality might not have been completely verbatim, but the epiphanic dumbness of the original cartoon frame or Brillo pad box is intrinsic to the effect. Hamilton tried this once himself in a shield-sized blow-up of a badge bearing the slogan "Slip it to me" – he called it *Epiphany* (1964). But in paintings of the late 1950s, such as *Hers is a Lush Situation* and *$he*, the subject matter is never simply dumped in front of the viewer with a disengaged shrug. It is always sifted and assimilated, broken down into its most significant particles – the angle of a fridge's open door, the precise curve of a fender, a toaster or a backless dress – then used as a catalyst for the making of a new composite image with the enduring quality of a contemporary myth.

Hamilton, said the critic Lawrence Alloway, was a new kind of "knowing consumer". Like fellow Independent Group member Reyner Banham, who loaned him some of the research material he drew on for *Hommage à Chrysler Corp*, he was obsessed with American auto-styling and the way in which these finned and bloated "vehicles of desire" – to use Banham's image – were presented in the ads. From the 1957 Buick to the Exquisite Form Bra, Hamilton was a highly literate connoisseur of advanced industrial styling, built-in obsolescence and the latest consumer trends. He made it his business to follow what was happening at design-conscious corporations such as General Motors, IBM, Olivetti and Braun. Dieter Rams's designs, he once confessed, "have come to occupy a place in my heart and consciousness that the Mont Sainte-Victoire did in Cézanne's". For another of his circuitous homages, a multiple called *The Critic Laughs*, he borrowed a Braun electric toothbrush, replacing the company's logo with his own name, the "i" raised in affectionate imitation of Braun's "a".

In his own work as a critic, Hamilton's range was impressive. As well as providing lucid expositions of his own procedures, he wrote or lectured on Duchamp (whose *Large Glass* he reconstructed for the Tate Gallery), art education, the books of Dieter Roth, the evolution of film projection technology and, of course, industrial design. Quizzed by *Design* magazine about the state of British design ten years after the Festival of Britain, he replied: "There is too little stress laid on product research in the consumer goods industries, too little initiation of product programmes at the design level, not enough probing of markets and too many curbs on imagination; production programming is all too often restricted by backward-looking sales executives." The year was 1961, but he might have been talking about today.

Given these interests, it was almost inevitable that Hamilton would be drawn into design. Although it has never been more than a sideline, he is an accomplished typographer. His typographic version of Duchamp's *Green Box*, the artist's unsequenced, hand-written notes for the *Large Glass* (1960), was a remarkable feat of transliteration – and an arcane delight. His design for his own *Collected Words* (1982), a book of writings, interviews and lectures, has the playful clarity one might expect of a teacher who (with Victor Pasmore) introduced a Basic Design Course partly modelled on the Bauhaus to Newcastle School of Art, and who had internalised, and moved beyond, the rationalist principles of Ulm. Hamilton mixes Times Roman with an upright sanserif and a more "intimate" italic. "A general lack of conformity helps to isolate and identify segments of a sporadic and diverse output," his preamble explains.

Hamilton's first venture into industrial design, at the invitation of Lux Corporation in Japan, produced strangely hybrid results. Accustomed to exploring the "illusion and paradox" of two-dimensional representations of form, he balked at the idea of a three-dimensional object. His solution, *Lux 50* (1979), was an abstract painting attached to a functioning amplifier which can be connected by plug-in leads to the other components of a hi-fi.

"Every day, perhaps every hour, I touch my radio or record player. Maybe a similar rapport could be achieved with a painting," he speculated. Presented as "art", he said,

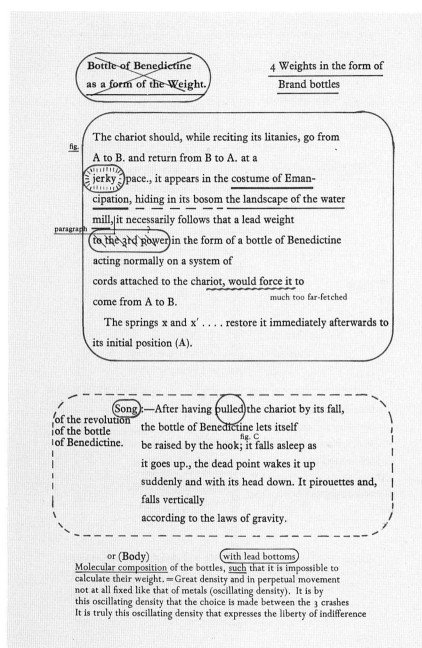

Bottle of Benedictine as a form of the Weight.

4 Weights in the form of Brand bottles

fig.

The chariot should, while reciting its litanies, go from A to B. and return from B to A. at a jerky pace., it appears in the costume of Eman-cipation, hiding in its bosom the landscape of the water mill, it necessarily follows that a lead weight

paragraph

to the 3rd power in the form of a bottle of Benedictine acting normally on a system of cords attached to the chariot, would force it to come from A to B.

much too far-fetched

The springs x and x′ . . . . restore it immediately afterwards to its initial position (A).

of the revolution of the bottle of Benedictine.

(Song):—After having pulled the chariot by its fall, the bottle of Benedictine lets itself be raised by the hook; it falls asleep as it goes up., the dead point wakes it up suddenly and with its head down. It pirouettes and, falls vertically according to the laws of gravity.

fig. C

or (Body) (with lead bottoms)
Molecular composition of the bottles, such that it is impossible to calculate their weight. = Great density and in perpetual movement not at all fixed like that of metals (oscillating density). It is by this oscillating density that the choice is made between the 3 crashes It is truly this oscillating density that expresses the liberty of indifference

The Bride Stripped Bare By Her Bachelors, Even. Page from a typographic version of Marcel Duchamp's *Green Box.* Artist/designer: Richard Hamilton. Edition Hansjörg Mayer, Stuttgart/London/ Reykjavik, 1976 (first published 1960)

the amplifier had as much chance of surviving as any of his other paintings. But if *Lux 50* seems on one level to suggest that we replot the boundaries of art and design, on another level – the display-worthiness of design in museums – it was as prophetic as ever of forthcoming trends.

In the 1980s Hamilton completed another lengthy industrial design project, this time for a Swedish manufacturer. The square, sharp-cornered, functional casing of the Diab DS-101 minicomputer owes an obvious debt to Rams. Computers clearly fascinate Hamilton, who spends much of his time writing programs in Unix, a notoriously difficult language to master. The same fearless embrace of new technology can be seen in his use of the Quantel Paintbox, shown in the BBC television series *Painting with Light* (1987). Paintbox's scissorless electronic cut-and-paste allows Hamilton to merge images with a seamlessness he never quite achieved in the early collage-paintings.

If Hamilton does, despite the twists and turns, have a characteristic theme, or at least one to which he always comes back, it is the contemporary interior. It was with an interior, after all, that he put down his marker. His tiny collage *Just what is it that makes today's homes so different, so appealing?* (1956) has become one of the defining images and most convenient image-banks of post-war consumer plenty – cited, quoted, adapted, appropriated and even restaged as the title sequence of a TV programme about advertising. "Any interior is a set of anachronisms," Hamilton writes in *Collected Words*, "a museum, with the lingering residues of decorative styles that an inhabited space collects. Banal or beautiful, exquisite or sordid . . . all tell a story and the narrative can be enthralling." He has filtered the residues and decoded the narratives of rooms inhabited by film stars, a fashion photographer's studio, a motel room, a hospital treatment room, a prison cell, a Berlin apartment, Langan's restaurant, La Scala, the bed chamber in Jan van Eyck's *Arnolfini Marriage*, and the entrance hall of a hotel.

The last, called simply *Lobby*, is arguably his masterpiece of the 1980s. Starting from a postcard image of a bland European hotel, Hamilton created a terrifying airbrush smooth anteroom of mirrorglass columns and polka dot-patterned carpet, a nightmare puzzle of reflections and misleading perspective in which the human presence is reduced to a small seated figure lost in the background. To Hamilton, now in his 70s, this nowhere which might be anywhere, familiar to any business traveller or holiday-maker, represents a kind of modern purgatory. "It's a reflection of life and death," he told an American magazine, "this lobby where you wait before you go somewhere else." With his usual painful accuracy, the artist the headline-writers still celebrate as the "Father of Pop" has once again hit the nerve. Perhaps it's his age. Then again, perhaps it's ours.

Blueprint, June 1992

THE WAR GARDEN
IAN HAMILTON FINLAY

With only a week to go before his latest exhibition opens at London's ICA, Ian Hamilton Finlay finds himself once again in a condition of battle alert. He has just received a letter from the Strathclyde Region. Technically he has been at war with the council – the Little Spartan War to give it its full title – since the end of the 1970s. But it is nine years since the notorious Budget Day Raid during which the sheriff officer entered Finlay's garden, Little Sparta, breached the Garden Temple and seized a number of works of art in reparation for unpaid rates on the building.

It took five years to recover these pieces and the dispute, in the meantime, has continued to smoulder. "It's a clear and straightforward question," says Finlay. "The law says that any building which is used wholly or mainly for religious purposes and is related to a body and not just an individual will be exempt from rates. So the question is: does the building fulfil these conditions or not? I say it does."

This time, however, bureaucracy's looters can expect to meet with little resistance. There will be no Finlay supporters styling themselves the Saint-Just Vigilantes to repel them, no campaign headquarters, no camouflaged "panzers", and quite possibly no propaganda – a medium at which Finlay is a master. So far as he is concerned the war may not be over, but the principle has long ago been won. "The issue is very important and to me it's one of the fundamental issues of our time. In the past, it was perfectly clear, even if it wasn't exactly categorised, that the arts overlapped with the spiritual or religion. In our age, we have a situation where the arts overlap with tourism. This has not been properly brought into the consciousness of the culture and that's what I wish to do."

Lately, Finlay's concerns for the garden have taken a more practical turn. He is 66 now and unwell. Stonypath, the abandoned hillside croft he and his wife Sue moved into in 1966, has evolved into a complex six-acre sculpture garden sought out by art enthusiasts and readers of the *Oxford Companion to Gardens* round the world. Every summer, from June to mid-October, they come to Little Sparta in the contemplative "ones or twos" that Finlay recommends, and sometimes by the coachload, to see for themselves the aircraft carrier fountain and bird table, the scattered fragments of stone carved with the inscription "The Present Order is the Disorder of the Future", the nestling homages to Claude, Poussin and Dürer, and the Garden Temple itself, which Finlay, in a provocative equation of harmony and destruction, has dedicated "To Apollo, His Music, His Missiles, His Muses".

And the garden is far from finished. In the last year alone, Finlay has added a mini-cascade with inscription, a pair of gates with finials, and a new swathe of woodland. A further pool is planned in time for the summer. No longer able to devote every

afternoon to his creation, he has finally engaged a gardener. He knows that some
kind of regulation is essential if the garden is to survive him. An activity that began
spontaneously, with no clear plan or end in view, has become the hub of Finlay's
artistic project, the far from still point around which his many endeavours turn.

"I didn't know anything about gardens," Finlay muses softly. "It was like one of
those old master paintings where a cloud descends. I've always worked like this. I get
a kind of feeling or inspiration and start something which I'm innerly certain about but
completely ignorant of. Then I read and look and discover what the antecedents are and
use tradition as a kind of instructor or clarifier. The process goes on until I become quite
knowledgeable. It's always at that stage that you feel the idea is beginning to die away
or change into something else. It's intuition clarified through contact with culture."

In retrospect, though, Finlay's youthful experiences seem oddly prophetic of the
pastoral and martial themes that would come to dominate his work. Called up to fight
during the Second World War, he entered London for the first time sitting astride
a bomb in the back of a lorry. After the war he worked as a shepherd in the Orkneys,
then as an agricultural labourer and writer. Early short stories with rural themes were
followed in the late 1950s by rhyming poems and the founding, in 1961, of The Wild
Hawthorn Press, which published his poetry magazine *Poor. Old. Tired. Horse.* from
1962 to 1967.

During this period, Finlay created concrete poetry and, in 1964, designed his first
environmental poem in sandblasted glass. After the move to Stonypath he began to
build model boats and planes. He was also exploring the idea of the one-word poem –
familiar from the work of Apollinaire and others (though not at this stage to Finlay) –
and its relationship to landscape. "One could (conceivably) have a one-word poem in
a garden," he conjectures in the last issue of *Poor. Old. Tired. Horse.*, "if the surroundings
were conceived as part of the poem."

Finlay's expanded definition of poetry has led him to embrace a wide range of media –
paper, bronze, wood, stone, glass, ceramics, tapestry, embroidery and neon – and brought
him a correspondingly varied team of collaborators. "I consider the interesting thing
in art is not the expression of self, of psychology, but the expression of tradition," he
explains. "If you work with other people it's really quite clear that you are not just

A Wartime Garden. Stone
carving from an artists' book.
Artists: Ian Hamilton Finlay,
John Andrew and Ron
Costley. Photographer:
Antonia Reeve. Graeme
Murray, Great Britain, 1990

expressing yourself. There's an obvious framework already."

He does not meet with his artists and craftsmen: he sends them a letter. It explains with the utmost clarity a piece's conceptual purpose and intended material effect, and includes rough sketches and photocopies of relevant information. Once Finlay has learned the strengths, preferences and "prejudices" of a collaborator, he creates work with these qualities in mind. The aim in all cases – and it is the reason he decided not to attempt to learn these skills himself – is to achieve the highest possible standards of manufacture.

It is all part of a process that Finlay, with his gift for the pungent phrase calculated to affront liberal preconceptions, has termed "neoclassical rearmament". Finlay's feud with the Scottish Arts Council in the late 1970s over his cancellation of an exhibition – "the absence of the works was a clearer statement of their content than the works themselves could have been" – and his skirmishes with the Strathclyde Region led to a literal armouring of his art. The fishing boat, a recurrent early image, was metaphorically torpedoed by the warship. The warship was reinforced by fighter planes, machine guns, bombers and tanks.

"I began to see the garden not just as a place but as a territory and the embodiment of an ideology. I made certain changes in the garden which made its ideology quite explicit. I thought it would be good to have a crisp phrase that said what I thought I was doing, which was a process of neoclassical rearmament. The phrase is quite provocative – deliberately so. I'm all for confronting the actual issues and making them as real and as vivid as possible, not muffling them."

And the real issue now, says Finlay, is power. "There's a great taboo on this subject, but it's quite clear to me that power is part of the given; the presence of power in the universe is a fact. You can pretend it's not there if you wish, but it seems to me that since it's there something has to be done with it. It has to be organised or dealt with or neutralised, and you can only do this by first admitting that it does exist."

In Finlay's view, the definitive neoclassical event was the French Revolution and he has deployed the thoughts of its Jacobin heroes (Saint-Just, Robespierre) and its style of rhetoric ("Terror is the Piety of the Revolution") with ballistic precision and barricade-storming zest. Finlay's "Instruments of Revolution", the scythes, hoes, spades and sickles, have impressive gravitas as objects, but works such as *Thermidor*, a collection of watering cans placed in a wheelbarrow, require a knowledge of the revolutionaries' agricultural calendar to yield their full allegorical import. How does he square this difficulty with the essentially public ambitions of neoclassical art?

"One has to face the fact that the public does not quite understand this art. But I don't think one should in any way talk down to people or diminish a work. One has to have faith that if a work is pure and true and exact it will in the end be understood." Documentation by Finlay and commentary by his critics are intended to form an essential part of the experience. He regrets the loss of a "common range of references" (bible stories, country pursuits, traditional lore) and is surprised that an American publisher was unacquainted with the tea-drinking habits of Scottish sailors on steamships.

Instead of drawing the obvious conclusions about cultural relativity, however, Finlay seems genuinely to believe that by invoking classical mythology, as well as his neoclassical heroes, he might be able to offer "what one supposes to be a fairly objective picture of the universe". The truth is that it could not be more personal.

Finlay politely rejects any suggestion of nostalgia. "No, I don't think that's ever been said." For him, neoclassicism remains aggressively, even dangerously, modern. Recently, he exhibited a number of maquettes in Frankfurt, one of them for an arch inscribed with the words "Neoclassicism has composed elegaic as well as triumphal arches". He hoped the invocation of elegy would forestall suspicions of fascist triumphalism, but it did no good. A proposed version of the project – "somewhere between a sculpture and an actual arch" – for a street in Munich bit the dust. "The authorities were delighted with the proposal and they were all ready to begin. But it had to be passed by the European Committee and they said it couldn't be built because an arch [as a symbol] was far too dangerous."

He has had more luck elsewhere. There have been gardens at the Kröller-Müller Museum in Arnhem, at the Max Planck Institute in Stuttgart, and even in Luton. Using a British Museum cast, he created a series of identical classical heads, each one named after a different French revolutionary, for O. M. Ungers's library of Renaissance manuscripts – "the point being, these people have set aside their own personalities to try to immerse themselves in a classical ideal" – and was subsequently asked to design a work for Ungers's Badische Landesbibliothek in Karlsruhe. He is about to work with Ungers again on a museum in Hamburg, though he has only ever spoken to the architect by phone.

Finlay prefers to remain at Little Sparta, the territory he has defended with such passionate fury and wit. "I've had a nervous dislike of travel for a long time. I have an associate who travels and of course you can understand places very well from photographs, writings and plans."

Nor did he plan to attend his latest opening at the ICA. "I'd rather there wasn't an opening. At the Fruitmarket in Edinburgh last summer I persuaded the gallery that they shouldn't have any wine, they should have tea, and bread and butter. Everybody likes a good cup of tea!" An innocent plea for sobriety? Only until Finlay points out that tea was the preferred refreshment of Robespierre's Jacobins.

Blueprint, March 1992

AIR CUT BY MATTER
SHIN TAKAMATSU

Buildings by the Japanese architect Shin Takamatsu rank among some of the strangest and most most provocative constructed in the 1980s. If André Breton's Bureau of Surrealist Research had been an office of architecture, rather than a gathering of poets and painters, its designs might have looked something like this. Takamatsu's buildings are uncensored reports from his own private dreamworld made brutally real in concrete, granite and steel. They are statements so extreme in their assertion of what architecture might become if it submitted to the imperatives of desire instead of logic or function that British squabbles about pitched roofs and pediments begin to look very dull by comparison. By any standards, except perhaps those of the sensation-hungry Japanese, Takamatsu's architecture is at the outer limits of taste and acceptability.

Takamatsu first began to attract attention in the West with Ark, the dental clinic he constructed in Kyoto in 1983. Occupying a site next to a railway track, the building has the look of an overscaled engine, with a silver-painted barrel vault and a row of ten chimney-like skylights along one side. (Recently, Ark received a pop-culture tribute of sorts in the film *Batman*, in which set designer Anton Furst cut up fragments of the building for the facade of the Flugelheim Museum.) The following year, Takamatsu completed Pharoah, a second dental clinic for the city. Like Ark, it was the architectural equivalent of a white dwarf star, with enormous density and power relative to its size. And as with Ark, its equation of cruel machine forms with dental unpleasantness encouraged some critics reviewing the building to indulge their most nightmarish fantasies.

In Takamatsu's burgeoning oeuvre, Ark and Pharoah occupy a pivotal position. His earlier buildings, concrete drums and boxes with metal insertions like front-loading washing machines, owe an acknowledged debt to Tadao Ando. Only Origin 1, completed in 1981, gave much hint of the developments ahead. Beneath a mysterious elliptical eye, the granite facade erupts in a vertical mouth like an open vice lined with metal studs.

Since Ark and Pharoah, which now look relatively restrained, Takamatsu's liking for ornamentation has run riot in a baroque proliferation of detail. Origin 111 (1987), the third and final stage of a building for a Kyoto textile company, has an unearthly, blood-red dome ringed by jagged skylights and a side elevation that resembles a cross-section of a motor with wheels and pistons. The forms are arbitrary, the fantasy is perverse, but the intensity is undeniable.

Takamatsu is based in the outskirts of Kyoto in a narrow five-storey office he designed himself, surrounded by paddy fields. An audience with the silver-haired master and his support team is less than relaxed. Time is limited; a good deal of it goes on getting the video of Takamatsu's first underground building in Tokyo, Sub-1, to work. In it, Takamatsu takes a walk round a computer-generated visual of the project, stopping

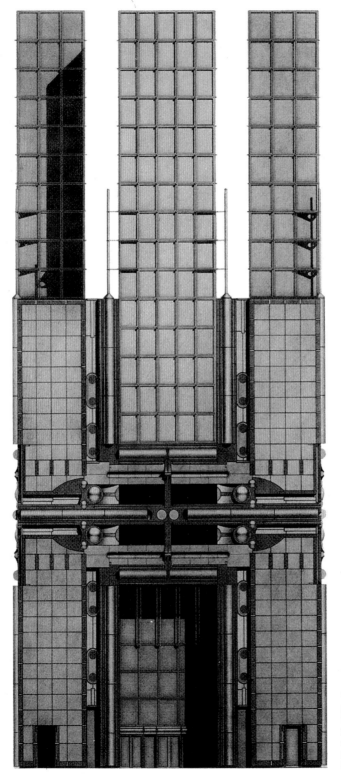

The Killing Moon and other projects. Drawing of Shin Takamatsu's Kirin Plaza building published in a boxed set. Artist: Shin Takamatsu. Architectural Association, London, 1988

every so often to shoot a meaningful glance at a point of particular interest. With
a doctorate from Kyoto University and a massive Yamaha bike on which he likes to
be photographed but rarely rides, Takamatsu is a peculiarly Japanese combination of
intellectual and fashion victim. His writings are notoriously impenetrable, suggesting
that his conversation, too, will be taxing. His references range from Thomas Pynchon's
"Entropy" to Tarkovsky's *Solaris*, from Marinetti to the rock group Echo and the
Bunnymen. But his answers are laconic in the extreme. Asked to illuminate the idea
of "non-conceptual form" broached in one of his essays, he says only, "Hmmn, aah,
very difficult" and shows another slide.

Takamatsu has an awful lot of slides to show. He has so many projects under way,
in fact, that there is little time to linger over even such basic details as function and
location. Takamatsu has always been astonishingly prolific by western standards –
in the past decade there have been more than 30 buildings in Kyoto alone, as well as
projects in Osaka, Nagoya and Tokyo. But now, riding on the crest of Japan's construction
boom, he has almost as many projects again at various stages of development. The
Kirin Plaza commercial building completed for the Japanese brewery in Osaka last year
("a facade as exciting as self-induced pain", confessed one writer, apparently without
irony) has propelled Takamatsu into the big league. The early houses, shops and clinics
have given way to office buildings, a gymnasium, a music school, a pachinko hall and
Takamatsu's first museum, devoted, surreally enough, to the subject of sand.

How much Takamatsu will be forced to compromise the intensity of his architecture
by this switch in scale remains to be seen. But there are signs already that he is
beginning to soften. Takamatsu once said that he didn't like to use aluminium cladding
because it was too much like human skin, yet a number of his most recent designs are
sheathed in the material. Why? "Because I'm old," says Takamatsu, now 41. His talk,
however, is of "power" and "strength" rather than of human frailty. Architecture, he
once wrote, is "air cut by matter"; buildings, he says, cut through the surface of the city.
Takamatsu's exhibition in 1988 at the Architectural Association was accompanied by
a ceremonial sword of his own design called "The Killing Moon" and touches like these
give his output an undertone of ritual and menace. But Takamatsu and his assistants
won't be drawn on the fantasies of violence that squeamish westerners have discovered
in his work (or projected on to it). According to Takamatsu, his use of red, whatever its
other associations, is merely intended to be a reference to the historical architecture
of Kyoto, a way of connecting the building to the city, though in anything other than
a symbolic sense it has precisely the opposite effect.

Takamatsu's relationship with Kyoto is undoubtedly complex. Repeatedly, he
compares the city to literature. His own architecture, he claims, is a "new language"
grafted on to the ancient city of Zen gardens and temples wreathed by hills. For
Takamatsu, as for other Japanese architects, architecture is an act of resistance as much
as of celebration. "When architecture has the power to withstand its surroundings,
there is a message for the city," he has said. Outside Kyoto, the message would seem to
be one of solipsism and withdrawal. In Kirin Plaza, Takamatsu countered the "seething
compression" of central Osaka by creating a building that addresses the city with four
equal, undifferentiated elevations, its upper storeys towers of emptiness and light
that make no concessions to the surrounding streetscape and want nothing in return.
Confronted by the possibility of "instant dissolution" in the urban inferno, architecture
turns in on itself.

But not all Takamatsu's buildings attain the degree of presence and power achieved by Kirin, Ark or Origin III. A tour around Kyoto, which is fast becoming a Takamatsu museum, reveals just how lightweight some of his architecture can be. Restaurant buildings such as Station (1989) and the Maruto building (1987) in the heart of the city's entertainment district are not much more substantial, despite the quality of their finishes, than unusually decorous greenhouses, thrown up to satisfy short-term commercial needs and unlikely to see out the century. Even larger projects which look promising on paper, such as the Week commercial building (1986), can prove to be disappointingly flashy and exhibitionistic in the flesh. In his interiors and furniture designs, too, Takamatsu can be tacky, piling on the glitz where brooding restraint might have been more fitting. The inevitable corollary of his more tormented exteriors are fractured internal spaces that permit the mind and body no peace.

These are not the buildings by which Takamatsu will be remembered, or even, to judge by the highly selective publicity, the ones by which he wants to be known. They are his own equivalent of bread-and-butter jobs and it is hardly surprising when a team of twenty works at this pace that there should be periodic drops in pressure.

Takamatsu's best buildings, as Peter Cook observed at the time of his AA exhibition, are extraordinary, their formal daring and exhilarating invention a powerful example to the younger architects of the West. He is already something of a cult in California. How Takamatsu himself might translate his sensibility into forms agreeable to American or European taste could soon become apparent. He is working with Jean-Michel Wilmotte, a long-time admirer, on a speculative office building in Nîmes. All they need now is a backer. It's a fusion of cultures, given the French origins of Surrealism and the Gallic toleration of the subversive, Sadeian intellectual, that could not be much more appropriate.

Blueprint, October 1989*

FORM FOLLOWS IDEA
DANIEL WEIL & GERARD TAYLOR

In 1987's *South Bank Show* lecture, "The Englishness of English Design", Peter York put Daniel Weil's *Small Door* radio on a pedestal. He did this not to celebrate or explain the piece to his audience (too boring, too obvious!) but to hold it up to national ridicule. According to York, Weil's "lopsided mousetrap" exemplified all that was wrong with contemporary British design. "They call it design, but you can tell from the price that it's actually art," he opined. "Now the compilers of *New British Design* think that this is an important little radio. They think it's a milestone in British design. They put it on the cover. My instinct is to step on it."

Perhaps it is unedifying experiences of this kind that Weil's partner, Gerard Taylor, has in mind when he says: "You should never make things too comfortable for yourself." If a marketing man of York's sophistication can miss the point of such research so disastrously, what chance do Weil and Taylor have of talking round blunt-speaking British industrialists?

One wonders sometimes why they stay here at all. Taylor has already made his escape once: after studying industrial design at the Royal College of Art alongside Weil, he was invited by Ettore Sottsass to join Sottsass Associati and to work with Memphis, who were keen to produce his pieces for their second collection. He was still there in 1984, when Weil arrived in town with an exhibition of see-through clocks and dismembered radios. For Taylor, his friend's persistence in the face of British indifference was an eye-opener. "What Daniel was achieving through that show held up for me the failure of what was going on in Milan," he recalls. "Milan had ceased to be a place that I felt was creative."

So Taylor came back to London to join Weil in partnership. Two and a half years later, the bulk of their work is still undertaken for international clients, leaving Taylor, at least, feeling detached from the London design scene. They both talk like members of a global community, of which Italy, almost in spite of themselves, remains the capital. As well as projects in Australia for Esprit, in association with Sottsass Associati, there has been a shop in Bari for Alessi; an executive furniture project for Knoll International; and unsuccessful proposals for JC, a Swedish jeans store, and Driade – though the furniture designed for the latter will now be launched in Milan by Rainer Krause's German company Anthologie Quartett.

Quartett will also produce Weil and Taylor's *Jour* clock. This, a rare brush with the design establishment, was a Design Council-funded consultancy project for a Birmingham manufacturer, who took fright when he saw the model and refused to pay the designers a penny. One can only wonder, as the Council did, at the client's lack of imagination. Constructed out of inexpensive plywood panels, *Jour* posits a return to the multi-planar Cubist imagery of Weil's 1984 clock, *Hinge*, a connection reinforced by its title – displayed on the clockface – which is a pun on the newspaper fragments (*Le Journal*) found in early Cubist collages, as well as the hours in the day.

Similar concerns inform *Quasimodo*, also for Anthologie Quartett. Driade's original brief to Weil and Taylor asked them to reinterpret nineteenth-century drawing-room furniture in a contemporary manner. In the course of their research they became fascinated by the eccentric construction of the concealed joinery in these upholstered pieces. As a result, *Quasimodo* combines a mock traditional approach to construction in wood with a Cubist treatment of structure to produce a chair that must be viewed in the round, like a piece of sculpture, before it can be fully understood. The wayward asymmetry, random Cubist perforations, eccentrically deployed colours and essential simplicity can be read as an implicit criticism of the modernist tyranny of steel, which, Weil and Taylor readily admit, leaves them cold.

But it would be a mistake to dismiss the Cubist gestures of these pieces as a stylistic fixation, still less as an empty exercise in historicist double-coding. For Weil, Cubism is just a handy device in the analytical toolbox. The clocks and radios he made in the early 1980s demystified the technology of the object by rendering the container transparent, disclosing the frail components for inspection (and, of course, remystified the object as a *presence* in the process). Similarly, Cubism potentially allows Weil to open up and reconstitute the object by breaking flat, enclosing surfaces into a sequence of shifting, interpenetrating planes.

This willingness to draw on the vocabulary of art is no doubt one reason for the accusation, from Peter York and others, that Weil's early pieces are in reality art posing as design. But it rests on a crucial misunderstanding. Unlike the showy one-offs touted by the colour supplements as examples of the new design, most of Weil's work is designed for mass-production. If prices have been high, it is only because Weil has been obliged to produce short runs of the pieces himself. "Even those things that are made in small quantities are conceived as repeats," he stresses, "and they address the idea of reproduction in some way. That is an area of interest that modern art has also touched on."

That Weil and Taylor's emphasis on art should seem almost wilful is a measure of how blinkered – "incestuous", says Weil – British design has become. Weil's desire to enrich design by closing the divide between the two disciplines has been there in his work since his time at the RCA. He originally planned, after leaving the college, to do a doctorate at Essex University, examining the role of humour and irony in art and design. He was searching not for off-the-peg formal solutions, but for ideas. "Design has to separate idea from form to be able to reposition form successfully," Weil insists. "You have to be able to deal with the abstract before you deal with the form. Design has dealt for too long with the form first: form follows function."

For Weil, form follows idea, but this does not mean he is any respecter of "essences". In Weil's surreal imagination, contraries – a table, a waste-paper basket – can and should collide and blur. If this sounds misguided, absurd, consider Weil and Taylor's proposal for the ICA's "Metropolis" exhibition, to be mounted in summer 1988. Their intention is to transform a normally useless parked car into a wired-up extension of the home, an extra room that can be used for work or leisure. The aim, to bring people back out into the streets, is public-spirited and responsible.

Weil and Taylor argue that collection and observation are also essential to the design

Jour. Cubist clock. Designer:
Daniel Weil. Anthologie
Quartett, Great Britain, 1987

process. Drawing, as ever, on Italian examples, they speak admiringly of Castiglioni's studio, a museum of inspirational objects, and of Sottsass's ability to freeze his observations of the world in his work. Their own drawers are full of old components, springs, light bulbs – industrial objects on the edge of extinction – and there are gardening books on the shelf. "Those are gardening dust, actually," quips Weil.

An encounter with Weil and Taylor is scattered with jokes like these. In conversation, Weil, in particular, veers unpredictably from earnest explanation to verbal anarchy. "Let's jump forward a bit," I suggest at one point, as the conversation trips up on the minutiae of who did what when at the RCA. Led by Weil, they simulate the sound of two accelerating tapewinds: "Dulululululu . . . pip!" Driving along Threadneedle Street in Weil's battered Renault 4, we see a man get out of his car and threaten a taxi driver. His number plate ends in "XYX". "Too many chromosomes!" exclaims Weil, neatly demonstrating that "observation" is a full-time occupation.

Weil acknowledges that the jokes and puns may, in the past, have led observers to question his seriousness. There is no doubting his seriousness now. Weil and Taylor's disenchantment with design in the late 1980s, particularly retail design, borders on disgust. "I think Oxford Street is an extremely depressing street," says Taylor. "It's design as comfort, design to pacify, design to round the edges, design to give a soft light. None of those shops take anything like an assertive stance. They actually do the opposite. They negate complexity. They negate clarity."

"Design is totally prostituted as a profession," adds Weil. "It has become a purely servile profession, as opposed to a service profession. It lacks self-confidence. You couldn't ask a doctor to become an engineer, but you can ask a designer to become a hairdresser."

Challenged to offer a vision of how the "cycle of making and selling" might be broken in design's favour, Taylor falls back on the example of Italy. "Design is only as good as its industrialists. In Italy, the industrialists you deal with are culturally sophisticated people. They know a little about art, literature and music. What it needs is people who perceive industrial manufacture to be a long-term process." Weil offers the familiar example of Alessi as a company prepared to make this kind of cultural investment.

Culture, for Weil and Taylor, is the key word. The primary responsibility of the designer, they believe, is not economics, employment or wealth creation – all of which are the proper business of the manufacturer – but cultural enrichment. To fulfil this duty, designers must design for themselves, in a spirit of unfettered research, as well as for the client – a process Weil and Taylor refer to as "academic" design. Drawing, a neglected art in the age of the slick visual, is a crucial part of this process of discovery. The guitar-shaped body and tubular components of *H-Arp*, Weil and Taylor's new lamp for Anthologie Quartett, can be traced back, across Weil's drawings on long rolls of lining paper, to early sketches offering a profusion of simultaneously developing possibilities.

By any standards, *H-Arp* is an extraordinary piece of work, as unexpected in its way as *Bag Radio* or *Small Door*. Its name is a *petit-hommage* to the Dadaist poet and sculptor Hans Arp, whose curiously organic abstract wooden reliefs were among the inspirations for the piece. Fringed by a ready-made cake mould (Duchamp is never far away), the lamp is concealed in a bulb-like casing in the centre of a long rod with handles at either end. The rod, which pivots on a green pole, is the switch. To turn on the lamp it is lifted from a rubber pad at the end of the steel scroll into its centre.

Formally, *H-Arp* is quite unlike anything either Weil, or Taylor in his Memphis manner, have produced before, but this is not perhaps the most crucial difference. Much of the shock created by Weil's early pieces came from the disparity – the misalignment – between the complicated imagery of the object and its routine technological function as clock or radio. Weil knew that his imagery would be better suited to sophisticated products, but through his ontological games he hoped to drive home the point that, while technology is expected to undergo a rapid rate of change, design is advancing at a much slower pace. The bland boxes we continue to favour are a hopelessly inadequate reflection of the marvels which they contain.

In *H-Arp*, the gap between technology and image has narrowed to a point of much greater intelligibility. The piece is strange, but it is accessible too. "Given the proper technology to deal with and the proper budgets," insists Weil, "we would be able to align the image with the technology and nothing will look out of place." It is high time that a British industrialist had the vision, the taste and the cultural conviction to take up this challenge.

Blueprint, July 1988

BIBLIOGRAPHY

Publications, articles and other sources mentioned, quoted, drawn on, or reviewed in the text. References to pages where specific citations occur are indicated in brackets at the end of the entry.

Aldersey-Williams, Hugh, *New American Design: Products and Graphics for a Post-industrial Age*, New York: Rizzoli, 1988 [42]

Aldersey-Williams, Hugh et al., *Cranbrook Design: The New Discourse*, New York: Rizzoli, 1990 [49, 74]

Aldrich-Ruenzal, Nancy and Fennell, John, *Designer's Guide to Typography*, Oxford: Phaidon Press, 1991 [43]

Alexander, Valerie, "An interview with April Greiman", in Kansas City Art Institute magazine, summer 1982 [43]

Berger, Warren, "Graphics acrobat" (on David Carson), in *New York Times*, 15 May 1994 [225]

Blackwell, Lewis, *The End of Print: The Graphic Design of David Carson*, London: Laurence King Publishing, 1995 [219–20, 224]

Blauvelt, Andrew (ed.), *New Perspectives: Critical Histories of Graphic Design*, Visible Language, 28.3, July 1994; 28.4, October 1994; 29.1, January 1995 [30–31]

Boxer, Mark, "*Ark*: The Journal of the Royal College of Art", in *Graphics RCA: Fifteen Years' Work of the School of Graphic Design*, London: Royal College of Art, 1963 [267]

Brighton, Andrew, "John Goto and photography as high art" (on Andrzej Klimowski), in *Modern Painters*, vol. 7 no. 1, spring 1994 [173]

Brody, Neville, "Small is more creative", in *Eye*, no. 1 vol. 1, 1990 [90]

Brody, Neville and Wozencroft, Jon, "Protect the lie", in the *Guardian*, 2 December 1988 [106]

Bürer, Catherine (ed.), *Kirei – Posters from Japan 1978–1993*, London: Thames and Hudson, 1994 [19–21]

Carson, David, "Influences: the complete guide to uncovering your next original idea", in *How*, April 1992 [222]

Coupland, Douglas, *Microserfs*, London: HarperCollins Publishers, 1995 [244]

Deleuze, Gilles, "Mediators", in Crary, Jonathan and Kwinter, Sanford (eds.), *Zone 6: Incorporations*, New York: Zone, 1992 [254]

Dent Coad, Emma, "Dumbar girds up for the Royal summons", in *Design & Art Direction*, no. 42, October 1985 [59]

Dumbar, Gert, "How designers get their own way", in *Design Review*, no. 2, summer 1991 [60]

Eno, Brian, Mills, Russell and Poynor, Rick, *More Dark Than Shark*, London: Faber and Faber, 1986 [152, 156]

Fern, Dan, *Breakthrough*, catalogue to an exhibition celebrating 25 years of illustration, London: Royal College of Art, 1988 [151]

Fern, Dan, *Works With Paper*, London: Architecture Design and Technology Press, 1990 [163–68]

Frayling, Christopher, *The Royal College of Art: One Hundred & Fifty Years of Art & Design*, London: Barrie & Jenkins, 1987 [151]

Friedman, Mildred and Freshman, Phil (eds.), *Graphic Design in America: A Visual Language History*, Minneapolis: Walker Art Center/New York: Harry N. Abrams, 1989 [179]

Gaiman, Neil and McKean, Dave, *The Tragical Comedy or Comical Tragedy of Mr Punch*, London: Victor Gollancz, 1994 [242–43]

Gibbs, David (ed.), *Nova 1965–1975*, London: Pavilion Books, 1993

Glaser, Milton, *Graphic Design*, New York: The Overlook Press, 1973 [181]

Gottschall, Edward M., *Typographic Communications Today*, Cambridge, Mass.: MIT Press, 1989 [30]

Green, Jonathon, *Days in the Life: Voices from the English Underground 1961–1971*, London: William Heinemann, 1988 [197]

Greiman, April, *Hybrid Imagery: The Fusion of Technology and Graphic Design*, London: Architecture Design and Technology Press, 1990 [16, 44, 213]

Greiman, April, *it's not what you think it is*, Bordeaux: Arc en Rêve Centre d'Architecture/Zurich, Munich and London: Artemis, 1994 [41–44]

Hall, Peter, "Word up!" (on Roger Black), in *Graphics International*, no. 16, August/September 1993 [253]

Hamilton, Richard, *Collected Words*, London: Thames and Hudson, 1982 [272, 274]

Hebdige, Dick, "The bottom line on Planet One: squaring up to *The Face*", in *Hiding in the Light*, London and New York: Routledge, 1988 [106]

Heller, Steven (ed.), *Innovators of American Illustration*, New York: Van Nostrand Reinhold, 1986 [156, 184]

Heller, Steven, "Moving on" (on Robert Weaver), in *Print*, XLIII:II, March 1989 [161]

Heller, Steven, "Cult of the ugly", in *Eye*, no. 9 vol. 3, 1993 [34–37]

Heller, Steven and Chwast, Seymour, *Graphic Style: From Victorian to Post-modern*, London: Thames and Hudson, 1988 [32]

Hollis, Richard, *Graphic Design: A Concise History*, London: Thames and Hudson, 1994 [105]

Hyde, Karl and Warwicker, John, *mmm . . . skyscraper i love you*, London: Booth-Clibborn Editions, 1994 [140]

Ionesco, Eugène, *The Bald Prima Donna*, London: Calder and Boyars, 1966 [246]

Jones, Chris, *Art Meets Science: The Cover Art of New Scientist*, London: IPC Magazines, 1986

Jones, Derek (ed.), *Once Upon a Time in Cyberville*, edited transcript of a programme first shown on 11 December 1994, London: Channel 4 Television, 1994 [259]

Jones, Mike, "Going public, going bust", in *Design*, January 1991 [90]

Karasek, Paul and Mazzucchelli, David, *Paul Auster's City of Glass*, New York: Avon Books, 1994 [243]

Keedy, Jeffery, "A conversation with Edward Fella and Mr Keedy", in *Emigre*, no. 17, 1991 [74]

Keedy, Jeffery, *Fast Forward*, Valencia: California Institute of the Arts, 1993 [253–54]

Keedy, Jeffery, "I like the vernacular . . . NOT!", in Glauber, Barbara (ed.), *Lift and Separate: Graphic Design and the Quote Vernacular Unquote*, New York: The Cooper Union, 1993 [77]

Keedy, Jeffery, "Zombie Modernism", in *Emigre*, no. 34, 1995 [77, 81]

Kinross, Robin, *Modern Typography: An Essay in Critical History*, London: Hyphen Press, 1992 [37]

Klimowski, Andrzej, *The Depository: A Dream Book*, London: Faber and Faber, 1994 [174]

Koolhaas, Rem, Mau, Bruce and OMA, *S,M,L,XL*, New York: The Monacelli Press/Rotterdam: 010 Publishers, 1995 [234–36]

Lamacraft, Jane, "Michael Peters on the spot", in *Direction*, November 1990 [90]

Larbalestier, Simon, *The Art and Craft of Montage*, London: Mitchell Beazley, 1993 [185]

Lehrer, Warren, *Nicky D. from L.I.C.*, Seattle: Bay Press, 1995 [246]

Lott, Tim, "My decade: John Hegarty", in the *Sunday Correspondent*, 10 December 1989 [93]

Lupton, Ellen and Miller, J. Abbott, *Design Writing Research: Writing on Graphic Design*, New York: Kiosk/Princeton Architectural Press, 1996 [28]

Mason, Robert (ed.), "Radical Illustrators", special issue of *Illustrators*, no. 38, autumn 1981 [152]

McCloud, Scott, *Understanding Comics: The Invisible Art*, Northampton, Mass.: Kitchen Sink Press, 1993/New York: HarperCollins Publishers, 1994 [241–43]

McQuiston, Liz and Kitts, Barry, *Graphic Design Source Book*, London: Macdonald Orbis, 1987 [53]

Meggs, Philip B., "Massimo Vignelli vs. Ed Benguiat (sort of)" in *Print*, XLV:V, September/October 1991 [217]

Meggs, Philip B., *A History of Graphic Design* 2nd edn., New York: Van Nostrand Reinhold, 1992 [30, 105]

Mellor, David, *The Sixties Art Scene in London*, London: Phaidon Press, 1993 [265–66]

Melly, George, *Revolt into Style: The Pop Arts in the 50s and 60s*, London: Allen Lane, 1970 [269–70]

Middleton, P. Lyn and Davis, Meredith, "Personally speaking: a discussion with April Greiman, Rick Valicenti and Nancy Skolos", in *Statements*, spring 1991 [43]

Mills, Russell, "Between Tides – an explanation of the cover artwork", in *Opal Information*, no. 8, March 1988 [160]

Mitchell, C. Thomas, *Redefining Designing: From Form to Experience* (on Brian Eno), New York: Van Nostrand Reinhold, 1993

Morris, Dean, "Please don't let me be misunderstood" (on April Greiman), in *Blueprint*, no. 47, May 1988 [42]

Neville, Richard, *Hippie Hippie Shake: The Dreams, the Trips, the Trials, the Love-ins, the Screw Ups . . .*

the Sixties, London: Bloomsbury Publishing, 1995 [196]

Owen, William, *Magazine Design*, London: Laurence King Publishing, 1991

Perkins, Sean (ed.), *Experience*, London: Booth-Clibborn Editions, 1995 [232–33]

Peters, Michael, "Design: a new vision", speech delivered at the PIRA/RSA Design Conference, London, 23 March 1990 [90]

Pijbes, Wim (ed.), *Behind the Seen: Studio Dumbar*, Mainz: Verlag Hermann Schmidt, 1996 [59–64]

Poynor, Rick, "Album cover artist", in *Exhibition/Exposition: Vaughan Oliver*, Nantes: CRDC, 1990 [125]

Poynor, Rick, "Reputations: Alan Fletcher", in *Eye*, no. 2 vol. 1, winter 1991 [91]

Poynor, Rick, *The Graphic Edge*, London: Booth-Clibborn Editions, 1993

Poynor, Rick and Booth-Clibborn, Edward (eds.), *Typography Now: The Next Wave*, London: Booth-Clibborn Editions, 1991

Rand, Paul, *A Designer's Art*, New Haven, Conn. and London: Yale University Press, 1985 [15]

Rand, Paul, *Design, Form and Chaos*, New Haven, Conn. and London: Yale University Press, 1993 [24–25, 217]

Remington, R. Roger and Hodik, Barbara J., *Nine Pioneers in American Graphic Design*, Cambridge, Mass.: MIT Press, 1989 [16]

Rocque, Melony, "Multimedia at the cutting edge" (on Max Whitby), in *XYZ*, June 1992 [251]

Savage, Jon, "The age of plunder", in *The Face*, no. 33, January 1983 [103, 114]

Seago, Alex, *Burning the Box of Beautiful Things: The Development of a Postmodern Sensibility*, Oxford: Oxford University Press, 1995 (PhD thesis: Royal College of Art, London, 1990) [267]

Smith, Joan, *Misogynies* revised edn., London: Faber and Faber, 1993 [173]

Sontag, Susan, *Against Interpretation*, New York: Dell Publishing, 1978 [43]

Sontag, Susan, *On Photography*, London: Penguin Books, 1979 [248]

Spencer, Herbert, *Pioneers of Modern Typography* revised edn., Cambridge, Mass.: MIT Press, 1983 [120, 129]

Takamatsu, Shin, *The Killing Moon and other projects*, Folio XII, London: Architectural Association, 1988 [281]

Taylor, Mark C. and Saarinen, Esa, *Imagologies: Media Philosophy*, London and New York: Routledge, 1994 [32, 33]

Ten Duis, Leonie and Haase, Annelies, "April Greiman", in *Zeezucht*, no. 3, October 1990 [43]

Thackara, John (ed.), *New British Design*, London: Thames and Hudson, 1986 [283]

Tschichold, Jan, *The New Typography*, Berkeley: University of California Press, 1995 [22–23]

VanderLans, Rudy, interview with April Greiman, *Emigre*, no. 14, 1990 [41]

VanderLans, Rudy, interview with David Carson, *Emigre*, no. 27, 1993 [222]

VanderLans, Rudy and Licko, Zuzana, *Emigre: Graphic Design into the Digital Realm*, New York: Van Nostrand Reinhold, 1993 [211–13]

Walker, John A., *Cross-overs: Art into Pop/Pop into Art*, London and New York: Methuen, 1987

Wittgenstein, Ludwig, *Tractatus Logico-Philosophicus*, London: Routledge & Kegan Paul, 1933 [139–40]

Woods, Gerald, Thompson, Philip and Williams, John, *Art Without Boundaries: 1950–70*, Thames and Hudson, 1972 [11]

Wozencroft, Jon, *The Graphic Language of Neville Brody*, London: Thames and Hudson, 1988 [100, 103, 105, 111, 213]

Wozencroft, Jon, *The Graphic Language of Neville Brody 2*, London: Thames and Hudson, 1994 [105, 110–111]

Wurman, Richard Saul, *Information Anxiety*, New York: Doubleday, 1989 [230–31]

Yelavich, Susan, *The Edge of the Millennium*, New York: Whitney Library of Design, 1993 [32–33]

INDEX